WA 1259657 4

D1643800

MUSEUM BUILDERS II

LAURA HOURSTON

Acknowledgements
Thanks to the many architects and museum professionals who so generously gave of their time to supply information and images on the featured museums. I would also like to thank the publishing team at Wiley-Academy, and especially Abigail Grater and Mariangela Palazzi-Williams, the staff at Artmedia Press, my colleagues in the School of the Built Environment at the University of Nottingham, my parents, Kate, and Phil.

Illustration Credits
Every effort has been made to locate sources and credit material but in any cases where this has not been possible our apologies are extended. All drawings are courtesy of the first-named architects or engineers, as are all photographs except the following: Cover © Enrico Cano; Frontispiece © Duccio Malagamba; pp. 12 left, 22 top left and bottom, 26–7, 44, 46 bottom, 47 bottom, 49 bottom; © Laura Hourston; pp. 10 right, 13 left, 29, 31, NMS/Trustees of the National Museums of Scotland; pp.8 left, 18 right, 19 left, 32 –7 © Canadian Museum of Civilization, photos Henry Foster; pp. 14 left, 38–43, © Jasmax Limited; pp. 9 right, 45, 46 top, 47 top, 48, 49 top, Studio Daniel Libeskind; pp.23 top left and bottom left, 50, 53–4, 57–8 © Jewish Museum Berlin, photos Dieter and Si Rosenkrant, Berlin; pp.51–2, 55; © Jewish Museum Berlin, Studio Daniel Libeskind; pp. 23 bottom right, 56, 59; © Jewish Museum, Berlin, photo Jens Ziehe; pp. 24 left, 60–3, © U.S. Holocaust Memorial Museum, courtesy of USHMM; pp. 11 left and right, 64–9 © Tadao Ando Architect & Associates; pp. 70–9, © Studio Hollein/Arch. Sina Baniahmad; pp. 80, 82–6, © Kisho Kurokawa Architect and Associates, photos Koji Kobayashi; pp 9 left, 92–3 © T. Loveless, photos Bob Berry/NMMC; p.94 © Kunsthal Rotterdam, photo Ernst Moritz; p. 95 C© Kunsthal Rotterdam, photo Gert-Jan van Rooij; pp. 96–9, Rem Koolhaas, OMA; p. 100 © Kunsthal Rotterdam, photo Hans Werleman; pp. 10 left, 102–7, © Philippe Ruault; p. 108 © Pino Musi; p. 110–1, 113, © Robert Canfield; p. 114, 117–18, 121–2, © Enrico Cano; pp. 124–7, 129, © Josef Paul Kleihues, Berlin, photo Hélène Binet, London; p. 128 © Josef Paul Kleihues, Berlin and Dülmen-Rorup; pp. 130, 133, 136, 139–40, 152, 156, © Duccio Malagamba, Barcelona; pp. 131–2, 134–5 © FMGB Guggenheim Bilbao Museoa, photos Erika Barahona Ede; pp. 142,145–6, 148, 149 bottom, 151, photos courtesy CGAC; pp.158 top, 161–2, © Toshiharu Kitajima; pp. 164–5, 169–71, © Kisho Kurokawa Architect & Associates, photos Tomio Ohashi; pp. 172, 175 right, 176, 180–1, © 2003 Paul Warchol; p. 175 left, © courtesy Zaha Hadid Architects; p. 178, © 2003 Hélène Binet, courtesy Hélène Binet Photography; pp.182–7 © Zaha Hadid Architects; pp.188–91 © Studio Daniel Libeskind, renderings Miller Hare; pp.192, 195, Tate Enterprises © Tate, London, 2003; pp. 193–94, Herzog & de Meuron; pp. 17 right, 196–9 © OMA; pp. 200–1, 203 bottom, 204 top, 205, © Don Barker; p. 202, © Ellis Williams Architects, sketch Dominic Williams.

Cover: Mario Botta and Giulio Andreolli, Modern and Contemporary Art Museum of Trento and Rovereto, Rovereto, Italy
Frontispiece: Frank Gehry Guggenheim Museum Bilbao, Bilbao, Spain

Published in Great Britain in 2004 by Wiley-Academy, a division of John Wiley & Sons Ltd

The Atrium, Southern Gate, Chichester
West Sussex PO19 8SQ, England
Telephone (+44) 1243 779777

Email (for orders and customer service enquiries): cs-books@wiley.co.uk
Visit our Home Page on www.wileyeurope.com or www.wiley.com

ISBN 0-470-84943-6

Other Wiley Editorial Offices

John Wiley & Sons Inc., 111 River Street, Hoboken, NJ 07030, USA
Jossey-Bass, 989 Market Street, San Francisco, CA 94103-1741, USA
Wiley-VCH Verlag GmbH, Boschstr. 12, D-69469 Weinheim, Germany
John Wiley & Sons Australia Ltd, 33 Park Road, Milton, Queensland 4064, Australia
John Wiley & Sons (Asia) Pte Ltd, 2 Clementi Loop #02-01, Jin Xing Distripark, Singapore 129809
John Wiley & Sons Canada Ltd, 22 Worcester Road, Etobicoke, Ontario, Canada M9W 1L1

Design and Prepress: ARTMEDIA PRESS Ltd, London

Printed and bound in Italy by Conti Tipocolor

CONTENTS

Introduction

ISSUES OF IDENTITY

Throughout its long history, although the museum has escaped easy definition, the same fundamental concerns have remained at its core. It has had a poignant and enduring role as a cultural repository, or 'treasure-trove'. The collection and preservation of material heritage has been at the heart of the museum's remit, and has even at times taken on a quasi-religious aspect. One need only consider the 'pilgrimage' of many millions of visitors to the contemporary museums discussed in the following pages to attest to this. More abstractly, knowledge is intrinsically bound up with the museum, and this link is twofold. The museum has been an influential forum for the *promotion* of ideas, with whole structures of thought being transposed onto the museum to be validated and legitimised. Beyond this, the museum, in raising certain fundamental questions, has acted as a *generator* of knowledge. Particular theoretical frameworks have been produced in order to resolve the problems and dilemmas cast up by the museum itself. As such, museums have in the past created, and still are creating, modes of knowledge:' ... the museum ... has been actively engaged over time in the construction of varying rationalities.'[1] The dissemination of this knowledge in the museum has altered dramatically over the institution's history, however, with didactic education, enlightenment and entertainment vying for supremacy. It is another constant factor in the story of the museum that will form the focus here though: its role as a significant site for the construction and depiction of identity.

Historically, issues of identity have been inseparable from the construct of the museum. During the Renaissance, the collections of noblemen – variously named *studioli*, *cabinets des curieux*, *Wunderkammern* and *Kunstkammern* – heavily influenced the manufacture of social and political hierarchies and identities. Typically, royal or aristocratic collections, which were intended to represent the world in miniature, were housed in secret, darkened rooms of their influential owners' palaces. The patrician alone was allowed access to the closed wall cupboards to view the exhibits, meaning he alone was empowered to comprehend the universe. The 'studiolo' therefore embodied a very specific knowledge-power interdependency, 'reserv[ing] to the prince not only the knowledge of the world constituting his supremacy, but the possibility of knowing itself'.[2] Monarchs used the forum of the museum as a source of prestige, and through such collections of *objets d'art* and curios, legitimised and enhanced their control. To ensure the wider continuation of this influence, it became necessary for such private displays of omnipotence to be moved into a more public context, as in the removal of the previously exclusive collection of Francesco I de Medici into the Uffizi Gallery in 1584. Occupying this newly prominent and increasingly accessible space, the collection then better served to impress the gravitas of the ruling family on its subjects. This lineage of private collecting and patronage has extended to the present day, and is apparent in sponsored projects like the Lois & Richard Rosenthal Center for Contemporary Art in Cincinnati, commercially driven commissions such as that for the Cartier Foundation in Paris and vast private art empires like that of John Paul Getty. Richard Meier's restrained and gleaming Getty Center, high above the sprawling downtown of Los Angeles, is undoubtedly a contemporary embodiment of the grandeur and palatial origins of the earliest royal collections: 'Los Angeles genuflects before the might of the Getty citadel'.[3]

By the late eighteenth and early nineteenth centuries, with the inception of modern Enlightenment ideas and the new hegemony of the nation-state, the public, national museum was born. This transition from an exclusive culture of collecting based around the private patron, to a public one centred on the nation-state, is evidenced by the number of national museums instigated at this time. In 1764 the Hermitage in St Petersburg opened, and Sweden, Italy, Austria, Poland and Spain all founded public, national museums between 1772 and 1789. In America, the idea of a national museum can be traced back to 1792, following pressure from the influential collector, Peale, while in France the former King's collection was placed on open display in the Grande Galerie of the Louvre in 1793. It was the British Museum, founded 250 years ago in 1753, which led the way, however, moving to its present home nearly a century later. Its Scottish equivalent, the Industrial Museum of Scotland, opened in 1854, and the National Museum of Ireland was inaugurated in 1890. In order to purvey state wealth, power and stability, neo-Classical and neo-Gothic edifices were largely favoured to house these nascent national institutions. Despite this transmutation to a national form, the museum maintained its previous influence, merely shifting its focus. Collections that had previously been intended as demonstrations of royal power, began rather to be managed in order to accentuate national cohesion, prosperity and identity: 'the wealth of the collection is still a display of national wealth and is still meant to impress. But now the state, as an abstract entity, replaces the king as host.'[4] The museum had begun to occupy the imagined and invented space of nation.

These concerns of nationhood and the museum, which first converged in the early years of Modernity, are still bound together in the contemporary national museum. The planning, architecture and the exhibitions of these institutions reveal much about contemporary national and sub-national ethnic identities, and the museum as a whole may be seen as an embodiment of the nation's own self-critique. Three contemporary national museums, the Museum of Scotland, the Canadian Museum of Civilization and Te Papa Tongarewa the National Museum of New Zealand, form the main focus here, and also critically inform our reading of the other, non-national museums. All three are positioned at a fertile crossroads or cultural loci, both demonstrating and generating aspects of their wider cultural, civil and political societies.

In the last 50 years, the museum's effectiveness as a tool for the communication of ideas and identities has increased. The 'white heat' of the 1960s technological revolution heralded a significant increase in leisure time, and the heritage sector capitalised fully on this new market opportunity, with museums proliferating at a previously unseen rate.[5] This trend has continued unabated into the twenty-first century, with the phenomenon of cultural tourism experiencing a sustained boom. Incredibly, by the late 1980s, museums in Britain were being opened at a rate of one every fortnight, and this pattern has been mirrored across the Atlantic. With this increase in museum numbers has come an increase in variety. Thematic specialisation has resulted in museums, within this volume alone, covering issues as diverse as war and the holocaust, to maritime history and volcanoes. Regional museums address topics of local relevance or supplement the programmes of their national counterparts, in an attempt to decentralise and thereby democratise collections, enhance the image, identity and fabric of a region, and kickstart or secure the local economy. It is the art museum, though, that has been most prolific over recent years – a point illustrated by the many contemporary examples in this volume. Architects of art museum projects have been faced with a dilemma. On one hand, their architecture should be complementary to the art on display, which often necessitates the production of neutral and passive spaces. On the other hand, architecture has become increasingly critical to the success of museum institutions, prompting museum designers to inject a new level of Expressionistic bombast into their buildings. The resultant tension between architecture and artwork is now a constant theme in such museums. The Guggenheim, Bilbao, is surely the most lauded example of this exuberant architectural Expressionism, although in this case the dramatic shell has not overtly compromised the success of the gallery spaces within. The Guggenheim is also a prime example of the museum's regenerative effect, although all of the museum buildings explored have impacted to some extent on their social or economic environments.

Although superficially a straightforward development, there is a deeper anomaly inherent in this recent growth of museums: 'museums occupy an intriguingly paradoxical place in global culture ... Bound up with much that is heralded to be nearing its end – stability and permanence, authenticity, grand narratives, the nation-state, and even history itself – their numbers are growing at an unprecedented rate.'[6] Whatever the contradictions may be, however, more people than ever before are now visiting museums and being exposed to the constructed narratives and identities presented through their architecture and displays. As in the past, the power of these museum narratives to inform and alter perception is considerable:

> The contradictory, ambivalent position that museums are in makes them key cultural loci of our times. Through their displays and their day-to-day operations they inevitably raise questions about knowledge and power, about identity and difference, and about permanence and transience. Precisely because they have become global symbols through which status and community are expressed, they are subject to appropriation and the struggle for ownership.[7]

This dialogue of 'identity and difference' finds many and varied architectural expressions in the contemporary museum building.

A NATURAL SOLUTION?

Many contemporary museum designers have turned to the natural landscape for inspiration, often for aesthetic or pragmatic reasons, but at times to invest their buildings with a specific identity. A large proportion of the projects displayed on the following pages have been planned to take advantage of waterfront sites, which permit dramatic, reflected vistas towards the buildings, refreshing, orientating glimpses of water from the interior spaces, and popular river – or seaside outdoor areas. However, at Te Papa Tongarewa the National Museum of New Zealand, designed by Jasmax Architects to 'powerfully express the total culture of New Zealand', the planning and orientation of the building on its waterfront site in Wellington take on much deeper cultural significance.[8]

In New Zealand, the natural landscape is intrinsically linked to the indigenous Maori ethnie. The Maori have traditionally maintained a balanced and pastoral relationship with their natural environment, with nature also providing the basis for societal structuring, spiritual beliefs such as the creation theory, and land settlement patterns:

> ... early dwellings ... were often imbued with magic and situated according to a strict directional orientation and alignment with

The triple-height glazed façade of the Grand Hall at the Canadian Museum of Civilization, was designed by Douglas Cardinal to represent the frozen 'wall' of a glacier

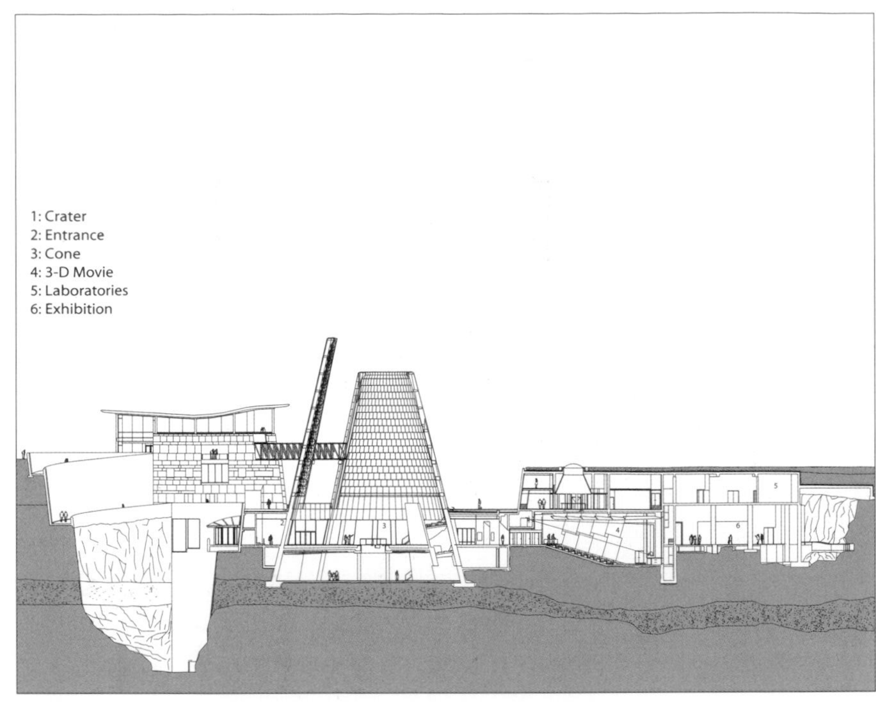

This cross section of Vulcania: the European Centre of Volcanism, designed by Hans Hollein, shows the downwardly spiralling, sunken Calderra, excavated to a depth of over 20 metres below ground level

> the heavens, or with an important topographical feature such as a distant mountain or sacred place, or an important feature of the immediate surrounding landscape ... In this way dwellings could be integrated with the order of the infinitely larger world outside them.[9]

Jasmax noted a preferential trend in the siting of traditional Maori dwellings and meeting houses, 'which involved orientation towards the most open landscape aspect, towards the rising sun, with enclosure behind', and bearing in mind their remit to represent the total culture of the country, decided to adhere to these distinctive patterns of land settlement in their planning of Te Papa.[10] These cultural preferences were transposed onto the finalised design in the alignment of the section containing the marae, or meeting house, and the Maori Art and History Gallery, which was consciously not as strongly part of the traditional museum culture. This area 'face[s] northeast along an axis directed towards the most open landscape features (the longest dimension of the harbour and the low saddle formed by the Taita valley beyond), towards the rising sun', with Mount Victoria providing the necessary enclosure behind.[11]

The architectural form of Te Papa Tongarewa also forges a basic and compelling connection with the national geological landscape. The dominant design theme to emerge is the awesome power and latent danger of the land. One of the faultlines underlying the capital and surrounding countryside, running adjacent to the Te Papa site and oriented from land to sea, provided a stimulus to the design. To express this idea of geological power or Ruaumoko – the Maori god of earthquakes – a mighty wall running in parallel to this fault line slices diagonally through the building. Clad in both polished and coarse-grained grey marble slabs, this prominent component provides a symbolic link to the uncontrollable might and intrinsic unpredictability of the 'shaky isles' of New Zealand.[12] Jasmax thereby derived design concepts from the most basic element of nation: the earth on which it is founded.

The new Canadian Museum of Civilization was inaugurated in Ottawa in 1989, and similar to Te Papa Tongarewa, its architecture was expected to be, 'a symbol of national pride and identity'.[13] With this goal in mind, the architect Douglas Cardinal, and his firm, TSE, decided to use landscape – again in its geological dimension – as an architectural leitmotiv. Related natural phenomena were chosen to be represented abstractly in the museum's forms, such as the Canadian Shield and glaciers, as seen in the curatorial and exhibition wings respectively. The pronounced horizontal bands of the museum's administrative wing evoke the stratified aggregates found within the massive rocky expanse of the Canadian Shield. This horizontality is emphasised by the long, narrow and unbroken strip windows, the glazing of which is very dark in contrast to the building's chalky-coloured Tyndall limestone cladding. To enhance the analogy, the museum building has a cantilevered or stepped construction, recalling the glacial undercutting and overhanging of exposed areas of the Shield.[14] The museum's public display building is intended to symbolise glacial forces that transformed the Canadian Shield. The most dramatic feature of the wing, the vast glazed window that faces the river and encases the Grand Hall, is emblematic of the great wall of the melting glacier itself. Above this, the brown and weathered green copper roof vaults represent the vegetated eskers and drumlins of the glacial landscape. Indeed, the architectonic mass of the building as a whole recalls land carved and sculpted by glaciers: 'the convoluted swirls

The National Maritime Museum Cornwall's round, almost lighthouse-like tower, sits out in the harbour, allowing views through the reinforced glazing of its tidal gallery deep into the sea

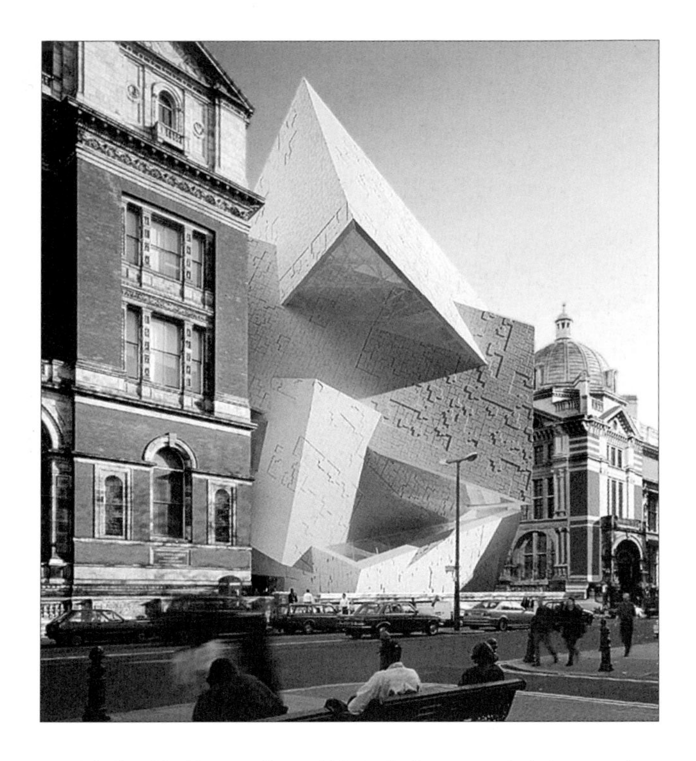

Daniel Libeskind has envisaged his Boilerhouse, or Spiral, extension to the Victoria & Albert Museum in London bursting out into the restrained formality of Exhibition Road

shaped by glacial action are reflected in the rounded, sinuous forms of this Hall'.[15] This curvilinear, organic quality to the design is strikingly obvious in the museum's plans, but is rather lost in the building's three-dimensional massing. The man-made stream, which flows down between the two wings, represents the meltwater that flowed away from the glaciers, cutting into the rock shelf beneath. This watercourse is a series of carefully stepped and landscaped pools, which, by originating at the top of the plaza between the two buildings, give the effect of having eroded one single sculptural rock form into the two discrete buildings now visible.

Many museums exhibit a more basic connection to the land, being buried either partially or deeply into the earth. At the Serralves Museum in the outskirts of Oporto, Alvaro Siza has embedded the new museum building into the site, to hide it from the original Art Deco villa, Casa de Serralves, to the east of the park. Staff, service and storage spaces are housed in the basement areas. A different motivation has led Tadao Ando to incorporate underground spaces at the Chikatsu-Asuka Historical Museum in Osaka. Here the subterranean chambers symbolise the *kofun*, or burial mounds, which surround the site and form the subject of the museum's displays. The most extreme example of this retreat underground, however, is Vulcania, the European Centre of Volcanism, at St Ours-les-Roches, where Hans Hollein has excavated galleries into the volcanic terrain to a depth of 20 metres, achieving a seamless fusion of site, architecture and exhibition programme. Analogously, the architects at the National Maritime Museum Cornwall in Falmouth, Kentish & Long, have also exploited the depths, but this time of the sea rather than the land:

> The tidal gallery in the base of the tower, with its multi-layered laminated windows which are submerged as the water rises, was complex and expensive to construct. It sounds like a gimmick, but descending from the open views at the top to this slightly threatening space is impressive, and the translucent shrimps which nestle up against the glass, and the shoals of tiny shiny fish are mesmerising: it is an encounter with real sea.[16]

There is undoubtedly a common ambition to integrate the natural landscape into recent museum architecture: 'Our buildings must be part of nature, must flow out of the land; the landscape must weave in and out of them so that, even in the harshness of winter, we are not deprived of our closeness with nature', and more subtle strategies than excavation have been used to achieve this ambiguity between inside and out.[17] At the Canadian Museum of Civilization, Cardinal attempts to achieve this fusion with swirling organic forms, heavily glazed in parts, extending out into the building's natural setting. Albeit at a highly contrasting site – a tight urban infill in London's South Kensington – Daniel Libeskind also sought the 'interlocking of inside and outside' in his design for the Victoria & Albert Museum's Spiral or Boilerhouse extension.[18] The fractured planes of his façade, clad in glazing panels and ceramic tiles, will burst out way beyond the street line of Exhibition Road, drawing the building into its site, and vice versa. Zaha Hadid's 'urban carpet' at the Center for Contemporary Art in Cincinnati, creates a similar dialogue between museum and city. This giant concrete element – which constitutes the rear wall of the museum – sweeps down to form the floor plane of the lobby, and then flows out onto the city pavement beyond, blurring the divide between inside and out. Frederick Fisher takes this ambiguity between the museum proper and its surroundings further at P.S.1 in New York, with

At Jean Nouvel's Cartier Foundation in Paris, cedar trees grow between the floating glass planes of the street façade, dissolving the distinction between inside and out

The Museum of Scotland's planted roof garden creates a strong dialogue with the natural backdrop of Arthur's Seat

a staged or layered entry promenade. Here, between the open courtyard and the enclosed museum, a series of concrete roofless rooms, practically provide viewing space for hardy, outdoor exhibits, whilst spatially creating a transitionary or intermediate zone between exterior and interior space. It is at the Cartier Foundation in Paris, however, where this notion of architectural layering and the fusion of natural and man-made finds its most refined articulation. Jean Nouvel expertly evaporates the building's threshold through a series of extruded, glass screens that float seamlessly between the Parisian pavement and the glass box of the gallery behind. It is the cedar trees growing between these hovering transparent planes, though, that truly permit 'the landscape [to] weave in and out' of the museum.[19] Planting is also used to contextualise the Museum of Scotland within its natural setting, particularly with relation to its fifth façade. The treatment of the roofscape required sensitivity, in light of its prominence from the city's other vantage points – Calton Hill, Arthur's Seat, Salisbury Crags and the Castle esplanade. Conversely, this fifth façade permitted the opportunity of a dramatic 360-degree vista. The architects' approach was to create a heavily planted, open-air roof terrace, or 'hanging valley', in order to 'mediat[e] between the major elements of the city's natural landscape'.[20] This elevated and suspended glen speaks of the rugged and evocative highland terrain of bens and glens, which is deeply imbued with a national romance. This is exploited in the roof garden where, in the words of its architects:

> selected archaeological and geological fragments would be placed ... where they could be viewed in a natural landscape of Scottish grasses, shrubs and wild flowers, rather than the decontextualised environment of a museum interior. The fragments could be seen in the wind and rain, against a backdrop of Arthur's Seat, the Salisbury Crags and Castle Rock.[21]

The roof garden then became a part of a larger narrative or symbolic journey:

> The long ascent from sedimentary compression to this aerial release [of the roof terrace], place[s] the visitor himself in the larger showcase of Edinburgh and its environs, [and] reveals the central force of nature – and specifically Scotland's landscape – as the constant factor in the story.[22]

Materiality is also used by museum designers to blur the divide between internal spaces and the external environment, as in the Clashach stone that clads the outer shell of the Museum of Scotland on its two street-facing façades, and is charged by its architects with esoteric significance. Gordon Benson names the stone the museum's oldest exhibit, and the occasional fossilised imprint is highlighted as a powerful reminder of this legacy. Ideas of the incomprehensible magnitude of time, along with its dual transience and permanence, are linked to the use of this stone, which, 'really once windblown sand, [is] now fixed for all eternity'.[23] The sandstone facing of the prominent northern and western façades penetrates or 'leaks' into the entrance tower, processional route and main orientation hall, creating continuity across the threshold and sustaining the memory of the building's exterior within: 'landscape infects and leaks through the architecture'.[24] It is the paradoxical use of the stone as a cosmetic veneer or cladding, rather than as a compressive, load-bearing construction element, that is most distinctive though, and it is this visual anomaly that answers the question: 'And ... how, incidentally, is it possible for a building clad in million year old material to appear so contemporary?'[25]

This sombrely-lit gallery at the Chikatsu-Asuka Historical Museum is keyhole-shaped and buried underground, in order to evoke the adjacent imperial *kofun*, or burial mound, of Ono-no-Imoko. Appropriately, the gallery houses relics recovered from this and other surrounding tombs

Sketch revealing the influence of the surrounding *kofun*, or burial mounds, on the form of the Chikatsu-Asuka Historical Museum

The natural landscape is a recurring theme in the architecture of many contemporary museums, and is particularly striking in the three national museums discussed. As the Jasmax team explained, the 'celebration of qualities of the New Zealand environment seemed integral to a building attempting to express "the total culture of this country"', but why is this?[26] One explanation is the positivistic bond between the natural landscape of a country and its people's sense of collective national identity. An empirical link is evident between national landscape and identity: aspects of nation directly influenced by a country's terrain, such as security and prosperity, in turn influence the national 'personality'. However, important though these practical connections are, it is surely a more aesthetic, abstract and emotional tie to the landscape of 'home' upon which the architects are drawing in their designs. At the Canadian Museum of Civilization, for example, Cardinal has both understood and attempted to exploit the Canadian people's innate consciousness of their own piece of, and place in, the natural world.

BUILDING A HERITAGE

'If Architecture has national peculiarities impressed upon it, then it must be history – the world's history written in stone.'[27]

Beyond the natural environment, built heritage has also inspired recent museum builders. Rich archaeological and architectural caches have been plundered by designers in a quest to give identity to their built form. At the Museum of Scotland, such architectural allusions – both ancient and modern – abound. The 'In Touch with the Gods' exhibition space, located in the basement of the round tower, is strikingly and poignantly reminiscent of circular prehistoric burial cairns. This powerful visual analogy begins with the gently sloping, dark and enclosed passageway that leads northwards from the central triangular space, and the similarities continue as this 'tunnel' opens out into a round, high-ceilinged cavity, of similar scale to many such prehistoric tombs. Aptly, the display exhibited within this 'burial chamber' contains inscribed gravestones, and other relics and artefacts of death. An almost identical approach has been adopted by Tadao Ando at the Chikatsu-Asuka Historical Museum in Minamikawachi-gun, Osaka. Here, in a landscape of ancient *kofun*, or burial mounds, Ando has hollowed an underground chamber out of the hillside. Keyhole shaped in plan, in order to resemble one of the four imperial tombs on the site, this dark evocative space houses the treasures recovered from the *kofun*, creating an integrated dialogue between site, architecture and programme.

Returning to the Museum of Scotland, the building's form as a whole resembles that of the Iron Age brochs that cover the country from Galloway to Shetland. Such circular towers of dry-built masonry had extremely thick walls and contained a large central courtyard. The base section of the walls was solid, but above this the construction was always hollow, containing galleries, and stairs leading up to the top of the structure. This characteristic constructional envelope of the brochs is clearly echoed at the Museum of Scotland, most prominently in the double-layered eastern wall adjoining the Royal Museum. To make this historical reference complete, this wall follows a slight curve and contains a staircase.

Other allusions to the fortified or castellated tradition within the Museum of Scotland's built fabric are plentiful, the most striking and overtly defensive element being the promontory tower. This corner tower, which stands near to the site of a former gate in the sixteenth

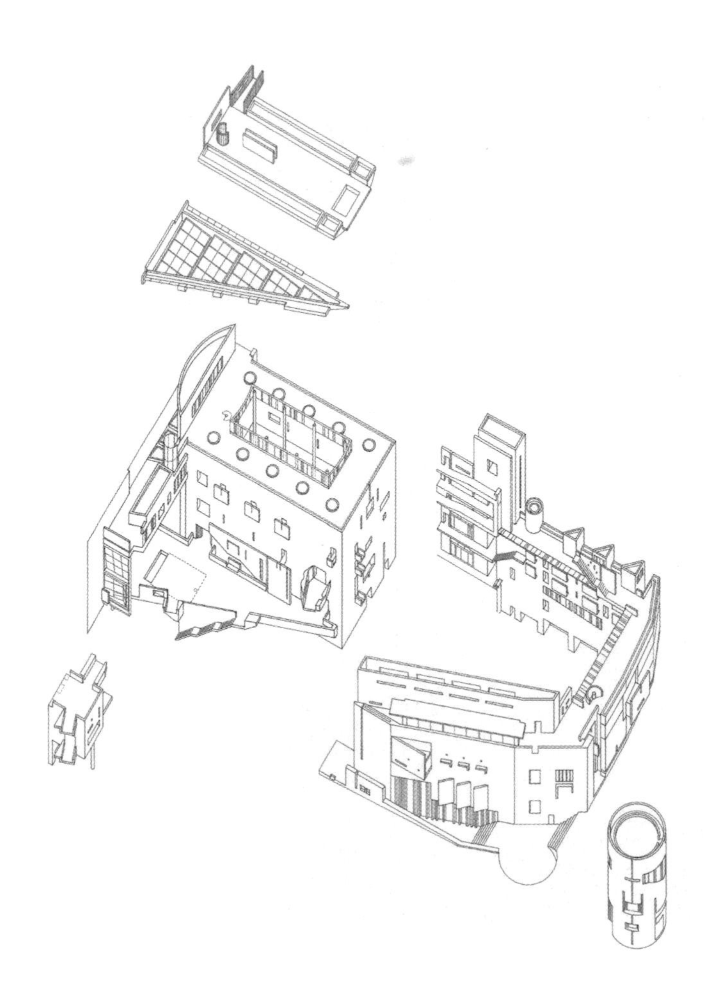

Above Benson + Forsyth have drawn on the national romanticism of nearby Edinburgh Castle to promote their own nascent national museum building

Right Exploded isometric of the Museum of Scotland, revealing the composition of cylinder, cuboid and triangular prism often favoured by Benson + Forsyth

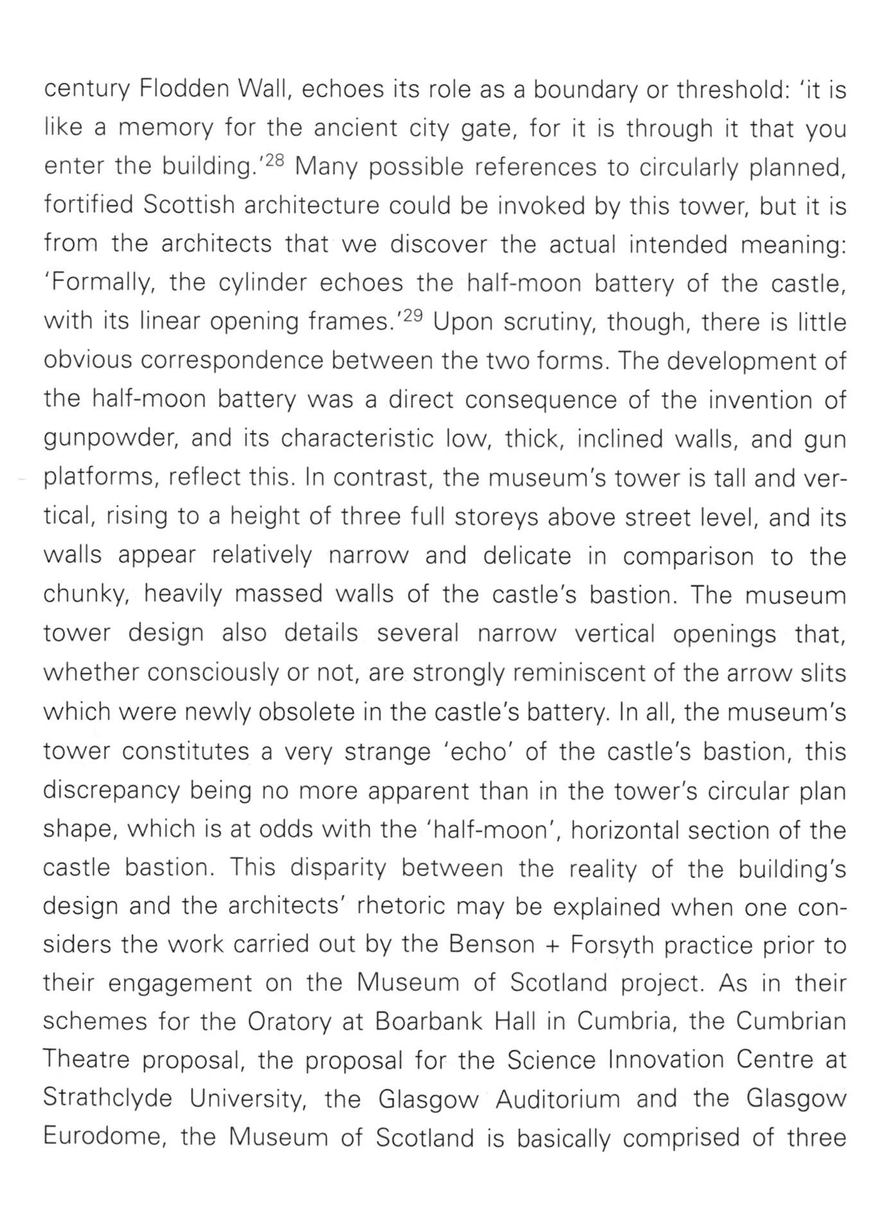

century Flodden Wall, echoes its role as a boundary or threshold: 'it is like a memory for the ancient city gate, for it is through it that you enter the building.'[28] Many possible references to circularly planned, fortified Scottish architecture could be invoked by this tower, but it is from the architects that we discover the actual intended meaning: 'Formally, the cylinder echoes the half-moon battery of the castle, with its linear opening frames.'[29] Upon scrutiny, though, there is little obvious correspondence between the two forms. The development of the half-moon battery was a direct consequence of the invention of gunpowder, and its characteristic low, thick, inclined walls, and gun platforms, reflect this. In contrast, the museum's tower is tall and vertical, rising to a height of three full storeys above street level, and its walls appear relatively narrow and delicate in comparison to the chunky, heavily massed walls of the castle's bastion. The museum tower design also details several narrow vertical openings that, whether consciously or not, are strongly reminiscent of the arrow slits which were newly obsolete in the castle's battery. In all, the museum's tower constitutes a very strange 'echo' of the castle's bastion, this discrepancy being no more apparent than in the tower's circular plan shape, which is at odds with the 'half-moon', horizontal section of the castle bastion. This disparity between the reality of the building's design and the architects' rhetoric may be explained when one considers the work carried out by the Benson + Forsyth practice prior to their engagement on the Museum of Scotland project. As in their schemes for the Oratory at Boarbank Hall in Cumbria, the Cumbrian Theatre proposal, the proposal for the Science Innovation Centre at Strathclyde University, the Glasgow Auditorium and the Glasgow Eurodome, the Museum of Scotland is basically comprised of three simple solids – a cylinder, a triangular prism and a cuboid – of the corner tower, Hawthornden Court and main gallery respectively. It seems that the architects wished to continue working to this tried and tested design formula, and realised that through unavoidable proximity and manipulated alignment, the museum's tower could be linked to the half-moon bastion of Edinburgh Castle, and as such be symbolically aligned with an extremely potent symbol of the strength and identity of the Scottish nation.

The museum exhibits other vestigial defensive features. The architects intended that their massed forms should resemble the central keep and enclosing curtain walls of Edinburgh Castle, and sought to achieve this by, 'wrapping a lower, outer building, containing the study galleries and the temporary exhibition space and following the precise undulations of the field roads, around the higher, rectilinear, main gallery and the triangular entrance space'.[30] The main gallery block of the museum, set back from both street façades, represents the rectangularly sectioned keep of St Margaret's Chapel in Edinburgh Castle, and this aesthetic echo is aided by the relative height of the tower, that stands proud not only of the other elements of the museum, but also of its neighbours. This feature is not specifically representative of Scottish architecture, though, as 'the characteristic Norman keep of England is unknown in Scotland, unless we accept that St Margaret's Chapel formed part of one.'[31] In fact, the museum contains several design details more reminiscent of the traditional Scottish tower house form than the Norman keep. As well as the obvious visual similarities of plan form, both also exhibit vertical organisation. At the museum, this vertical architectural promenade linked to the displays is immediately apparent, and jars against the strongly horizontal planning

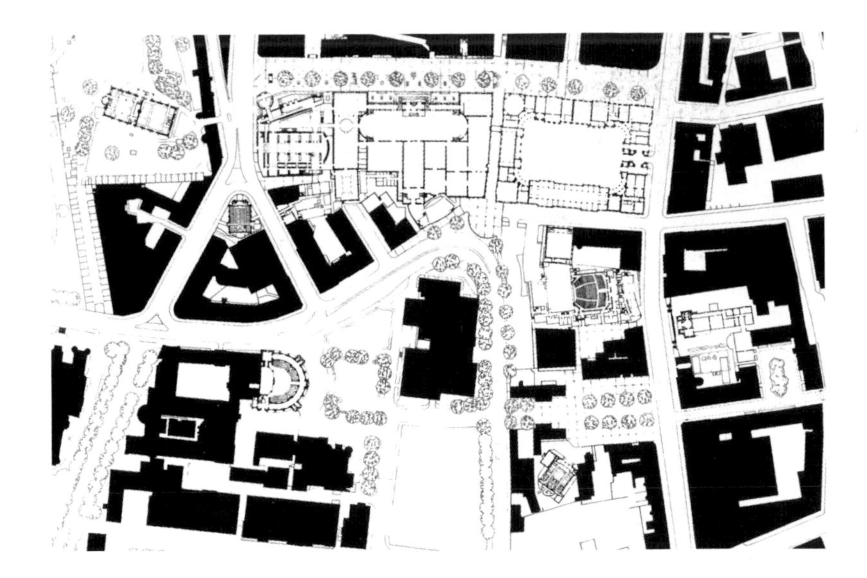

Left Contemporary cantilevered turnpike stairs within the Museum of Scotland evoke traditional castellated and tower house forms

Above Plan view, from east to west, of the Royal Museum of Scotland, the Museum of Scotland and Greyfriars Kirk. Benson + Forsyth used a manipulated axial alignment to spatially and symbolically link their new museum to Greyfriars Kirk and the National Covenant

of the adjacent Royal Museum. Similarly, in Scotland's many tower houses,' ... all the elements – stores, kitchen, hall, chamber and bedrooms – were set on end, served by one or more turnpike stairs as vertical corridors.'[32] Even this turnpike stair form favoured in tower houses is used by the architects at three points around the perimeter of the museum.[33] In an avoidance of banal pastiche, however, the steps cantilever from a central column and stop just short of the wall, creating the unusual and dramatic effect of light passing between tread and wall. A further suggestion of the medieval tower house within the museum's form is rather more subtle. Such tower houses typically grew organically over time, resulting in 'fortified homes: quirky, asymmetrical, casually human', and the irregularity of the museum's massing and detailing, as seen in the stone courses, door, window and slit openings, and its roofline, reflect this type of piecemeal and picturesque construction.[34]

The second part of this reference to castellated architecture, the museum's lower curved perimeter wall, mirrors the defensive curtain wall at Edinburgh Castle as it turns the corner from the north to the west façade. Often associated with this enceinte castle arrangement was a defensive moat, and echoes of such a fortification are also observable: 'The round tower on the corner suggests castles and a deep basement area beneath the facade could be a dry moat.'[35] This enceinte organisation is also mirrored aesthetically at the very heart of the museum in the form of the triangular orientation court that 'does not feel like an ordinary indoor space, more indoors-outdoors like the courtyard of a castle'.[36] Although not specifically national, the 'keep and curtain wall' arrangement deployed did help to resolve disjuncture in height lines and scale of the surrounding buildings. The keep-like main gallery block is the highest point in the immediate vicinity, but its height is successfully negated by both its set back position on the site, which largely obscures it from pavement level, and its white rendered finish. The most decisive element regarding sensitivity to height lines and scale is the curtain wall: this outer form of the building exactly matches the cornice height of the old Royal Museum of Scotland at that juncture, with the prominent line at ceiling height of the second floor also being reflected, but then reduces in height according to the slope of the site, to equate with the height and scale of the buildings on Bristo Port and Bristo Street. Similarly, there is a step down again to the diminished height of the third element, the circular corner tower: a further concession to the reduced scale of the medieval Greyfriars area.

Another spatial device, 'a poetic interpretation of the myths and memories of the local landscape', was critical to the generation of the museum's two-dimensional plan.[37] At the initial planning stage, the architects encountered two particular difficulties. Practically, they needed to knit together the opposing geometries and scales of medieval and 'New' Town Edinburgh, which converge on the site. Even more critical, though, was the search for symbolic meaning or validation with which to unite and embolden their design strategy. Thus, the architects were desperately searching for a design generator that would resolve this physical disjuncture, impose the necessary structure and order and, most importantly, endow the museum building with the resonance befitting such a seminal national institution. The National Covenant, 'a public petition which presumed a direct Scottish relationship with God, without "all kinds of Papistry" ', and more specifically the adjacent Greyfriars Kirk where the Covenant was signed in 1638, provided this linchpin.[38]

The marae, or Maori tribal meeting house, which is located at the heart of the National Museum of New Zealand, is both contemporary and inclusive

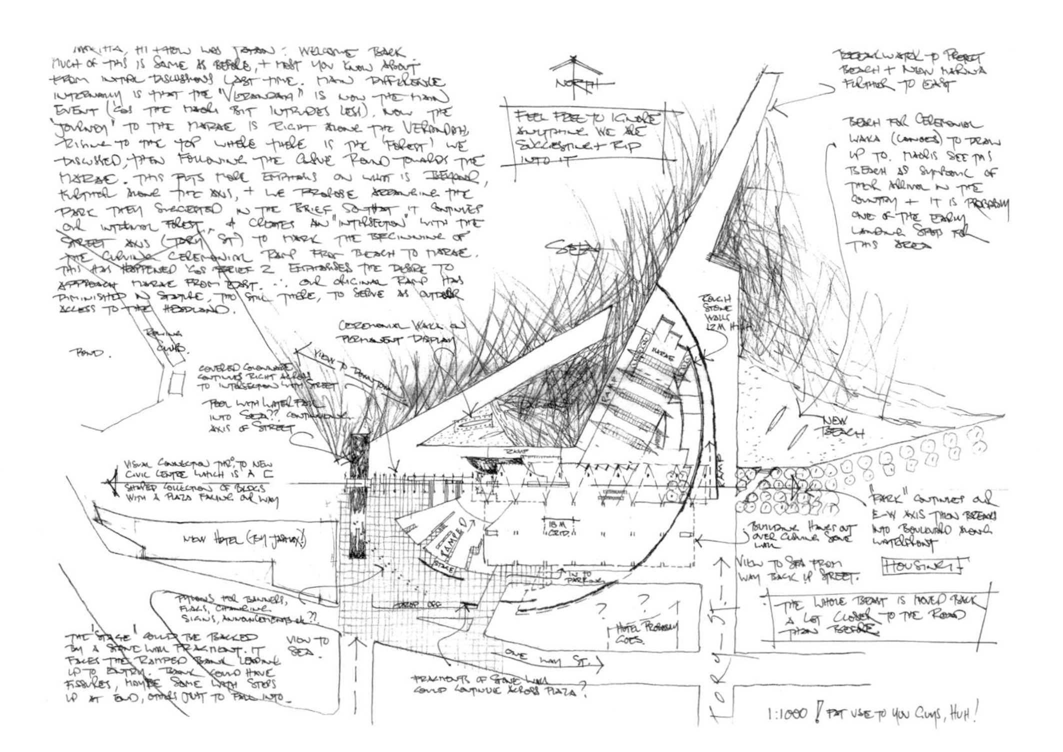

This very early sketch by Jasmax Architects shows the National Museum of New Zealand's marae almost surrounded by the sea in Wellington Harbour, with views from within the space across 'the most open landscape aspect' of the bay. The city's orthogonal urban grid is also clearly represented

This significance of Greyfriars Kirk and hence the signing of the Covenant manifests itself in the Museum of Scotland building, whilst at the same time solving this difficult problem of juxtaposing scales and orders, through the manipulation of principal design axes. The main axis of the Royal Museum runs lengthways through the 'nave' of its main hall, parallel to Chambers Street. In order to ensure continuity with this 'parent' building, the architects identified the node at the intersection of this line of symmetry with the threshold to the Museum of Scotland, as key.[39] The pivotal point of the new building, the apex of the Hawthornden Court, was then formed by continuing the axis from this point, to a point at the centre of the gate leading into Greyfriars Kirk. Thus, the principal line of orientation was generated from an imaginary extension or link to Greyfriars Church. Although not entirely precise in its execution, this symbolic intention with its latent meaning is clear. Through this device, and associated architectural signposts to it, the museum highlights and privileges the history of the National Covenant. Claiming a special link between God and the people of Scotland, the Covenant not only defined and reinforced the idea of Scotland the nation, but also honoured and empowered the Scottish people. In using the most tangible remnant of the Covenant, Greyfriars Kirk, as the main planning generator of the new museum building, the architects sought, by association, to promote and privilege the new national museum.

The historical and cultural layering of the Museum of Scotland's site – 'a hinge between the rationalist, orthogonal, and horizontally proportioned buildings of Chambers Street and romantic, crumbly, massive pre-Enlightenment Edinburgh' – further influenced the building's design.[40] Six approach roads intersect at the western edge of the site, of which four follow the course of the original medieval fieldroads, and the irregularly graduated curve of the museum's stone clad curtain wall reflects these erratically winding medieval streets in, 'a metaphorical transformation of medieval types'.[41] However, two of the six roads which converge on the western perimeter of the museum's site postdate the medieval period, being a part rather of the substantial, Enlightenment-based city improvement drives of the eighteenth and nineteenth centuries. This wave of building, with its ordered and symmetrical grid layout, was explicitly located within the new ideology of rationality and progress. In stark contrast to the 'Old' Town, which appears to have grown organically out of the rock, the thoroughfares of the 'New' Town were imposed onto the landscape, and these developments have informed the design of the museum. In complete contrast to the undulating curtain wall, which mirrors the façades of the Old Town dwellings lining the winding field roads, the museum's internal construction and resultant spaces are strictly ordered around a regular grid system. This 7.5 metre square structural system, constructed from reinforced concrete columns and beams, is most clearly defined in the main gallery block or 'donjon', which comprises five bays from east to west and three from north to south. Beyond this, the grid, although not determining the two-dimensional plan, still at times suggests it. This orthogonal organisation is intended to be a reduced reflection or embodiment of the new 'enlightened' pattern of urban settlement, which so transformed Edinburgh in the eighteenth and nineteenth centuries. As the architects themselves explain, 'the juxtaposition of the plastic outer wall with the formal geometry and axiality of the main gallery mediates between the Old and New Towns, whose respective characteristics both overlay the site'.[42]

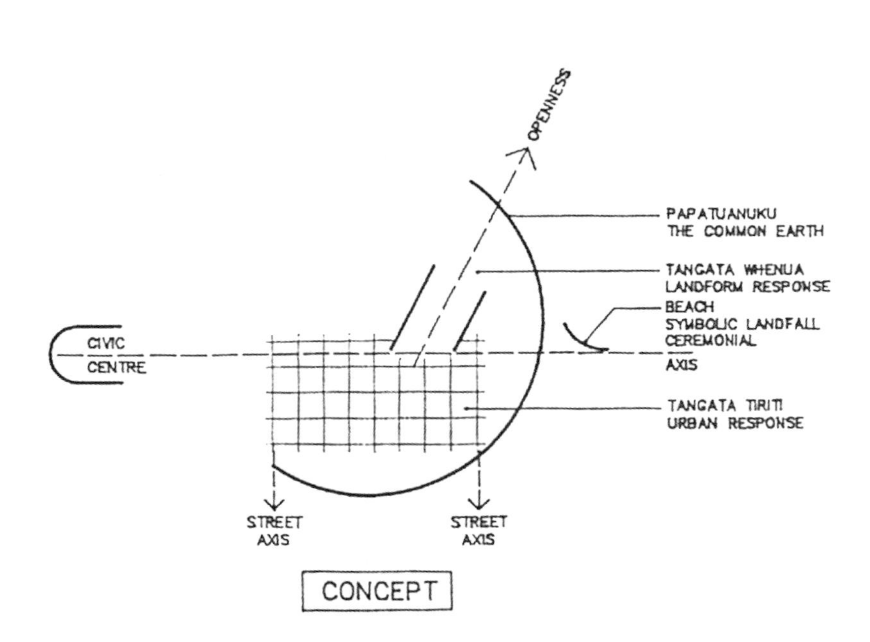

Concept diagram revealing how Wellington's colonial grid has generated the form of Te Papa's pakeha wing

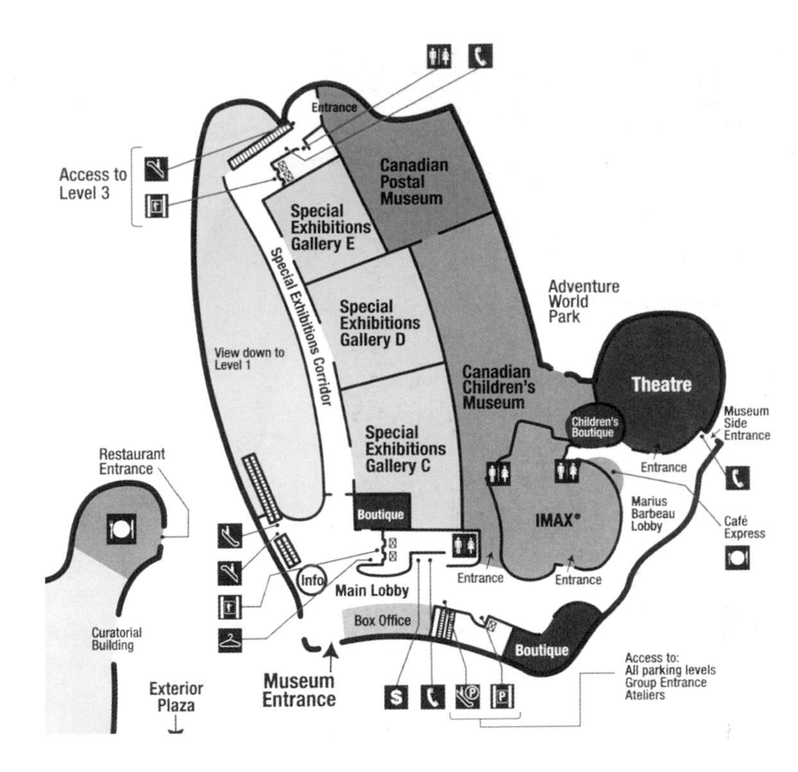

Douglas Cardinal's design for the Canadian Museum of Civilization is roundly sinuous in plan form, and separates the Curatorial Building from the Exhibition Wing to admit views of the national Parliament buildings across the Ottawa River

This reflection of land settlement patterns is also the principal organisational motif at Te Papa. The display areas pertaining to Maori art, history and life are housed in a homogeneous block in a roughly triangular wing of the museum building adjacent to Lambton Harbour, deferring to naturalistic mythology in a subtly symbolic representation of Maori culture. However, the museum's brief explicitly requested a building to represent the 'bicultural nature of the country, recognising the mana and significance of the two mainstreams of tradition and cultural heritage and provide for each to contribute effectively to a statement of the nation's identity'.[43] Jasmax therefore needed to ally this reference to Maori culture with a representation of *pakeha* or 'colonial' society. In order to achieve this, exactly the same device was used by the New Zealand design team as was employed in the Museum of Scotland: 'the original Jasmax concept group ... finally developed the use of settlement patterns to express the differences between Maori and pakeha'.[44] They used the city's orthogonal European settlement pattern – laid out by Edward Gibbon Wakefield in 1840 – as a design generator and continued this grid framework, although on a diminished scale, into the built fabric of the museum. Appropriately, as Bossley explains, 'the galleries which sat traditionally within the European museum tradition (History, Art, Natural Environment), were oriented within [this] structural grid which responded to the city grid directly behind the site'.[45] At this point the container was designed to reflect the contained, with the plan of the Tangata Tiriti, or 'People of the Treaty' galleries, being influenced and generated by the colonial grid.

The wish to create a strong and positive image of nation was also paramount in the Canadian Museum of Civilization, and determined its very site, which it was decided should form a part of the National Ceremonial Route and Confederation Boulevard. This is an avenue constructed to incorporate various political, cultural and diplomatic landmarks, which mostly date from the nineteenth and early twentieth centuries when the Enlightenment project of Canadian nation building was at its peak, into one national promenade. Taking its place within such a strong chain of national symbols, the Canadian Museum of Civilization itself becomes a part of this Modernist agenda, as Confederation Boulevard, powerfully 'link[s] the principal images every visitor to the capital is likely to retain of national symbols'.[46]

As well as the choice of site, this desire to communicate national pride also influenced the architectural planning of the Canadian museum. It was identified in the *Architectural Programme Synopsis*, that, 'a major attribute of the site is the availability of commanding views towards the Parliament buildings and the river'.[47] This led the architect to separate the curatorial and exhibition accommodation, admitting fine views between these two wings and across the Ottawa River to the nation's Parliament, as iconised on the national one-dollar bill. Beyond this obvious visual alignment, an axis exterior to, although exactly parallel with, the Grand Hall's line of symmetry, precisely connects the midway point between the museum's two wings to the Parliament's prominent Peace Tower. This connection is heightened by the use of copper cladding on the three barrel-vaulted roofs of the Exhibition Wing. Although initially a copper-brown colour, these panels have weathered sufficiently to turn green, reflecting the emerald roofs of the Parliament buildings. By forging this strong visual connection with the Parliament, the architect intended to create a deeper, symbolic link. The Parliament buildings are the ultimate symbol of Canada's great nineteenth century 'nation-building' project, and

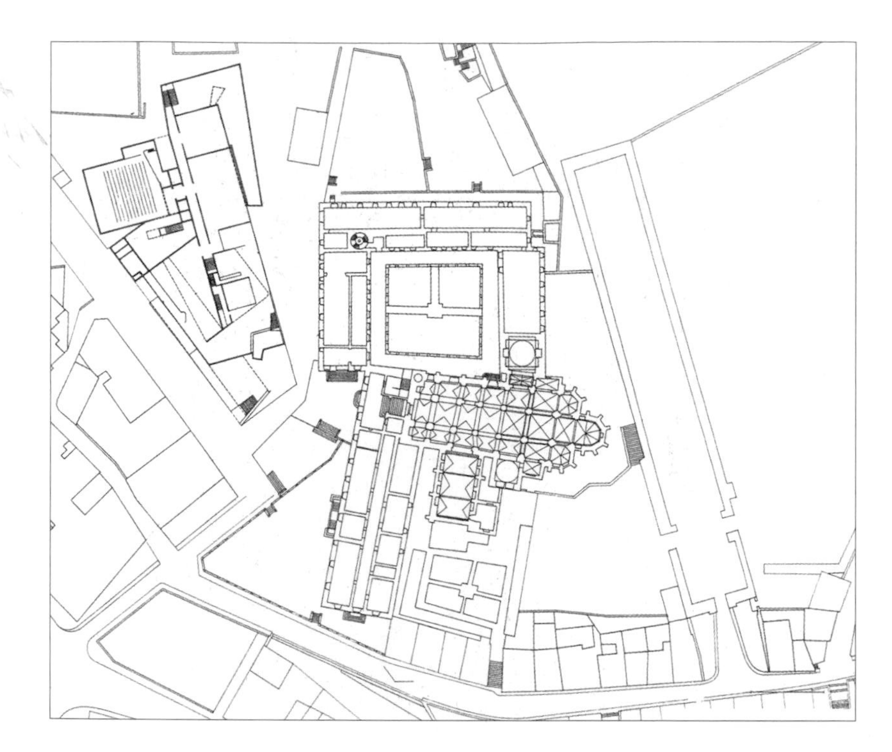

Site plan of the Galician Centre for Contemporary Art in Santiago de Compostela, showing its position adjacent to the seventeenth century monastery of Santo Domingo de Bonaval

In his design for the large modern art and architecture museums complex in Stockholm, Rafael Moneo shows sensitivity to the scheme's prominent and historic site on Skeppsholmen Island, beneath Skeppsholmen Church

although constructed a century later, the Canadian Museum of Civilization is a continuation of that project and may well become a key visual icon of Canadian identity far into the twenty-first century.

Although not always as laden with symbolic intent as these national examples, many of the museums explored here are well contextualised into rich and historically sensitive surroundings. At the Galician Centre for Contemporary Art in Santiago de Compostela, for example, Alvaro Siza has created a dialogue with the adjacent seventeenth century monastery of Santo Domingo de Bonaval. This is achieved formally by mirroring the unusual double corner entrance to the Baroque church and cloisters with the interlocking 'L'-shaped volumes of his own design, and materially through the use of the same granite as a cladding material. The contemporary application of this stone is clearly signalled, especially on the south elevation, where a granite plane hovers, seemingly weightless, above a corner-to-corner strip window. Rafael Moneo's Stockholm Museums of Modern Art and Architecture is similarly respectful of its historic site on the island of Skeppsholmen in the Swedish capital. The building sits reserved and unassuming within its setting, confining a statement of its identity to the distinctive series of lantern lights at roof level. In a further attempt at contextualisation, Moneo's decision to specify a grey colour for the exterior rendering was overturned by the museum's board, who advocated a terracotta-coloured finish, to lighten the drab greyness of Stockholm's winter skies and, more importantly, to respond to the similar warm, earthy colours of the capital's vernacular architecture. However, as Yoshio Taniguchi proves at the Toyota Municipal Museum of Art, it is not just the historic vernacular tradition that is celebrated by modern museum designers. In a city with a split personality, the architect has ably acknowledged both identities by framing views in one direction towards the historic heart of the castle town, formerly known as Koroma City, and in another direction towards a modern urban centre, which has flourished as a result of the Toyota Motor Corporation's relocation to the city. Kleihues + Kleihues were similarly unafraid to reference Chicago's more recent past in their Museum of Contemporary Art for the city. In a downtown city block, the architects sought to fuse the European Classical tradition with Chicago School Modernism, and this latter influence is probably most visible in the textured aluminium panels of the curtain wall, which recall the power and craftsmanship of the Chicago School's prolific, trademark use of cast metals.

Clearly, the national, civic and immediate architectural context has been a strong influence on many museum designers, but for those architects involved in an adaptive reuse scheme, another dialogue, that with the existing building itself, is critical. Two mid-twentieth century industrial buildings in Britain, Bankside Power Station on the south bank of the Thames in London, and the Baltic Flour Mill on the River Tyne, have both been converted to house art, but in each case their industrial strength and character has been retained, with the architects favouring relatively minimal intervention. In the Gateshead commission, Ellis Williams Architects were forced to remove the tightly packed grillage of concrete silos from the mill's interior, in order to free up studio and gallery space, although they retained the rest of the structure, replacing the bricked east and west elevations with glazing, to physically and metaphorically open the building up to its new public. In London, Herzog and de Meuron centred their thoughtful and refined intervention around the splendid volume of the existing turbine hall, but stamped their own identity on the scheme with an extended

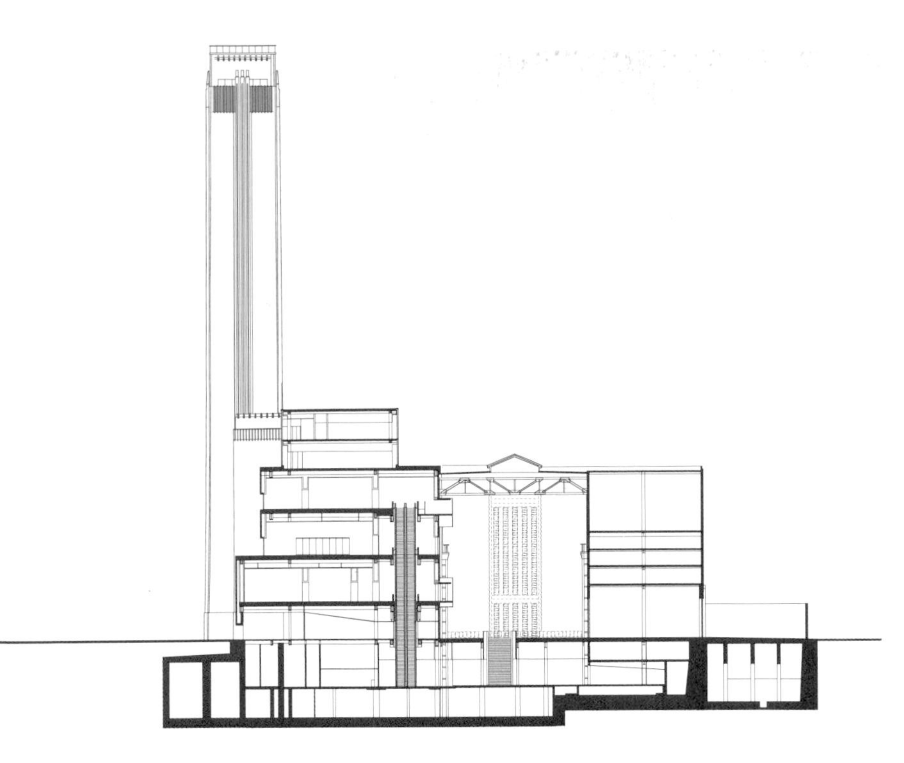

Tate Modern; cross section through the Turbine Hall and exhibition galleries

At BALTIC The Centre for Contemporary Art in Gateshead, Ellis Williams Architects chose to replace the brick screens to the east and west elevations of the former mill building with curtain glazing. This design strategy allows natural light to penetrate deep into the galleries and studios within, and invests the building with a more open and accessible character

'light beam' at roof level, which draws natural light into the top floor galleries during the day, and shines, beacon-like, over London at night. Another conversion scheme, Frederick Fisher's P.S.1 gallery in New York, takes positive advantage not only of the structure, but also the embedded memories, of the existing building – a late nineteenth century elementary school. Fisher retained partitions and fittings, such as doors and sinks, in order to leave a trace, or ghostly reminder, of the building's past history. The most startling interventions into an existing building, however, are surely the Guggenheim Las Vegas and the Guggenheim Hermitage that have been calmly inserted into the theatrical Baroque pastiche of the Venetian Hotel on the Las Vegas strip. An incongruous dynamic between the cool and refined functionalism of Koolhaas and the glitzy kitsch of Vegas has emerged, but ultimately this highly unlikely marriage has proved successful.

EXHIBITING ENCOUNTERS

In the progression towards the formation of modern nations, the meetings of cultures were undoubtedly defining moments, and these encounters have left a tenacious legacy on the architecture and exhibitions of our contemporary national museums.

In the early decades of the seventeenth century both the French and the English established permanent colonies in what is present-day Canada, and despite forming mutually advantageous trading alliances with the native 'Indians', conflict, both random and strategic, inevitably occurred. A similar pattern of encounter occurred in New Zealand, when Abel Tasman, the Dutch East India Company explorer, first landed in New Zealand and disturbed its inhabitants' centuries-old peace. This highly symbolic meeting brought together a Maori ethnie whose culture and society continued to be dominated by myth, with a newly 'enlightened' western culture, and the ramifications of this collision were to be far-reaching.

At that time, such 'enlightened' European societies viewed their cultures as superior to those of the indigenous peoples whom they increasingly encountered through the imperialist projects in the New World. These indigenous cultures were often subjugated, or at least marginalised, by the new dominant colonial core culture, which created and sustained an imperialist grand narrative of identity. However, this belief that a single, authoritative narrative can adequately represent the past, has, of course, been fundamentally challenged, most recently by:

> The condition of Postmodernity [which] is distinguished by an evaporating of the 'grand narrative', – the overarching 'story line' by means of which we are placed in history as beings having a definite past and a predictable future. The Postmodern outlook sees a plurality of heterogeneous claims to knowledge, in which science does not have a privileged place.[48]

This new plural perspective has challenged the hegemony of each country's dominant ethnie, which throughout the era of Modernity remained unassailable. In the case of New Zealand, 'the pakeha culture has always seen itself as universal, the answer to everything. But Maori – and other ethnicities – have a different way in which we want to make things happen.'[49] In this context, the three national museums have debunked the notion of a dominant or 'universal' national identity and embraced the diverse 'stories' or identities of Postmodernism to varying degrees.

The approach to identity displayed at the Museum of Scotland has strayed least from the traditional course. Throughout the displays, and

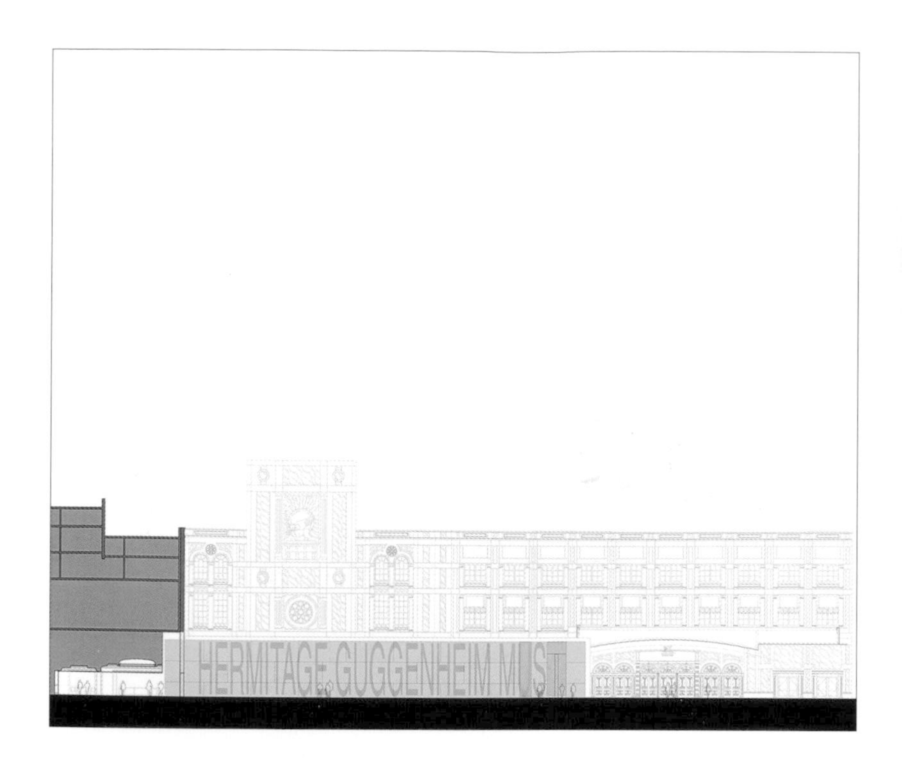

OMA's sleek, minimalist Guggenheim Hermitage Museum creates a startling collision with the surrounding pastiche of its parent building; the Venetian Hotel, Las Vegas

Authentically reconstructed indigenous dwellings line the length of the Canadian Museum of Civilization's Grand Hall

even to a large extent in the twentieth century gallery, a rich but ultimately *homogeneous* Scottish national identity is presented. Most telling of this is the 'Scotland and the World' display located on level 5, which is devoted to the migration of Scots overseas in the eighteenth- and nineteenth centuries, and includes 'the world map which introduces this theme [and] traces Scottish place names all over the world, and suggests just how much of a mark Scots have made'.[50] In contrast, there is no similar exhibit charting the influx of people of other identities into Scotland, which, although a much smaller phenomenon, is still a constituent in the identity of the contemporary nation. Within the broader historical and political context, this 'universal' approach to identity is explicable with reference to Scotland's long-standing position as a 'stateless nation'.[51] From the time of the Union with the English Parliament in 1707, the Scottish nation has been denied its own autonomous state, and, 'one of the first reactions [of such a disempowered minority group] is that it draws in on itself, it tightens its cultural bonds to present a united front against its oppressor. The group gains strength by emphasising its collective identity'.[52] The opportunity presented by the Museum of Scotland project to promote just such a unified and coherent national identity has clearly been seized, even though a degree of political control has recently returned to Scotland through the establishment of a devolved national parliament.

In the Grand Hall of the Canadian Museum of Civilization, the curators have avoided falling in line with an imperialist paradigm, forging instead a balanced and pluralist approach. Here, on the length of the hall opposite the glazed façade and across the polished marble 'sea', are exact replicas of the houses of a traditional coastal village. These were made by the descendants of each tribal group, using traditional methods, in an attempt to achieve authenticity. The resultant' ... walk along the shoreline represents a walk from the southern to the northern coast – from the Coast Salish house past the Nuu-Chah-Nulth, Central Coast, Nuxalk and Haida houses to the Tsimshian.'[53] The potentially problematic decision was taken to depict indigenous life and culture in the Grand Hall at a time *after* the arrival of European settlers, at this very period of European 'colonisation' or 'invasion'. This forced the curators to address contentious and sensitive issues, such as the decimation of the native population through the introduction of European diseases, and in taking up this difficult challenge in a purposefully impartial and academic manner, a rich and vital tableau of life on the British Colombian coast over the last two centuries has been achieved: 'The arrival of explorers, followed by fur traders, missionaries, the British Navy, and settlers, brought tragedy, opportunity and dilemmas to every family on the coast. The last years of the eighteenth century, and the nineteenth and twentieth centuries represent a period of innovation, change, resistance, loss, recovery and, ultimately, survival.'[54]

The three mainstream Canadian identities, native, French and English, are represented in the Grand and History Halls, and although largely autonomous, some attempt has been made to interweave these narratives. Significantly, though, the museum's curators have looked beyond these respectively indigenous and 'dominant' ethnies, and presented the arrival and subsequent experiences of other peripheral ethnic groups in Canada: 'although designated the History Hall, it does not restrict itself to the story of French and English settlement but also illustrates the relationship between the European newcomers and the established natives as well as the role of other immigrant

Canadian Museum of Civilization

This mighty, marble-clad wall slices through Te Papa Tongarewa from city to sea, symbolising an adjacent fault line deep in the earth

groups in the development of the country.'[55] Indeed, it is recognised that 'immigration from non-Western countries can be expected to become an increasingly important component of population growth, with the resulting need to integrate foreign values and traditions into the national self-understanding.'[56] The museum's director, George Macdonald, waxes lyrical on this theme:

> At the very heart of CMC's ambition is to be a crossroads of cultures, in a much wider sense than just a cultural marketplace. As a *national* museum, CMC belongs to, and serves, all Canadians and represents Canadian heritage and identity to both Canadians and non-Canadians. It has no valid choice other than to be concerned with all regions, cultures and eras in Canadian history. The multicultural nature of Canadian society seems to be the best theme for use in organising and making sense of CMC's resources and products.[57]

Certainly then, the displays at the Canadian Museum of Civilization attempt to portray the 'plurality of heterogeneous' Canadian identities, but, overriding this, the construction and promotion of a single, all-encompassing national identity is still the key priority.[58]

> Pluralism as an ideology makes a peripheral place for new possibilities without allowing them to challenge the central idioms of 'Euro-centered art.' Most often, this incorporation occurs under 'categorisations of "ethnic art" as primitivistic and folkloric' – that is, on much the same terms that African and Oceanic art have entered comprehensive art museums.[59]

The Canadian museum can be accused of allowing the culture of Canada's ethnic minorities into the museum in only a superficial or peripheral way, leaving white, European culture to determine its very structures, as at no point has this traditional model of European-style exhibition space been challenged. This is further borne out because the non-European art and material culture collections, as well as being housed in traditional European-style galleries, are indeed separately displayed under just such 'ethnic', 'primitivistic' and 'folkloric' categorisations as the *Native* Art Gallery, the *Folk* Arts Hall, and the Arts and Traditions Hall. This 'gives the opportunity to treat *ethnic* cultures, and *folk* or *popular* culture generally, more broadly than in the History Hall'.[60]

Both 'mainstream' New Zealand identities have been acknowledged and celebrated within the architectural planning of the Te Papa museum building, but the most challenging and potentially rewarding space is undoubtedly the interface between these two wings. This space is triangular, or wedge-shaped, and was created from the angled slant of the Maori wing in relation to the horizontal, north–south axis of the pakeha wing, that runs parallel to Cable Street. Bossley from the Jasmax team explains that

> during development the central space became a Wedge expressing the idea 'to cleave', which means both 'to split' and 'to adhere'. This allowed us to usefully develop the space as sitting between (separating) and also arching over (linking), thereby expressing the shifting nature of the relationship between the two cultures in a process of continual redefinition.[61]

With such a strong architectural meaning or discourse, it was decided that this intermediate space should house the exhibition on the Treaty of Waitangi – an agreement of 1840 which controversially passed sovereignty of the islands of New Zealand to the British Queen – with its location at the hub of the building metaphorically expressing the centrality of the Treaty to the New Zealand psyche. Its linking and

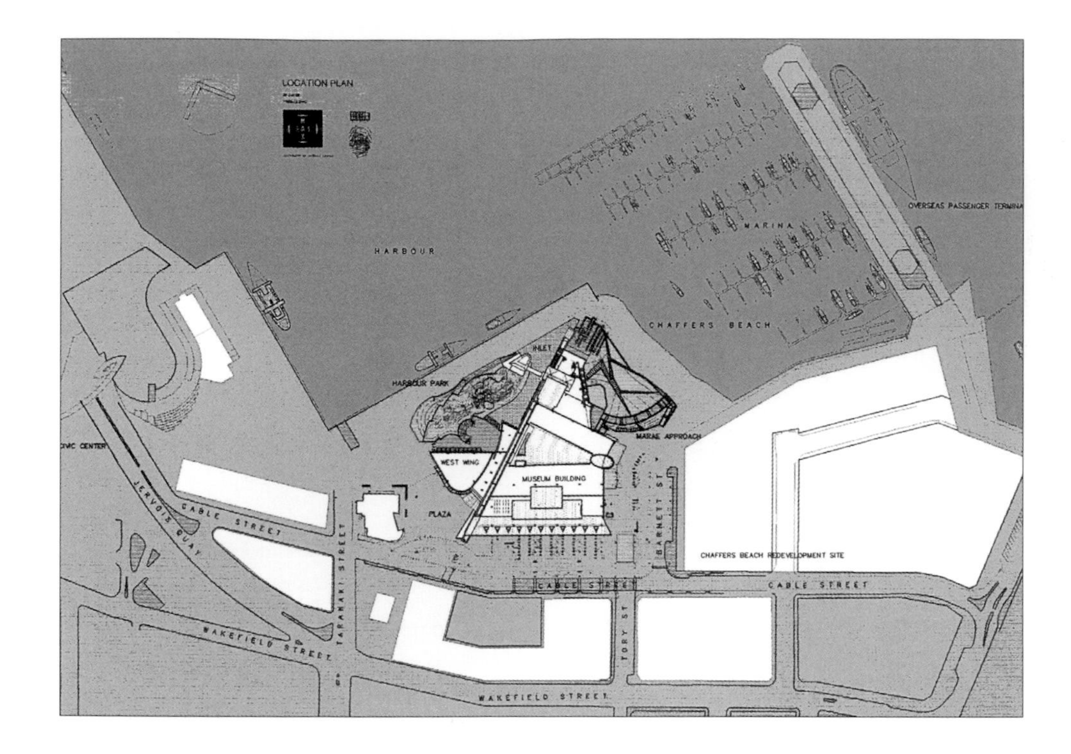

Site plan of the National Museum of New Zealand showing the Maori wing facing the rising sun and the openness of the bay beyond, in accordance with indigenous tradition, and the pakeha wing addressing Wellington's gridded street pattern

separating function of the Maori and pakeha wings allows dialogue and mediation between the two distinct cultures, highlighting both their uniqueness and similarity. Via this symbolic manipulation of the plan form, the architects hoped to create a shared space of encounter within the museum, where comparisons and contrasts could be formed.[62] The design team intended to treat this symbolism abstractly, in order to avoid clumsy pastiche: 'The main level 4 space is of monumental proportions under the expanding conical roof and between the 11m-high, exposed concrete walls on each side. The vaulted ceiling is of triangulated fibrous plaster and macrocarpa slats, suggesting interwoven links between the pakeha and Maori sections across the space.'[63]

Handling of the Treaty exhibition itself, which occupies a total area of 650 square metres and is housed on level 4 and on the level 5 mezzanines, was undoubtedly a sensitive and contentious issue. However, this was addressed openly and directly by the architectural team, who recognised' ... that many visitors may potentially have a fair degree of antipathy towards any exhibition regarding the treaty'.[64] Adding to the difficulties of representation was the scarcity of material evidence relating to the Treaty of Waitangi, that was compounded because the original documents were to remain at the National Archives. This dearth of material culture inevitably led to a curatorially controlled narrative approach that begins on the main level 4 hall most unusually, with three clusters of rusted steel poles, varying in height and diameter, symbolically representing the basic themes of governance, land and cultural heritage and citizens' rights. Significantly, the poles incorporate graphic panels depicting stories of individuals affected by the Treaty, and this fragmentation or personalisation is further emphasised by, 'the soft murmuring of many voices telling their varied stories ... '[65] Such plurality and egality in this depiction of the effects of the Treaty on all the people of New Zealand embraces the multiple and non-hierarchical narratives of Postmodernity. Moving further into the display area beyond the clusters,' ... a huge, 7 x 5m suspended glass relief acknowledges, in two layers, the history of the document itself. The front layer contains all the signatures of the Waitangi document, while the rear layer represents, in moulded and coloured surfaces, the parchment as ravaged by ill treatment and hungry rats.'[66] This is a powerfully iconic example of the inauthenticity of Postmodern reconstruction. To complete this space, two large-scale translations of the Treaty in English and Maori are suspended on the respective walls of the 'wedge', creating a quietly charged display, far removed from the object-based academicism of the early Modern museum display. Jasmax then, in association with the Te Papa curatorial team, largely discarded the framework of Modernity in their attempt to produce a balanced, plural and inclusive interpretation of the Treaty of Waitangi: 'The Treaty is therefore seen in a variety of contexts – historical, monumental, awe-inspiring, troublesome, flawed, under constant reinterpretation as part of the ongoing debate, but above all, relevant.'[67]

A radical approach to the depiction of plural identities was found to be lacking in the Canadian Museum of Civilization. However, those driving the national museum project in Wellington appear to believe that a' ... liberal, ameliorative agenda is not enough, that a more fundamental challenge to the canon, to the principles of a core historical heritage, is required', and just such a fundamental challenge to the pakeha canon can be discerned at all levels of Te Papa's structure.[68]

At Te Papa, biculturalism, or the place between the two worlds of pakeha and Maori culture, is apparent even at the smallest scale of the

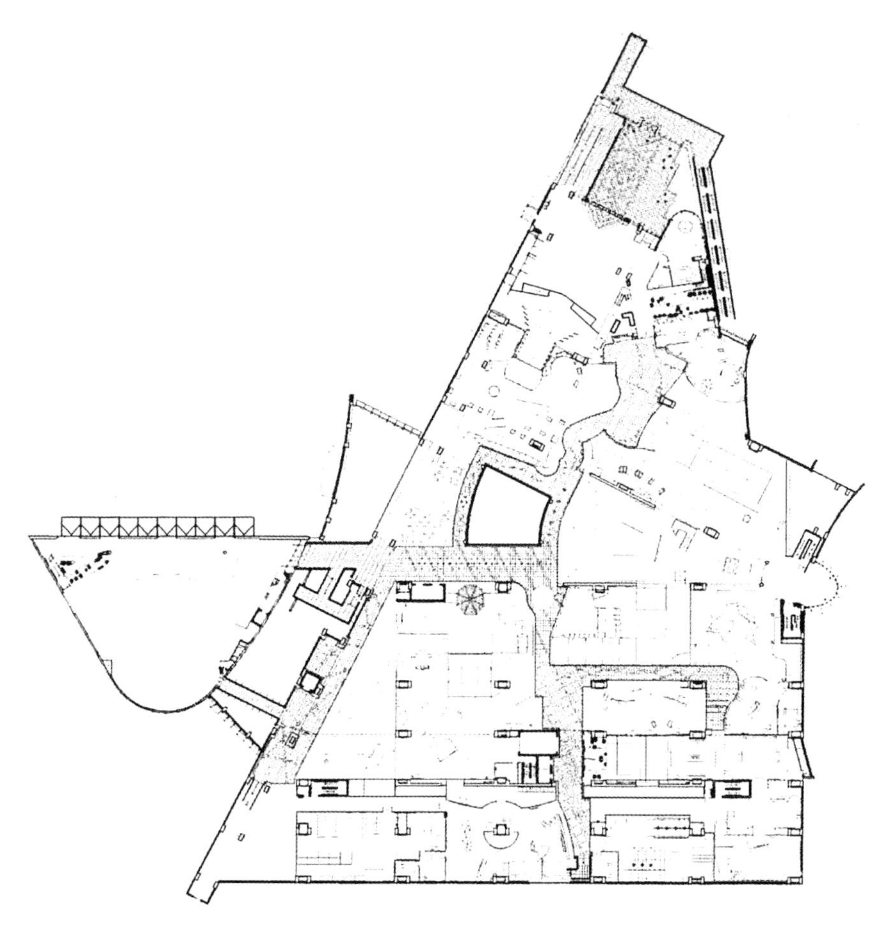

The wedge-shaped space at the heart of Te Papa Tongarewa houses an exhibition on the Treaty of Waitangi

museum: the individual exhibit. Throughout New Zealand's 'colonial' history, Maori *taonga*, or treasures, have consistently been appropriated without consent by pakeha collectors and museum curators. However, throughout the 1980s and 1990s this practice was radically amended, with the Te Papa Development Board instead engaging in consultation with *iwi*, or Maori tribal leaders, in order to acquire such *taonga*. The resultant shared concept of *mana taonga* has meant that *iwi* have a right to be consulted in the way their *taonga* are handled, used, exhibited and interpreted within the museum, and this joint or bicultural policy has had a significant effect on the way the Mana Whenua exhibition was developed, and more generally on the acceptance of the museum by the Maori community.

The most visible and potent sign of Te Papa's commitment to a bicultural identity is its marae, Rongomaraeroa, which occupies the harbour-side space of level four. Based on the traditional and sacred Maori tribal meeting house, this marae is unique, both in its contemporary design and decoration, which are based on traditionally used forms and materials, and in its embrace of a shared *Whakapapa*, or genealogy, of all the peoples of New Zealand. This symbolic openness is continued outside on the museum's promontory, where the *wahoroa*, or gateway, celebrates the arrival of all those who have come to New Zealand including, in addition to the expected representation of Kupe – an early Maori discoverer of Aotea-roa – European explorers such as Tasman and Cook. This marae is a deeply significant cultural gesture, which is all the more significant and lasting for being integrally located at the heart of the building:

> Here you get a marae structure that's built into the building. It's not added to, it's not put on top of, it's built into the architecture of the place. And of course, it's going to be very difficult to change it, especially now that it's there in people's minds. I've always said that this goes a long way towards the recognition of the bicultural approach in the building.[69]

On a larger scale, a commitment to biculturalism is also apparent in the museum's organisational operations, which are run jointly by Maori and pakeha, and hinge around negotiated compromise:

> [Biculturalism is] difficult because integration is not only about content but also about world-view, about values, about issues of time, of collaboration, disputational style, and the issues of supervision. In short, real biculturalism demands an understanding and acceptance by leadership of entirely different work and thinking patterns, and creating pathways, for it to work effectively in running an organisation.[70]

The most holistic approach to biculturalism, however, is revealed in the literature surrounding Te Papa, which describes the influence of the natural environment on the museum's architectural design in the following terms: 'In these shaky isles the land has many powers. It broke off from Gondwanaland more than 60 million years ago and drifted south. Rising and sinking many times, scoured by sea and sky, fished from the sea by Māui, it slowly formed itself ... '[71] That such a description in the building's official architectural guide can and does integrate the almost diametrically opposed languages of Maori native mythology and *pakeha* scientific rationalism, is surely indicative of the sincere commitment to create a truly bicultural museum.

Unlike the Canadian Museum of Civilization, Te Papa's much-vaunted attempt to achieve this biculturalism has gone beyond the museum's material contents to reassess the very ordering and guiding principles

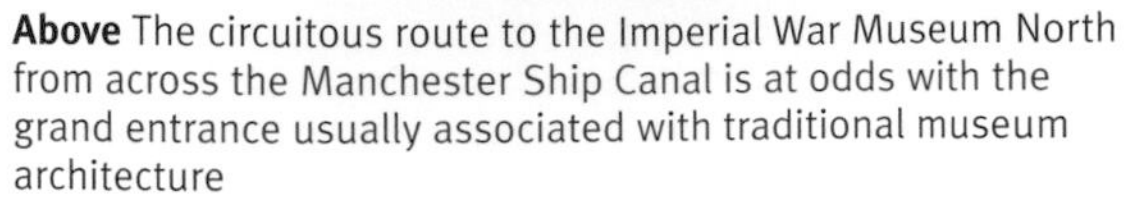

Above The circuitous route to the Imperial War Museum North from across the Manchester Ship Canal is at odds with the grand entrance usually associated with traditional museum architecture

Right, top Daniel Libeskind's concept of global fragmentation for the Imperial War Museum North

Right The Air Shard at the Imperial War Museum North on Salford Quays

Far Right The openness and angularity of the Imperial War Museum North's viewing platform promotes a sense of vertiginous unease

present at every level and in every activity of the institution. However, beyond these two main identities of Maori and pakeha, none of New Zealand's other minority ethnic groups have received more than superficial representation within the museum's exhibitions.

The colonial encounter has certainly informed many aspects of the contemporary national museums discussed, but more recent and extreme confrontations have been dealt with in the Imperial War Museum North, the Jewish Museum, Berlin, and the United States Holocaust Memorial Museum.

Daniel Libeskind was commissioned by the Imperial War Museum to design a new northern outpost in Manchester to house displays on the history of conflict in the twentieth century, and the architect found both the semantics and reality of this remit a challenge: 'the project was extremely challenging, not least because it contains three of the most difficult words in the English language: "imperial", "war" and "museum".'[72] The building's chosen site on Salford Quays was not only strategic, extending the programme of rejuvenation of this formerly industrial, brown-field area, but also resonant, as many munitions factories had supplied the Allied war machine from there during the Second World War. Libeskind wished to debunk any imperialist glorification of war, and certainly achieved this in his entry promenade to the building. Approaching the museum across the footbridge, visitors must navigate a disconcertingly erratic and tenuous path around the side of the building, eventually arriving at the idiosyncratic, domestically scaled entrance. Far from an imperialist celebration of victories on the battlefield then, this uncertain and low-key route points to the confusion and deprivation of war. A similar sense of unease is generated by a trip to the observation platform at the top of the scaffolding-framed air shaft. Here, open-meshed floor plates and angled balusters cause vertiginous unease, playing on the fearful excitement of the sublime.

In addition to these architectural devices, Libeskind also intended the building as a whole to be abstractly symbolic of war: 'I have imagined the globe broken into fragments and taken the pieces to form a building: three shards that together represent conflict on land, in the air and on water'.[73] Although this conceptual approach could be discounted as 'soundbite symbolism', the elegant resolution between the form and function of the three shards, and the dramatic sculptural quality of the aluminium clad whole, serve to quiet such criticism.[74] The air shard viewing tower is the first to be encountered, with the water shard – housing support and visitor facilities, including the restaurant – addressing the canalside. The principal open-plan gallery is housed in the capacious earth shard, and despite following a traditional chronological sequence around its perimeter, like Te Papa it makes space for a diversity of opinions and experiences. This is most noticeable in one enclosed 'room' within the main volume of the hall, where the curators have presented the rich stories of individuals affected by war through their personal memorabilia. These artefacts are contained within stacked drawers which visitors can open to reveal the lives within. Similarly, the audio-visual show, which periodically animates the main gallery, personalises the experience of war, rather than presenting a single, definitive narrative.

It was in Berlin where Libeskind first focused on identity, with the highly contested commission for the Jewish Museum. He saw this as 'a means of portraying the enormous intellectual, economic and cultural contribution that Jewish citizens made to Berlin and a means of incor-

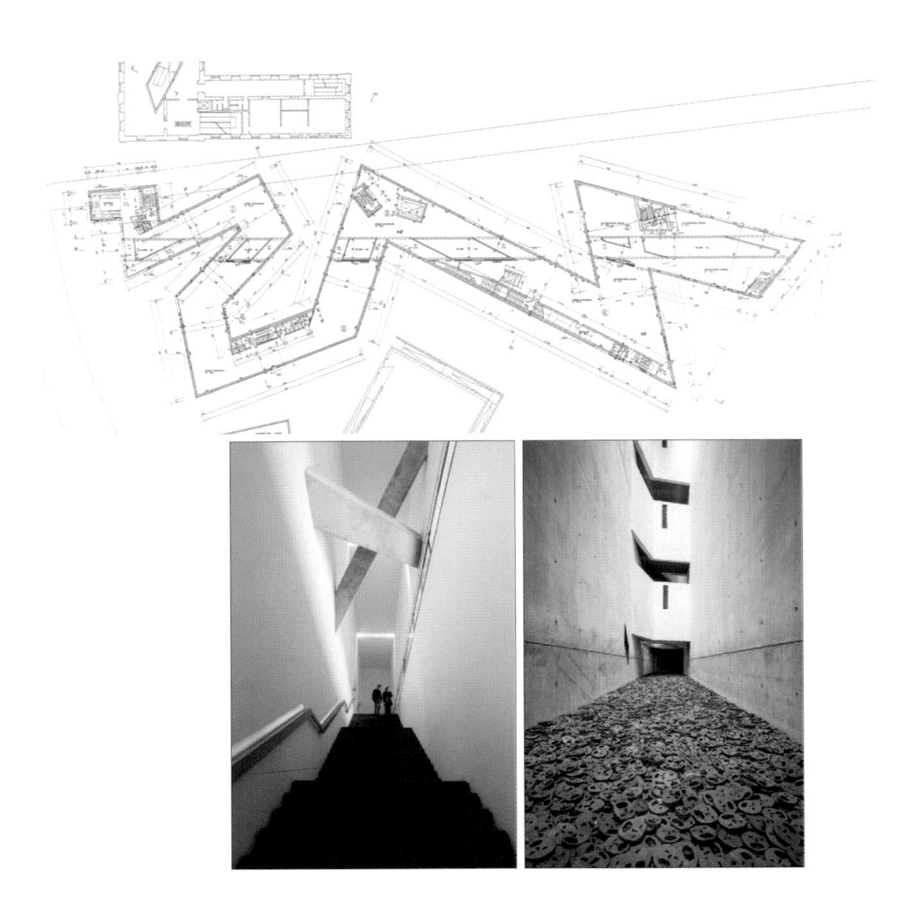

Above Libeskind's Deconstructivist symbolism at the Jewish Museum, Berlin, houses a contested and contentious space of encounter

Right, top First floor plan of the Jewish Museum Berlin, generated from poignant symbolism and an informed urban matrix

Right The staircase at the end of the Axis of Continuity leads from basement level to the historical installations above

Far Right The installation, 'Fallen Leaves', by Menashe Kadishman, heightens the chillingly sombre emptiness of Libeskind's Holocaust Void

porating the meaning of the Holocaust into the city's conscious memory.'[75] The very thought of a museum to the Jewish people in the heart of the city, which only a few decades earlier had been the seat of Nazi power, seemed unthinkable to many. However, combining sensitivity and symbolism, the architect has created an extraordinary space of encounter. Just as the overall spatial planning of Te Papa Tongarewa and the Museum of Scotland in particular, has been shown to be influenced by their immediate edge conditions and wider urban and natural contexts, so the design of the Jewish Museum was generated in part with reference to the fabric of the surrounding city. Libeskind identified the homes of prominent pre-war Jews around the city, and the intricate connection of these nodes to each other and the museum site began to generate the irregular footprint of the building. Superimposed onto this was a deconstructed synthesis of the potent symbolism of the Swastika and Star of David, and from the resultant plan, Libeskind extruded his four-storey building.

The new museum's situation adjacent to the existing nineteenth century Berlin Markische Museum was meaningful to Libeskind, who used the spatial conjunction between these two buildings to express the fluctuating and deeply troubled relationship between German and Jewish Berliners over the centuries. Libeskind was determined that the new building should be entered through the old, believing that the history of the city's Jews was inextricably linked to that of its German citizens, but this linking passageway was placed underground, to concretise the hidden shame of episodes in their joint history. In so doing, the architect was 'preserving the contradictory autonomy of both the old building and the new building on the surface and bound the two together in the depth of time and space.'[76] This entry arrangement has another resonant effect, making the doorless new museum appear solitary, almost mute. Inside the museum, this tense and metaphorical architectural language continues along three subterranean passageways, one leads to the most resonant space within the building: the Holocaust Void. Simply a dead end, this uncanny volume is powerfully disconcerting in its abrupt and echoing nothingness. Here, the desolation caused by history's most horrific encounter is given physical form, and the resulting experience is strangely moving.

Libeskind was not alone in tackling such a heavily laden commission, across the Atlantic, James Ingo Freed had been commissioned to 'symbolise the unspeakable' in his design for the United States Holocaust Memorial Museum in Washington DC.[77] Freed's design is rationalised into three main components that act rather as 'decompression chambers between the reality of the outside world and the hyper-reality of the Holocaust'.[78] The first of these to be encountered is an 'L'-shaped element, which addresses 14th Street with a rather static Neo-Classical façade reminiscent of the state architecture of National Socialism. On turning the corner, this element transforms into a blank, mute screen that encloses and contains the Hall of Witness, metaphorically shrouding the mechanisms of evil within a legitimate cloak of state. The Hall of Witness itself is the museum's principal volume, which pervades an uneasy tension thanks to its off-centre skylight and a large crack down the western wall. The brick walls and steel gates around its perimeter allude to the prison walls and gates of the Nazi death camps in eastern Europe, and the metal doors provide a chilling reminder of the camps' crematorium ovens. Four metal bridges spanning the space above roof level bring to mind the Warsaw Ghetto, and the volume as a whole is confined by two ranks

Above The form of the hexagonal Hall of Remembrance, which lies to the rear of the series of individual museum spaces, provides a calming space for meditation and reflection

Right Sketches by Pei Cobb Freed & Partners Architects, detailing the brick towers which line the Hall of Witness at the United States Holocaust Memorial Museum. These provide a chilling reminder of concentration camp watch towers

of imposing brick towers, reminiscent of the concentration camp watch towers. Together, these abstracted architectural metaphors fuse to create a highly charged atmosphere, concretising the horrific encounter between Nazis and Jews during the Second World War. The final volume of the design, the discrete hexagonal Hall of Remembrance, draws – as did Libeskind's Jewish Museum – on the Star of David, but also on the yellow triangles that demarcated Jews during the war. This space, like over three-quarters of the entire museum, is dedicated to contemplation and commemoration, and acts as an antidote to the Hall of Witness. In all, the United States Memorial Holocaust Museum is an extremely poignant physical monument to one of the most horrifying and inhumane encounters in human history, and is a most extreme example of the museum's lasting role in the construction and depiction of identities.

Notes

1 Eilean Hooper-Greenhill. *Museums and the Shaping of Knowledge* (London and New York: Routledge, 1992), p. 4.

2 Ibid., p. 106.

3 Robert Bevan. 'Treasure Island', *Building Design*, no. 1340, 27 Feb. 1998, p. 14.

4 Duncan and Wallach. Cited in Tony Bennett, *The Birth of the Museum* (London and New York: Routledge, 1995), p. 38.

5 This term was coined by Labour Prime Minister, Harold Wilson.

6 Sharon Macdonald and Gordon Fyfe. *Theorizing Museums: Representing Identity and Diversity in a Changing World* (Oxford and Cambridge: Blackwell Publishers, 1996), p. 1.

7 Ibid., p. 2.

8 Architectural Brief. Te Papa Tongarewa the National Museum of New Zealand, Wellington, 1989.

9 Norman Crowe. *Nature and the Idea of a Man-Made World* (Cambridge, MA and London: MIT Press, 1995), p. 30.

10 Pete Bossley. 'Concepts in Culture', in *Architecture New Zealand*, 'The designing of Te Papa', Special Edition, 1998, p. 18.

11 Ibid.

12 Pete Bossley. *Te Papa. An Architectural Adventure* (Wellington: Te Papa Press, 1998), p. 'the earth papatuanuku'.

13 Architecture and Planning Group, National Museums of Canada. *Architectural Programme Synopsis* (Ottawa: National Museums of Canada, 1983), p. 2.

14 Not an original concept, this architectural metaphor has a particularly famous precedent at Frank Lloyd Wright's 'Fallingwater', Bear Run, Pennsylvania, the design of which imitates the layered sedimentary stone outcroppings of its site.

15 Douglas Cardinal. 'A Vision for the National Museum of Man', 17 Jan. 1983, p. 22.

16 Martin Jackson. *Reflections* (Falmouth: National Maritime Museum Cornwall, 2002), p. 14.

17 Douglas Cardinal, CTV Documentary *Frozen Music*, in George F. Macdonald and Stephen Alsford. *A Museum for the Global Village* (Hull: Canadian Museum of Civilization, 1989), p. 13.

18 Charles Jencks and others. *New Science = New Architecture? Architectural Design*, vol. Sept./Oct. 1997, p. 65.

19 Ibid.

20 Gordon Benson. 'Benson + Forsyth', *Mac Mag*, p. 6.

21 Ibid., p. 6.

22 John Allan. 'In Search of Meaning: An Architectural Appreciation of the Museum of Scotland', in Gordon Benson and Alan Forsyth, *Museum of Scotland* (London: August Media in association with Benson + Forsyth, 1999), p. 127.
23 Duncan Macmillan. In Gordon Benson and Alan Forsyth, *Museum of Scotland* (London: August Media in association with Benson + Forsyth, 1999), p. 113.
24 Ibid.
25 John Allan. In Gordon Benson and Alan Forsyth, *Museum of Scotland* (London: August Media in association with Benson + Forsyth, 1999), p. 124.
26 Pete Bossley. 'Redirect, Redevelop', *Architecture New Zealand*, 'The Designing of Te Papa', Special Edition, p. 19.
27 C. R. Mackintosh, 1892.
28 Duncan Macmillan. In Gordon Benson and Alan Forsyth, *Museum of Scotland* (London: August Media in association with Benson + Forsyth, 1999), p. 110.
29 Gordon Benson. 'Benson + Forsyth', *Mac Mag*, p. 6.
30 Ibid.
31 George Hay. *Architecture of Scotland* (London: Oriel Press, 1977), p. 25.
32 Edith B. Hannah. *Story of Scotland in Stone* (Edinburgh and London: Oliver and Boyd, 1934), p. 47.
33 This is a uniquely Scottish term for a spiral staircase.
34 Duncan Macmillan. In Gordon Benson and Alan Forsyth, *Museum of Scotland*, (London: August Media in association with Benson + Forsyth, 1999), p. 113.
35 Ibid.
36 Ibid., p. 115.
37 William J.R. Curtis. *Modern Architecture Since 1900* (London: Phaidon Press, 1997), 3rd edn, pp. 132, 133.
38 John and Julia Keay. *Collins Encyclopedia of Scotland* (London: Harper Collins, 1994), p. 189.
39 This axis creates symmetry within the hall, although not the building as a whole.
40 Charles McKean. *The Making of the Museum of Scotland. Draft Text*, p. 5.4.
41 William J.R. Curtis. *Modern Architecture since 1900* (London: Phaidon Press, 1997), 3rd edn, pp. 132, 133.
42 Gordon Benson, 'Benson + Forsyth', *Mac Mag*, p. 6.
43 Pete Bossley, 'Concepts in Culture', *Architecture New Zealand*, 'The Designing of Te Papa', p. 18.
44 Ibid.
45 Ibid.
46 George F. Macdonald and Stephen Alsford. *A Museum for the Global Village* (Hull: Canadian Museum of Civilization, 1989), p. 8. Indeed, all five short-listed sites for the museum lay on this route, but the Parc Laurier site was always favoured because it aided the political agenda to assimilate the working-class district of Hull with Ottawa's affluent and vibrant community across the river.
47 Architecture and Planning Group, National Museums of Canada. *Architectural Programme Synopsis* (Ottawa: National Museums of Canada, 1983), p. 17.
48 Anthony Giddens. *The Consequences of Modernity* (Cambridge: Polity Press, 1990), p.2.
49 Anne French. 'Setting Standards', *Architecture New Zealand*, 'The Designing of Te Papa', Special Edition, 1998, p. 72.
50 Jenni Calder. *Museum of Scotland* (Edinburgh: NMS Publishing, 1998), p. 61.
51 David McCrone. *Understanding Scotland: The Sociology of a Stateless Nation* (London and New York: Routledge, 1992).
52 Madan Sarup. *Identity, Culture and the Postmodern World* (Edinburgh: Edinburgh University Press, 1996), p. 3.
53 Andrea Laforet. *The Book of the Grand Hall* (Hull: Canadian Museum of Civilization, 1992), p. 6.
54 Exhibition text from the Grand Hall, Canadian Museum of Civilization.
55 George F. Macdonald and Stephen Alsford. *A Museum for the Global Village* (Hull: Canadian Museum of Civilization, 1989), p. 72.
56 Ibid., p. 59.
57 Ibid.
58 Anthony Giddens. *The Consequences of Modernity* (Cambridge: Polity Press, 1990), p. 2.
59 Steven D. Lavine. 'Art Museums, National Identity, and the Status of Minority Cultures: The Case of Hispanic Art in the United States', in Ivan Karp and Steven D. Lavine. *Exhibiting Cultures. The Poetics and Politics of Museum Display* (Washington, DC and London: Smithsonian Institution Press, 1991), p. 83.
60 George F. Macdonald and Stephen Alsford. *A Museum for the Global Village* (Hull: Canadian Museum of Civilization, 1989), p. 89. My italics.
61 Pete Bossley. *Te Papa. An Architectural Adventure* (Wellington: Te Papa Press, 1998), p. 'the developed concept'.
62 As John Hunt explains, the first and most lasting concept forwarded by the design team was that 'the *marae* and Maori collection were to be located on this promontory, and its oblique relationship to the gridded spaces of the other galleries (reflecting the European settlement pattern of Wellington) was intended as an acknowledgement of cultural differences'.
John Hunt. 'Process of Selection', *Architecture New Zealand*, 'The Designing of Te Papa', Special Edition, 1998, p. 16.
63 Ibid.
64 Pete Bossley. 'The Treaty', *Architecture New Zealand*, 'The Designing of Te Papa', Special Edition, 1998, p. 64.
65 Ibid., p. 67.
66 Ibid.
67 Ibid.
68 Steven D. Lavine. 'Art Museums, National Identity, and the Status of Minority Cultures: The Case of Hispanic Art in the United States', in Ivan Karp and Steven D. Lavine. *Exhibiting Cultures. The Poetics and Politics of Museum Display* (Washington, DC and London: Smithsonian Institution Press, 1991), p. 86.
69 Anne French. 'Setting Standards', *Architecture New Zealand*, 'The Designing of Te Papa', Special Edition, 1998, p. 69.
70 Elaine Heumann Gurian. 'A Ray of Hope', *Architecture New Zealand*, 'The Designing of Te Papa', Special Edition, 1998, p. 78.
71 Pete Bossley. *Te Papa. An Architectural Adventure* (Wellington: Te Papa Press, 1998), p. 'the earth papatüänuku'.
72 Mark Lawson. Interview with Daniel Libeskind, Front Row, Radio Four, July 2002.
73 Daniel Libeskind. Imperial War Museum North, wall text.
74 Graham McKay. 'Old Paradigm Jencks', *Architectural Review*, vol. 213, no. 1274, Apr. 2003, p. 35.
75 Daniel Libeskind. *The Space of Encounter, Between the Lines* (New York: Universe Publishing, 2000), p. 23.
76 Ibid., p. 27.
77 James Steele. *Museum Builders* (London: Academy Editions, 1994), p. 177.
78 Ibid.

The imposing Museum of Scotland acts as both beacon and buffer on its corner site

Benson + Forsyth

MUSEUM OF SCOTLAND

Edinburgh **1998**

Just as Scotland was increasing its political autonomy in the 1990s through the formation of the Scottish Parliament, so it was asserting its cultural identity via the Museum of Scotland project.

The chosen architects, Benson + Forsyth, had to work within a confined city centre site adjacent to the existing Royal Museum of Scotland, prompting their decision to excavate a 'basement' level to increase the total permissible floor area. The site also threw up other challenges and suggested possibilities, being located at a confluence between Edinburgh's medieval 'Old' Town, and urban developments of the nineteenth century. In response to these rich site conditions, the architects mirrored the gridiron 'New' Town street pattern in the large, orthogonally framed main gallery block to the rear of the site and wrapped an undulating stone-clad curtain wall around the north and west perimeter to address the erratically winding medieval fieldroads: 'the juxtaposition of the plastic outer wall with the formal geometry and axiality of the main gallery mediates between the Old and New Towns, whose respective characteristics both overlay the site.'[1]

Between these two strong design elements, the triangular Hawthornden Court provides an orientation core and transitionary space between inside and out. Meanwhile the corner tower strikes up a dialogue with nearby Edinburgh Castle, reduces in height to bridge the scale differential across the site and acts as both beacon and buffer at the busy corner intersection.

1 Gordon Benson. 'Benson + Forsyth', *Mac Mag*, Nov. 1991, p. 6.

View of Edinburgh Castle from Museum of Scotland tower

Above Extruded model revealing the museum's formal reference to the fortified tradition of 'keep', 'curtain wall' and 'promontary tower'

Right Exploded isometric revealing the composition of cylinder, cuboid and triangular prism favoured by Benson + Forsyth

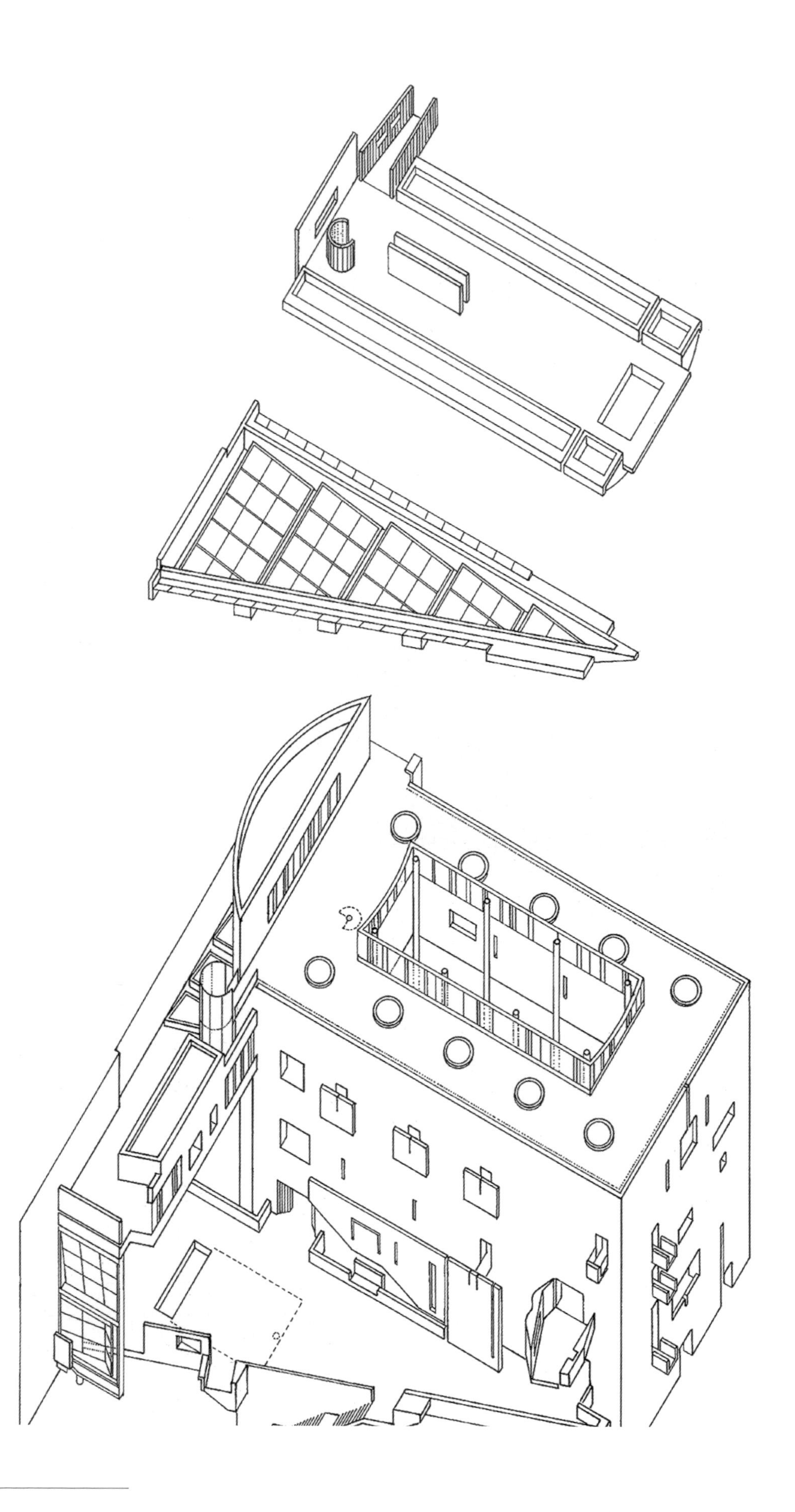

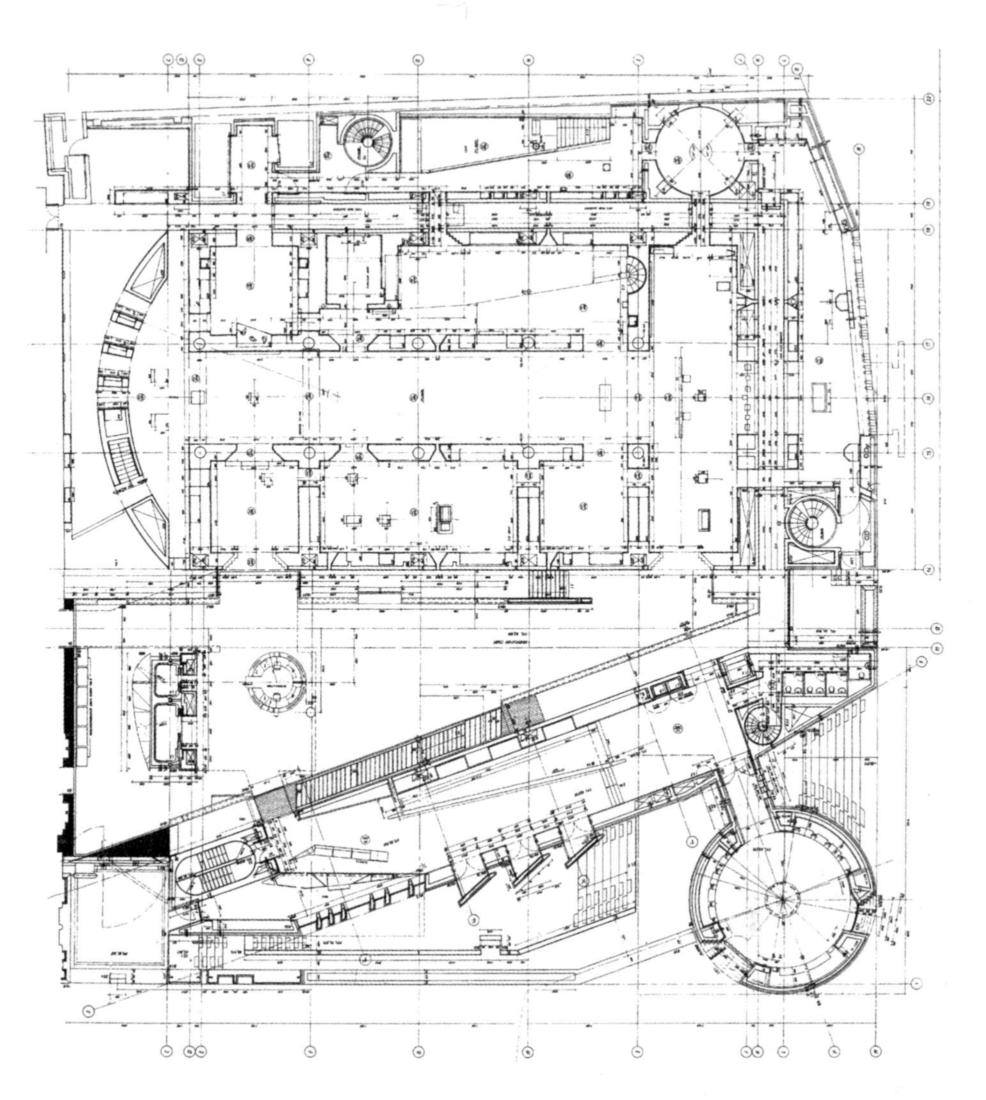

Above Ground floor plan

Left Contemporary cantilevered turnpike stairs evoke traditional castellated and tower house forms

Below Plan of the tower

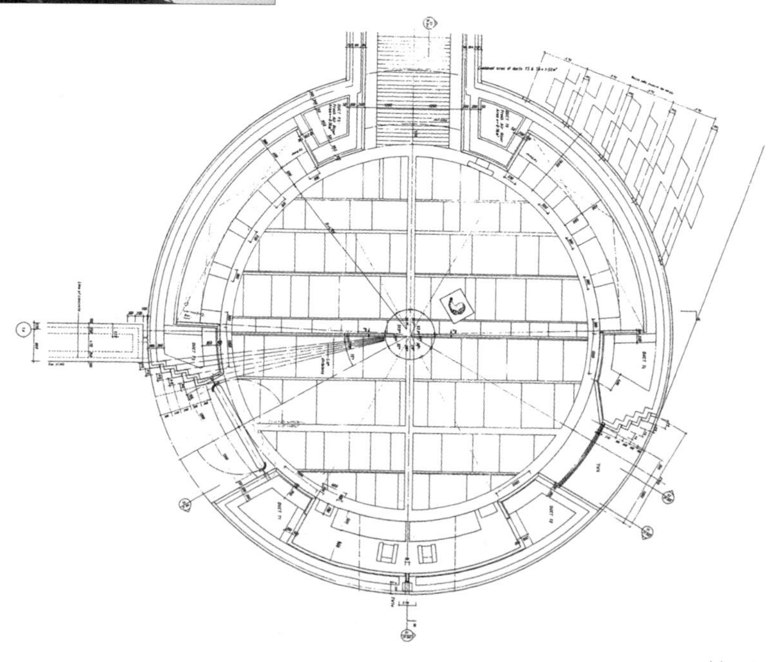

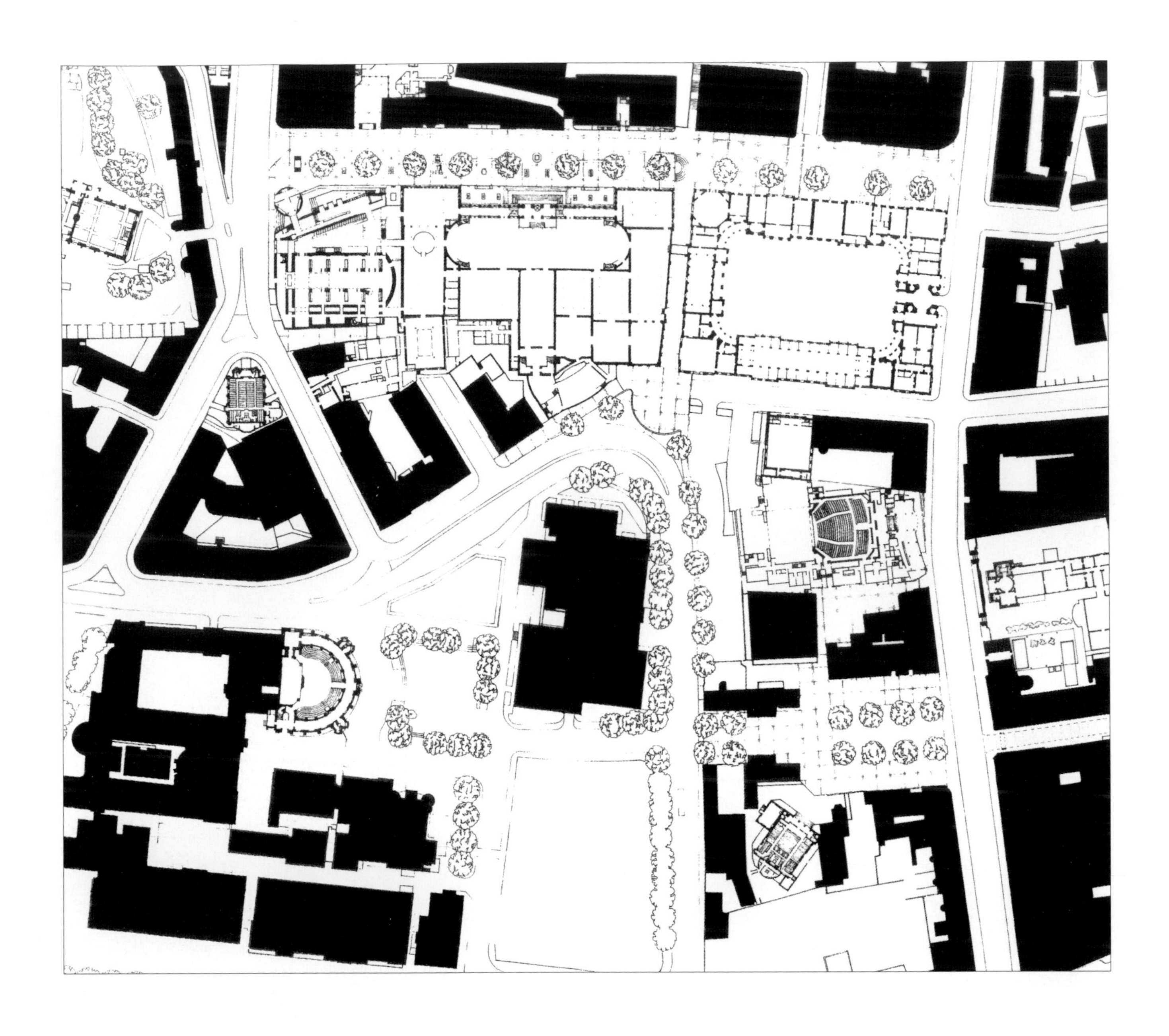

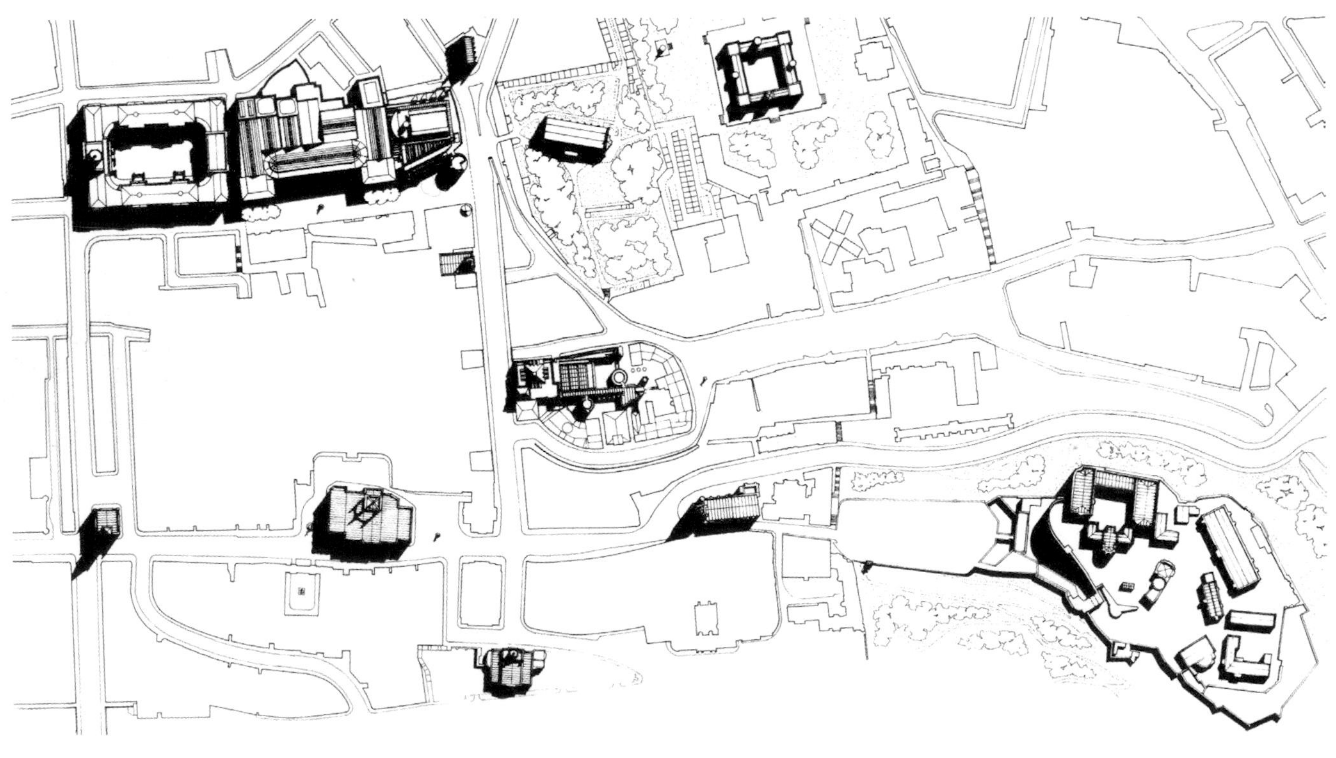

Above Arthur's Seat provides a backdrop to the museum, when viewed from Edinburgh Castle esplanade

Opposite top Site plan

Opposite bottom This shaded roof plan reveals the strong dialogue Benson + Forsyth have created between the Museum of Scotland (top left) and nearby Edinburgh Castle (bottom right)

Douglas Cardinal TSE

CANADIAN MUSEUM OF CIVILIZATION

Ottawa 1989

Nation building was central to Canada's cultural renaissance of the 1980s: the National Gallery of Canada, the Canadian Museum of Contemporary Photography, the National Aviation Museum and the Canadian Museum of Civilization were all built during this period. Arguably, the Canadian Museum of Civilization is the most symbolically important of these national commissions. This is because of its highly prominent location across the Ottawa River from the nation's Parliament buildings, its key position on the capital's National Ceremonial Route and its explicit design brief that called for 'the creation of a symbol of national pride and identity'.[1]

Douglas Cardinal certainly had this aim of the architectural programme in mind when he took the strategic decision to separate the museum into two discrete buildings – a display wing and a curatorial building – connected by an underground link. This design approach allows a framed vista from the museum complex to the Parliament buildings beyond, which is now iconised on the one-dollar Canadian bill. Architecturally, Cardinal adopted a free-flowing, organic approach to the design of both wings, to echo the undulating forms of the country's geological landscape. The very complexity of the resultant curvilinear masses necessitated the computer resolution of many thousands of simultaneous equations.

On an urban scale, the museum has been successful in boosting the flagging economy of the industrial sector of Hull, and reintegrating this area with the fabric of the more prosperous region of Ottawa over the river. However, the building is less successful in its small-scale marriage of exhibition to building design; the two processes at times being largely autonomous.

1 Architecture and Planning Group, National Museum of Canada. *Architectural Programme Synopsis* (Ottawa: National Museum of Canada, 1983), p. 2.

Fireworks display over the museum plaza and Ottawa River beyond

Opposite top View between museum wings to Parliament buildings beyond

Opposite bottom Banded administrative wing

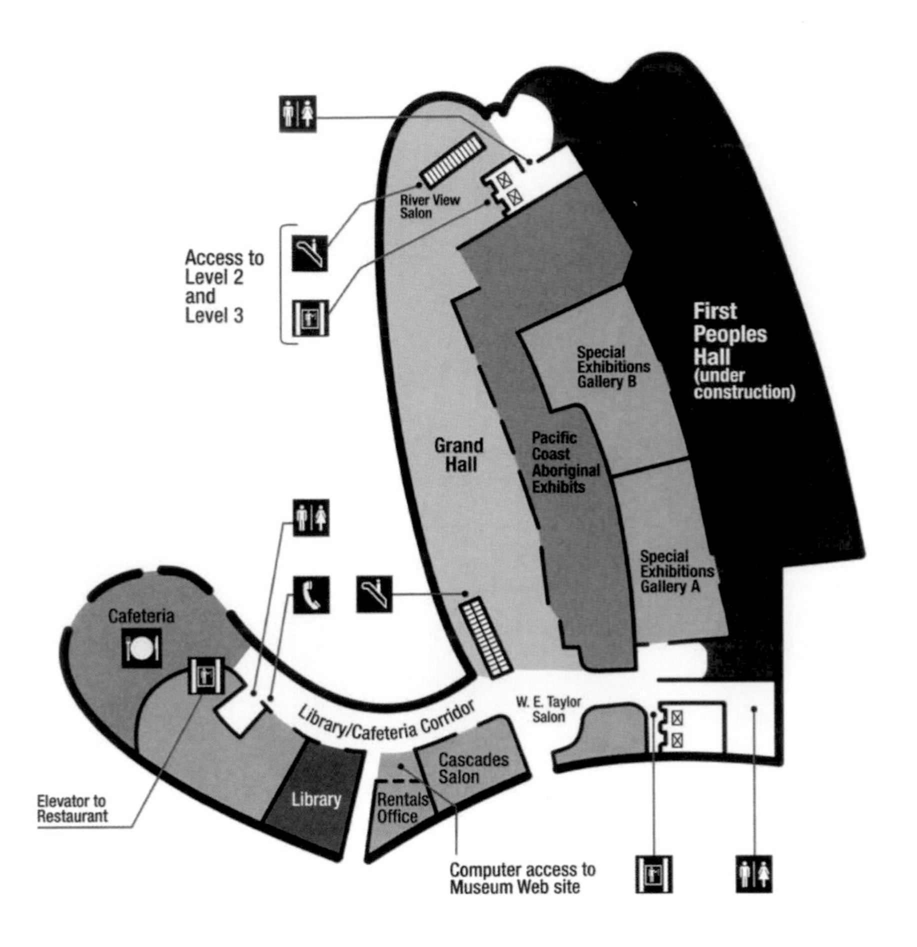

Above First floor plan: the Grand and First Peoples Halls dominate the ground floor plan of the museum

Below Second floor plan

Opposite top The horizontal limestone and glazing bands of the museum's administrative wing

Opposite bottom The main entrance to the museum conjures up images of indigenous masks and totem pole faces

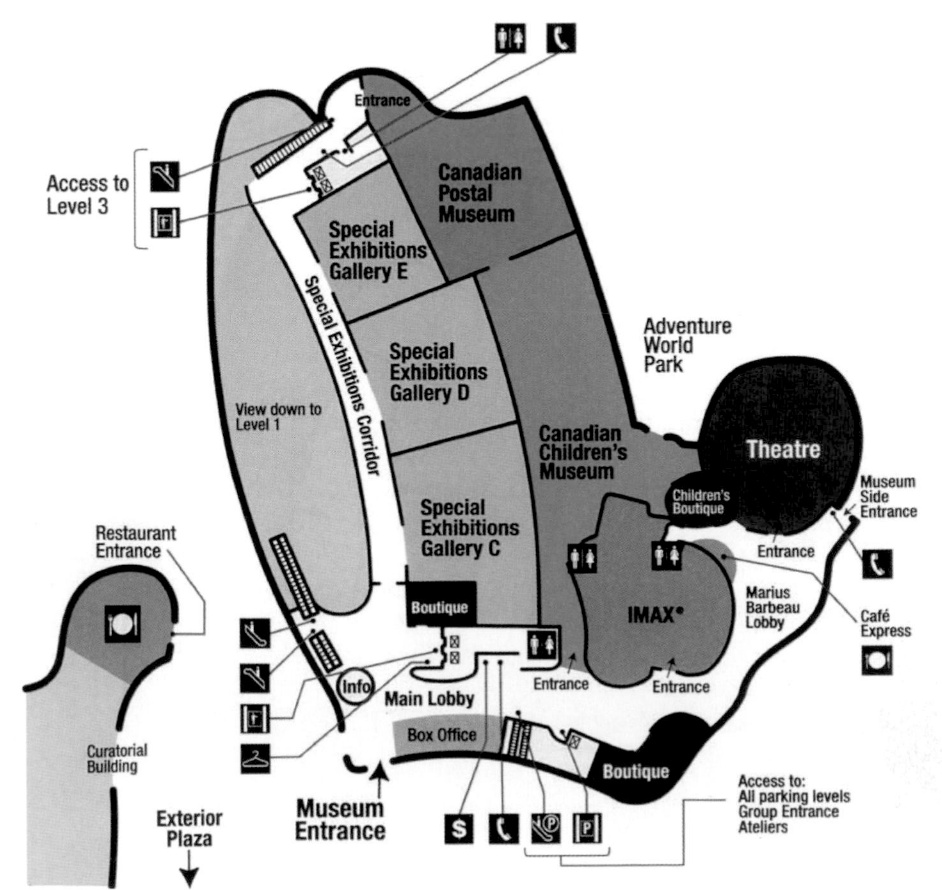

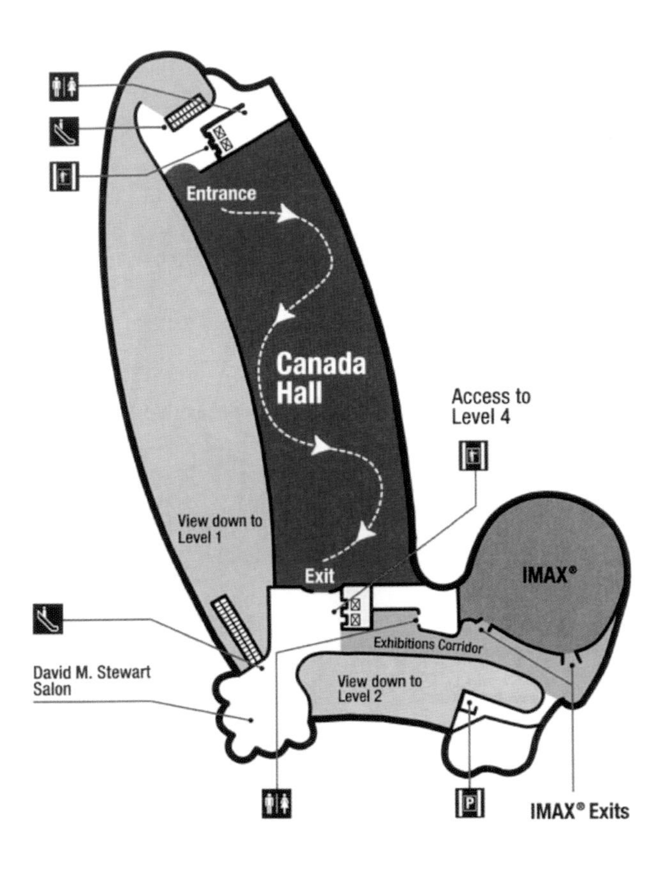

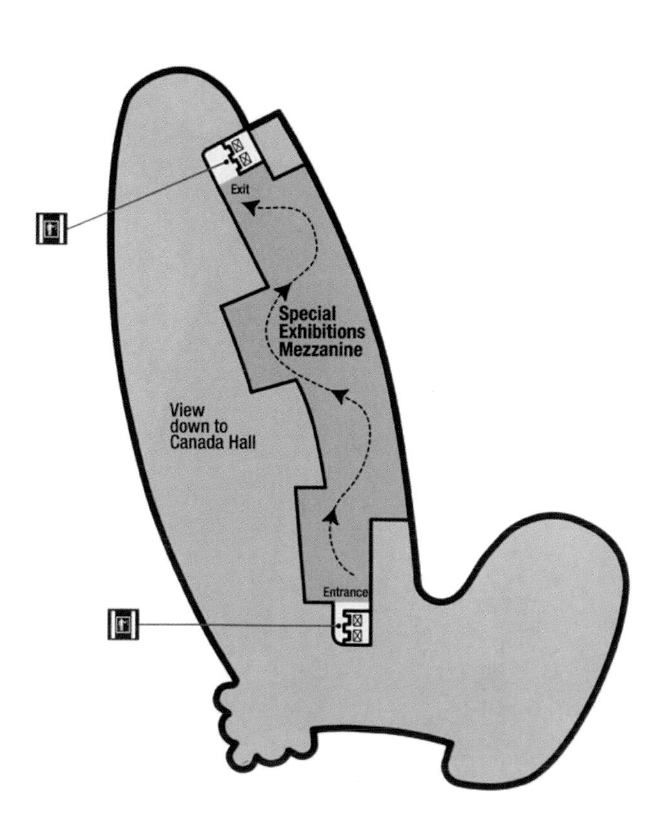

Above The Grand Hall at the Canadian Museum of Civilization is intended to represent the British Colombian coastline, with a marble 'sea', replica indigenous housing and a scrim 'forest' behind

Top left Second floor plan: visual connections occur between the Canada Hall on the second floor, and the Grand Hall below, which functions successfully as an orientation space

Bottom left Third floor plan: special exhibitions are housed on the third floor mezzanine level

Opposite top Façade of the Grand Hall

Opposite bottom Interior of the Grand Hall, with canoe-shaped ceiling

Above Night view from Cable Street

Opposite Site plan

Jasmax Group

TE PAPA TONGAREWA THE NATIONAL MUSEUM OF NEW ZEALAND

Wellington 1999

The design project for Te Papa Tongarewa the National Museum of New Zealand, undertaken by Jasmax Architects between 1989 and 1999, primarily addresses the key and linked issues of culture and context.

The design needed to represent the 'bicultural nature of the country, ... and provide the means for each to contribute effectively to a statement of the nation's identity ...', and its location proved pivotal in achieving these aims.[1] Pragmatically, the reclaimed waterfront site in Wellington was problematic, requiring lengthy compaction and an extensive foundation system. However, it was also the source of design inspiration, as 'it is at the edge of the sea, a symbolic place where both waka and European boats were drawn up ...'.[2] Taking this link between site and culture further, Maori and pakeha settlement patterns were then superimposed onto the design, resulting in a rational gridded aesthetic for the city-side pakeha galleries, and a more flowing, natural architectural language for the sea-facing Maori section. The wedge-shaped space, seen as both linking and separating the two wings, was symbolically given over to a display on the contentious Treaty of Waitangi. However, this is rather to simplify a very complex 36,000 square metre and NZ$280,000,000 project that, in addition to the four main galleries, contains a host of other primary and support spaces.

Curatorially, the museum is bold – disregarding allegations of populism and gimmickry to include a host of interactive displays. The most exciting of these, virtual bungee jumps and rollercoaster rides through time, break away from traditional academic restraints on the museum, forging a new and more inclusive path.

1 Design Brief. Te Papa Tongarewa, 1989.

2 Jasmax Competition Entry, 1990.

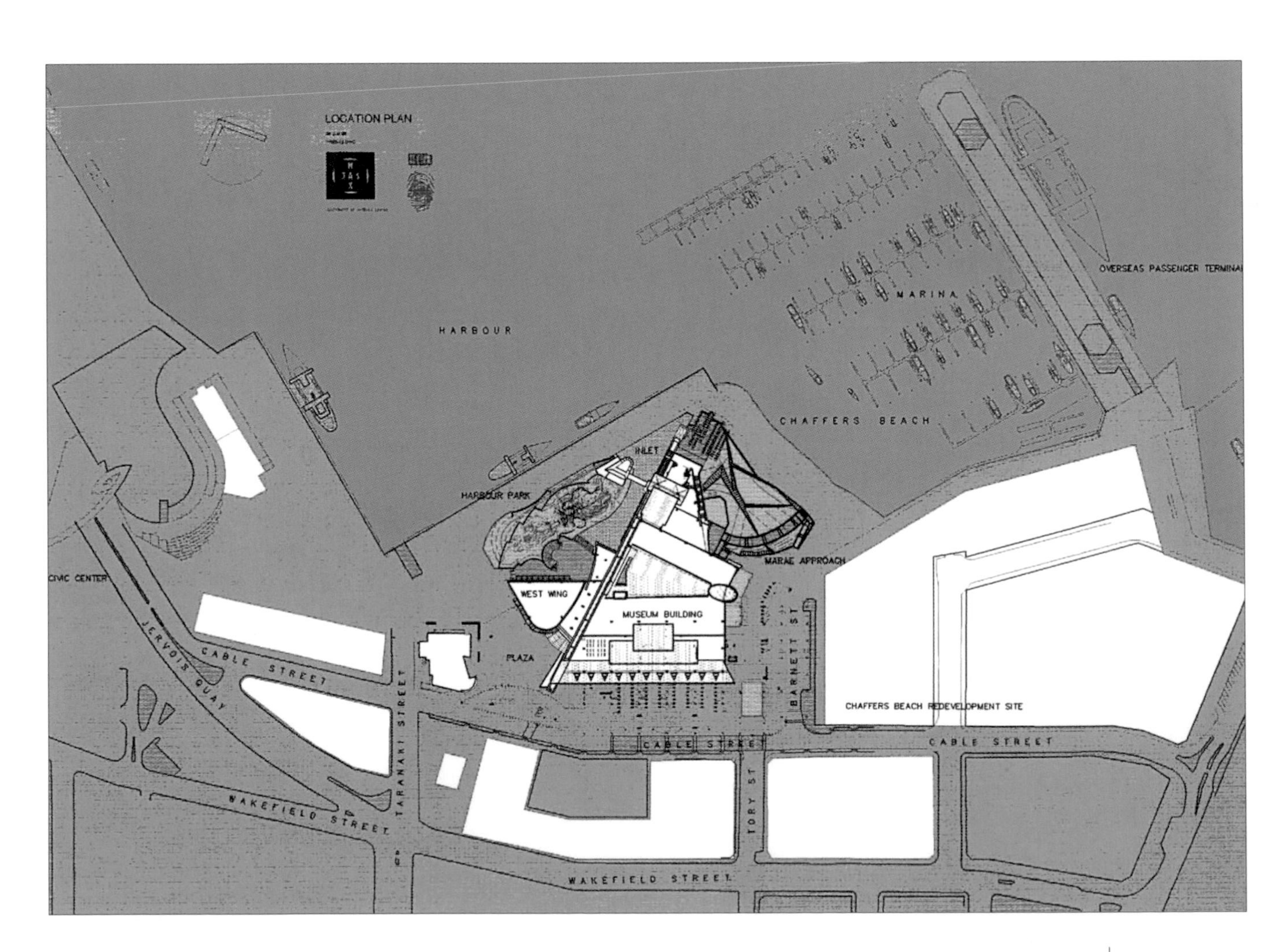

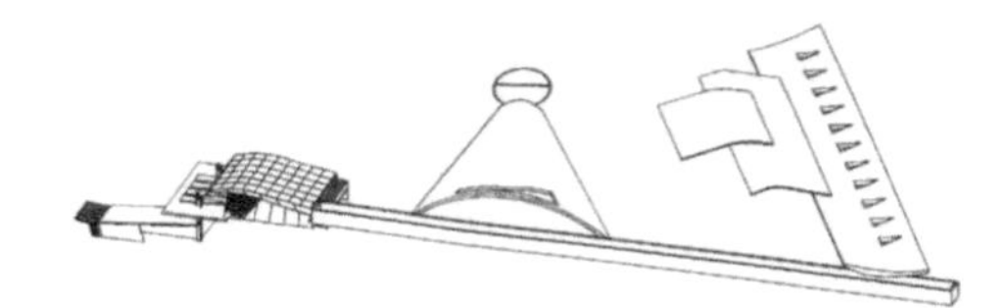

KEY

- Te Marae
- Exhibition Gallery
- Promenade and Public Circulation
- Auditrorium
- Commercial Areas
- Administration, Staff Offices and Workshops
- Service Area and Plantrooms
- Collections
- Parking

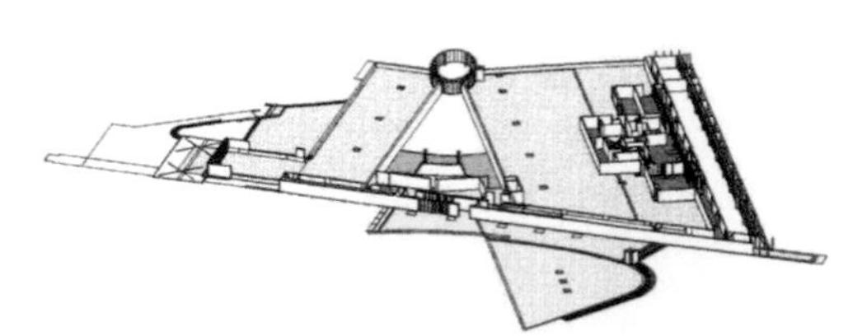

LEVEL 6 ROOF

Exhibitions
Public Roof Terrace
Public Viewing
Wedge
Promenade
Plant

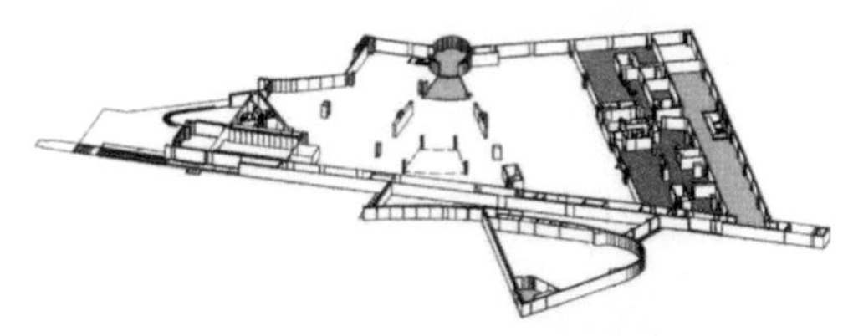

LEVEL 5 EXHIBITIONS

Exhibitions
Collections
Library
Marae Changing
Natural Light Gallery

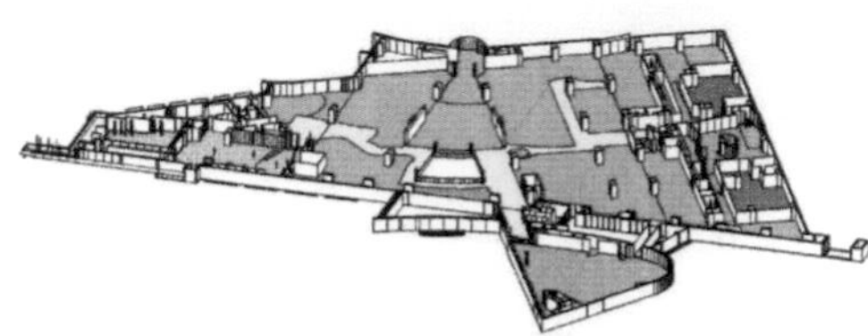

LEVEL 4 EXHIBITIONS

Exhibitions
Collections
Te Marae
Art
History
Intergrated Exhibitions

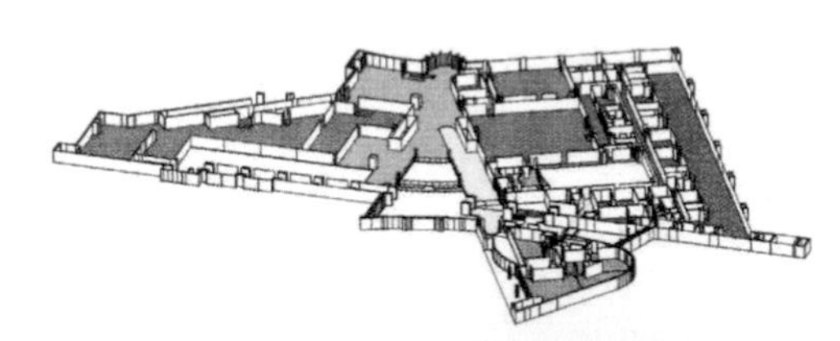

LEVEL 3 EXHIBITIONS & COLLECTIONS

Administration Offices
Conference Centre

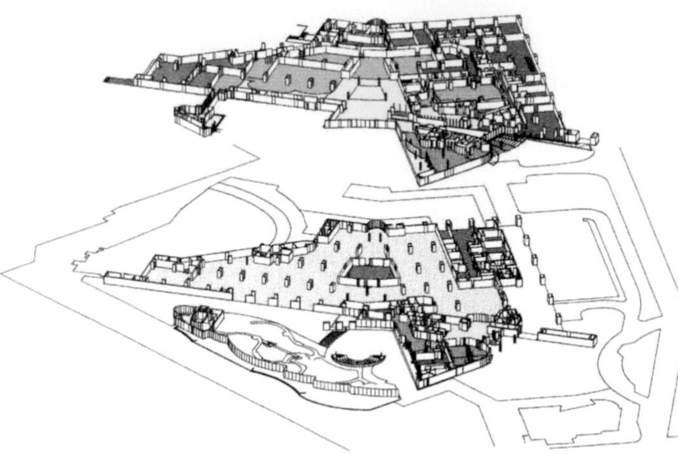

LEVEL 2 EXHIBITIONS

Auditorium
Collections
Offices
Workshops & Labratory
Restaurant
Orientation Lobby

LEVEL 1 ENTRANCE

Main Entry
Cloaks
Shop
Cafe
Classrooms
Plant
150 Carpark

ISOMETRIC LAYOUT

Plan views showing the organisation of the museum's accommodation

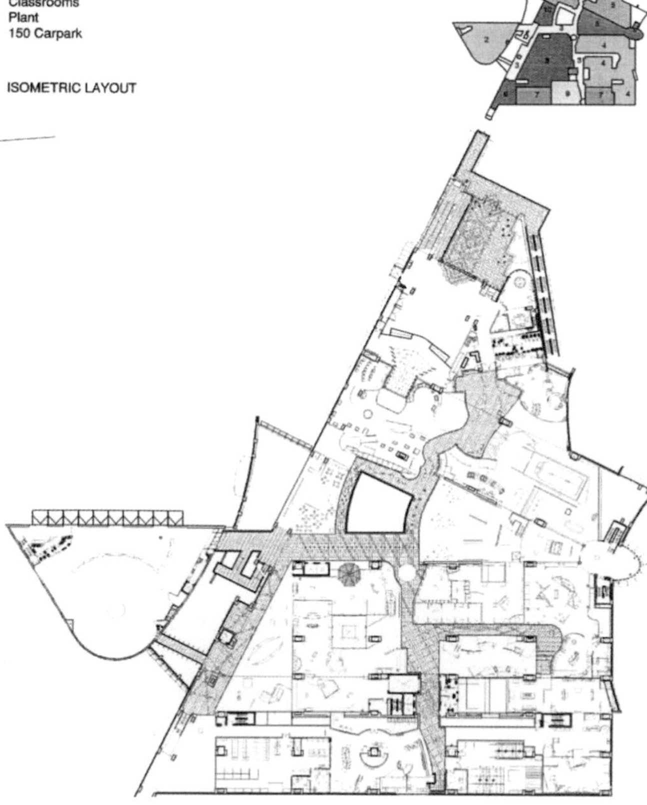

KEY

1 Te Marae
2 Touring Exhibitions Gallery
3 Promenade, Public Circulation and Toilets
4 Tangata Tiruti History Exhibitions
5 Tangata Whenua Exhibitions
6 Tangata Tiruti Art Exhibitions
7 Collections
8 Integrated Exhibitions · Treaty Exhibit
9 Resource Centers
10 Expresso Bar · Lounge

Above View of the contemporary Maori tribal meeting house

Below Concept sketch

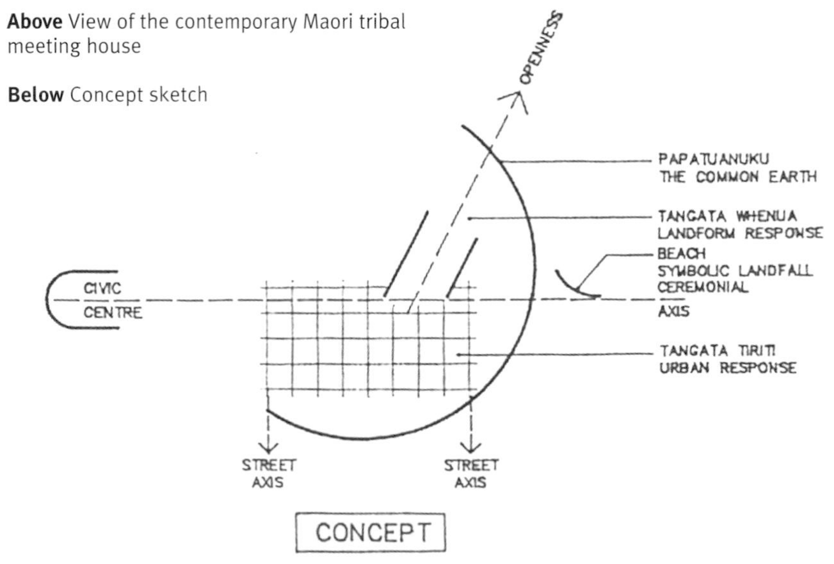

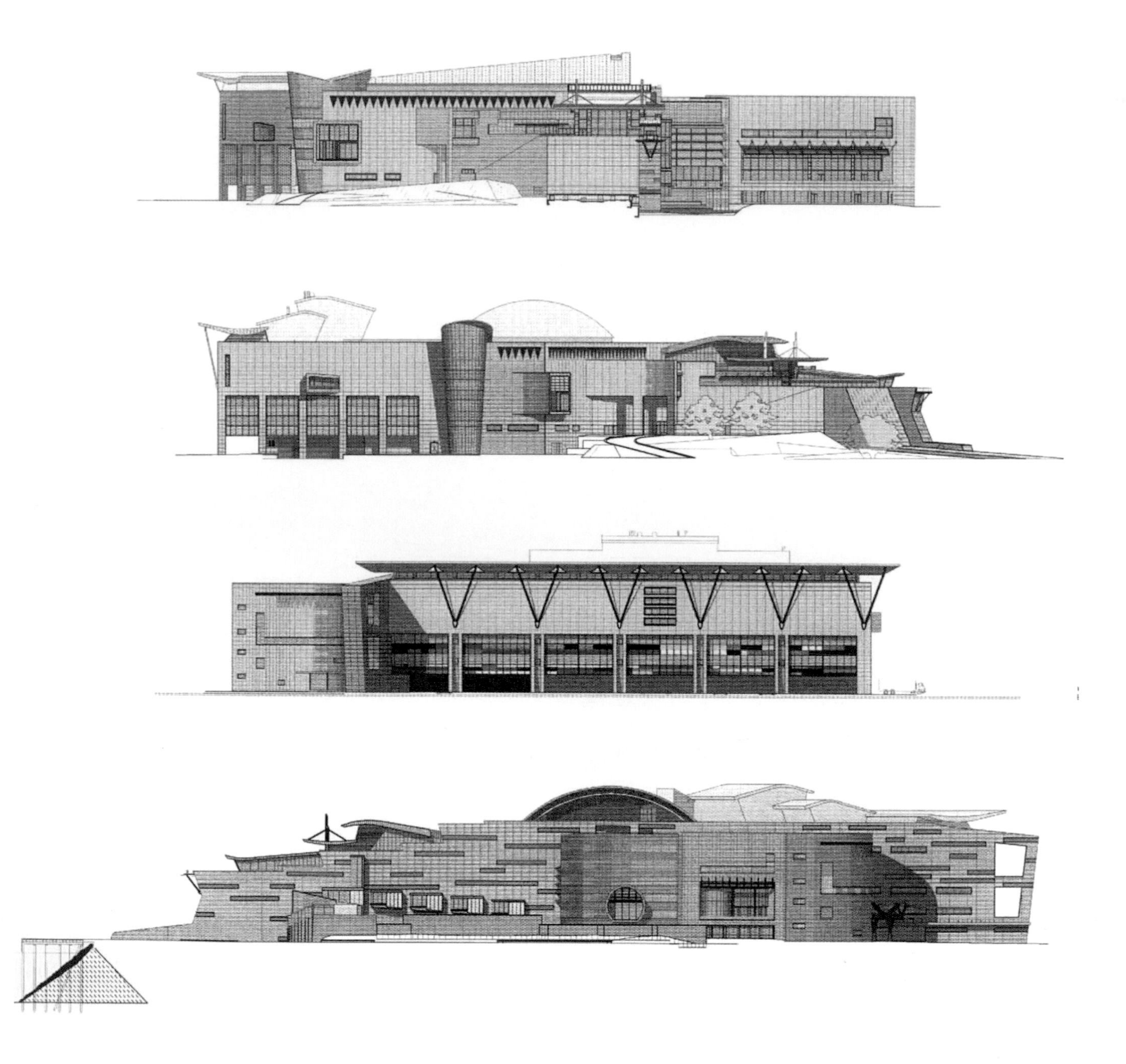

Above left These large glazed openings allow natural light into the museum's second floor Wellington Foyer

Above right The marble-clad element slices through the building from land to sea and creates the main entrance on the city side

Opposite from above North, east, south and west elevations

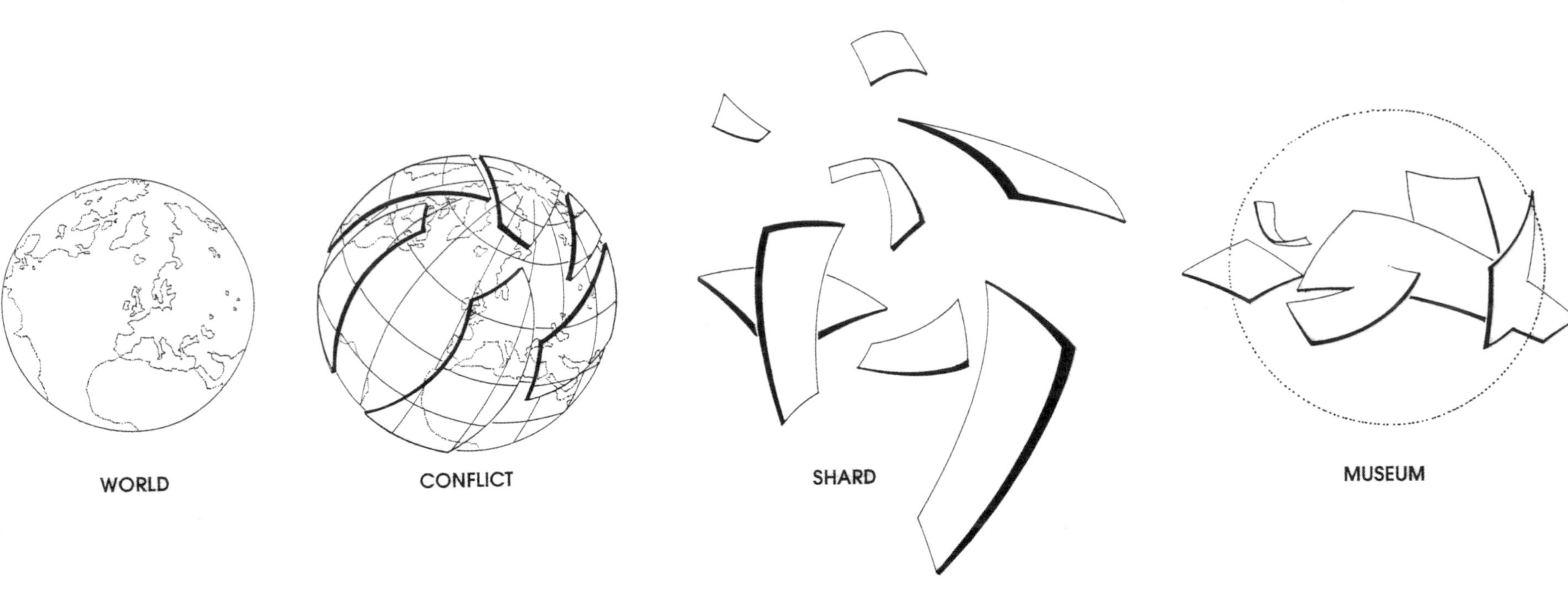

Top Concept drawings of shards

Bottom The zinc clad planes of the museum, seen from across the ship canal, are chameleon-like under Manchester's brooding, changeable skies

Opposite The site plan reveals the architect's Deconstructivist approach to landscaping as well as building design

Daniel Libeskind

IMPERIAL WAR MUSEUM NORTH

Manchester **2002**

In the past, the museum has often addressed controversial and contested subjects, and Daniel Libeskind's Imperial War Museum North certainly continues that tradition. The architect was charged with designing a building to house an exhibition on the history of conflict, and the startling result opened in 2002 on the quayside in Trafford Park, Manchester.

Libeskind's central concept was simple: 'I have imagined the globe broken into fragments and taken the pieces to form a building; three shards that together represent conflict on land, in the air and on water.'[1] This approach is most apparent from across the ship canal from where the exposed steelwork and aluminium cladding of the three fused fragments make a dynamic silhouette against the Mancunian skyline. Having first located the building's diminutive, idiosyncratic entrance – far from the grand 'Imperialist' entry the museum's title would suggest – the visitor experiences the air shard or shaft: an exposed, vertical web of steel beams that encases a lift, and rises to a walkway and viewing platform 30 metres above. Up here, the combination of askew barriers, and mesh flooring allowing views down to the ground, is sublimely vertiginous. Further into the heart of the building, the riverside 'water' section houses the café and restaurant, with the main gallery being contained within the vast, undulating volume of the earth shard. Here architecture and artefact exist happily together, with audio-visual shows intermittently transforming the space.

Rebelling against the ranks of uniformly rationalist museums, the Imperial War Museum North is testament to 'Libeskind's astonishingly assertive, metaphorical style of architecture, in which the building not only contains the story but becomes the story.'[2]

1 Daniel Libeskind. Imperial War Museum North, Wall Text.

2 Richard Morrison. 'A Mind like a Furnace', *The Times*, 3 July 2002.

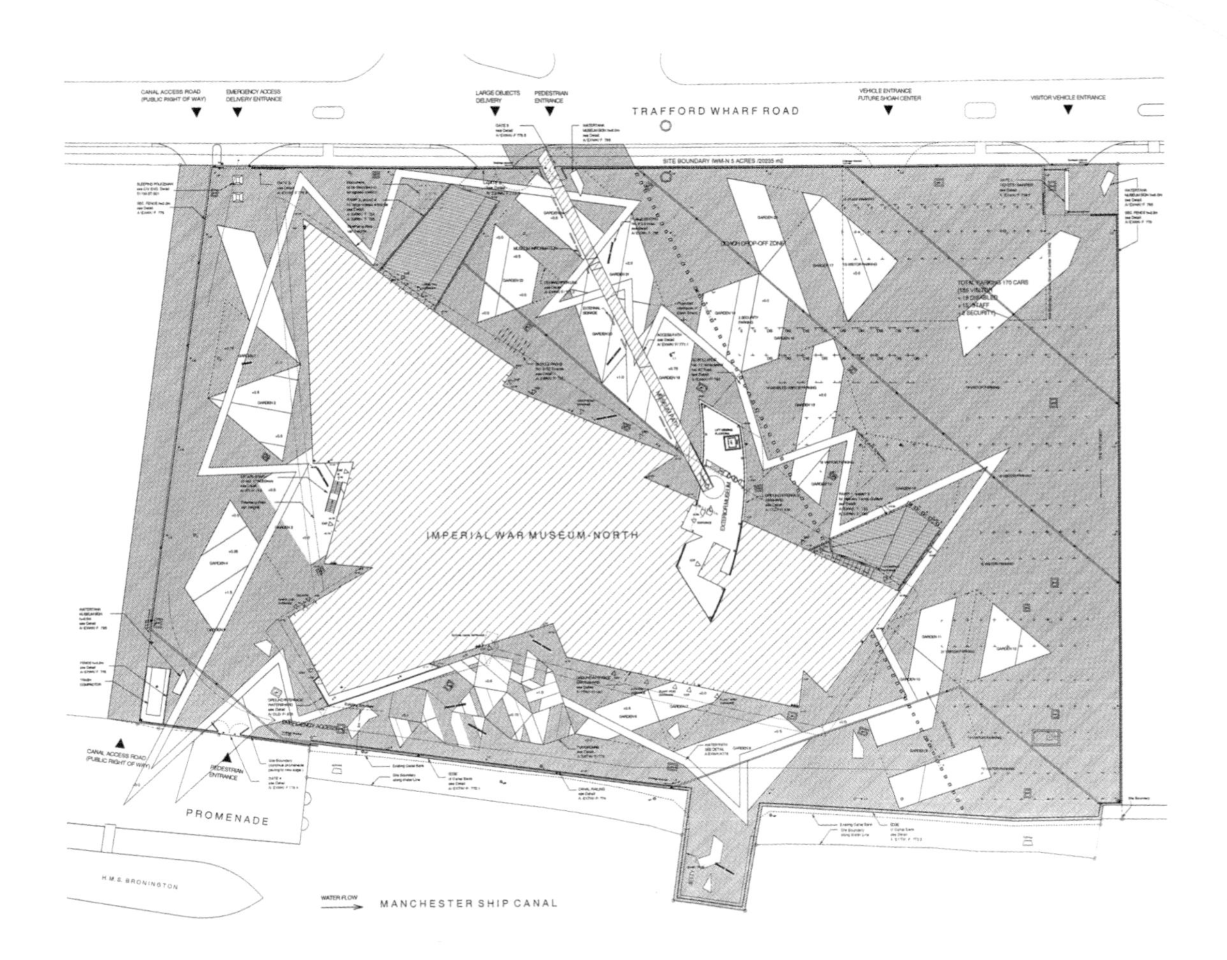

Right Street-facing elevation

Bottom left Air shard

Bottom right Viewing platform

Right Canalside elevation

Bottom left The museum's open air shard houses the viewing platform, and abuts the main entrance

Bottom right Inside a silo

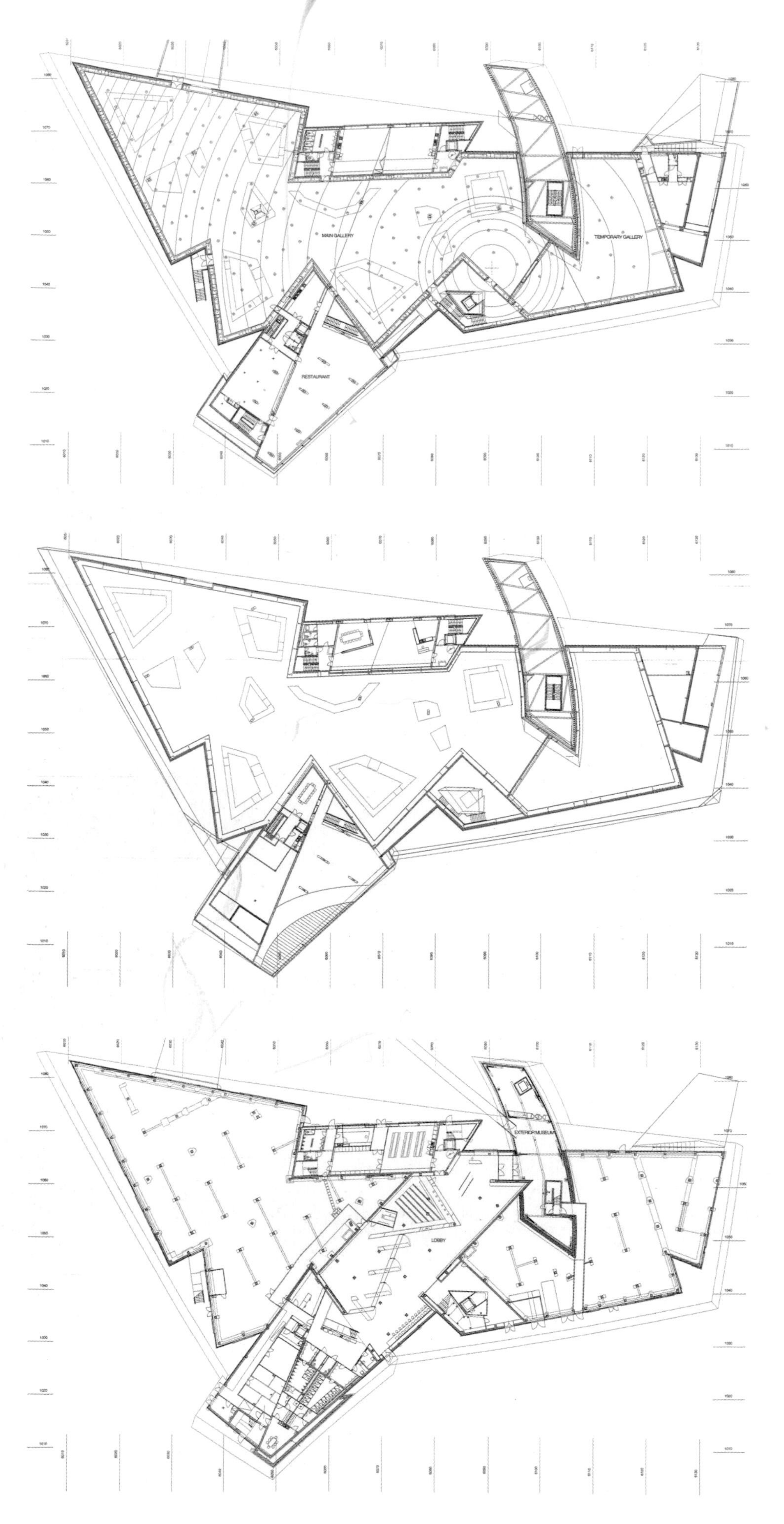

Top Gallery level floor plan

Centre Lobby, gallery and mezzanine level floor plans

Bottom Lobby level floor plan

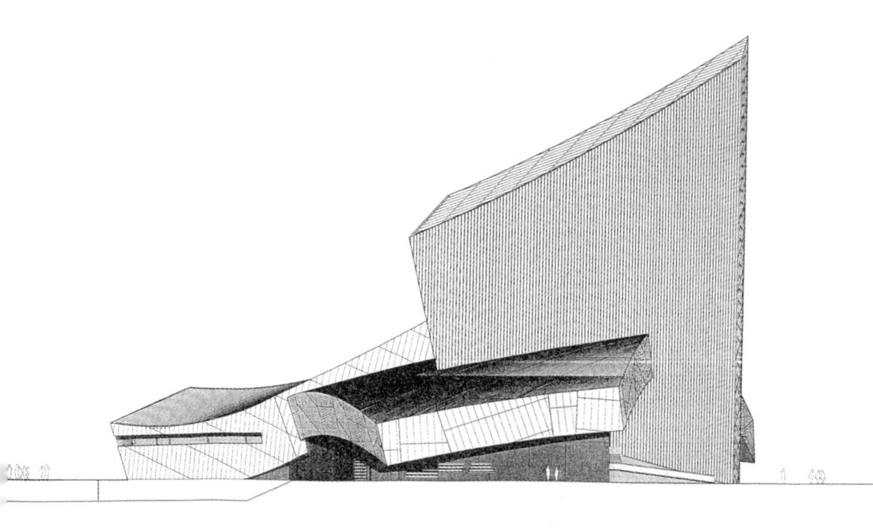

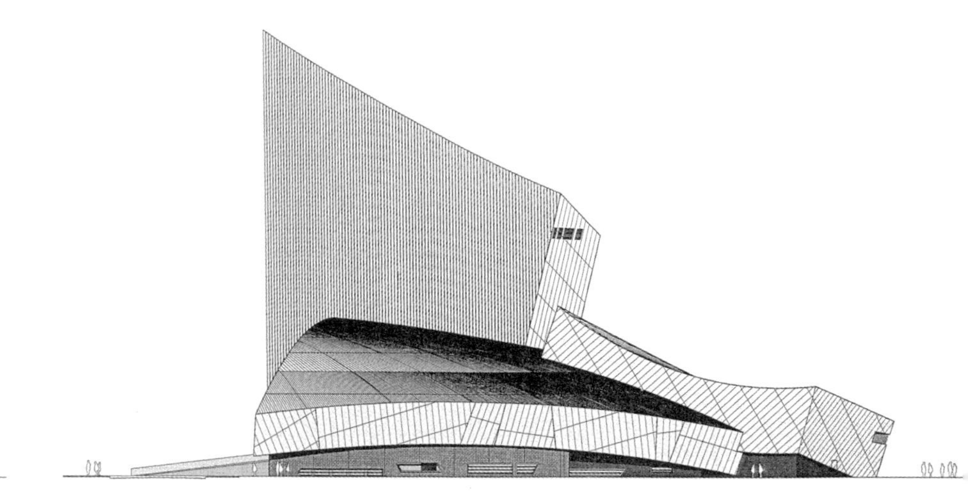

Top The museum's east and west elevations emphasize scale and disjuncture

Above left Route to entrance

Above right Collision of Libeskind's air, land and sea shards

Daniel Libeskind
JEWISH MUSEUM

Berlin | **1997**

Identity is all-important at the Jewish Museum, Berlin. The building's programme raised uncomfortable questions about the nature of Germanness and Jewishness at the end of an horrific century of conflict. On a more intimate scale, the Polish-born architect found himself in an unusual position of personal engagement with the project, having lost many of his family in the Holocaust.

Commissioned in 1988 to design the new extension to the Berlin Markische Museum, Daniel Libeskind adopted a Deconstructivist standpoint, synthesizing the powerful symbolism of the Swastika and Star of David, with an urban matrix connecting the homes of influential pre-war Jewish Berliners to the museum's site. A four-storey building arose, composed of interlocking fragments clad in zinc panels, the slashed openings in which bear no relation to the internal organisation within. Also symbolic is the connection between Libeskind's design and the parent museum: the architect placed the link underground to express the inseparable, but contentious, relationship between the two cultures, and this charged dynamic is heightened as both buildings nearly, but never quite, touch at three points along their perimeter.

Internally, the museum centres around three principal journeys: the first, the Stairway of Continuity, leads to historical and cultural installations; the second leads to the Hoffmann Garden that 'represents the exile and emigration of Jews from Germany'; and the third is the Holocaust Void, which is empty and terminates in a dead end.[1] This architectural metaphor has great resonance, and the space created is undoubtedly the most powerful in the museum. However, it highlights the tension between built form and exhibition content that characterises the whole project. Close to 350,000 visitors toured the empty building before the displays were installed, expressing an overwhelming sentiment that it should be left as a monumental piece of Expressionist sculpture.

1 Daniel Libeskind. *The Space of Encounter, Between the Lines* (New York: Universe Publishing, 2000), p. 27.

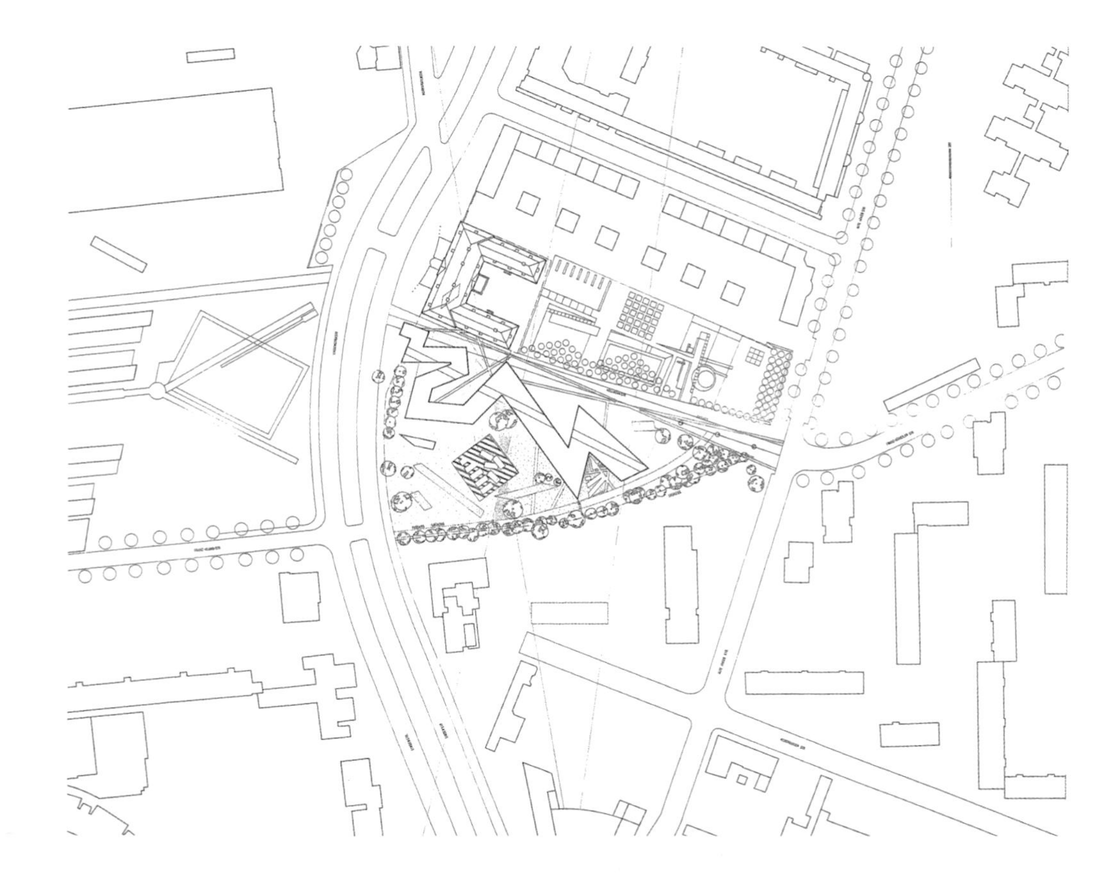

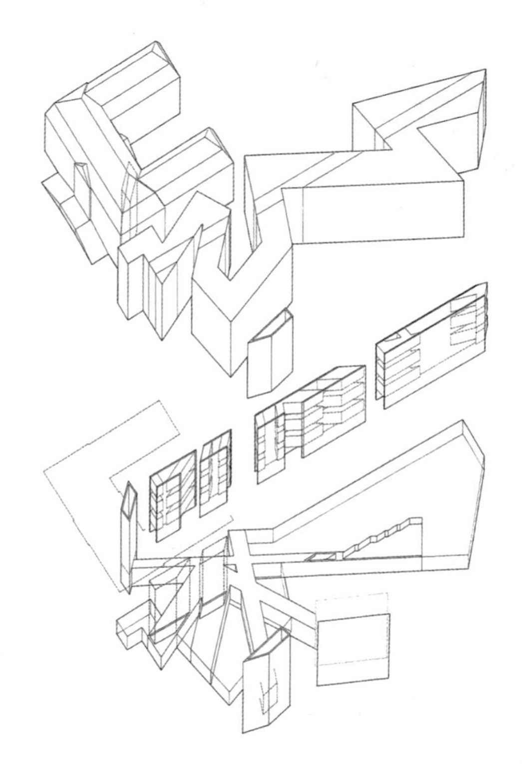

Above Axonometrics

Left Site plan

Opposite The slit openings in the museum's zinc planes give no clue as to the building's internal organisation

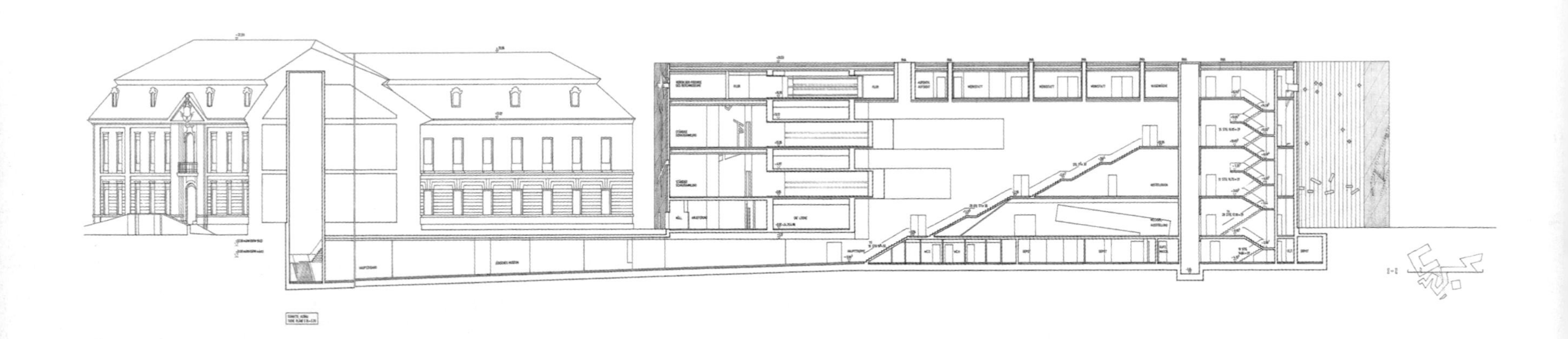

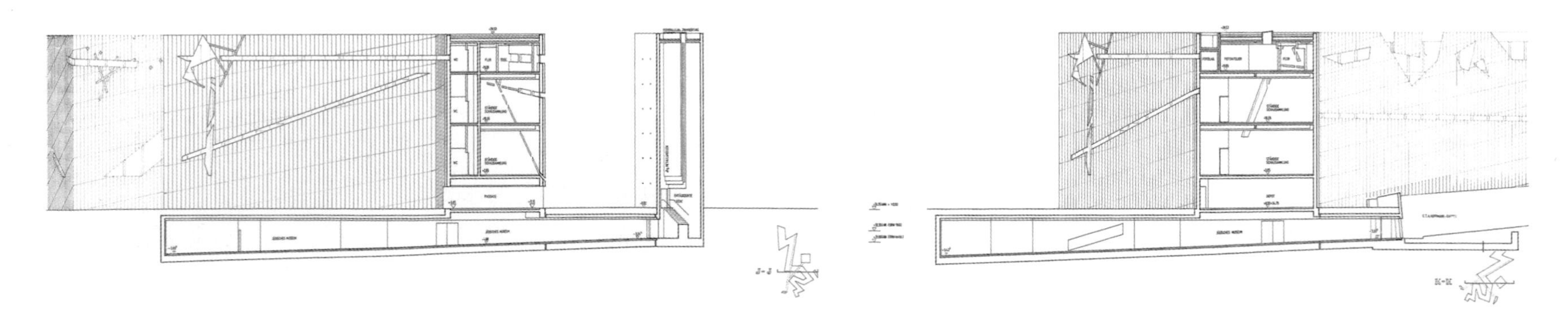

Sections through the museum, showing circulation routes

Opposite Libeskind's symbolic Deconstructivist architecture houses a contested and contentious space of encounter

The Garden of Exile provides a leafy space for rest and contemplation

Opposite Sections through the museum, showing circulation routes

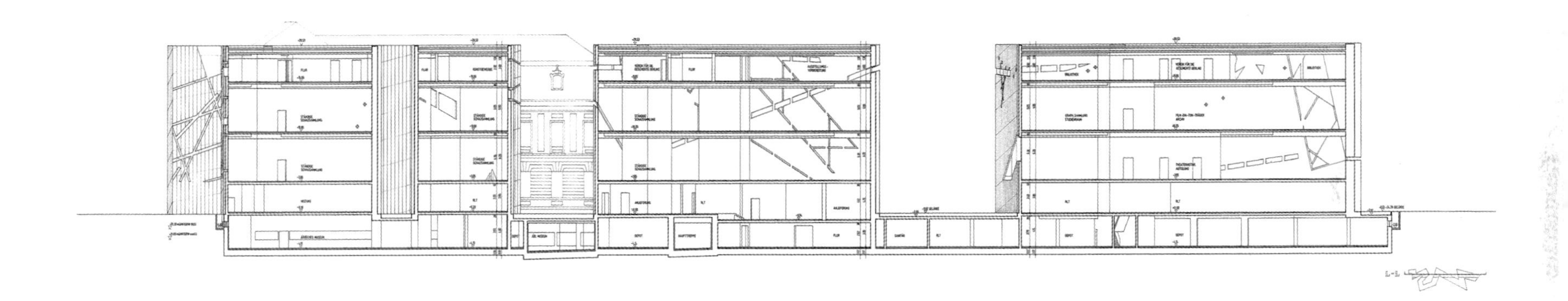

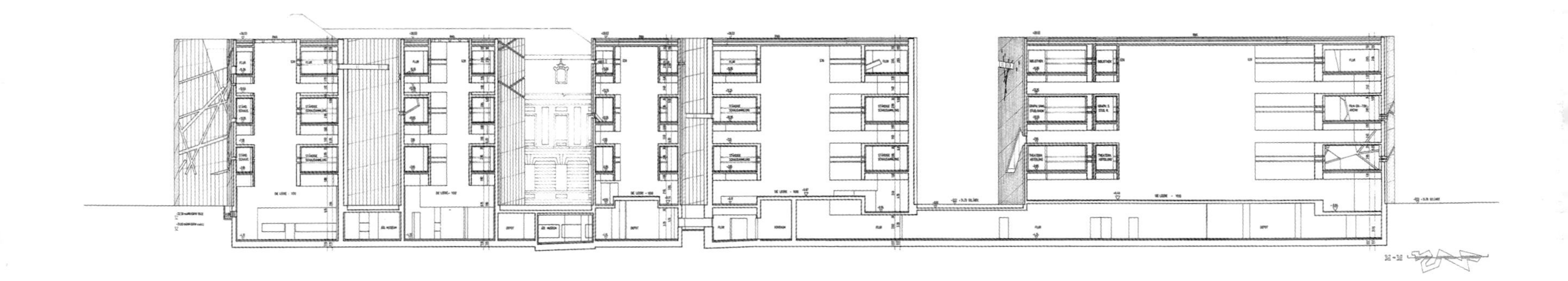

Installation, 'Fallen Leaves', by Menashe Kadishman

Opposite Staircase at the end of the Axis of Continuity

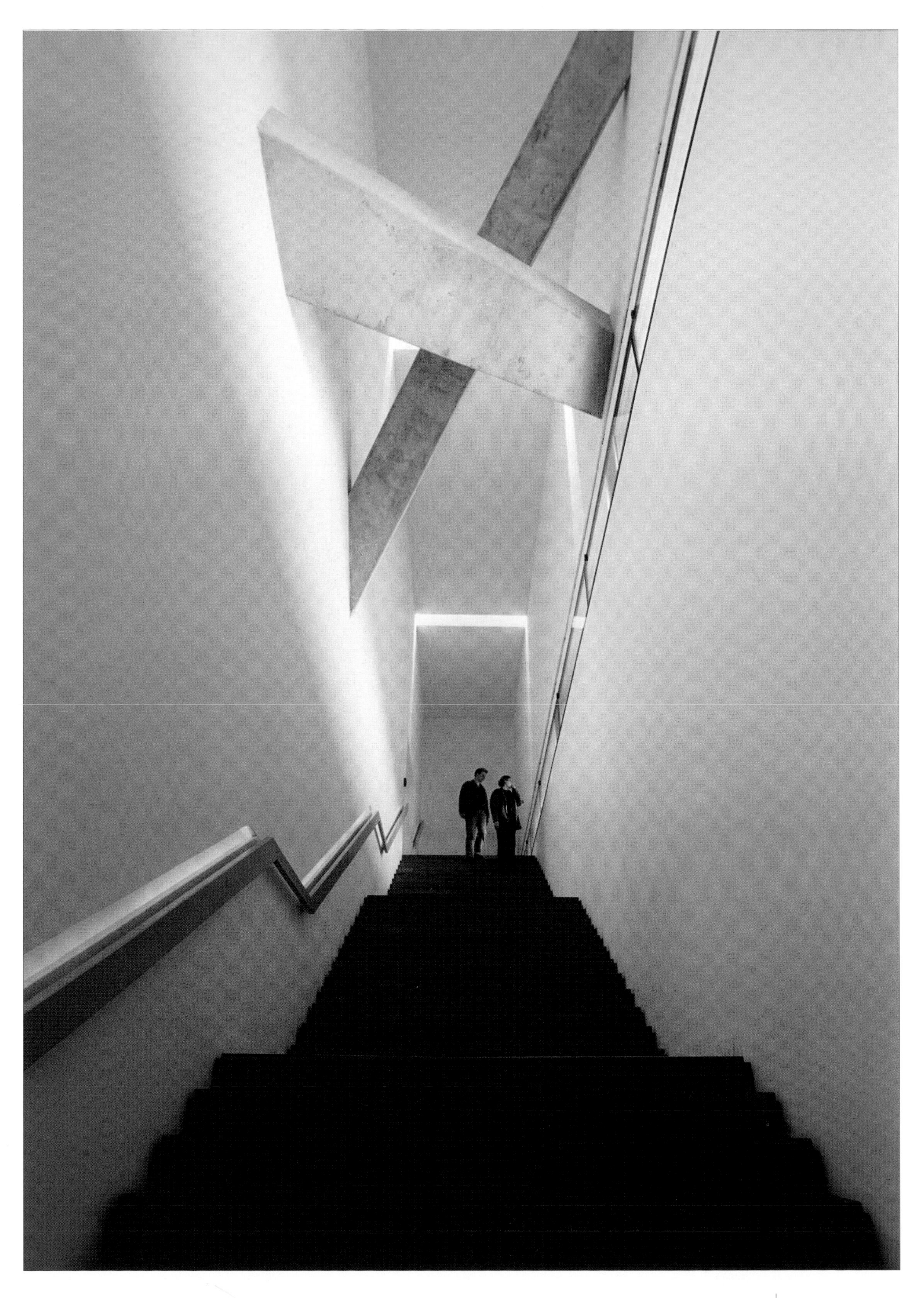

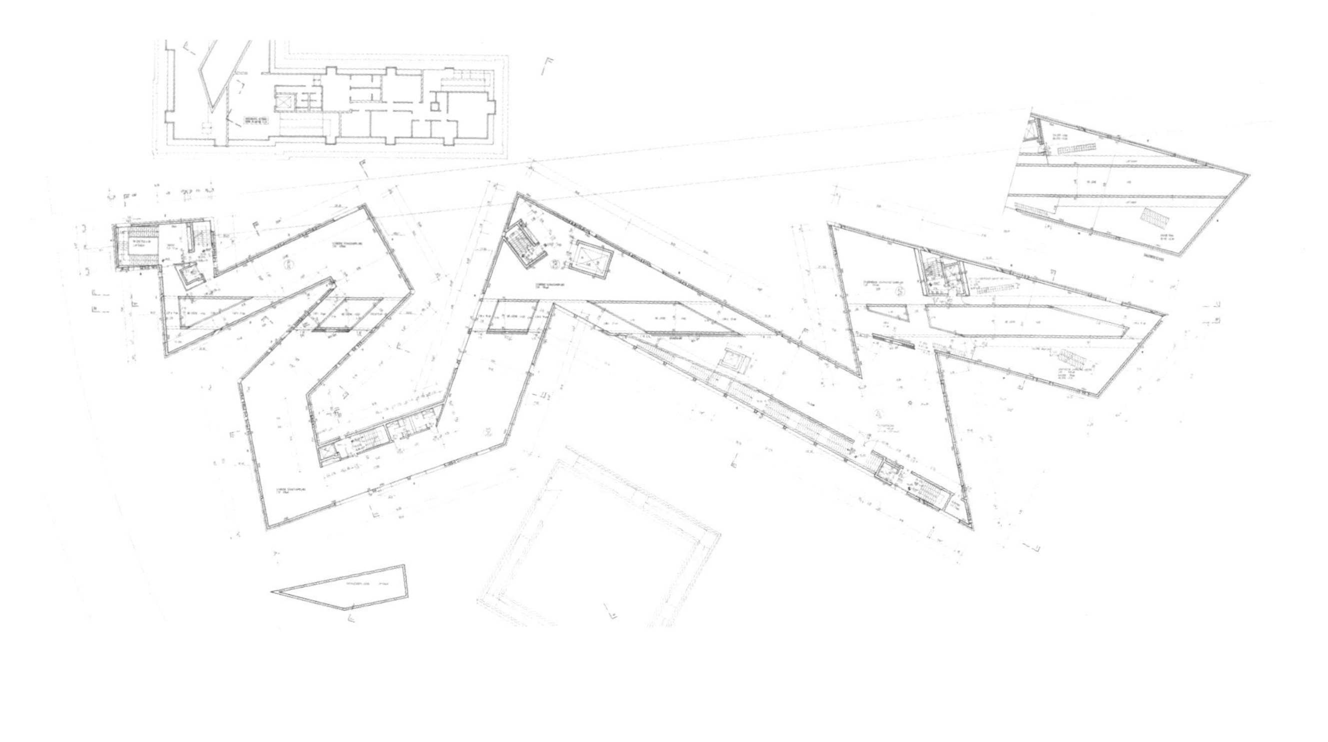

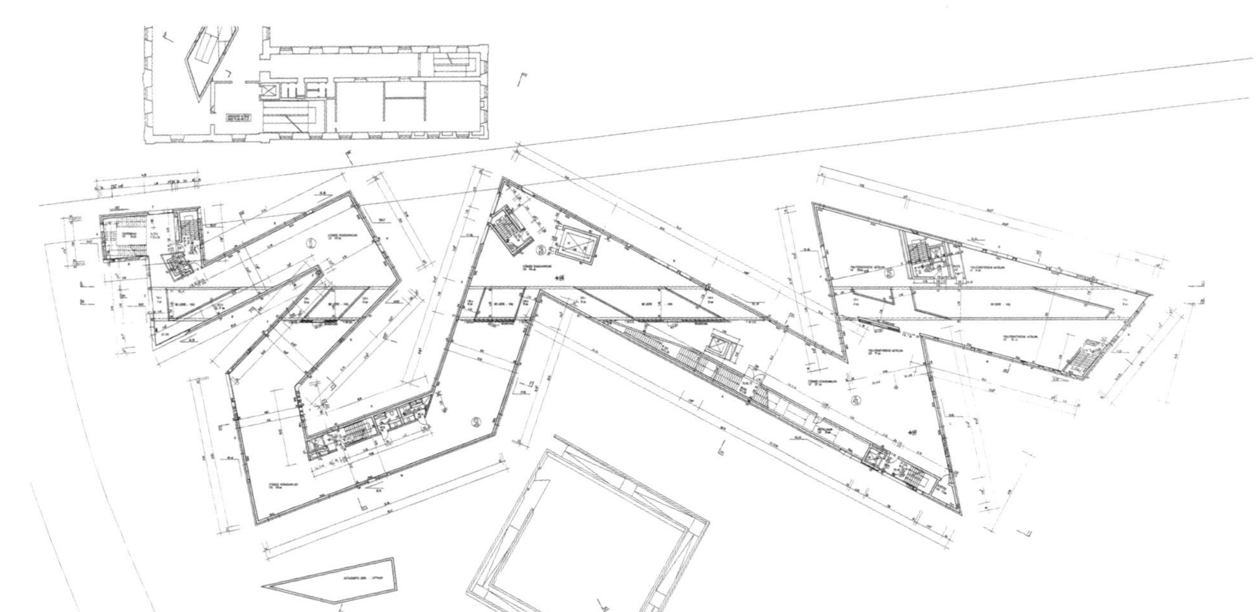

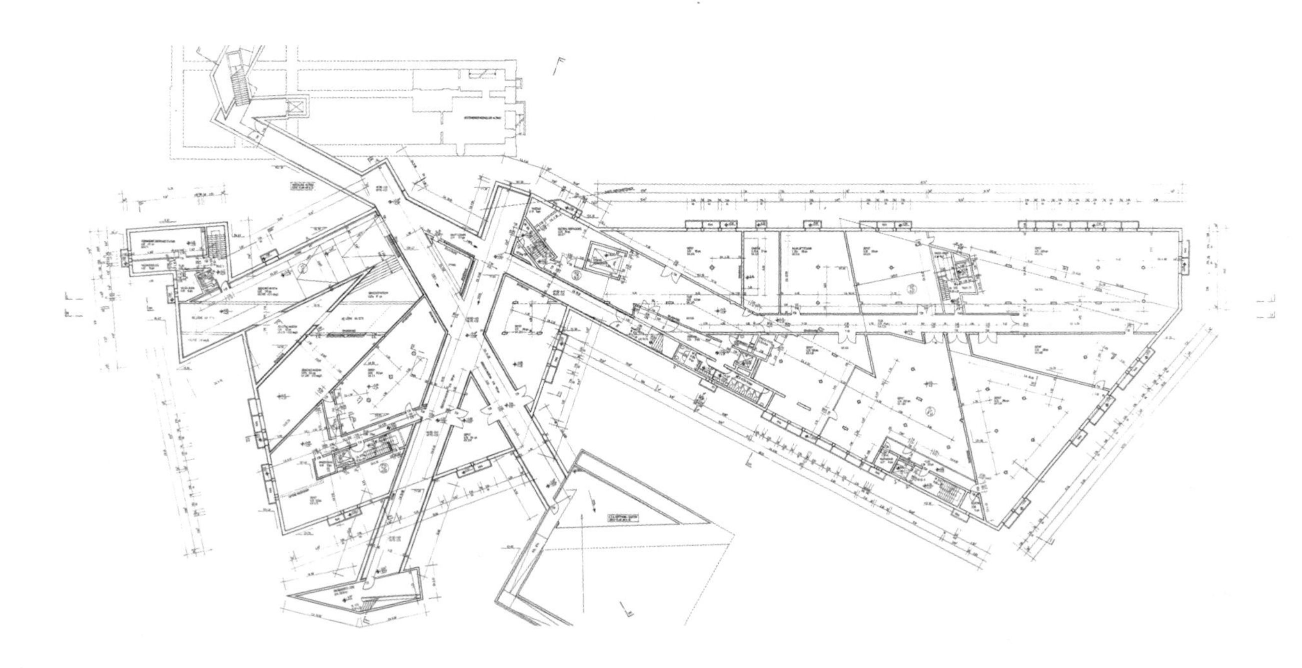

Top Second floor plan, showing the charged relationship between Libeskind's intervention and the adjacent Berlin Markische Museum

Centre First floor plan

Bottom Underground plan

Opposite The fact that hundreds of thousands of visitors toured the empty building prior to the exhibition fit-out, has led many to question the relevance of the displays themselves

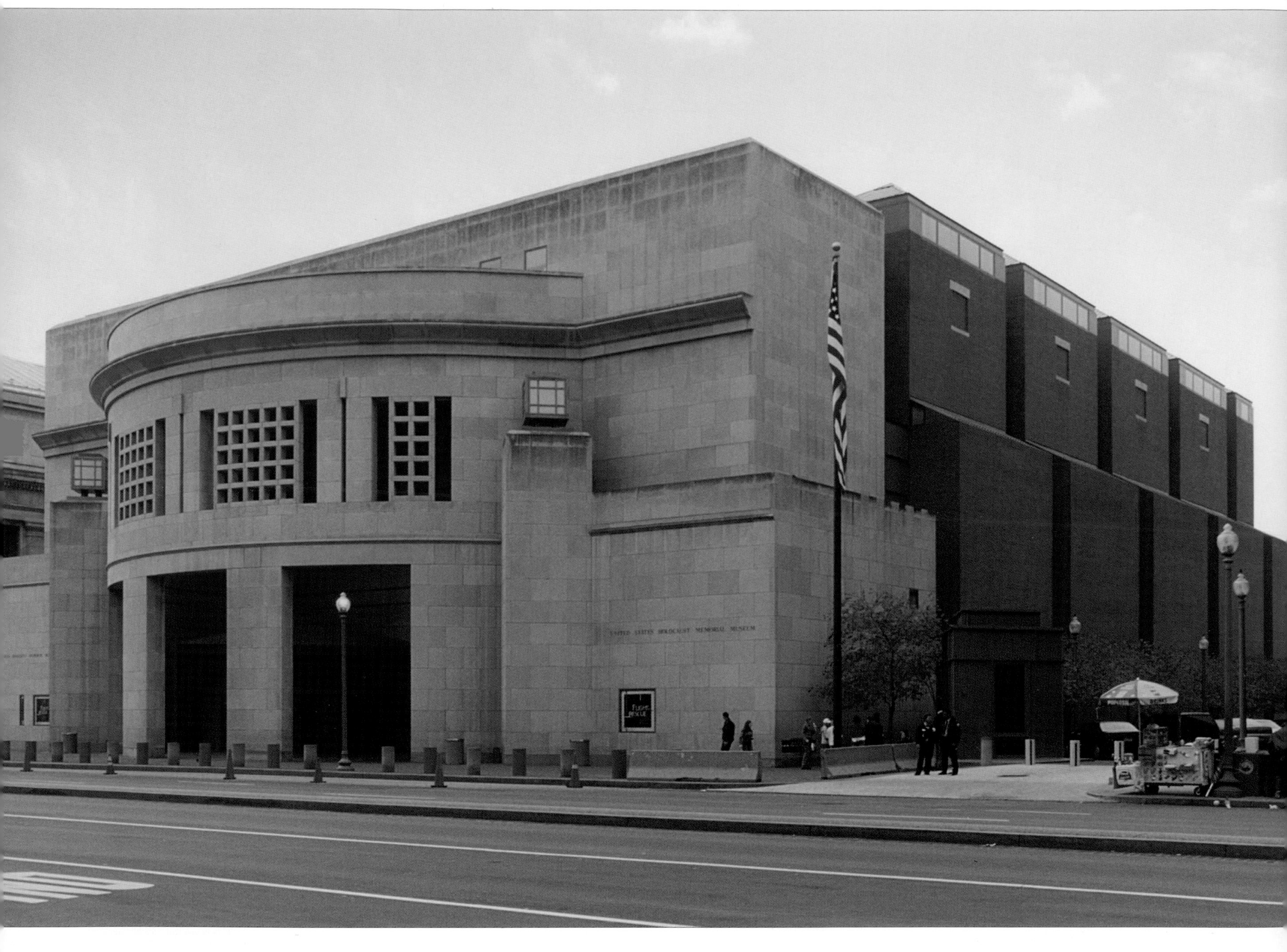

Above The museum's neo-Classical façade onto 14th Street acts as a metaphor for the shrouding of the mechanisms of evil within the legitimate cloak of state

Right Sketch of the brick towers

Opposite The form of the hexagonal Hall of Remembrance, which lies to the rear of the series of individual museum spaces, provides a calming space for meditation and reflection

Pei Cobb Freed & Partners

UNITED STATES HOLOCAUST MEMORIAL MUSEUM

Washington DC **1993**

Few architectural commissions are as highly charged as that which James Ingo Freed of Pei Cobb Freed & Partners undertook for the United States Holocaust Memorial Museum in Washington DC.

Following a research visit to the Nazi concentration camps of eastern Europe, Freed chose to draw on the chillingly rational architecture of the Holocaust, which he encountered, employing symbolism rather than literalism in his subsequent architectural interpretations. The principal volume within the building, the three-storey Hall of Witness, makes use of steel bracing, doors and gates, and rough brick walls, evoking the crematorium ovens, prison gates and high walls of the death camps. However, the distinctly unsettling nature of the space cannot be explained through this materiality alone. The strangely distorted skylight, the large crack in the west wall, and the four overhead bridges, 'reminiscent of those above the Warsaw Ghetto', all combine to magnify the sense of disquiet, and are 'watched over' by eight brick towers that stand sentinel around the Hall 'like the guard towers of the concentration camps'.[1] Far from being heavy-handed or disjointed, though, these allusions act together subtly as 'resonator[s] of memory, a stage for introspection, rather than a series of specific architectural metaphors'.[2]

Enclosing this central core on its south and west sides is a blank limestone screen that opens into a stolidly proportioned entrance façade on 14th Street. As well as creating a suitable dialogue with the other public buildings along the Washington Mall, and alluding to the heavy, austere, neo-Classicist architecture of National Socialism, this whole design element acts as a metaphor for the shrouding of the mechanisms of evil within the legitimate cloak of state.

The final space to be reached along the museum promenade is the hexagonal Hall of Remembrance. This is a large, discrete, skylit volume, empty for contemplation, in which 'the repeated use of the triangle form evokes both the Star of David and the yellow triangles Jews were required to wear during the Nazi years'.[3]

1 James Steele. *Museum Builders* (London: Academy Editions, 1994), p. 177.

2 Justin Henderson. *Museum Architecture* (Gloucester, MA: Rockport Publishers, 1998), p. 178.

3 Ibid., p. 181.

Sketch of the Hall of Witness

Opposite View of the Hall of Witness

Tadao Ando

CHIKATSU-ASUKA HISTORICAL MUSEUM

Osaka **1994**

Tadao Ando's Chikatsu-Asuka Historical Museum is a highly symbolic addition to the landscape of southern Osaka, being both metaphor and container of the *kofun* culture of death.

Dotted about the museum's picturesque site of plumtree-lined hills, there are around two hundred *kofun*, or burial mounds, dating from the fifth and sixth centuries. The museum's design brief required there to be views of this rich archaeological terrain from the building, but being located in a bowl of the hills, the realisation of this was far from straightforward. In a simple and elegant design solution, Ando's building both cuts into and rises above the surrounding hillside; the roof becoming a large open-air terrace and viewing platform. To reach this platform – which also plays host to performances and lectures – the visitor must ascend a majestic flight of shallow concrete steps, towards a starkly bold viewing tower. The overall aesthetic is austere but extremely compelling: 'Like a Mayan temple emerging from the deepest jungle, the building has a brooding, monolithic presence.'[1]

More than a vantage point or stage set though, the museum was also to house artefacts of death recovered from the *kofun*. The entry into the building is via a claustrophobic, diagonally slicing passageway in the grand flight of steps, and once inside, the building exudes a calm and dim funereal ambience. Beyond the entrance hall is the permanent collection, and further into the heart of the building there are views down to the basement level. Here, in a symbolic gesture, the tomblike, buried gallery space is keyhole-shaped in plan, resembling one of the four imperial crypts on the site – that of Ono-no-Imoko. The refined range of interior materials – natural wood, concrete and glass – gives subdued clarity to the internal spaces and, 'as with all of Ando's buildings, formal and spatial concepts are executed with a rigorous but poetic intensity.'[2]

1 Phoebe Chow. 'House of Shadows – Chikatsu-Asuka Historical Museum, Osaka', *Architectural Review*, vol. 198, no. 1182, 1995, p. 42.

2 Ibid., p. 44.

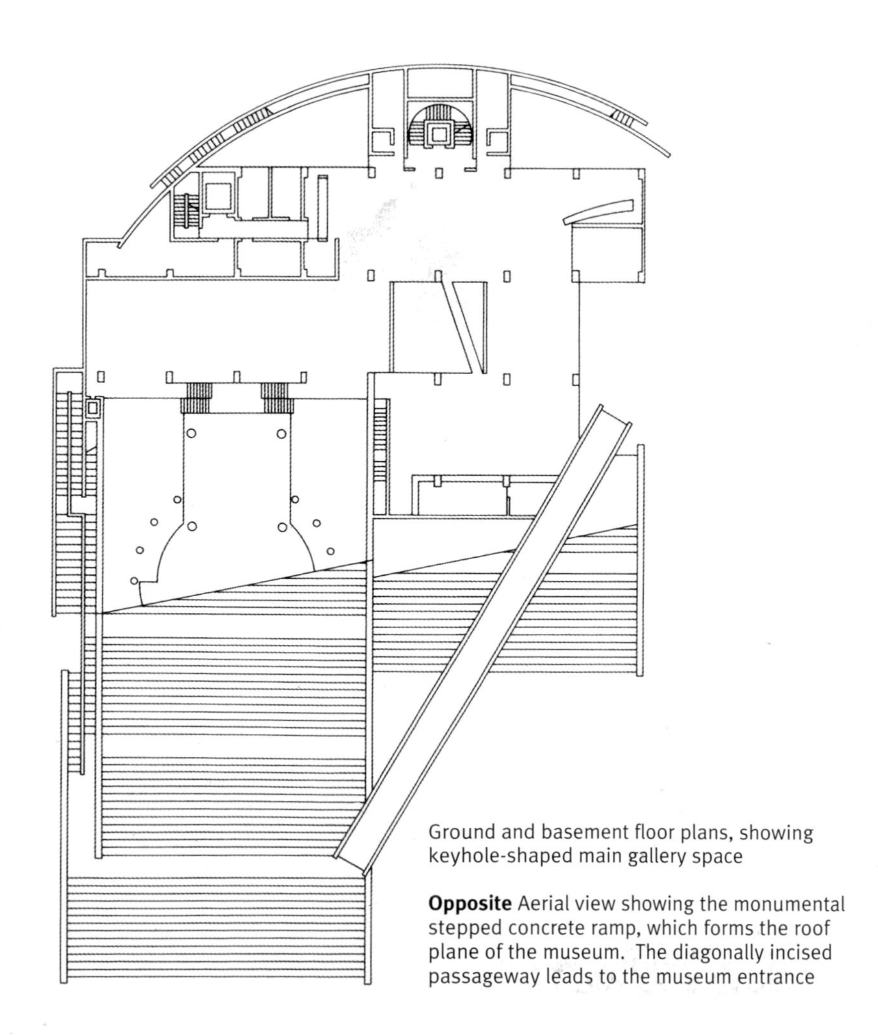

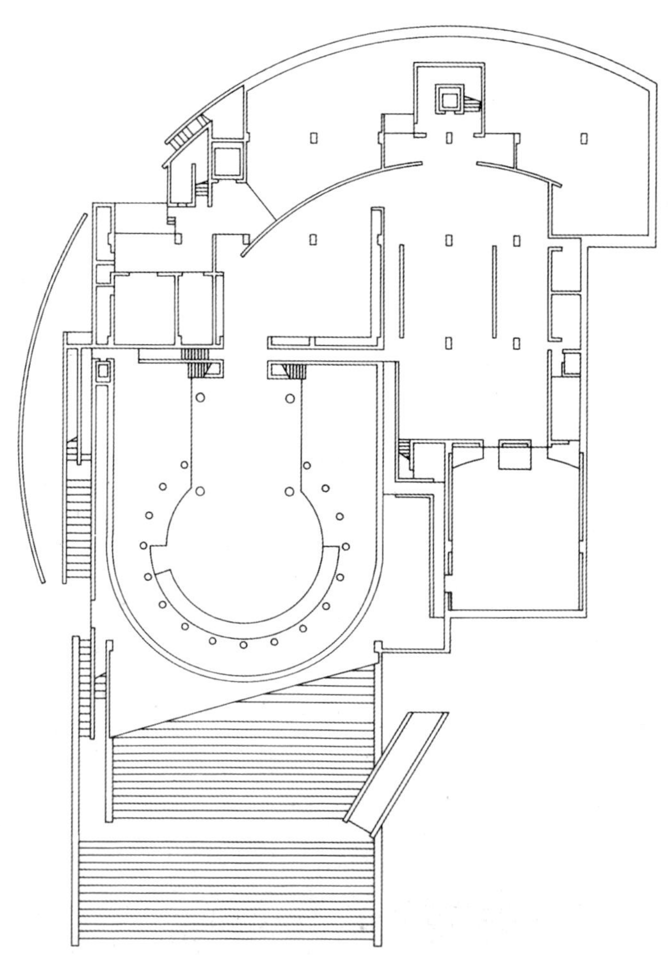

Ground and basement floor plans, showing keyhole-shaped main gallery space

Opposite Aerial view showing the monumental stepped concrete ramp, which forms the roof plane of the museum. The diagonally incised passageway leads to the museum entrance

Right Longitudinal section: Tadao Ando has cleverly utilised the slope of the wooded site in Minami-kawachi, both digging galleries into the hillside, and raising a platform and tower above, to provide views over the surrounding archaeologically-rich landscape

Below View of the gallery space

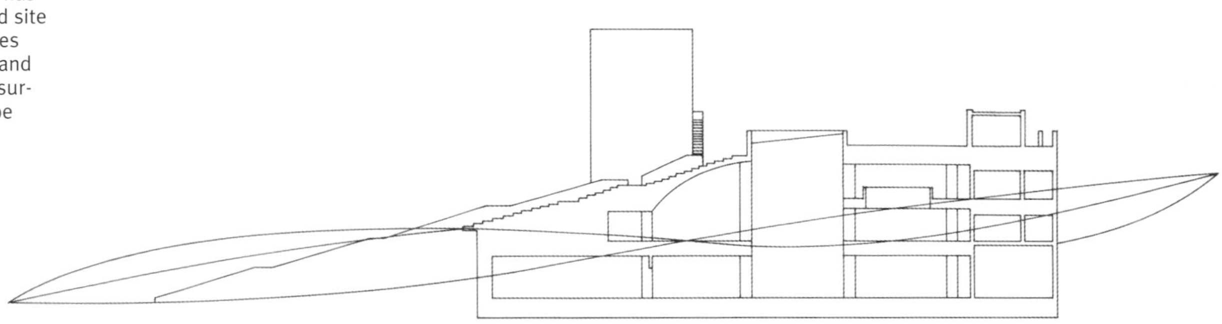

Right Longitudinal section

Below The grand flight of steps rises to a viewing tower and terrace, which doubles as a performance space

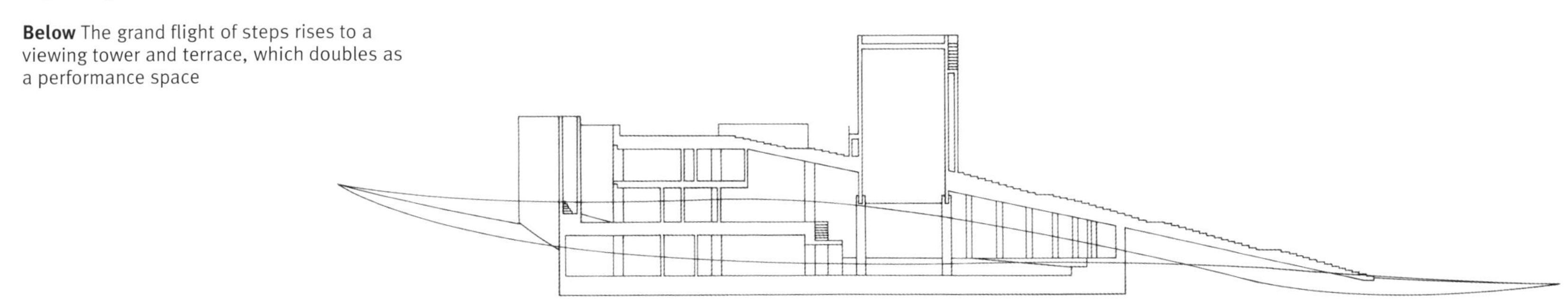

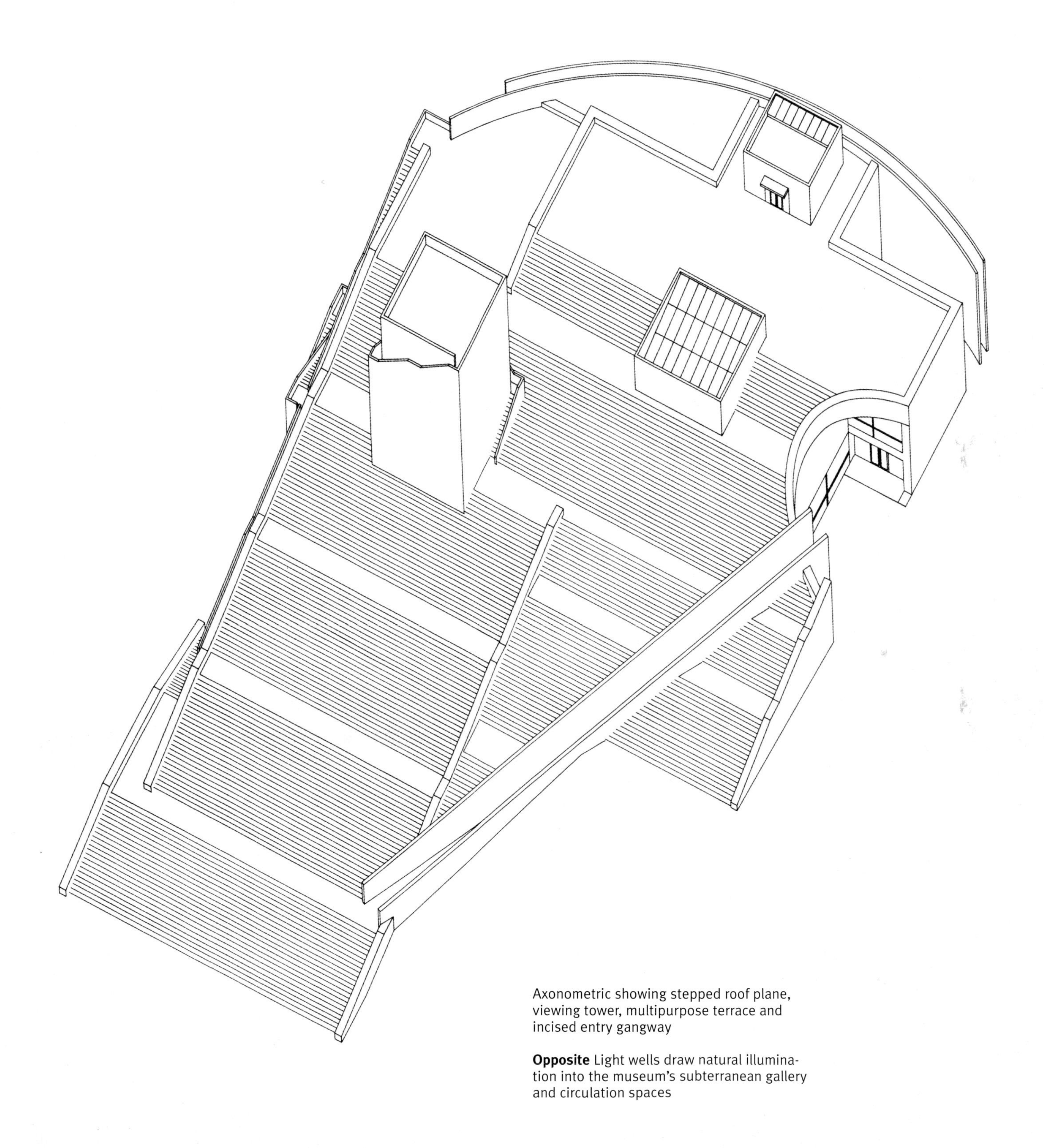

Axonometric showing stepped roof plane, viewing tower, multipurpose terrace and incised entry gangway

Opposite Light wells draw natural illumination into the museum's subterranean gallery and circulation spaces

Hans Hollein

VULCANIA: THE EUROPEAN CENTRE OF VOLCANISM

St Ours-les-Roches **2000**

Vulcania – or the European Centre of Volcanism – designed by Hans Hollein and opened in February 2002, is one of a new breed of scientific exploration parks. It is set in a landscape of extinct volcanoes at St Ours-les-Roches, Auvergne, and connects both practically and metaphorically to this primordial landscape: 'Vulcania has been sculpted and dug out of the basalt lava flows; there are no clearly marked boundaries between the buildings and surrounding countryside.'[1] Indeed, three-quarters of the construction is underground, bringing immediacy to the programme of display and a blurring of the divide between container and contained.

The first element on the journey, the Passage of the Lava Flow, is a landscaped route delineated by a wall clad in volcanic stone, predominantly hewn from the site itself. This path leads to the vertically incised, 28 metre high Cone, which externally evokes a volcanic plug, whilst internally acting as a giant reflector, bouncing natural light down into the heart of the museum below. Adjacent to this Cone is the open Calderra, which 'resembles a crater formed by the collapse of the roof of a magma chamber'.[2] A path spirals around the perimeter of this void, allowing views of the exposed rock strata, and descending deep into the subterranean exhibition and auditoria spaces up to 20 metres below. These house traditional exhibits, as well as experiential spaces such as the Rumbling Chamber.

1 Hans Hollein. In 'Vulcania, the European Park of Volcanism', *Press File*, p. 3.
2 Ibid., p. 9.

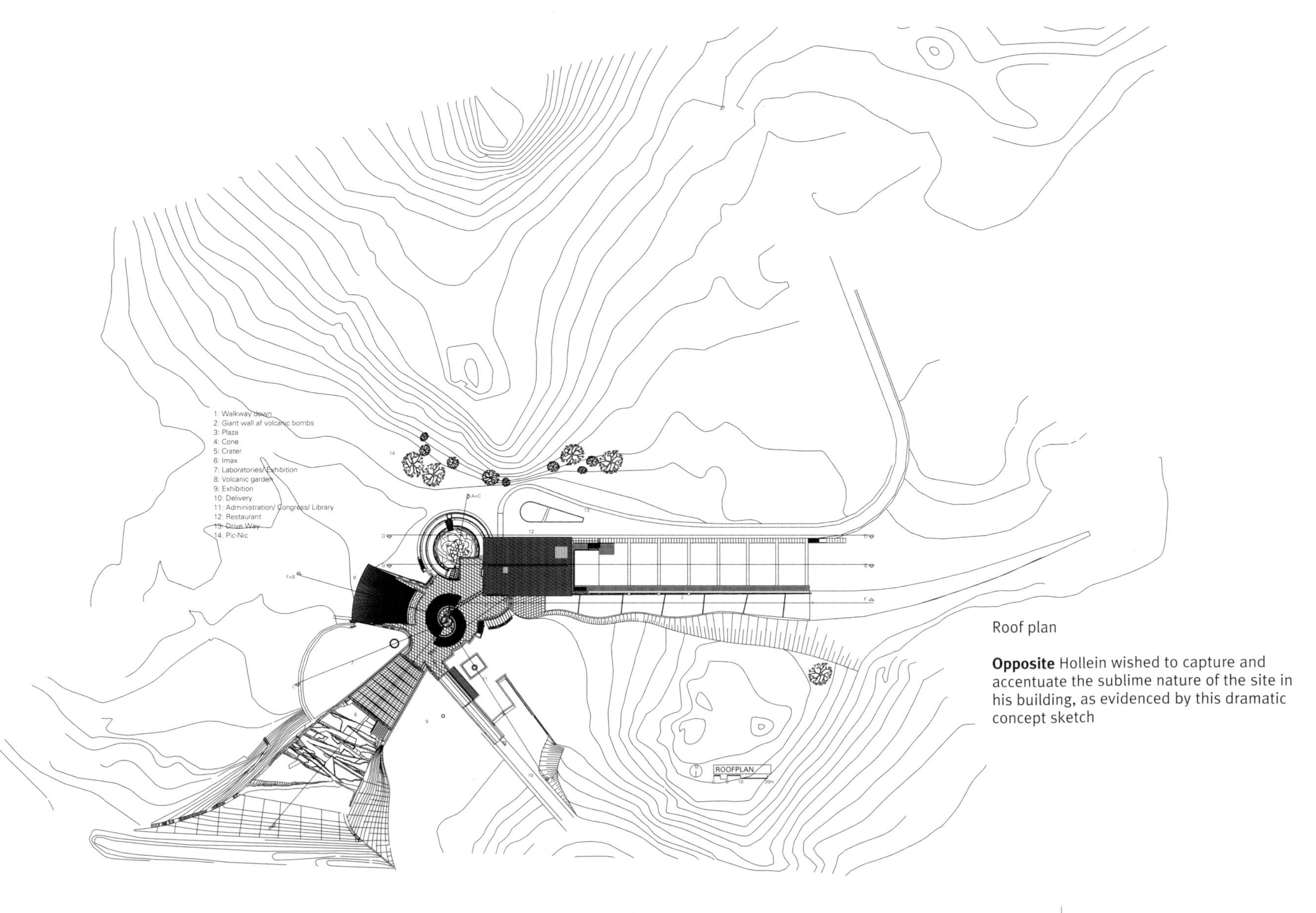

Roof plan

Opposite Hollein wished to capture and accentuate the sublime nature of the site in his building, as evidenced by this dramatic concept sketch

Top Exhibition space with glazed roofing

Bottom Computer rendering, showing the 28 metre high Cone and adjacent, downwardly tapering Calderra

Opposite top Sectional sketch revealing the embedded nature of the scheme

Opposite bottom Early concept sketch showing the major components of the scheme: the Passage of the Lava Flow; the Cone; and the Calderra

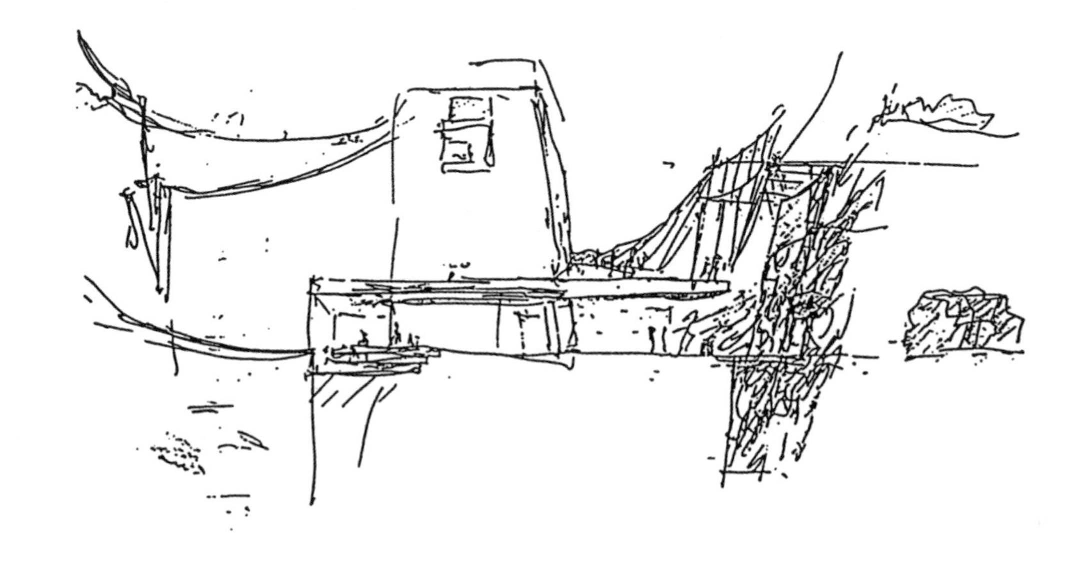

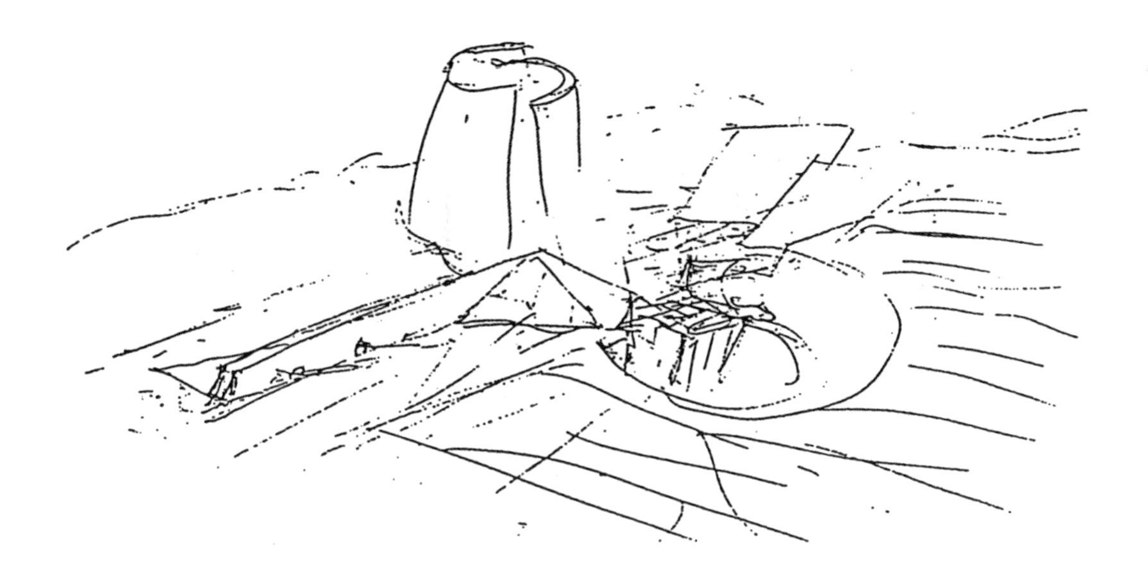

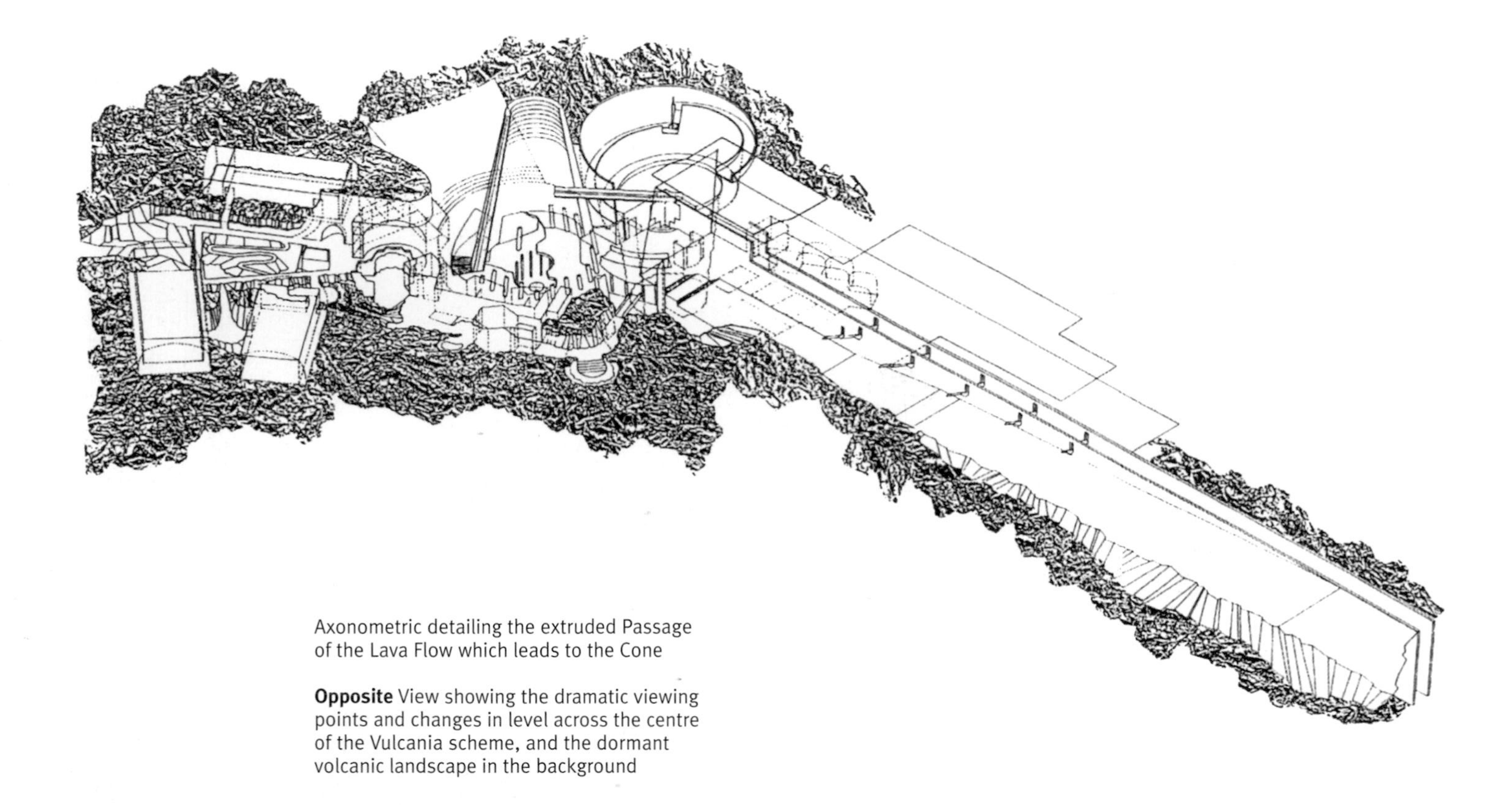

Axonometric detailing the extruded Passage of the Lava Flow which leads to the Cone

Opposite View showing the dramatic viewing points and changes in level across the centre of the Vulcania scheme, and the dormant volcanic landscape in the background

1: Crater
2: Entrance
3: Cone
4: 3-D Movie
5: Laboratories
6: Exhibition

Top Cross section showing the downwardly spiralling, sunken Calderra, excavated to a depth of over 20 metres below ground level

Centre and bottom Longitudinal sections

Opposite A bridge passing into the Cone structure

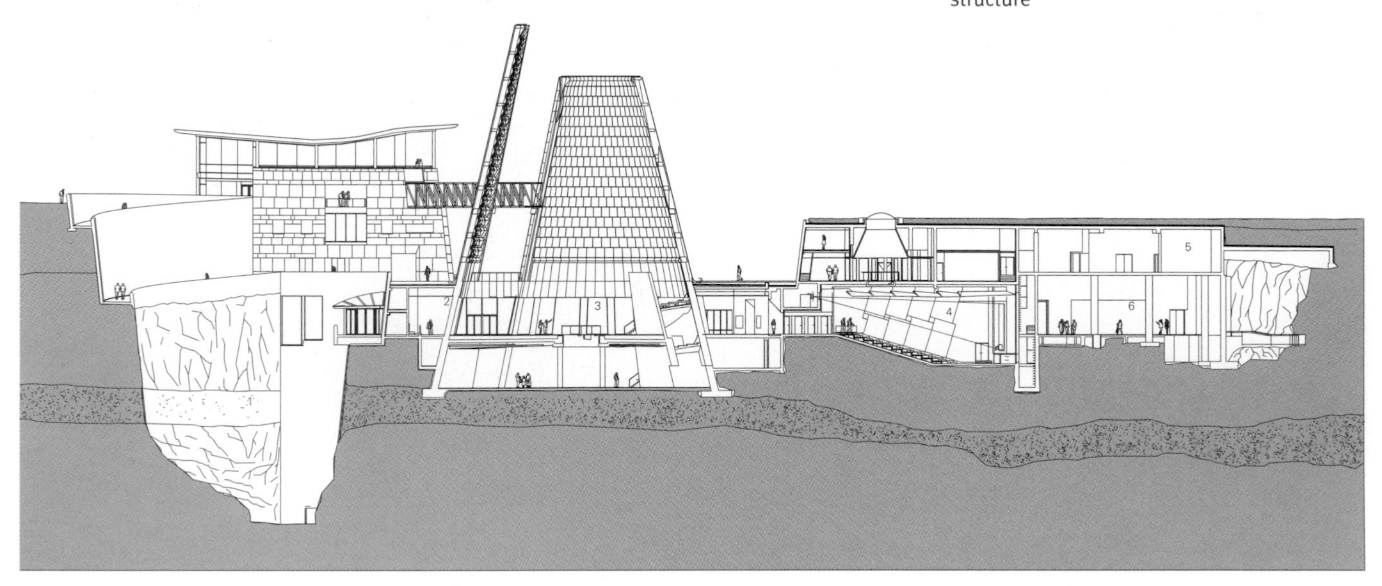

Section C – C

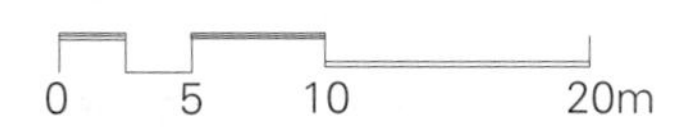

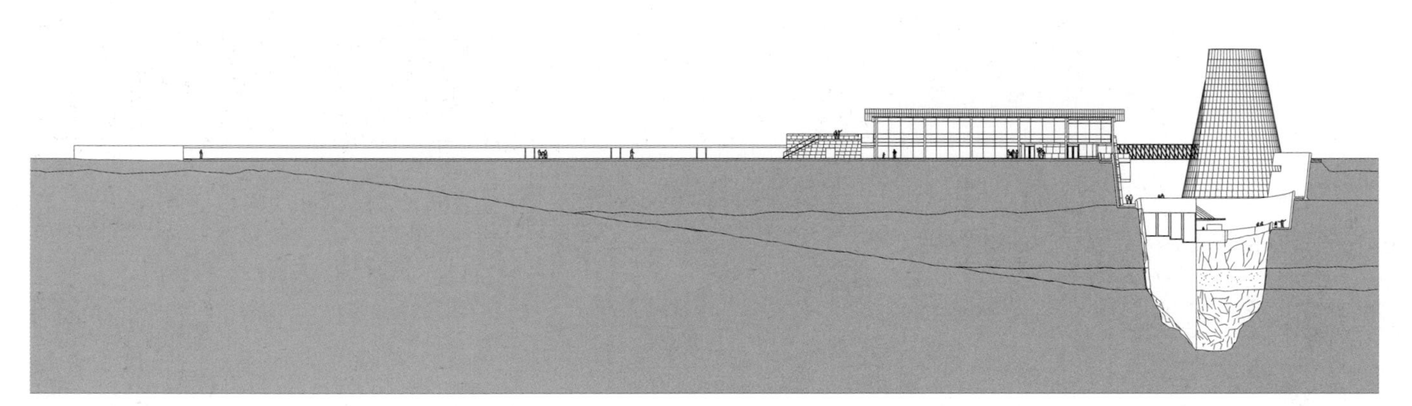

Section D – D

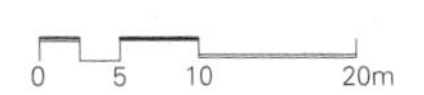

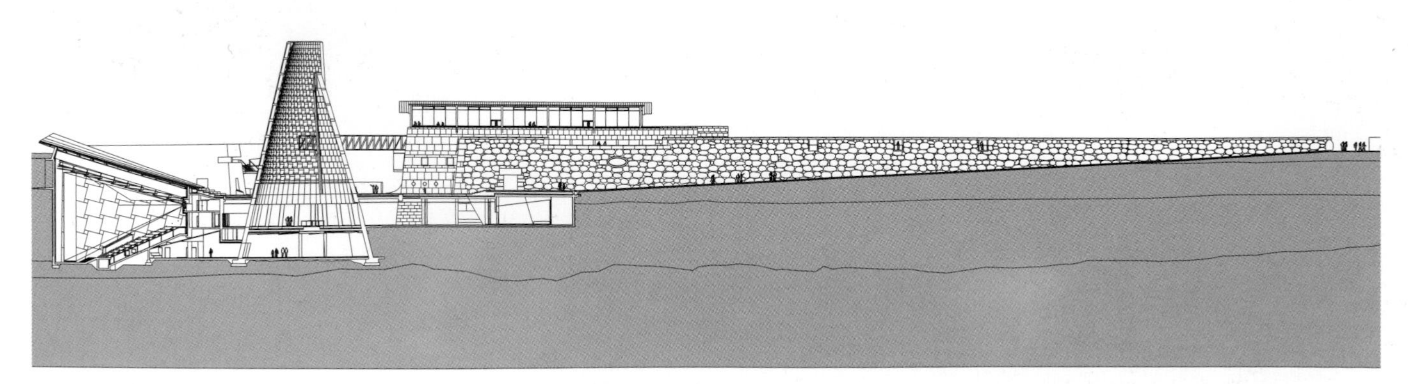

Section F – F

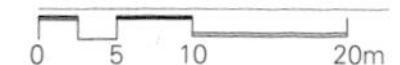

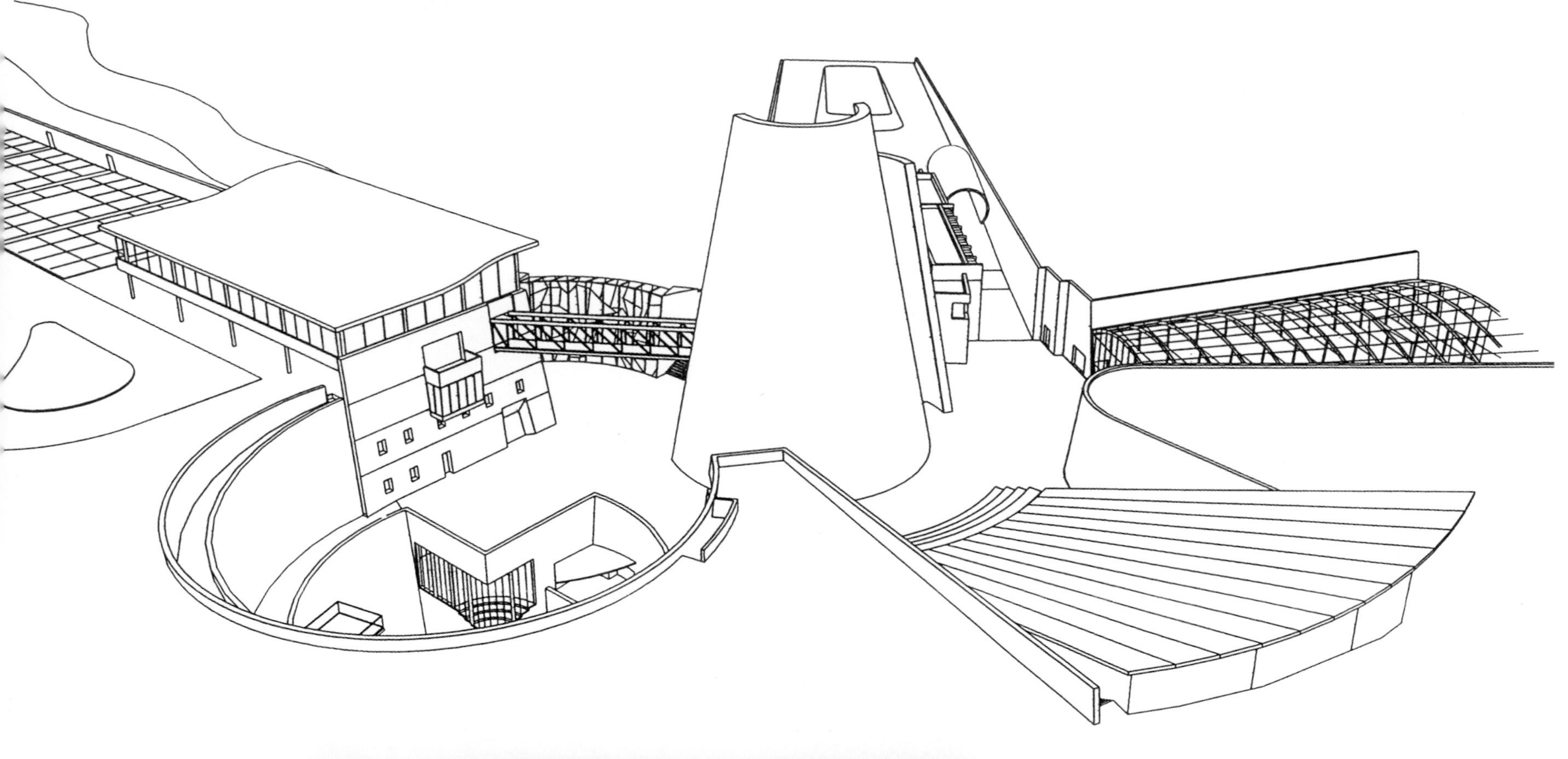

Top and bottom The vast Calderra, which 'resembles a crater formed by the collapse of the roof of a magma chamber', spirals deep into the volcanic terrain

Centre Axonometric revealing the simple geometric masses at the heart of the site

Top At night, the interior of the Cone glows with artificial lighting

Centre Sketch showing the building chiselled deep into the volcanic landscape, and the prominent, light-reflecting Cone at surface level

Bottom The textured interior of the Cone, or plug, serves to reflect daylight down into the exhibition spaces below

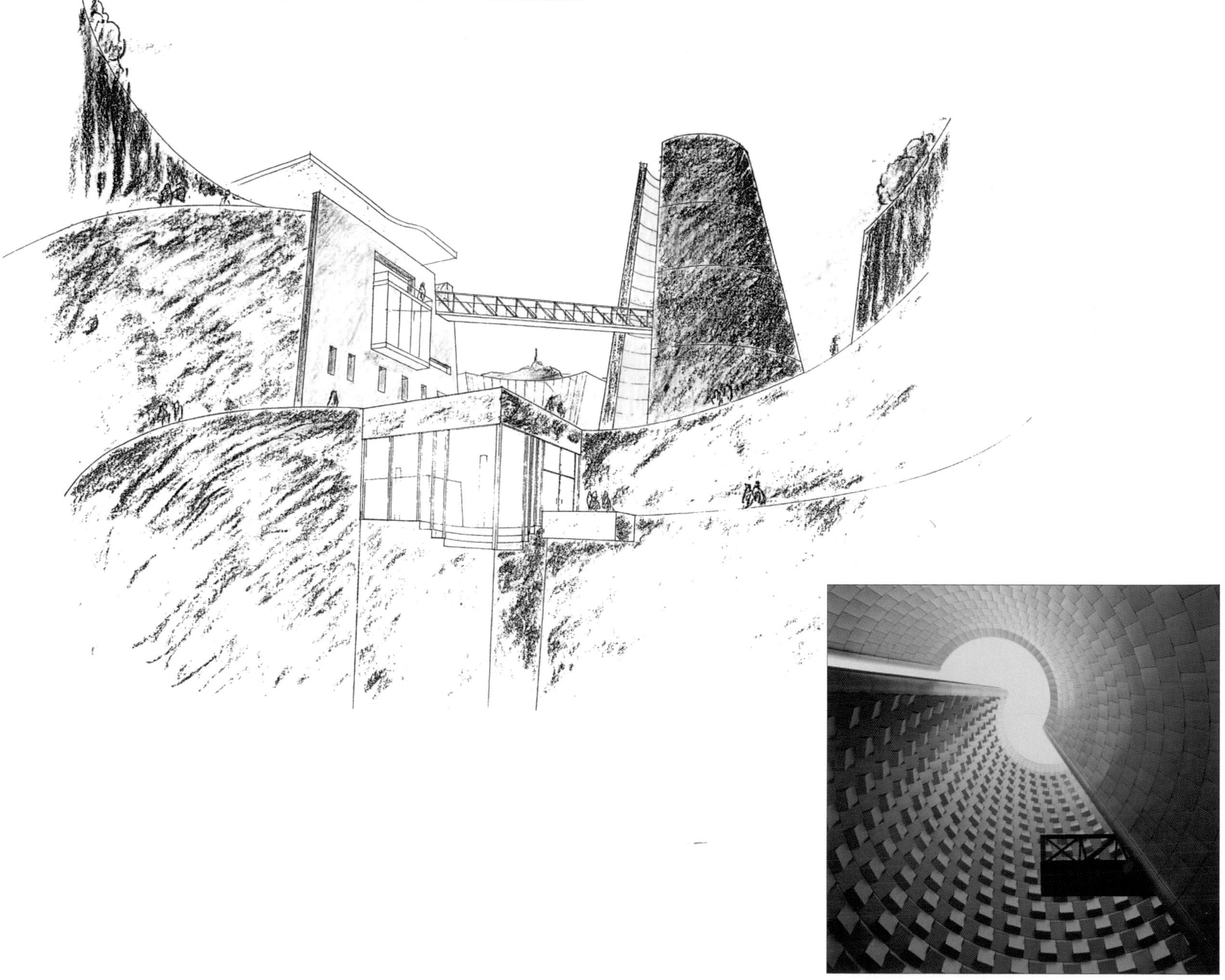

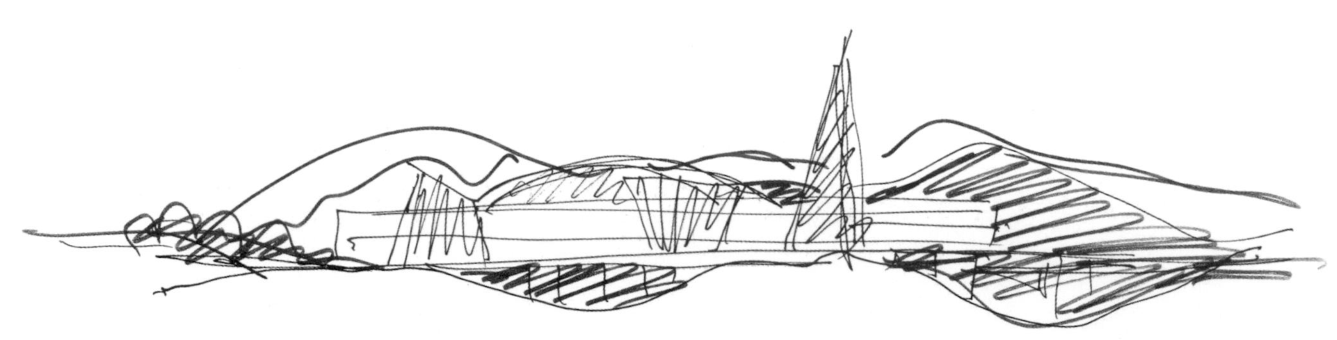

FUKUI PREFECTURAL DINOSAUR MUSEUM

Katsuyama City | **2000**

Kisho Kurokawa Architect and Associates' Fukui Prefectural Dinosaur Museum is located in Katsuyama City in an area that has been widely archaeologically excavated, 'resulting in the discovery of numerous dinosaur bones, fossilised footprints, and dinosaur eggshells.'[1].The purpose of the building is actually twofold, and this duality is revealed in its architectural configuration.

The first of the two key zones to be encountered is the Wing Building, which houses a palaeontology research facility, as well as visitor support services such as a shop and café. This is approached from the north and uses the contours of its site to disguise two of its three storeys. Glazing, special-order tiles native to Fukui and exposed and patterned concrete are all used for cladding, and in combination these suggest a cross-section of the earth's geological strata. The visitor enters into a modest ante hall before proceeding into a large elliptical atrium, dominated by escalators, which travel down to the first basement floor level. Here, the architectural promenade, or narrative, continues with the Dino Street – a tunnel in which the walls are embedded with fossils – and from which the visitor is led into the second principal element of the overall scheme: the Hall Building.

The dramatically ellipsoid Hall Building is devoted to public exhibition space, and, housing over 30 reconstructed dinosaur skeletons, it is one of the most extensive and comprehensive displays of dinosaur remains in the world. In order to accommodate these gigantic exhibits, a clear span space was required, and Kurokawa achieved a columnless volume, a maximum of 84 metres long, 55 metres wide and 37.5 metres high, through the use of structural iron-framed trusses of rotated oval shape. On the exterior, metallic cladding emphasizes the sculptural quality of this form and its geometric simplicity, in line with Kurokawa's self-confessed, 'abstract symbolism'.

1 Kisho Kurokawa Architect and Associates. 'Fukui Prefectural Dinosaur Museum: Design Concept', *Press File*, p. 2.

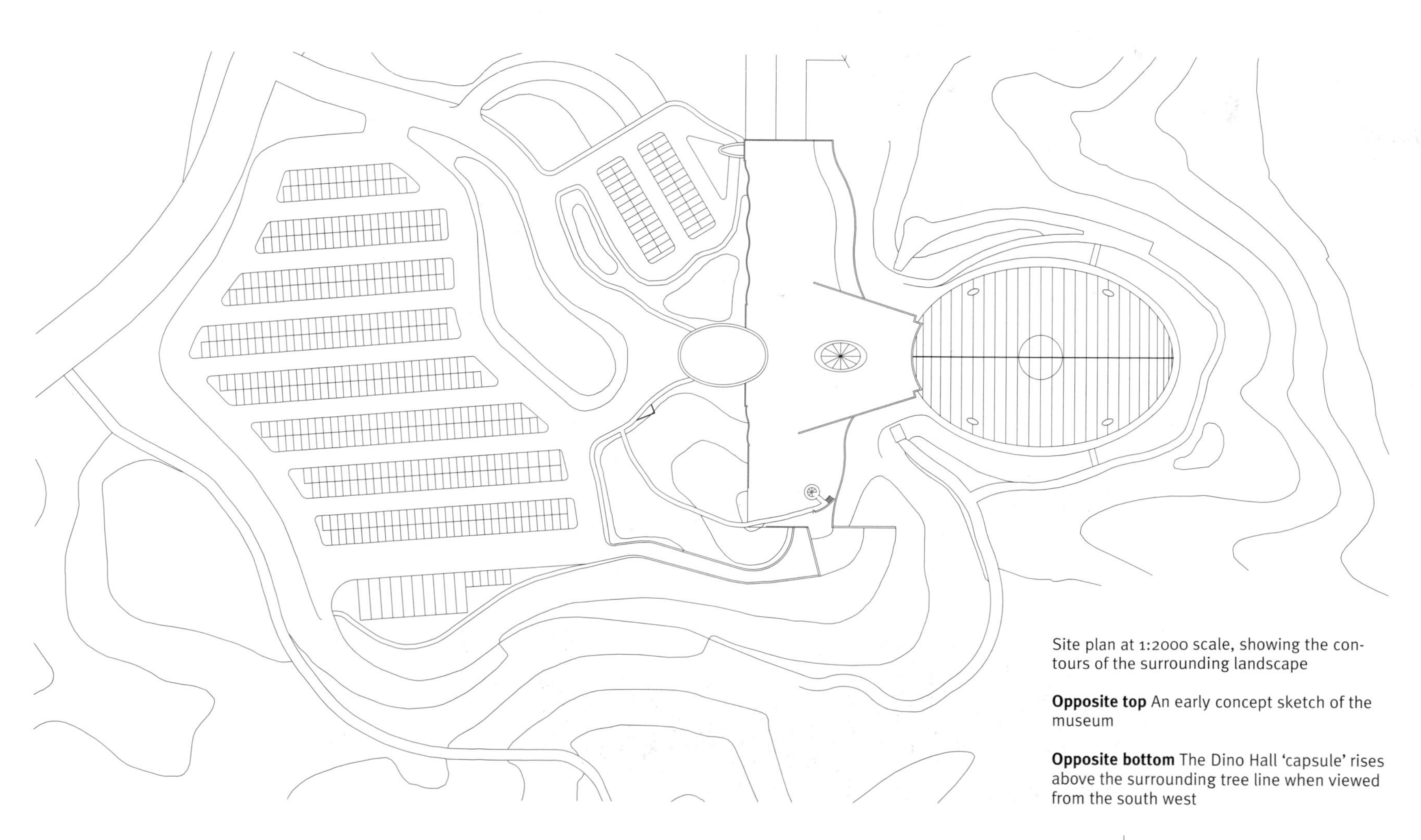

Site plan at 1:2000 scale, showing the contours of the surrounding landscape

Opposite top An early concept sketch of the museum

Opposite bottom The Dino Hall 'capsule' rises above the surrounding tree line when viewed from the south west

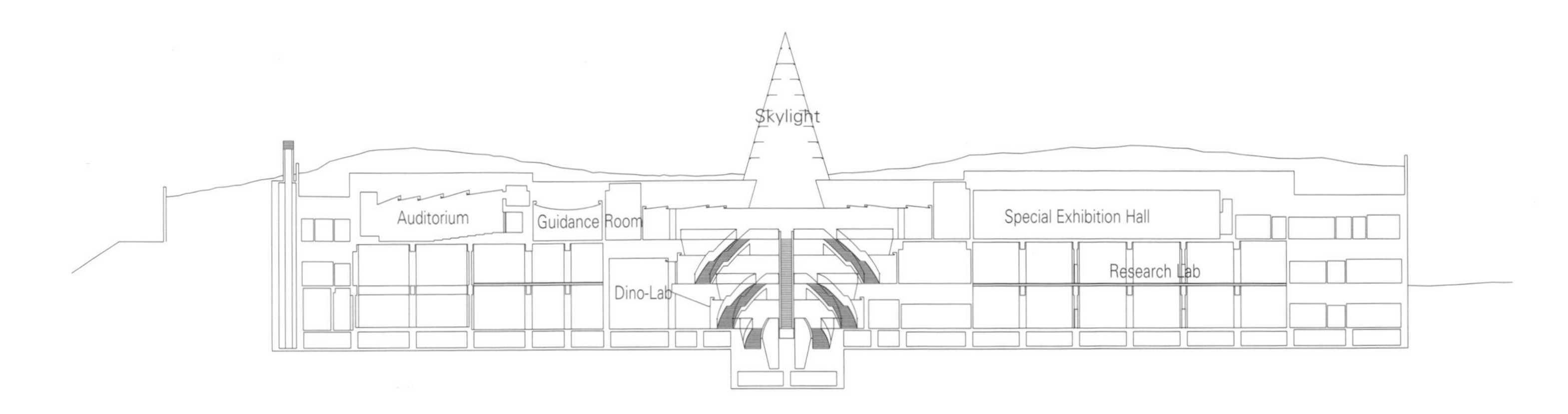

Above Cross section: The conical skylight draws natural light down into the Dino Street

Below The Dino Hall, Dino Street, and apex of the skylight from the north west of the site

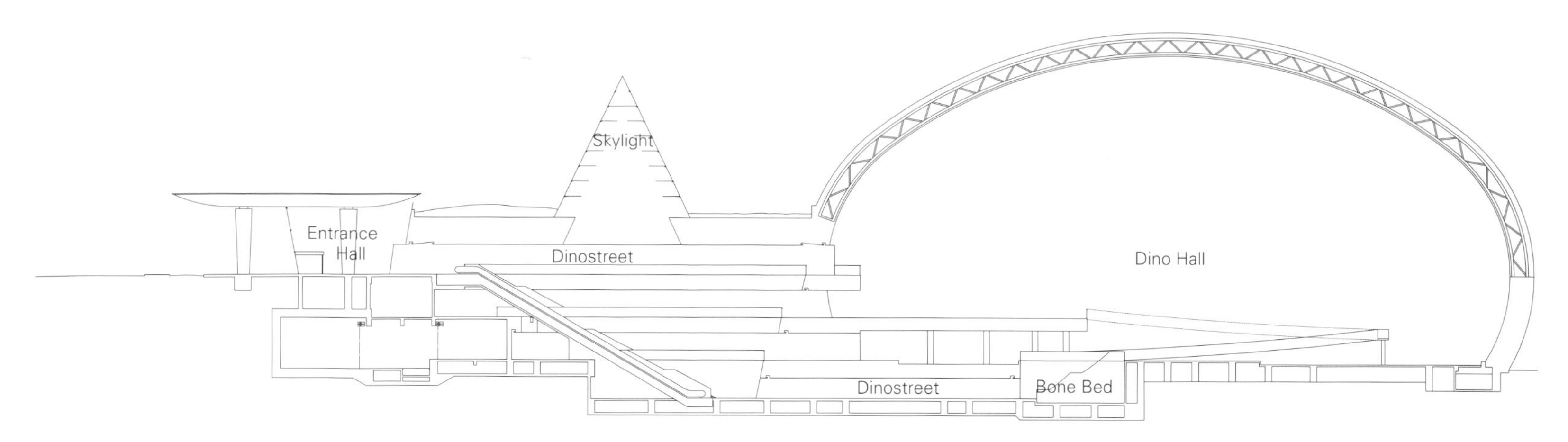

Above The longitudinal section reveals the trussed construction of the Dino Hall 'dome'

Below Kurokawa's 'abstract symbolism' is evident here in the pure Cartesian solids of the museum's form

The form of the Dino Hall is ideal for placing large scale exhibits within a diorama

Opposite Fossils are displayed along the Dino Street, which leads visitors to the monumental Dino Hall

Within the atrium, an escalator conveys visitors from the entrance hall down to the Dino Street below

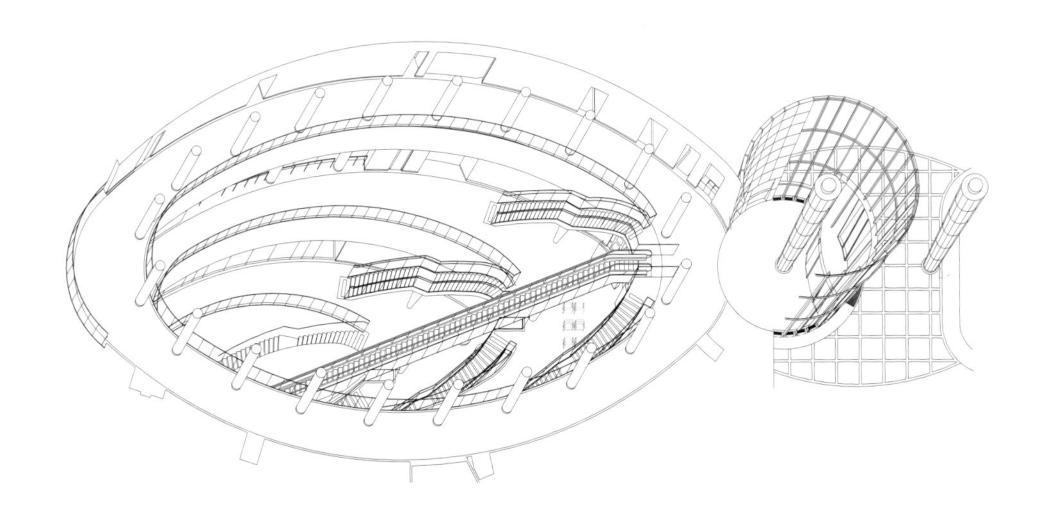

Above Axonometric showing the dramatic descent from entrance hall to exhibition spaces

Below First floor plan: The research wing to the north of the museum complex houses laboratories and a conference lecture hall, on first and second floor levels

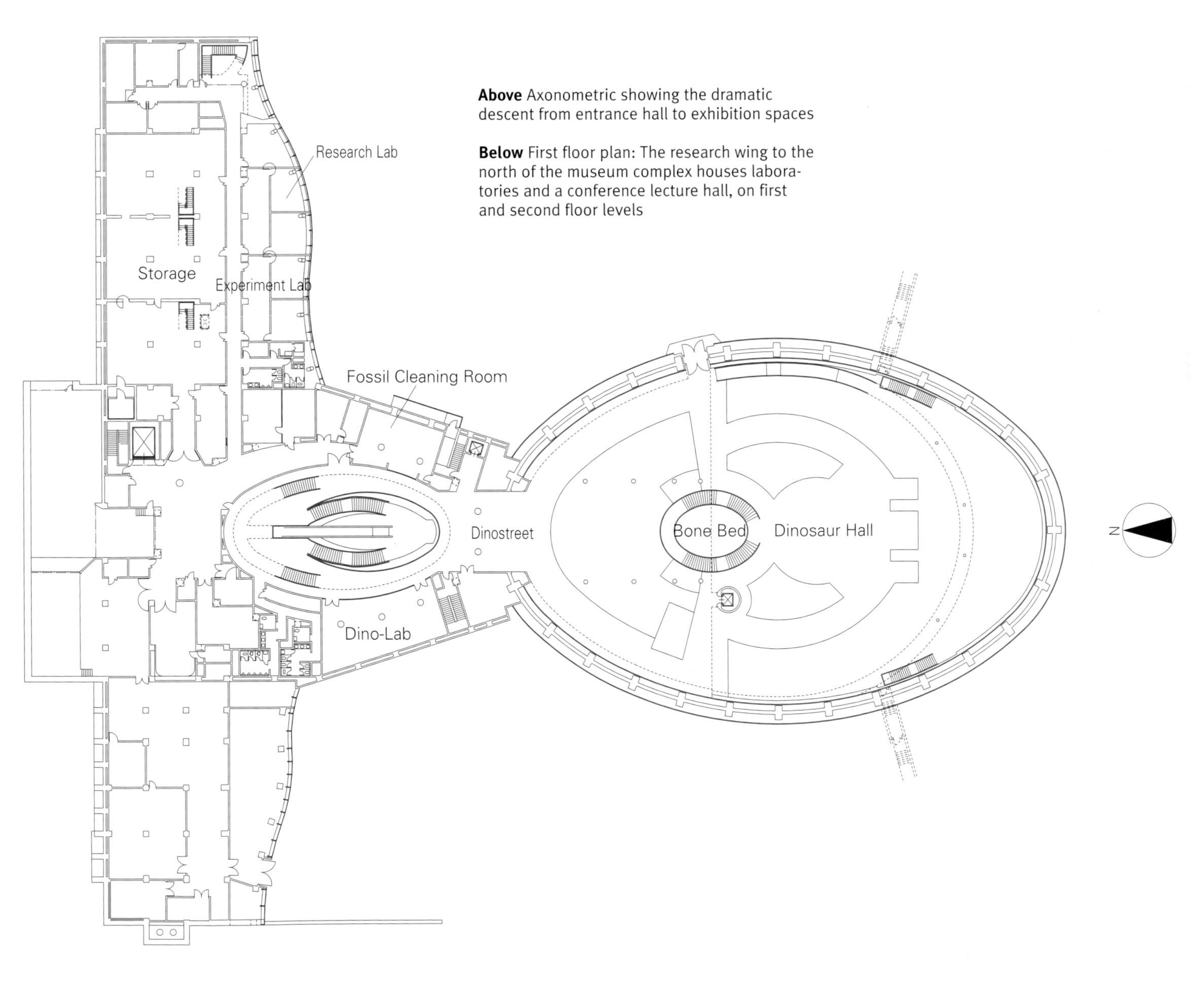

Top View of the concertinaed city-facing façade

Bottom Main gallery space

Opposite Detail of the seaward façade

Arata Isozaki and Cesar Portela

DOMUS, HOME OF MAN

La Coruña | **1995**

Domus, Home of Man, designed by the collaborative team of Arata Isozaki and Cesar Portela, has been described as the building 'most representative of our century in La Coruña'.[1] It certainly embraces the local, but, importantly, also looks beyond those confines.

Dramatically situated on a rocky promontory of the Galician coast, a bold and durable design was required for this cultural centre that would visually dominate the bay, beach and a large part of the city of La Coruña, and would physically have to endure the harsh, coastal conditions. In response, the architects produced a large, elemental two-way curving screen, constructed of precast concrete and clad in slate. From across the bay, the resultant form resembles a wave or wind-blown sail and, being largely windowless, provides an effective buffer to the elements. A skylight along its length washes the interior of this wall with natural light. In contrast to this element, the wall to the rear is eastern in influence, demonstrating the architects' desire for inclusivity and universality. Resembling a Japanese screen, this granite-clad façade addresses the urban scale of the city behind.

Internally there is a large, flowing exhibition space, with mezzanine levels, which follow the topography of the site, projecting from the rear wall. Ramps connect these different levels, and the space terminates in a multi-purpose hall. Sandwiching this principal floor are administration and research facilities above, and a glass-fronted restaurant below. Despite its relatively modest total surface area of 3,300 square metres, this building occupies its site boldly, conveying a degree of grandiosity, whilst the interactive displays within bring life to the story of man.

1 Information Pack, Domus, Home of Man.

The screen addressing the bay of La Coruña appears to 'billow', sail-like, because of its double curving form

Opposite A long roof light between the curving wall and ceiling planes allows natural light to flood the main gallery space

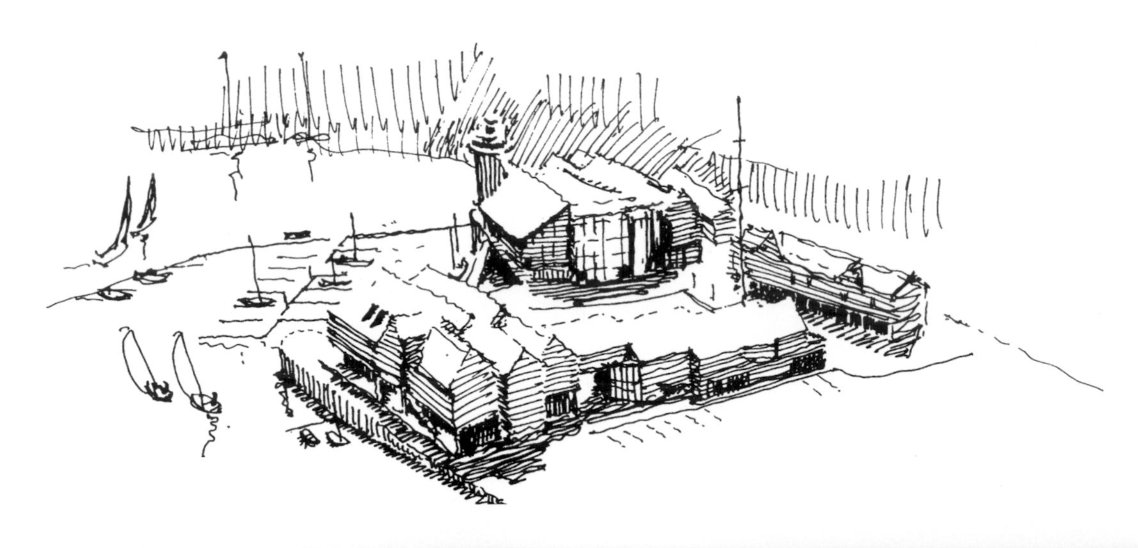

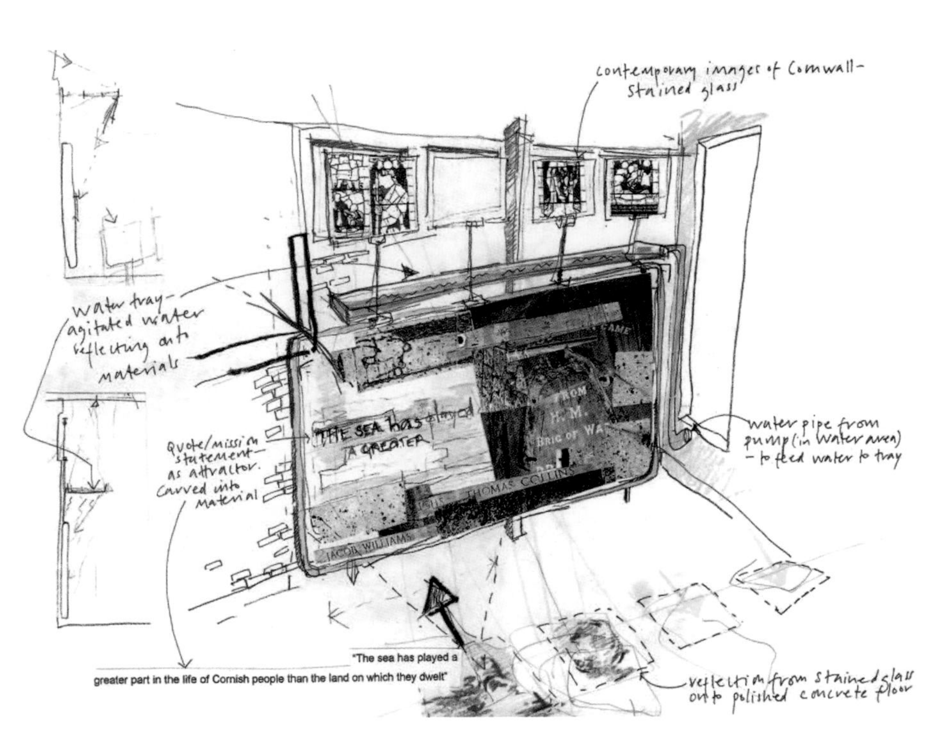

Top and bottom Concept drawings

Centre Detail of the front façade

Opposite Aerial view of the museum. The boat building sheds which formerly occupied the site provided the design inspiration

Long & Kentish

NATIONAL MARITIME MUSEUM CORNWALL

Falmouth **2002**

The National Maritime Museum Cornwall, which opened at the end of 2002, certainly bolsters a flourishing cultural regionalism in the West Country, kick-started by Evans and Shalev's Tate St Ives and Grimshaw's Eden Project. However, whilst it does on one hand respond to the particularities and memories of its immediate waterfront site, its design also transcends the local, to embrace a national and international collection and agenda.

The architects, Long & Kentish, won the international design competition in 1996, and '... outlined a building that would be attention grabbing – but not simply attention seeking'.[1] Design inspiration came from nineteenth century photographs of the site showing timber repair sheds, but this vernacular form was released from the purely traditional and local via a dramatically tilted roof, terminating in a tower structure at its eastern end. Pragmatically, this rising roof form provided the necessary three-storey high internal spaces for the boat galleries, acted as a backdrop to the large external public square and bridged a considerable gap in scale across the site: to one side the 30 metre tower addresses the industrial proportions of the dockyard, and on the other the extruded roof structure sympathetically reduces in height as it approaches the domestic scale of Falmouth.

Unlike many contemporary museums, which are tending towards the temporary, the Maritime Museum has been designed to last 100 years, and the simple granite masonry, slate roofing and unvarnished green oak cladding are sufficiently durable to withstand the, at times, harsh coastal conditions. Indeed, Long & Kentish revelled in the challenges of the seaboard site, positioning the imposing tower structure out in the water, allowing views deep into the sea through its glazed tidal gallery as the water rises.

1 Martin Jackson. *Reflections* (Falmouth: National Maritime Museum Cornwall, Nov. 2002), p. 23.

A planted roof garden softens the museum's cool functionalism

Opposite The museum's bright orange steel 'I' beam on its southern façade mirrors the speed and dynamism of the adjacent dual carriageway

KUNSTHAL ROTTERDAM

Rotterdam 2002

Early last century, Eric Mendelsohn described Holland's two great cities in the following terms: 'Analytic Rotterdam refuses vision: visionary Amsterdam does not understand objectivity'.[1] However, in the conception and realisation of the city's Boyman Museums Park, Rotterdam has embraced a startlingly bold vision of the city's cultural future that highlights the museum's strategic significance in the battle for civic identity and supremacy.

The Park evolved in the late 1980s around A. van der Steur's Boyman-van Beuningen Museum, with Koolhaas's Kunsthal – or museum for contemporary art – designed to terminate the site at its southern end. This location was certainly inauspicious, being hemmed in by tramlines and a dual carriageway to the south, and sliced in two by a parallel service road. The 6 metre change in level across the site from the higher road side down to the sunken Park side was also a constraining factor, although one which eventually served Koolhaas and OMA well, allowing them to produce interior spaces of considerable drama and tension. In resolving this level change, Koolhaas decided that the building should be entered at highway level via a ramp that straddles the dip of the embankment below. From here, the architect took 'the concept of the building as a continuous circuit', with one ramp leading upwards to a gallery space overlooking the busy road, and another heading downwards to a more tranquil exhibition space which fronts on to the Museum Park.[2] The main entrance was then articulated where the two ramps cross.

The split personality of the site is mirrored in the contradiction between inside and out, with the refined, diaphanous exterior box betraying little of the spatial gymnastics within. Only the massive orange steel I-beam 'architrave' and tree-trunk handrail give any clue as to the architectural excitement of the interior.

1 John Welsh. 'Double Dutch', *Building Design*, no. 964, 1 Dec. 1989, p. 18.

2 Rem Koolhaas. In *Kunsthal Rotterdam* (Rotterdam: Kunsthal Rotterdam/a+t ediciones, 2002).

Raked auditorium and café-restaurant to the south-west elevation

Opposite top Schematic isometric showing circulation routes through the building and the distribution of accommodation

Opposite bottom Site plan

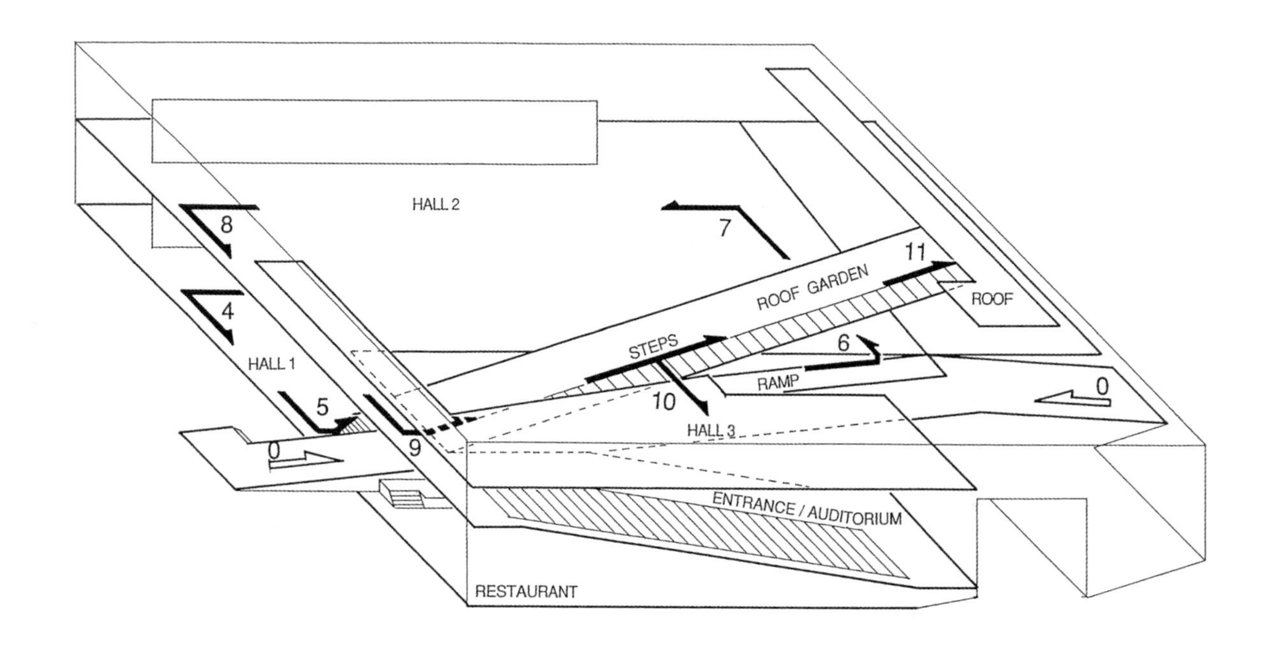
HALL 2
7
8
4
HALL 1
5
0
9
STEPS
ROOF GARDEN
11
ROOF
6
RAMP
10
0
HALL 3
ENTRANCE / AUDITORIUM
RESTAURANT

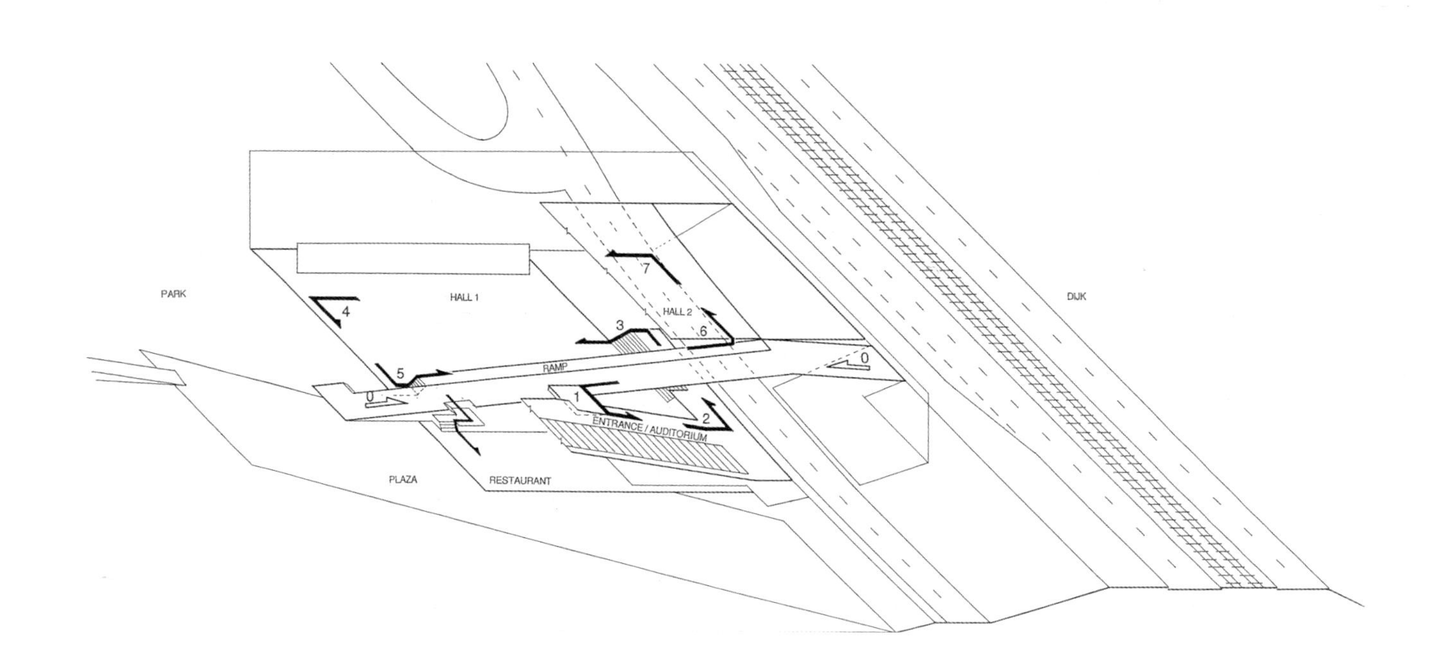
PARK
HALL 1
7
4
HALL 2
3
6
DIJK
RAMP
5
0
0
1
2
ENTRANCE / AUDITORIUM
PLAZA
RESTAURANT

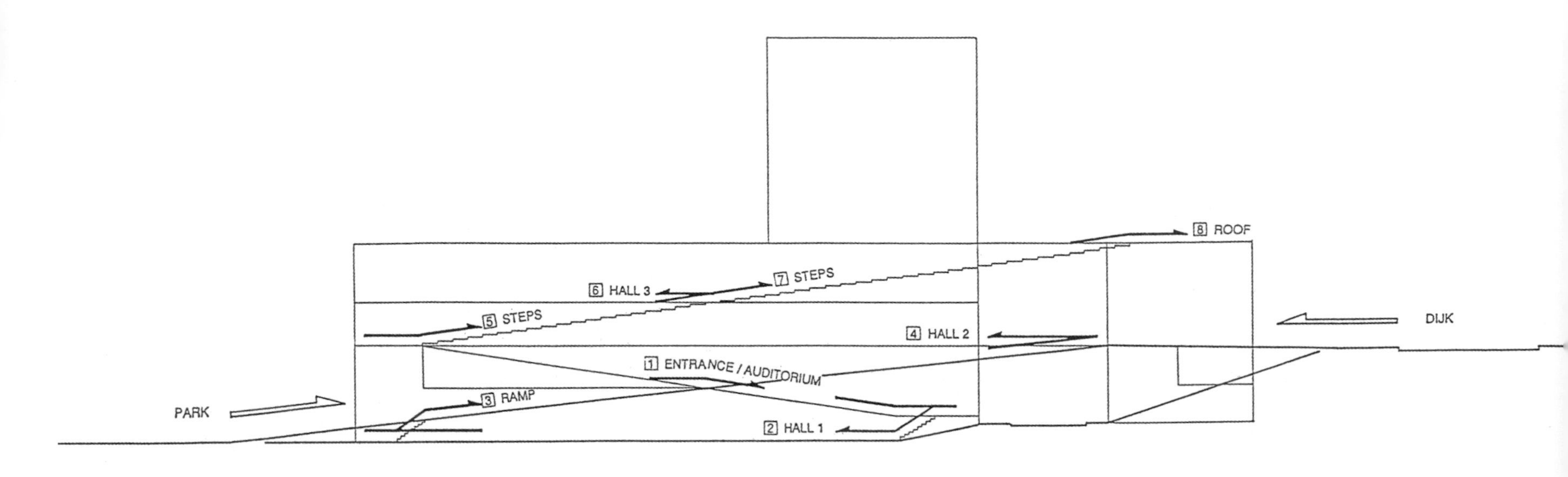
8 ROOF
6 HALL 3
7 STEPS
5 STEPS
4 HALL 2
DIJK
1 ENTRANCE / AUDITORIUM
PARK
3 RAMP
2 HALL 1

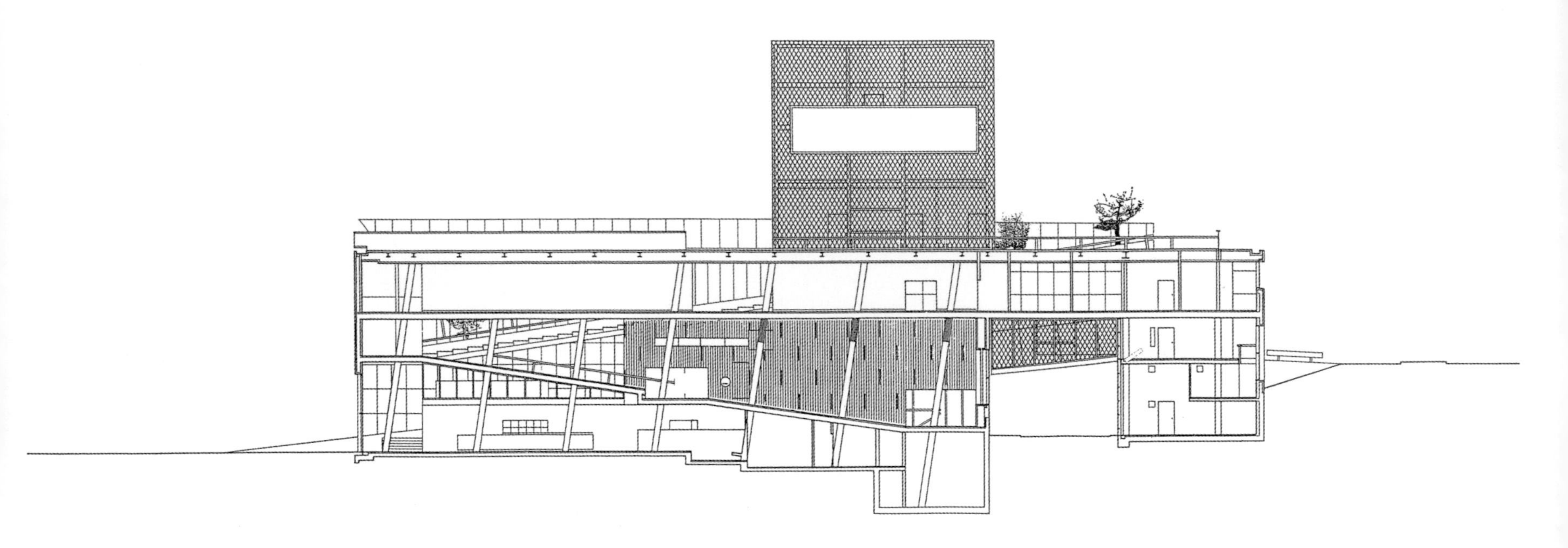

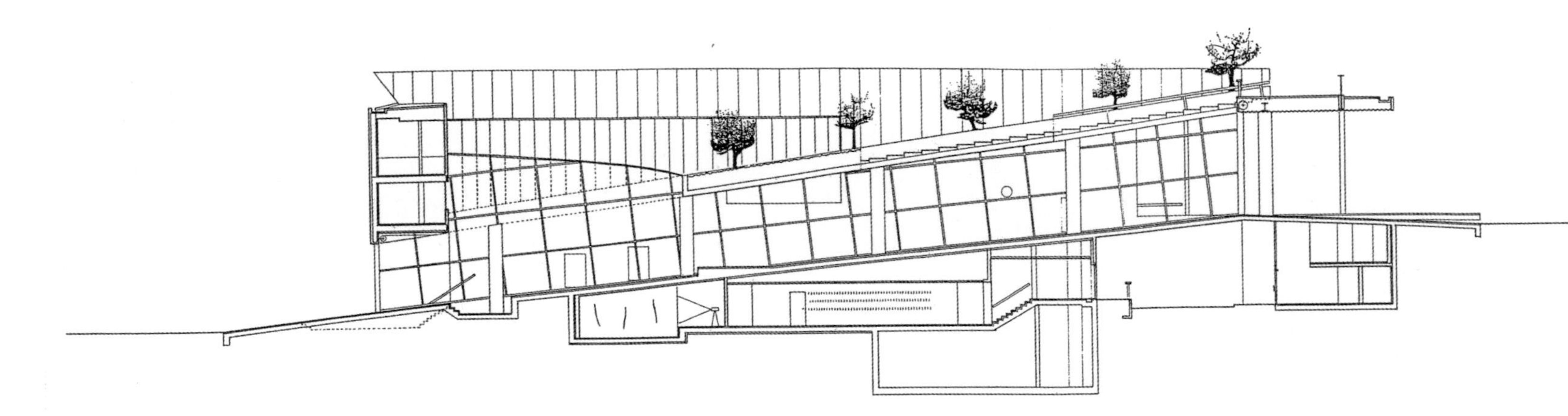

West side of the Kunsthal Rotterdam terrace seen from Museums Park

Opposite top Diagrammatic section showing the rise in level across the site from the Museums Park, up to the adjacent dual carriageway

Opposite centre and bottom Sections through the building, showing the buried accommodation, ramped entry and raked auditorium, and roof top garden

Koolhaas has used lighting to enliven the underside of the café-restaurant's concrete roof plane

Opposite top Plan of the upper road level

Opposite bottom Plan of the lower Museums Park level

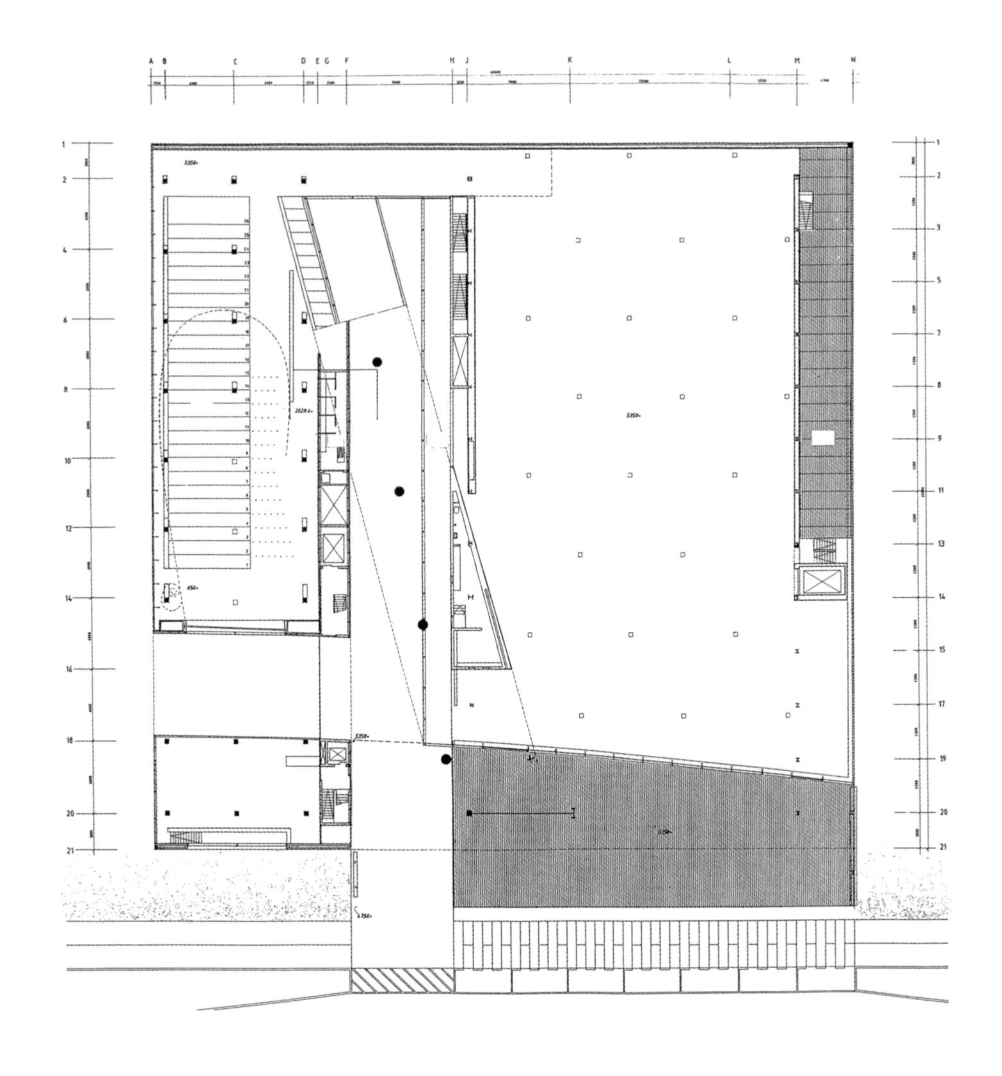

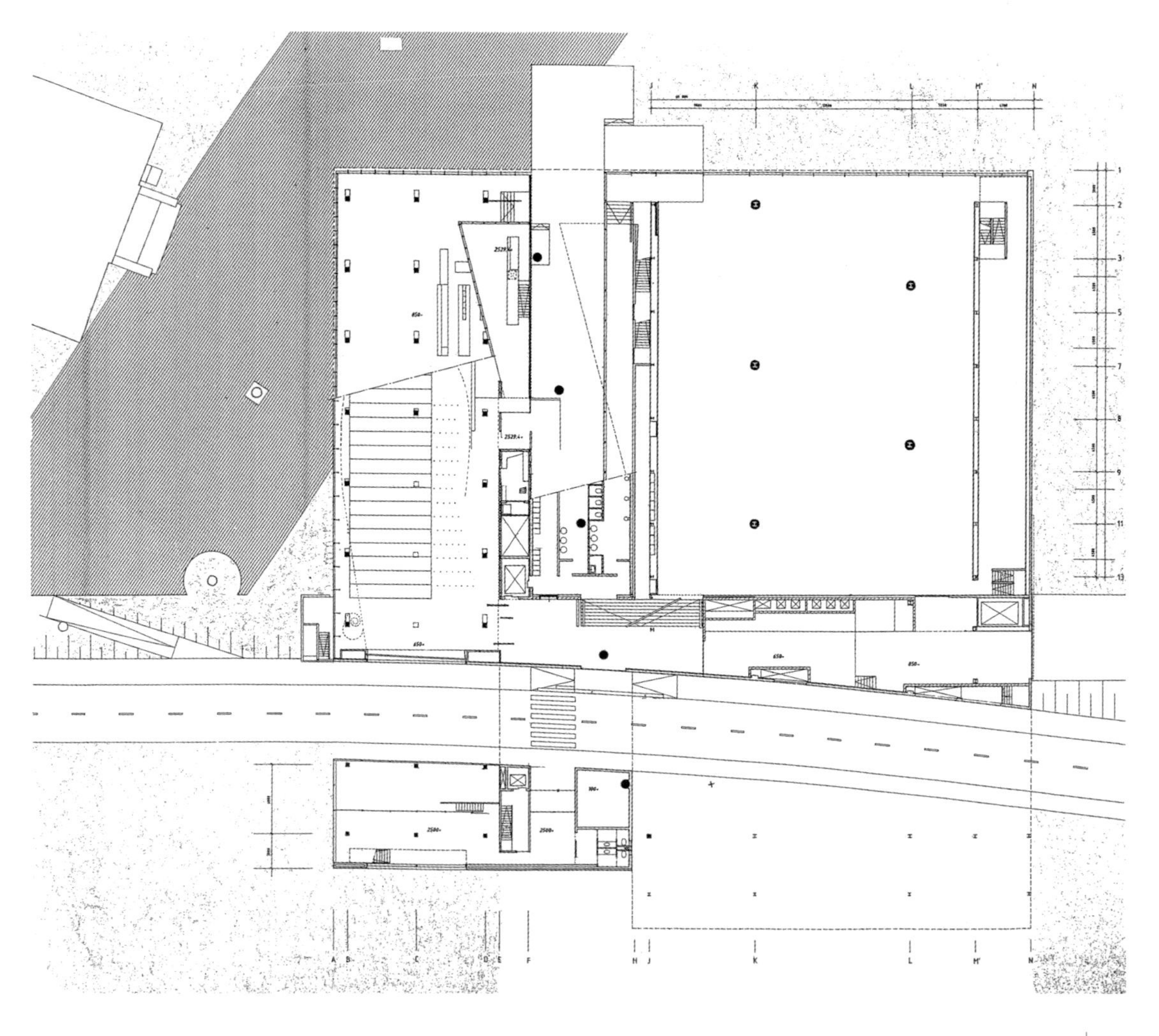

Temporal and seasonal variations in the quality of natural light alter the very character of the museum itself

Jean Nouvel

CARTIER FOUNDATION FOR CONTEMPORARY ART

Paris 1994

Occupying the relatively modest site of the former American Center on Boulevard Raspail in Paris, Jean Nouvel's Fondation Cartier pour l'Art Contemporain is a wonderfully refined exercise in the use of steel and glass.

In essence, the building is a symmetrical glass box, with glazed screens to front and rear, extending beyond its limits. This purist, 'post-Miesian' form accommodates a triple height gallery on ground floor, and a double height exhibition space below.[1] Seven floors of office space, including a roof terrace café, extend upwards, and with six further subterranean levels of workshops, storage and car parking, the building is almost as deep as it is high. Primary circulation is provided by central stairs from ground to mezzanine levels, which are thereafter replaced by glass lifts, and open metal stairwells at either end of the main façade ascend the Foundation's entire height behind the extruded screens.

However, to describe the building solely in these terms is to miss its magic. The shimmering transparency of the glazed façades enables the building to mirror and disappear into the surrounding sky, vegetation and nineteenth-century bourgeois villas. Chameleon-like, it is constantly shifting in different lights, creating ambiguity between inside and out. This uncertainty is heightened by the glass screens that glide seamlessly across the façades, framing and containing a number of cedar trees within and around them.

Jean Nouvel minimised structural details in an attempt to produce pure, abstract forms, and as a result, 'this is a glass and steel building that has nothing to do with high-tech'.[2] This approach certainly 'runs the risk of descending from the poetic to the realm of the vapid', but the simple beauty of the architect's final creation is hard to dispute.[3]

1 Nouvel's own classification of the architecture. In Clare Melhuish, 'Peering into the Void', *Building Design*, no. 1166, 1 April 1994, p. 8.

2 Editor. 'Art in a Void', *Blueprint*, no. 107, May 1994, p. 40.

3 Ibid.

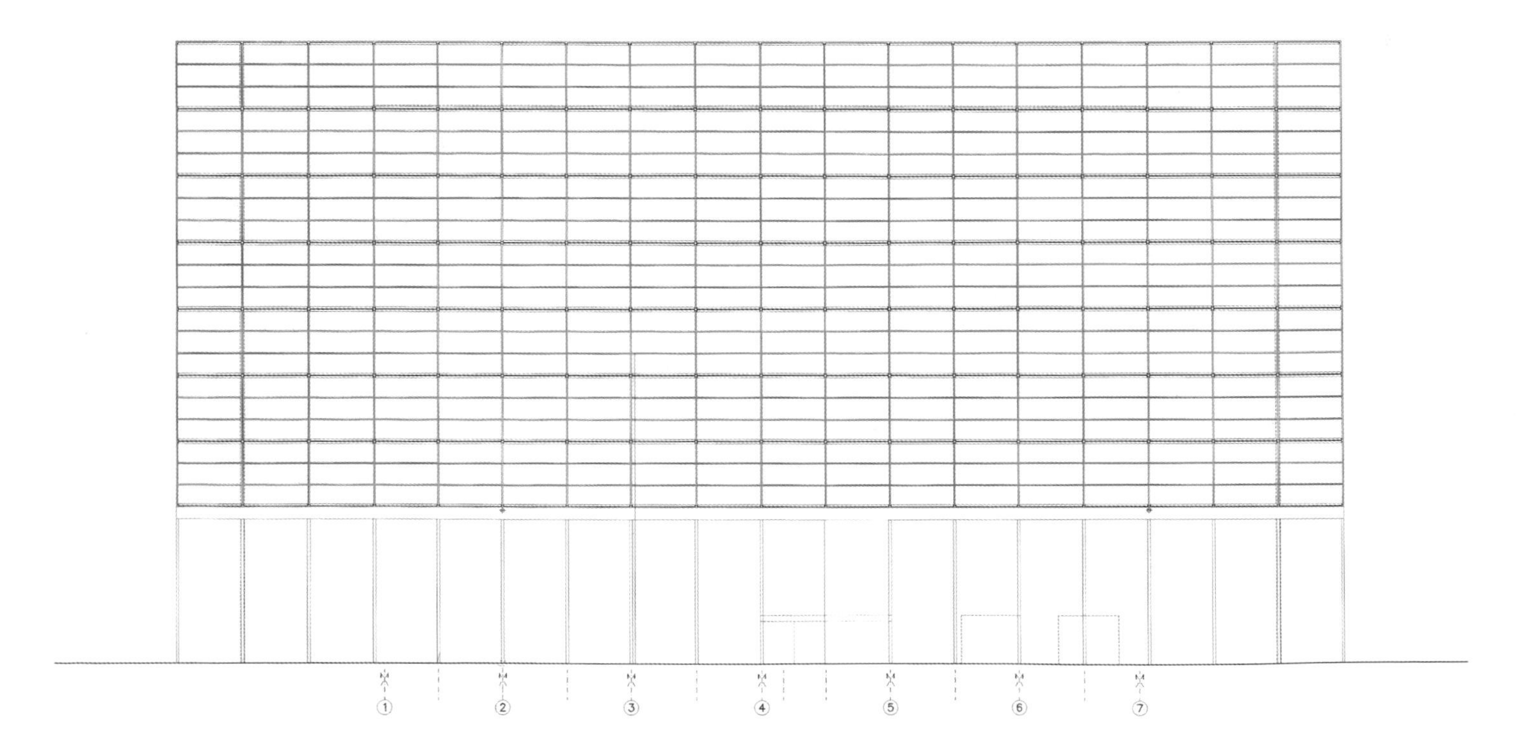

This west elevation highlights the refined simplicity and clarity of Nouvel's vision for the museum

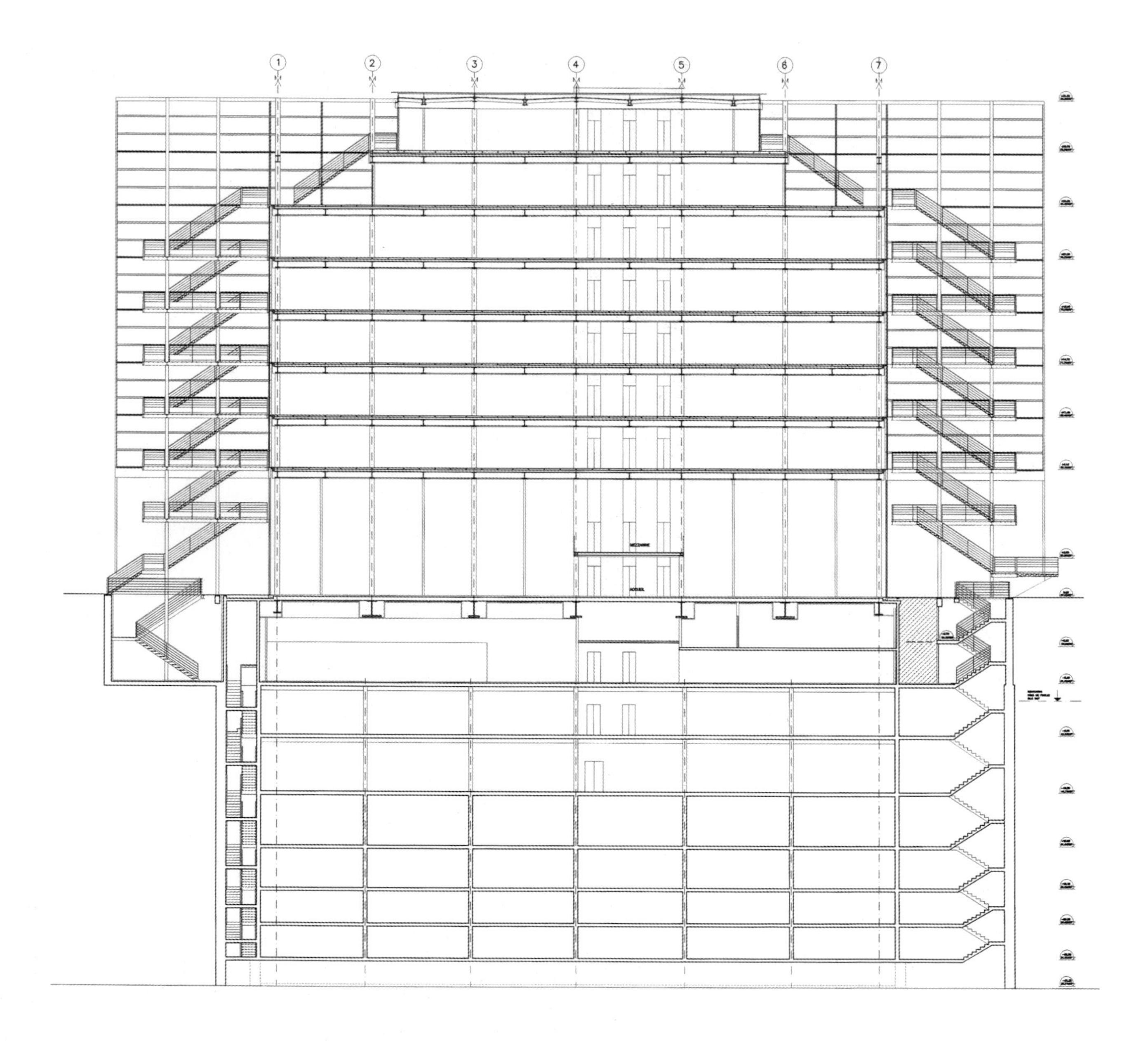

Above and Right These longitudinal and cross sections show the building's circulatory systems, and its depth beneath the Parisian pavement line

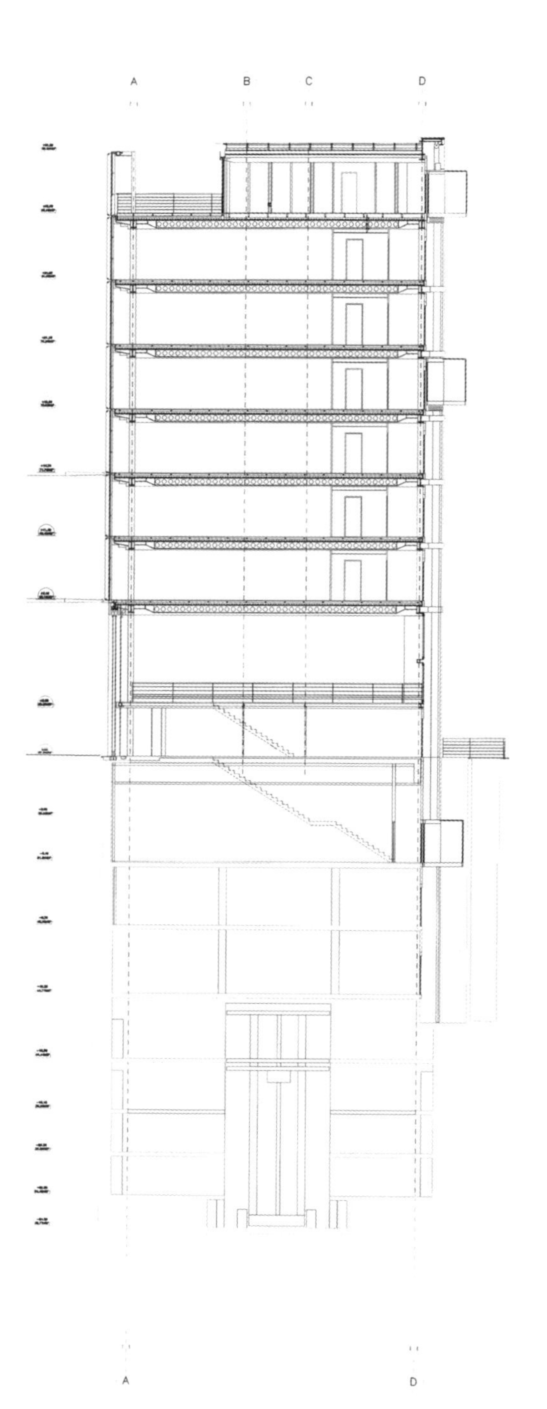

The building's simple transparency and reflectivity enable it to dissolve into the surrounding Parisian environment

Cedar trees grow between the floating glass planes of the street façade, dissolving the distinction between inside and out

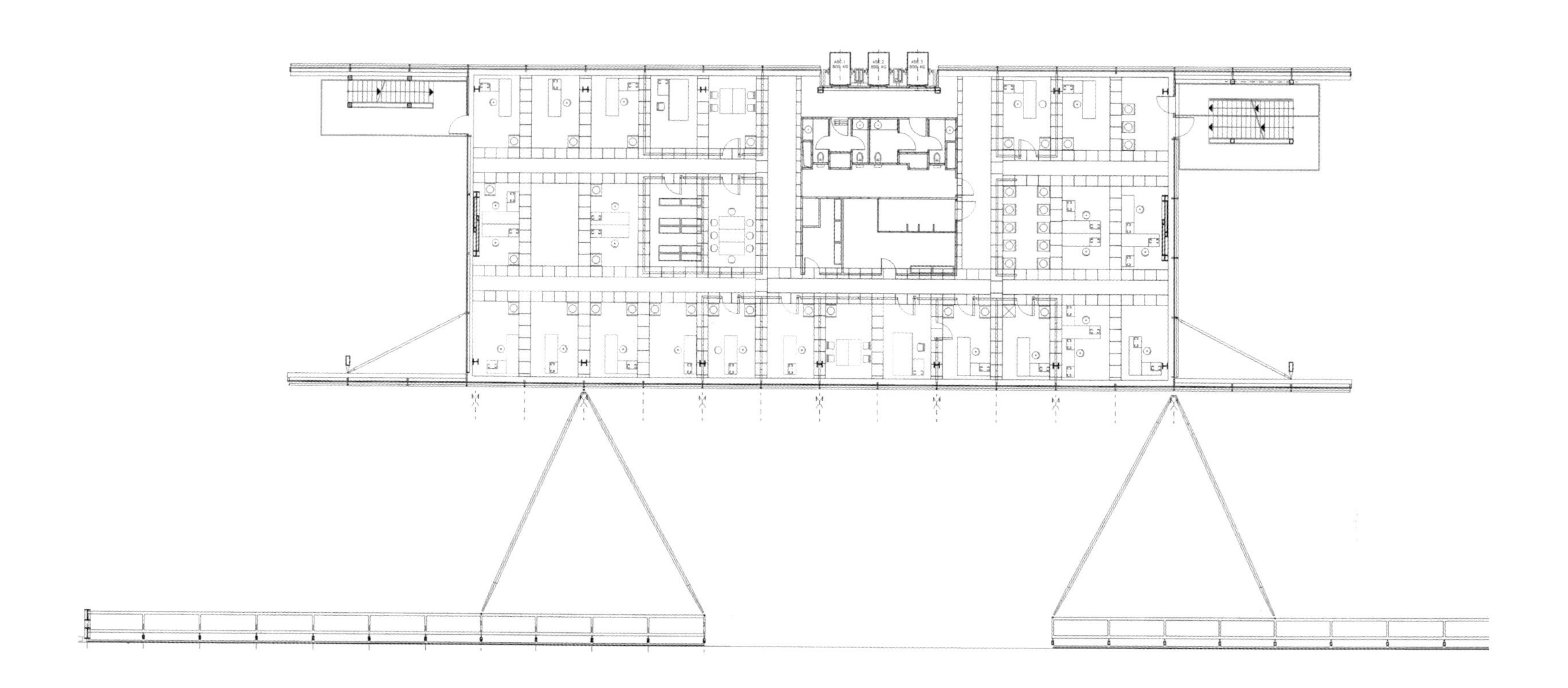

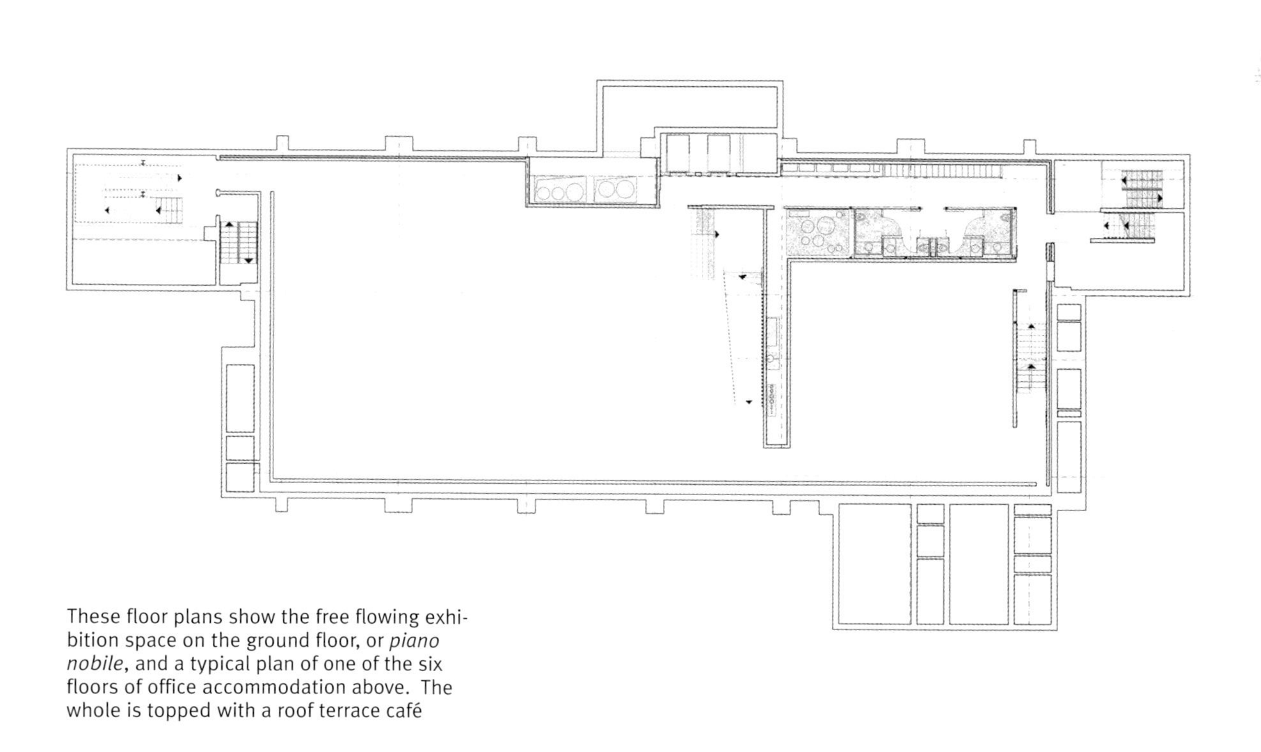

These floor plans show the free flowing exhibition space on the ground floor, or *piano nobile*, and a typical plan of one of the six floors of office accommodation above. The whole is topped with a roof terrace café

Top Mario Botta recessed the imposing brick-clad blocks in order to allow natural light into the heart of the deep plan building

Bottom Sketch: despite its diminutive scale in comparison to the adjacent skyscrapers, Botta's museum is sufficiently monumental to command its city centre block site

Mario Botta

SAN FRANCISCO MUSEUM OF MODERN ART

San Francisco **1995**

Mario Botta, the architect of San Francisco's Museum of Modern Art, recognises the pseudo-spiritual significance of the contemporary museum, declaring that 'in today's city, the museum plays a role analogous to that of the cathedral of yesterday'.[1] Indeed, the monumentality of his San Franciscan edifice is its defining feature, making it a fitting destination for cultural pilgrimage.

Located in the recently rejuvenated area south of Market Street, opposite the Yerba Buena Gardens arts complex, the building is boldly autonomous. Its composition of stacked and set back, heavy brick masses pervades a fortress-like aspect to the surrounding streets and buildings. However, this solid homogeneity is relieved both by the patterning of the brickwork, which 'creates subtle variations of light and shadow on the monochromatic surface', and, most notably, by the chamfered cylindrical funnel at its core that rises to a height of over 41 metres.[2] This element, clad in black and silver granite, accommodates a fenestrated lantern light that allows daylight to flood the atrium below. Additionally, the stepped section of the building permits light to enter the internal gallery spaces, despite the museum's deep plan.

Externally, the building betrays little of its interior organisation. On ground floor level, support spaces such as the bookshop, café and an auditorium, open out from the central atrium or piazza, and a double staircase ascends to the gallery spaces above. These occupy four floors and are arranged in long enfilades, stretching over 60 metres. Crowning the building is a bridge that crosses underneath the lantern high above the atrium, providing a bird's eye view of activity below.

1 Justin Henderson. *Museum Architecture* (Gloucester, MA: Rockport Publishers, 1998), p. 46.

2 Ibid., p. 48.

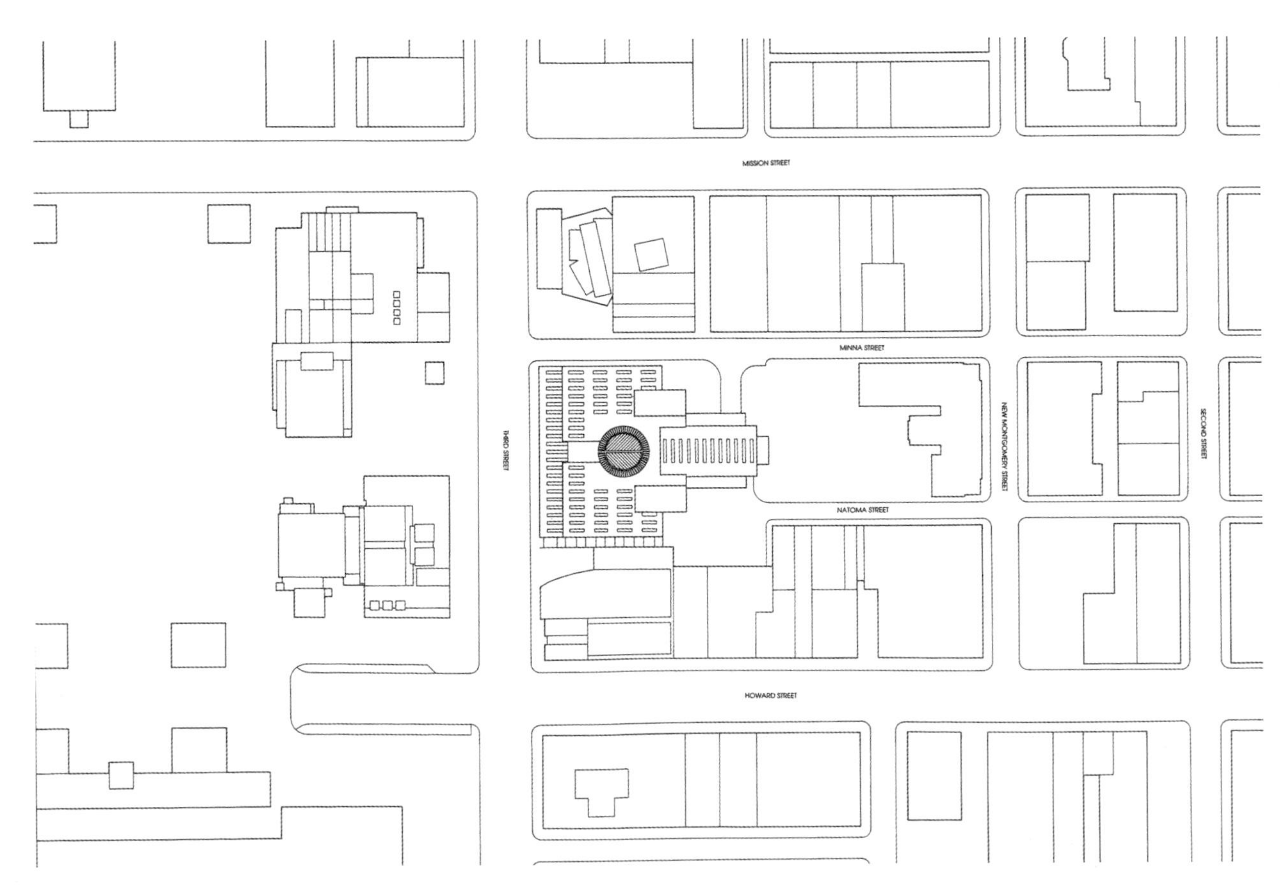

Site plan: the museum occupies a corner of its city block between Third, Minna and Howard Streets

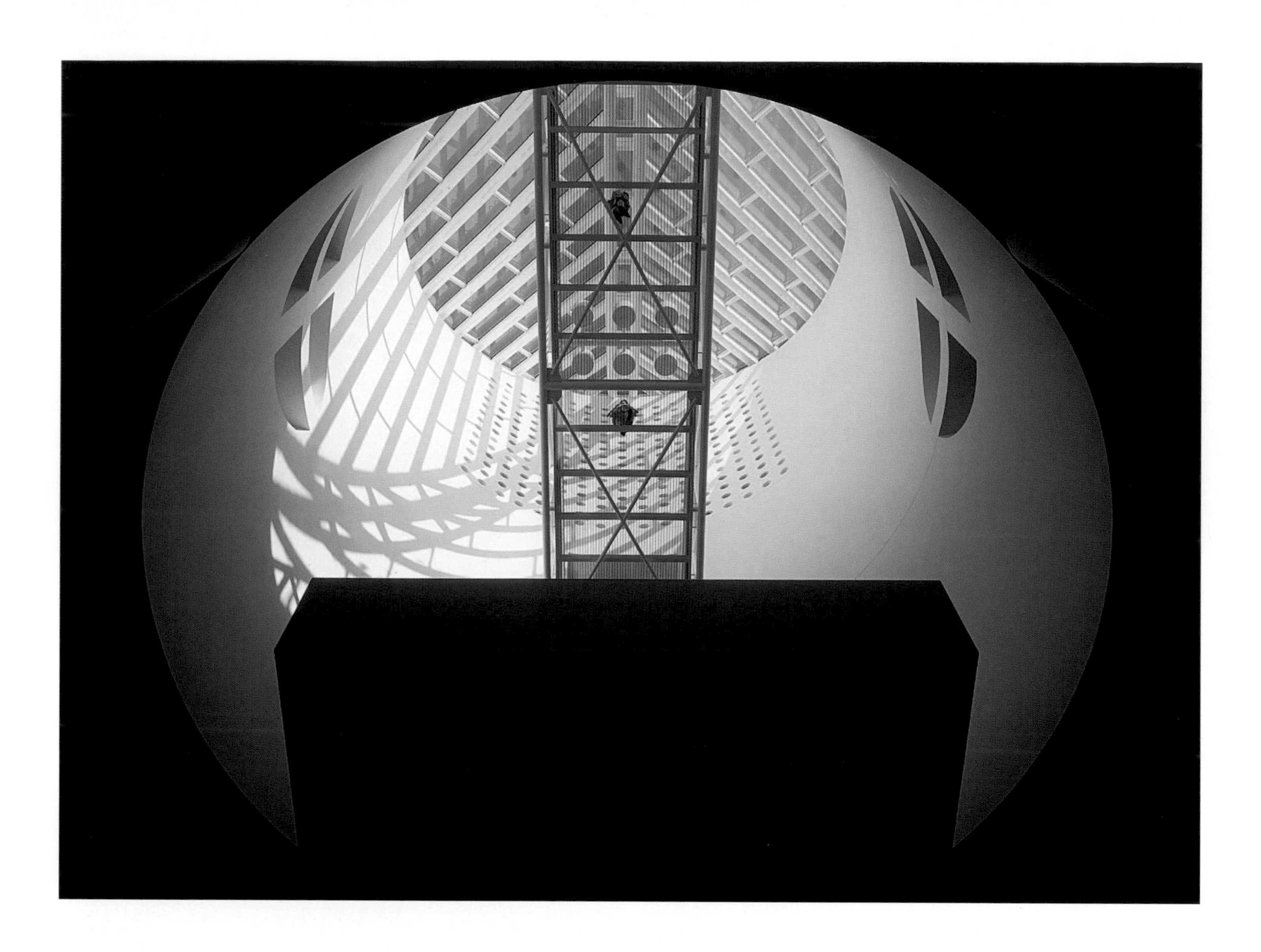

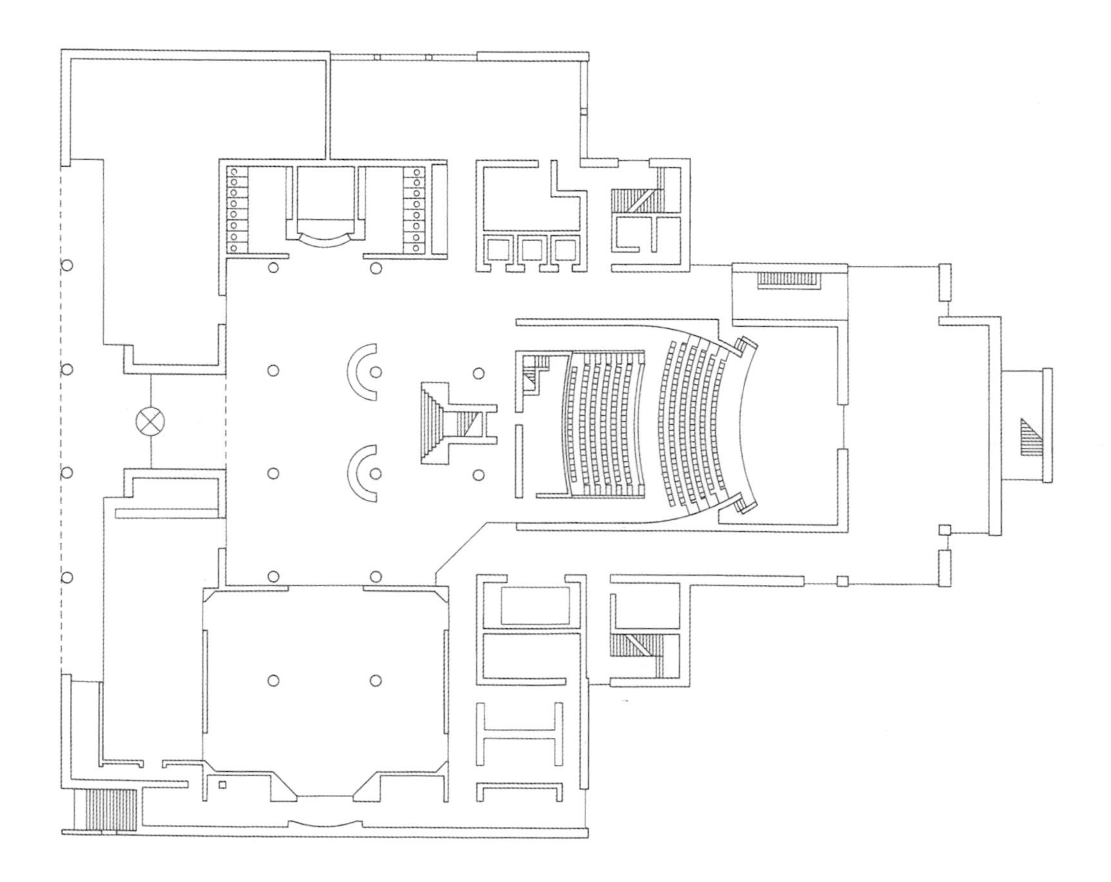

Top The central lobby, or orientation core, is flooded with natural light from the cylindrical chamfered skylight above. The bridge crossing underneath this provides dramatic views down into the lobby space below

Left The atrium or lobby is at the heart of the museum's ground floor plan, with the auditorium, event space, café, bookshop and education classroom all radiating out from this focal point. The galleries are located on the four floors above

Opposite The galleries and service spaces of the museum radiate from this central lobby area, which has a circulation core of stairs and lifts at its rear

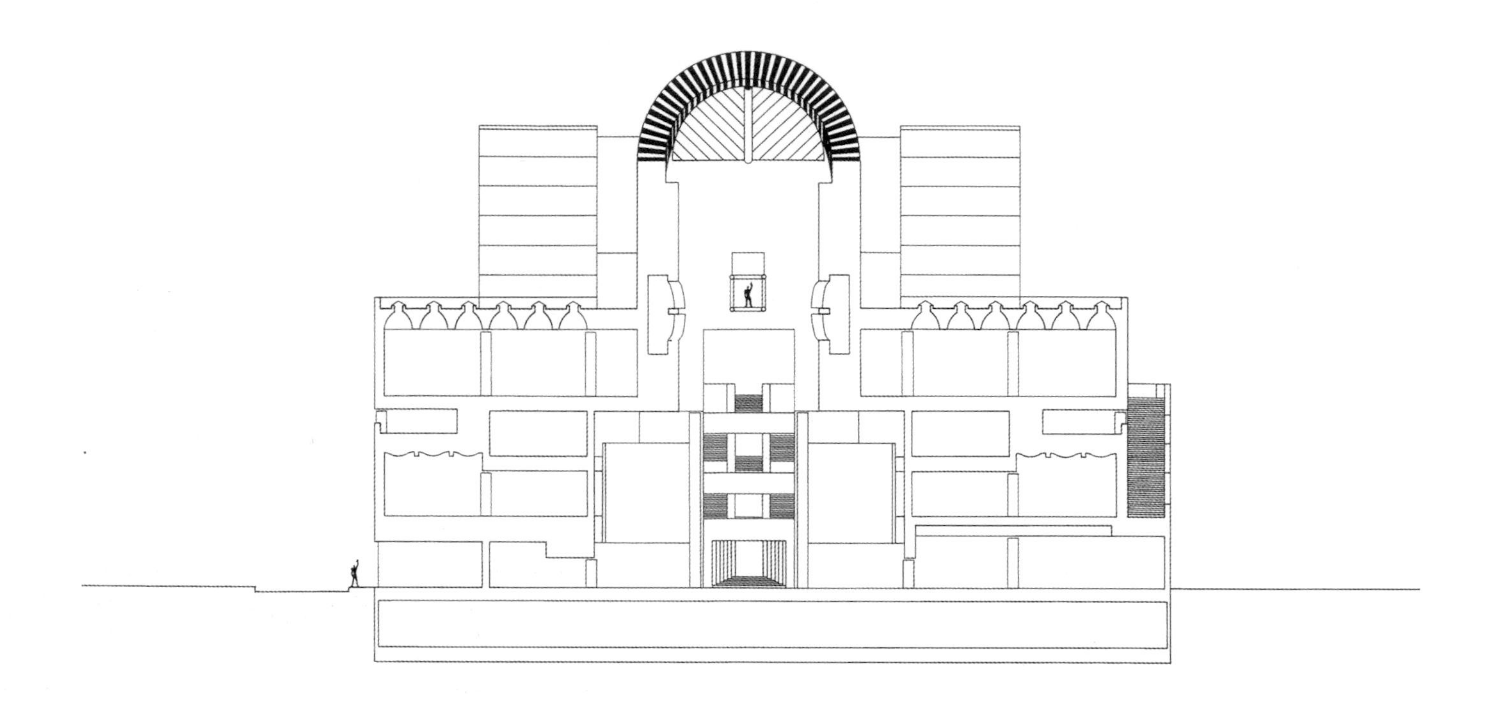

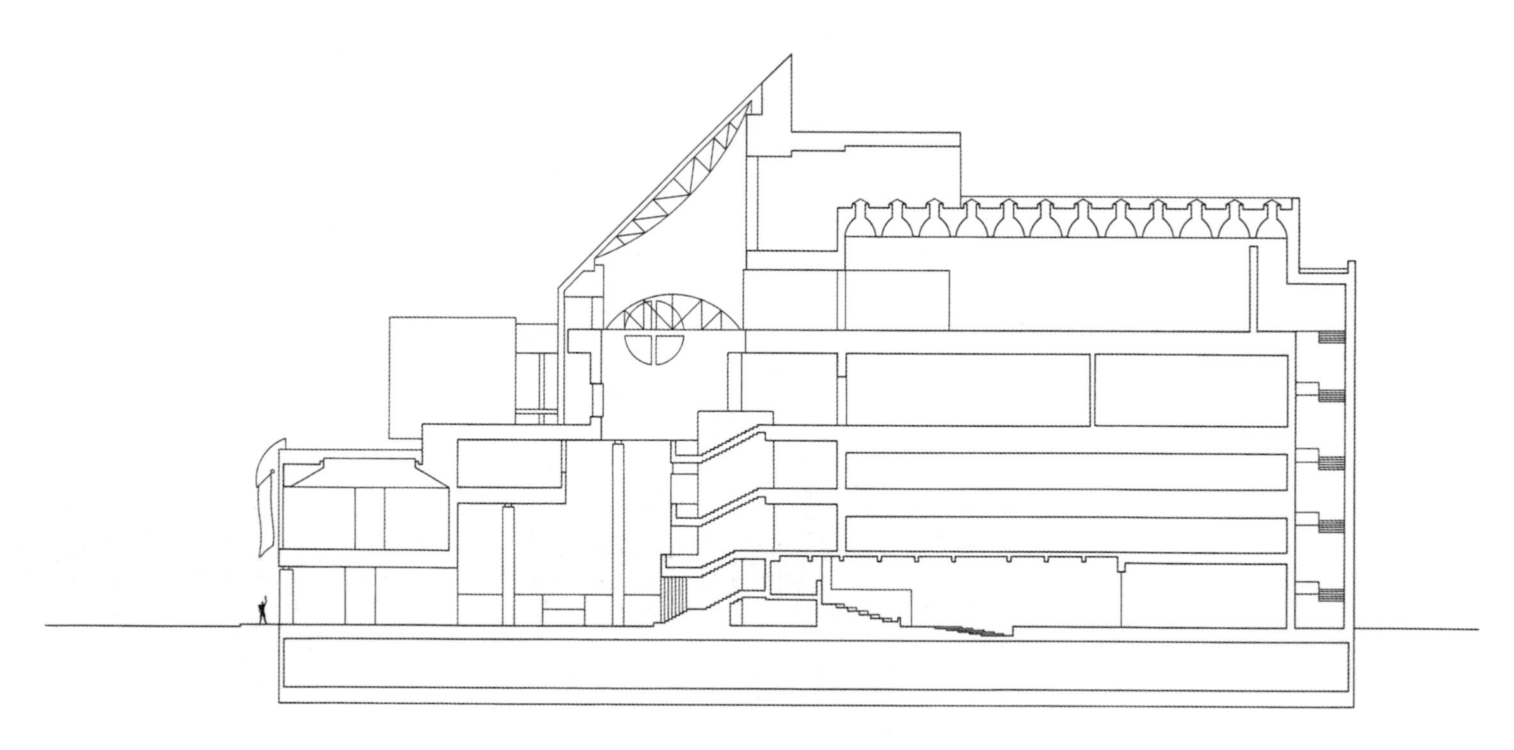

Top Cross section

Bottom Although dwarfed by its high rise neighbours, this longitudinal section reveals the still grand scale of Botta's design

Opposite Thanks to the stepping of the building's Third Street façade, many of the interior gallery spaces enjoy natural lighting

Mario Botta and Giulio Andreolli

MODERN AND CONTEMPORARY ART MUSEUM OF TRENTO AND ROVERETO

Rovereto | **2002**

MART, or the Modern and Contemporary Art Museum of Trento and Rovereto, designed by Mario Botta in collaboration with Giulio Andreolli, grafts onto the historical fabric of the northern Italian town of Rovereto almost seamlessly.

Originally conceived in 1987, but only completed between 1996 and 2002, the museum complex is located off corso Bettini, on a plot behind two eighteenth century buildings: Palazzo Alberti and Palazzo dell'Annona. Rather than plugging the gap between the two palazzos, to create a conventional street-facing façade for the new cultural institution, the architects left this as an open approach avenue, drawing the public into the heart of the scheme behind. This architectural route culminates in a new, round city 'square', topped by a towering glass and steel dome some 40 metres in diameter, beneath which up to 1,200 people may be seated. A fountain in the middle of the square aligns with an aperture in the roof structure above. All of the the museum's facilities are accessible from this covered city plaza, with the library and archives at basement level, visitor amenities situated on the ground floor and exhibition spaces occupying the upper two floors.

Both its recessed position in relation to the street line and its facing in the same yellow Vicenza stone as the adjacent palazzos are subtly deferential to the immediate urban fabric: 'the new structure, standing back from the two historical buildings with their dignified architectural language, does not present an autonomous image of itself with respect to the city.'[1] However, Botta's patchwork-like intervention into this historical quarter has doubtless had positive impact, not least in its creation of a new and vibrant civic meeting place.

1 Project Information, Architetto Mario Botta, 2003.

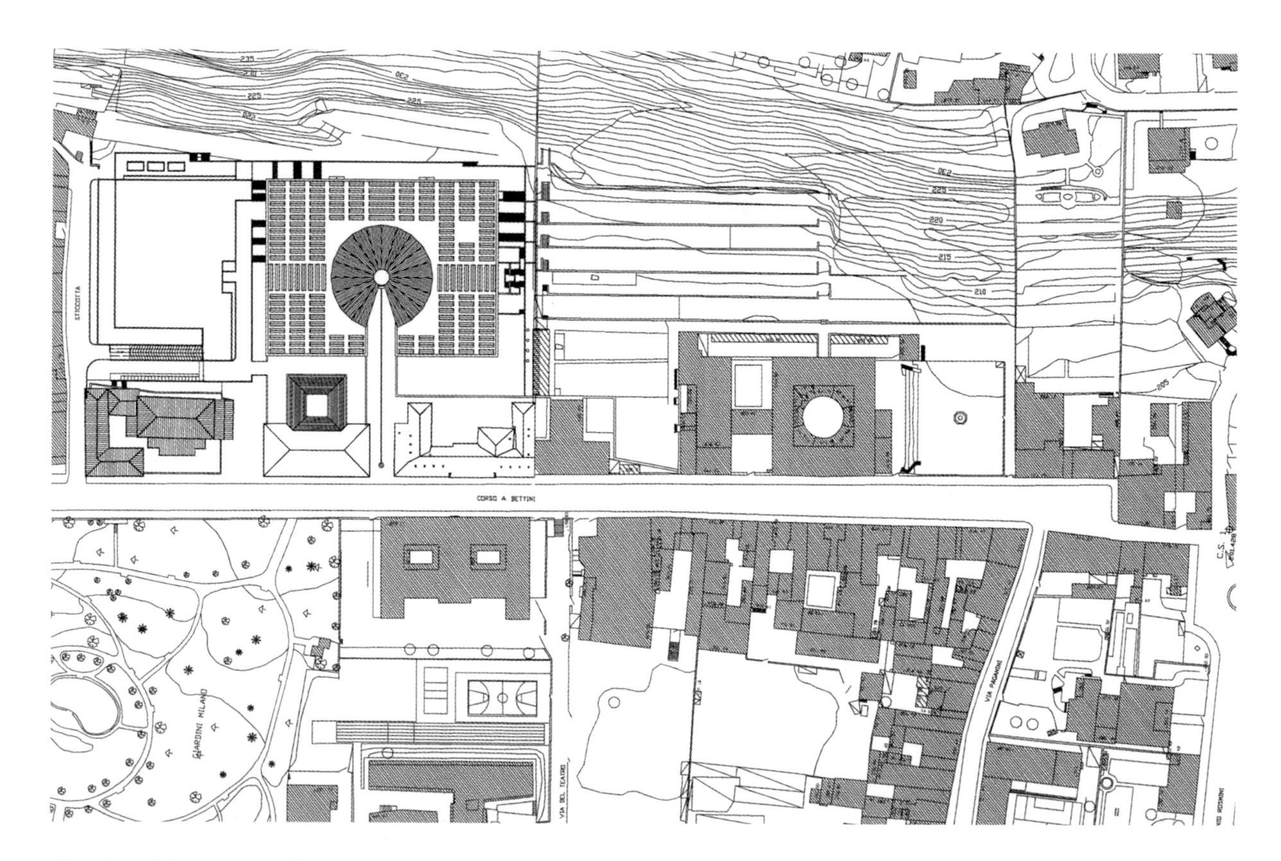

Site plan of the museum, showing its relation to the two adjacent eighteenth century palazzos

Opposite The museum nestles into the hillside behind

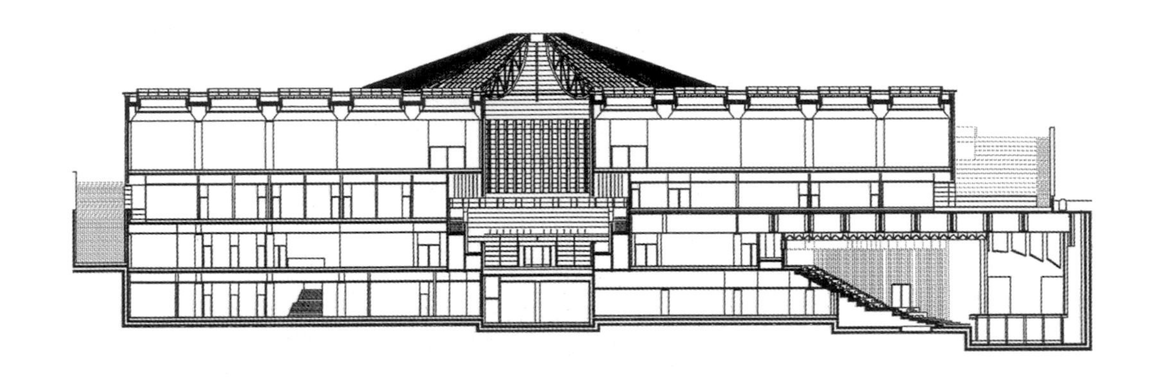

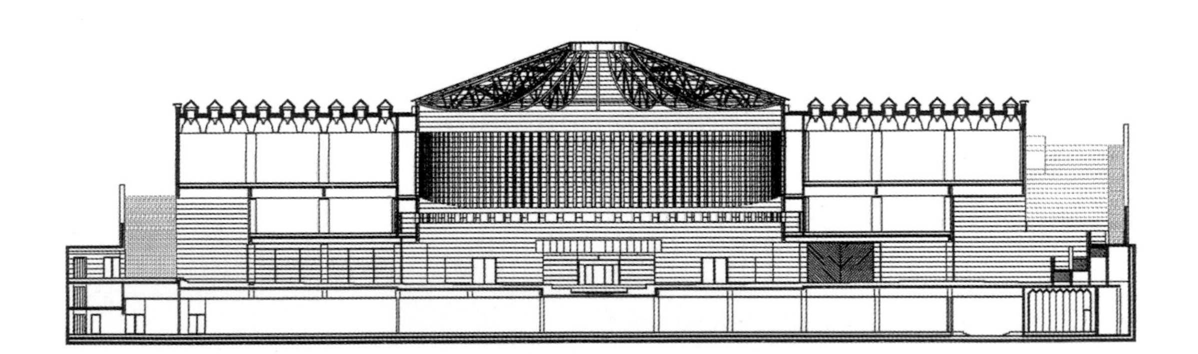

In order to respect the surrounding historical fabric of Rovereto, Botta has set the museum back from the street line, and this design strategy has resulted in an intriguing entry promenade

Opposite Sections showing the top-lit gallery spaces at second floor level

Skylights provide natural light to the top floor gallery spaces

Opposite Elevation and section showing the proximity of Botta's museum to the eighteenth century villas on corso Bettini

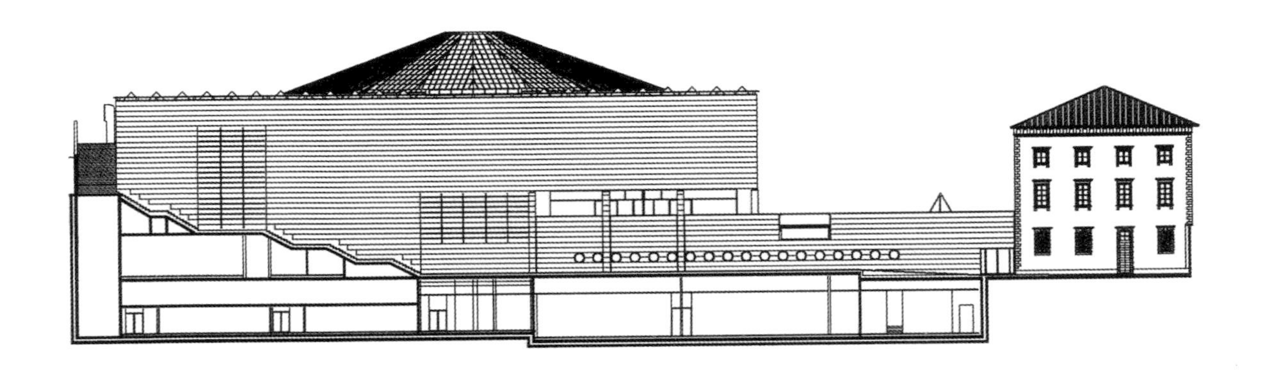

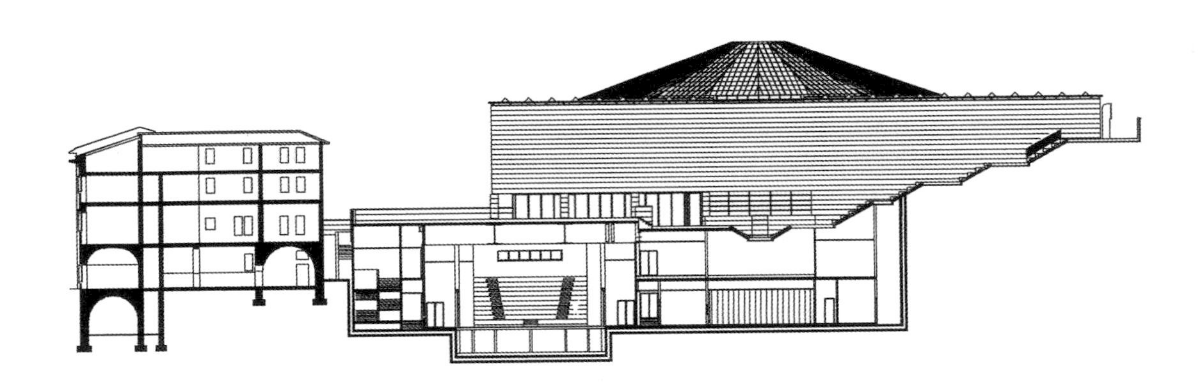

Developmental perspective sketch of the central atrium, looking towards corso Bettini

Opposite The entry route from corso Bettini draws visitors into the heart of the museum

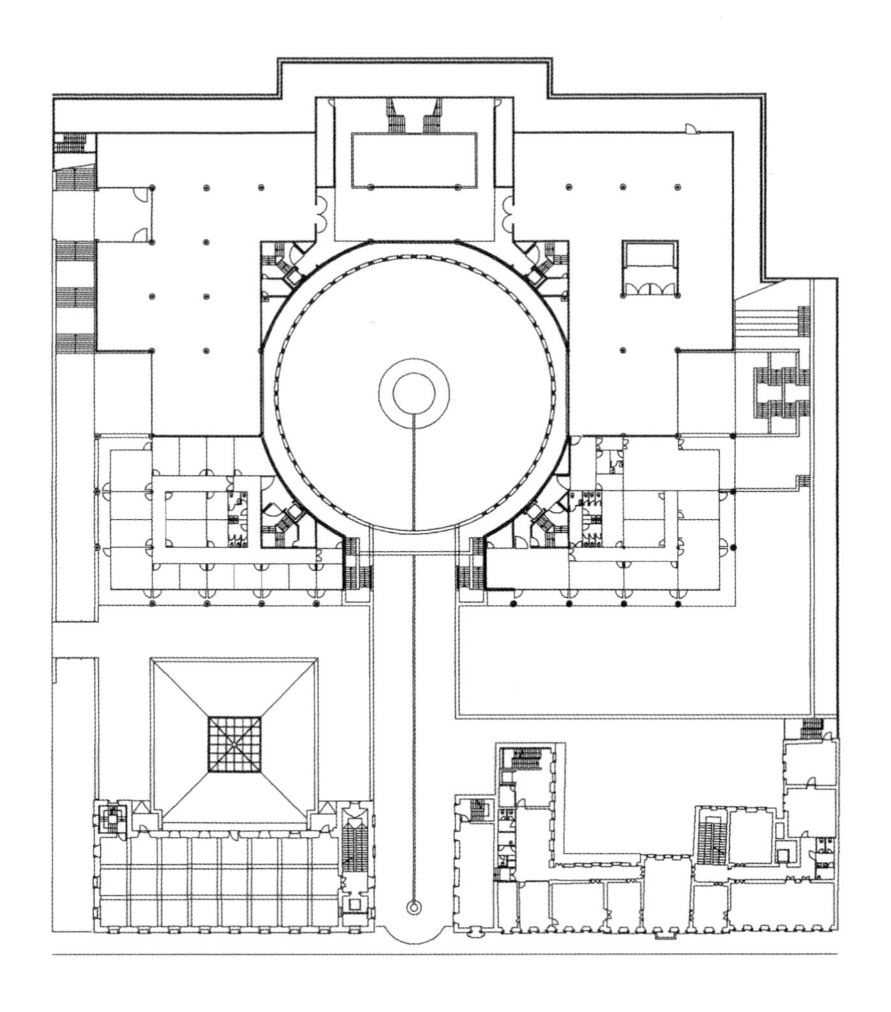

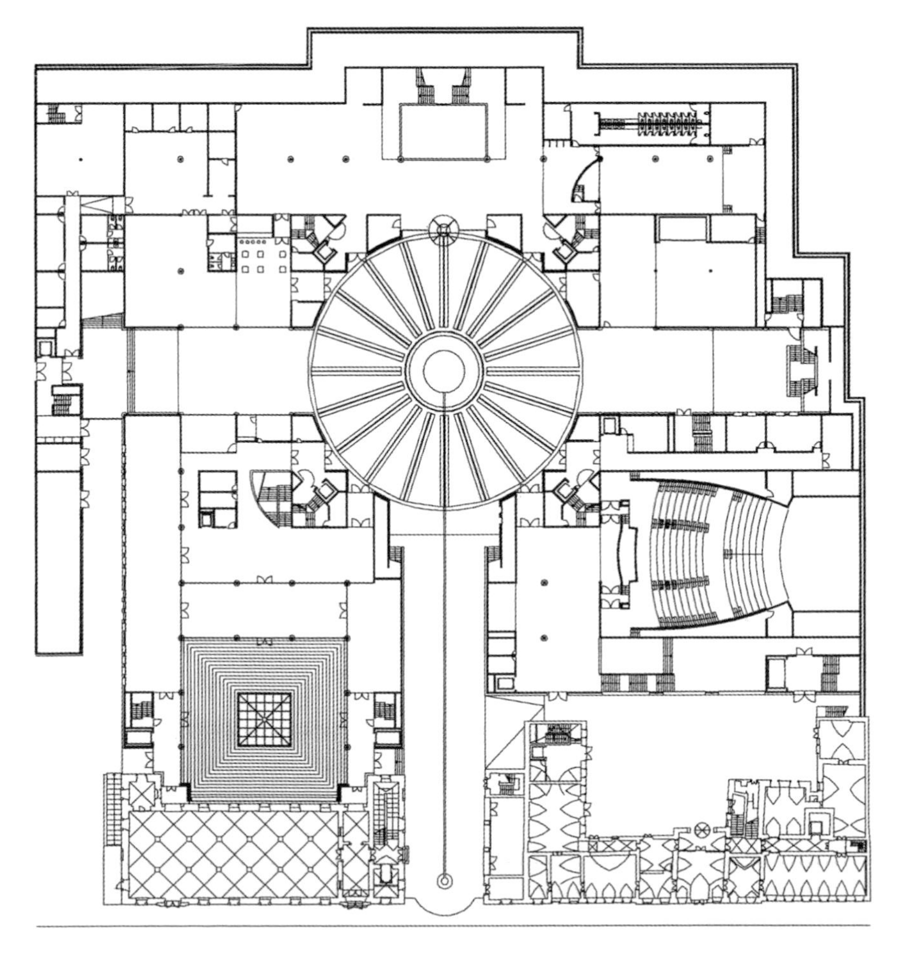

These ground (bottom) and first (top) floor plans show the museum's accommodation radiating from the central 'piazza'

Opposite A glazed, steel-framed dome soars above the museum's central plaza

Above Winter view of the museum's front elevation, as seen from Seneca-Park

Below This perspective section through the permanent galleries shows the intentionally simple, calm, and predictable nature of these spaces

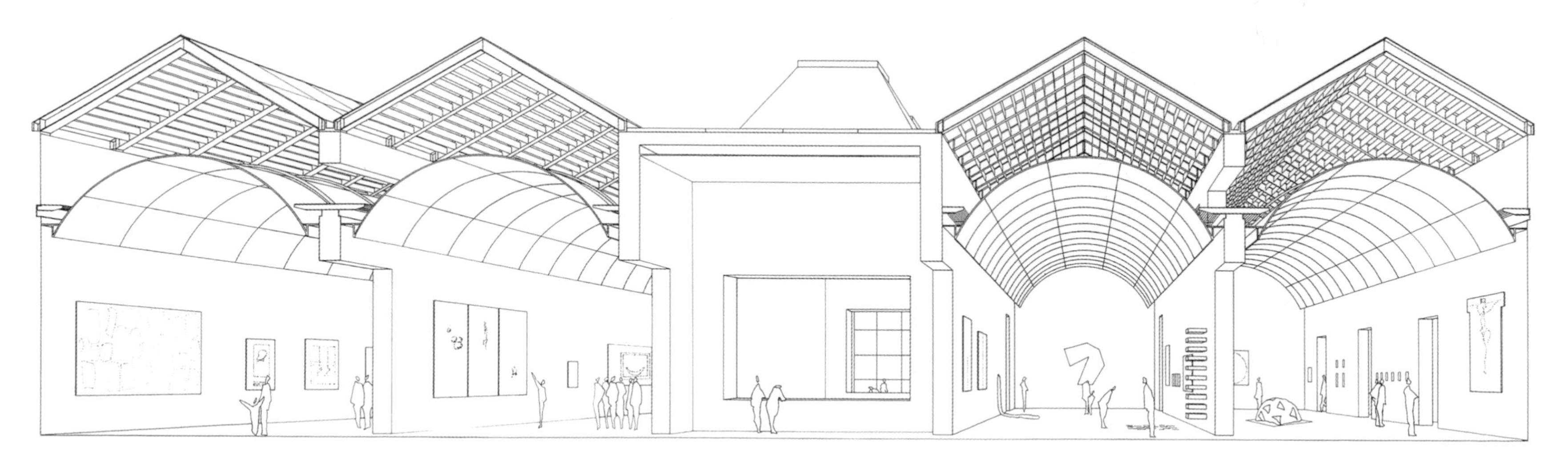

Kleihues + Kleihues

CHICAGO MUSEUM OF CONTEMPORARY ART

Chicago **1996**

Located in an 'urban-canyon' site, with the city's historic Water Tower to its west and Lake Michigan to the east, the Museum of Contemporary Art resides modestly, but confidently, in the thriving heart of Chicago's 'Magnificent Mile'.

The architects, Kleihues + Kleihues, sought a fusion between European Classicism and Chicago School Modernism and both of these strands are easily identifiable. The grand staircase, which rises from the first floor entrance to emerge in the main lobby, is the most distinctively classicist element of the design, consciously created in the tradition of the Propylaea of the Acropolis and the steps of Schinkel's Altes Museum, Berlin.[1] Materiality provides the building's most direct link to the Chicago School, with the textured aluminium panels of the curtain wall recalling the power and craftsmanship of the Chicago School's prolific, trademark use of cast metals.[2]

The basic spatial organisation of the museum is simple and geometric, with both the main building and the sculpture garden having identical square plans. Within the building, the architects make a clear distinction between the public service spaces, located in glazed atria on the east and west perimeters, and the enclosed galleries at the building's core. As a result, 'this quietly imposing, self-contained building is simultaneously open and transparent', resolving what Kleihues has described as the 'dialogue between transparency and containment [that] is characteristic of an art museum'.[3]

The architect stated from the outset that he 'would never build a museum that would interfere with the visitor's ability to concentrate on art.'[4] He was successful in this aim, as unlike some of the display spaces within the new breed of sculpturally expressive museums, the MCA's gallery spaces are deferential to the art they contain, being conventionally proportioned and using a muted palette of materials.

1 'A Walk through the Museum of Contemporary Art's New Building', Museum Information Pack, MCA, Chicago, p. 1.

2 Ibid., pp. 1–2.

3 Ibid., p. 1.

4 Ibid.

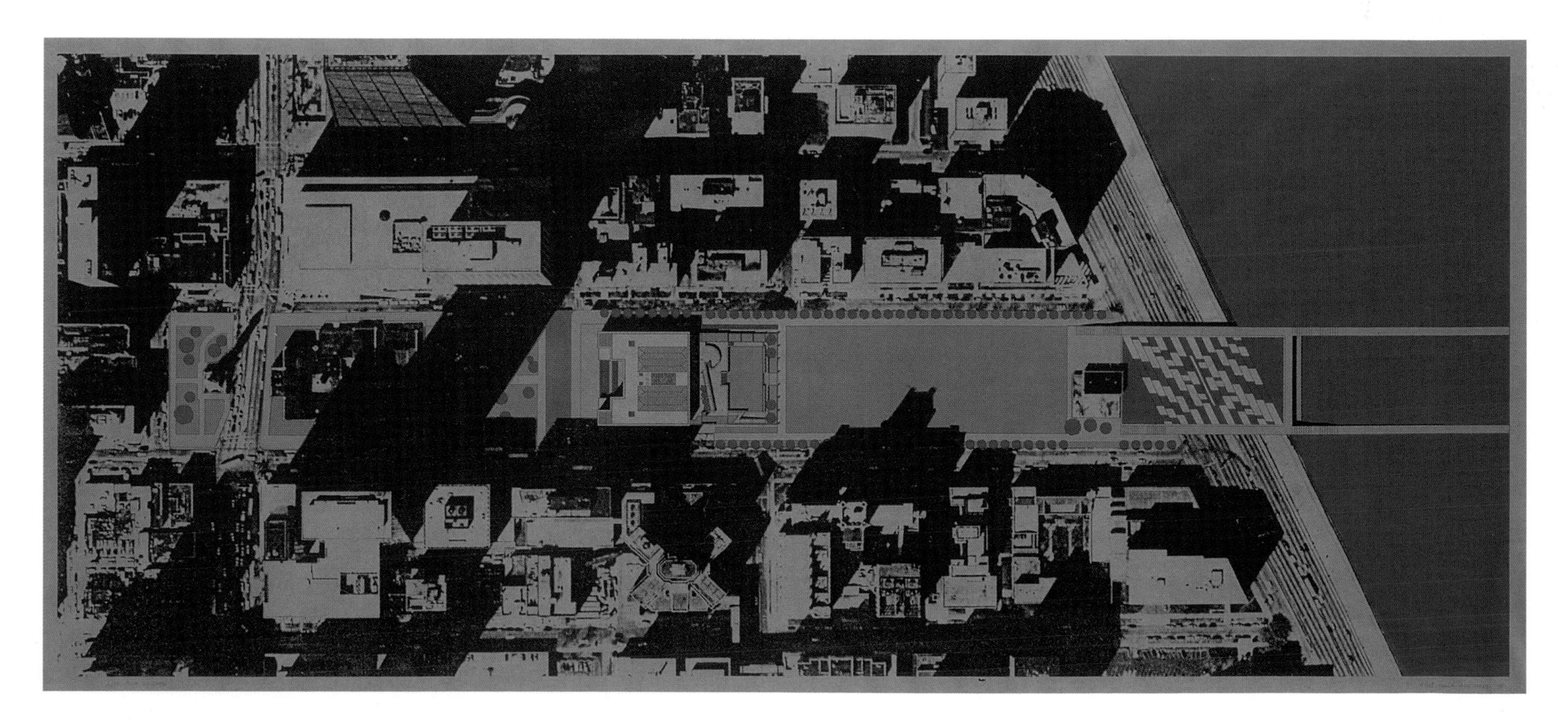

Screen print site plan showing the museum's proximity to Lake Michigan

Opposite and left These two views from the two-storey foyer, towards the sculpture garden and entrance area, demonstrate the 'interplay between transparency and containment', which Kleihues sought to exploit

Below left The 'grand stair', which springs from the entrance at first floor level, is the most identifiably Classicist element of the design

Below right The elevation to Chicago Avenue demonstrates the modest simplicity of Kleihues' composition

Aerial view of a model study of the realised project

Opposite This open stairwell, crowned with a sky-light, connects all the floors of the museum

Frank Gehry

GUGGENHEIM MUSEUM BILBAO

Bilbao | **1997**

Located on the bank of the River Nervion beside a main bridged entry to the northern Spanish city of Bilbao, Frank Gehry's Guggenheim Museum is a catalyst for cultural tourism and urban rejuvenation. It is an expression – albeit through an international aesthetic – of the fiercely independent identity of the Basque people, and one of the most renowned buildings of the late twentieth century.

Despite the building's exuberant Expressionism, which shatters the adjacent nineteenth century city grid just as Frank Lloyd Wright's iconic Guggenheim did in New York over half a century earlier, Gehry's building is responsive to its site: landscaping and views connect the city to the museum and the river beyond. The building itself is monumentally sculptural, combining glazed façades and limestone anchoring walls, with the dominant curving planes of titanium, which glide over each other seamlessly to create a dynamic and ever-changing aesthetic: 'One moment the sun ignites the voluptuous arrangement of tumbling titanium cubes in a molten flare; the next it goes behind a cloud, and the skin of the building goes soft and satiny, absorptive, contemplative.'[1]

Although the museum's form may appear instinctive or fanciful, it is closely bound up with the spatial requirements of the display programme. The design hinges around a capacious 50 metre high orientation core, from where ramps and stairs spring to the galleries and roof terraces above. Three branches radiate from this volume, with the spatial configuration of each relating closely to the artwork contained within: the temporary exhibitions are housed in a large, inherently flexible volume to the east, whilst more intimate and customised spaces to the south and west house the permanent collections and those of selected living artists. The north wing to the riverside is truncated by the huge glass façade of the central atrium. These disparate elements of the design have an holistic coherence, however, as the 'figural roof' form 'unif[ies] the composition'.[2]

1 Justin Henderson. *Museum Architecture* (Gloucester, MA: Rockport Publishers, 1998), p. 32.

2 Charles Jencks and others. *Contemporary Museums, Architectural Design*, vol. Nov./Dec. 1997, p. 33.

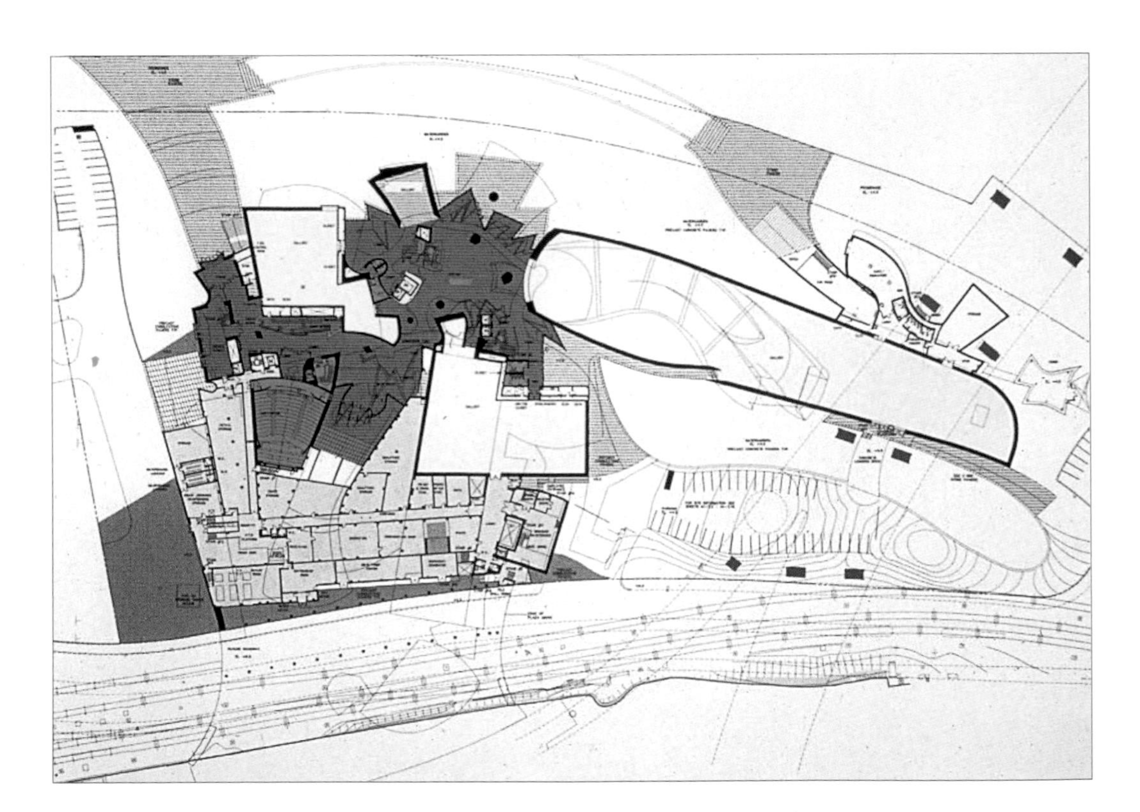

Site plan, showing the museum on the banks of the River Nervion

Opposite The bulging titanium clad planes of the museum fuse with glazed elements, and are anchored by lower level limestone walls

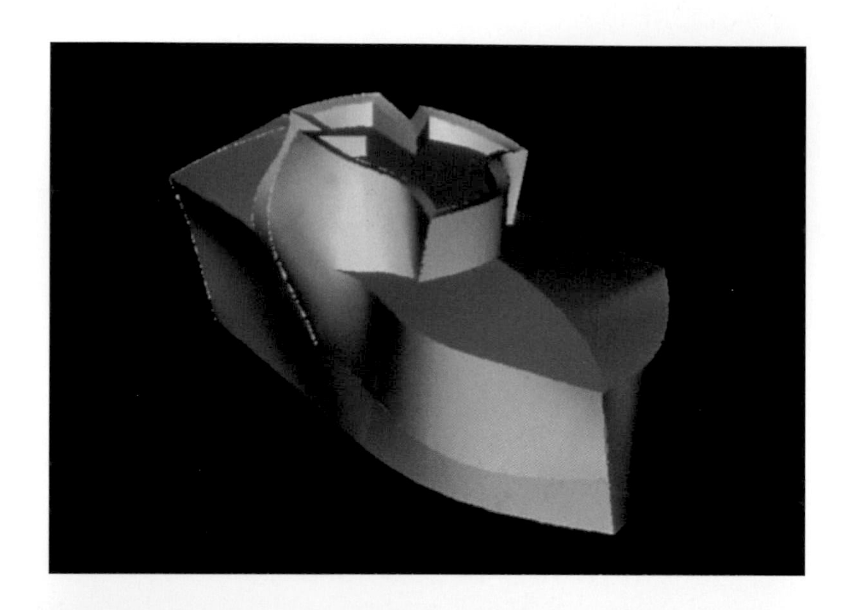

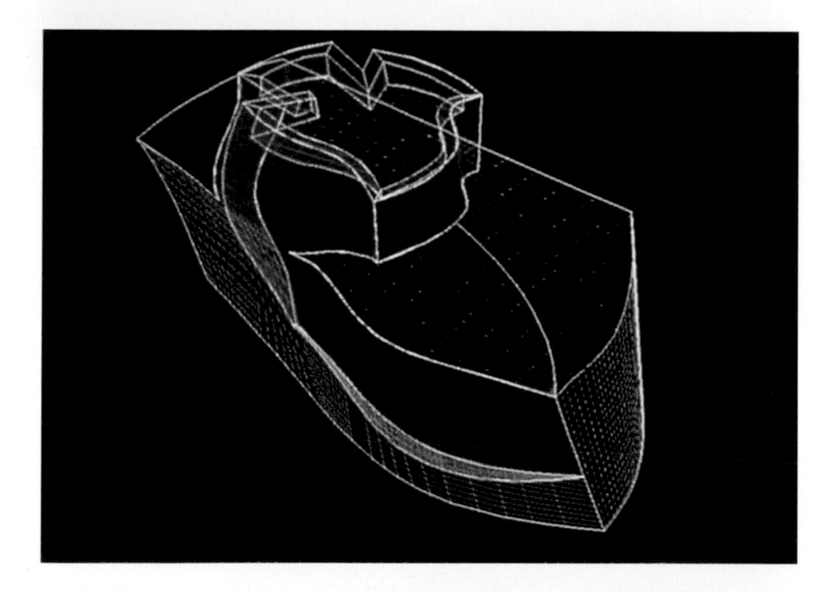

Computer models of the south wing of the building, which houses the museum's permanent collection

Opposite The three principal volumes of the museum radiate from this monumental central atrium

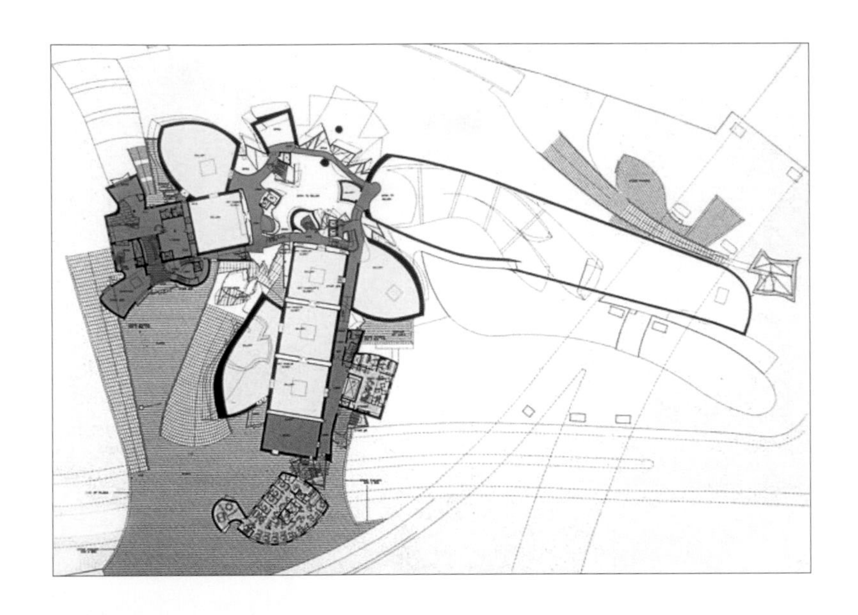

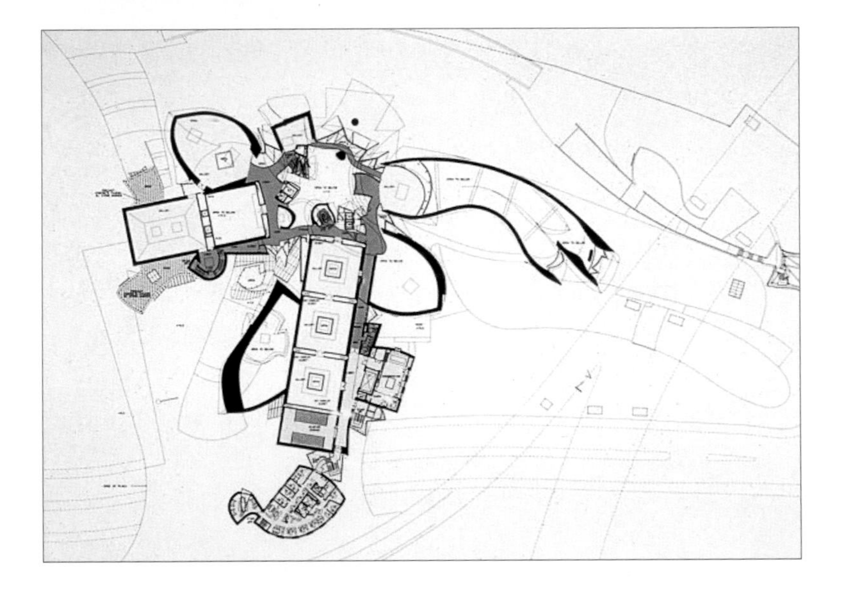

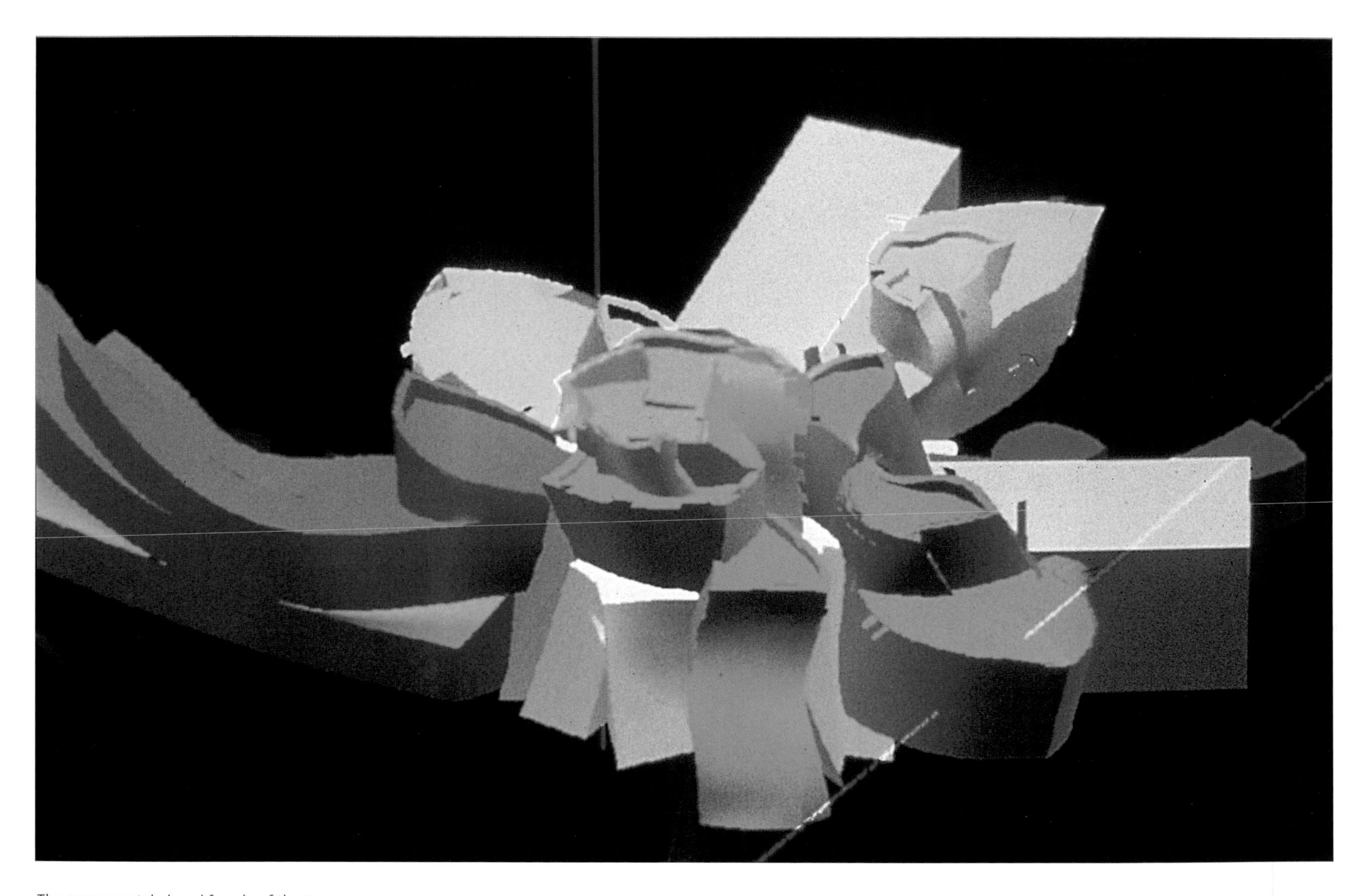

The monumental glazed façade of the truncated, river-facing north wing is evident on this computer-generated massing model

Opposite Second and third floor plans, showing the three main wings of the building branching from the central atrium

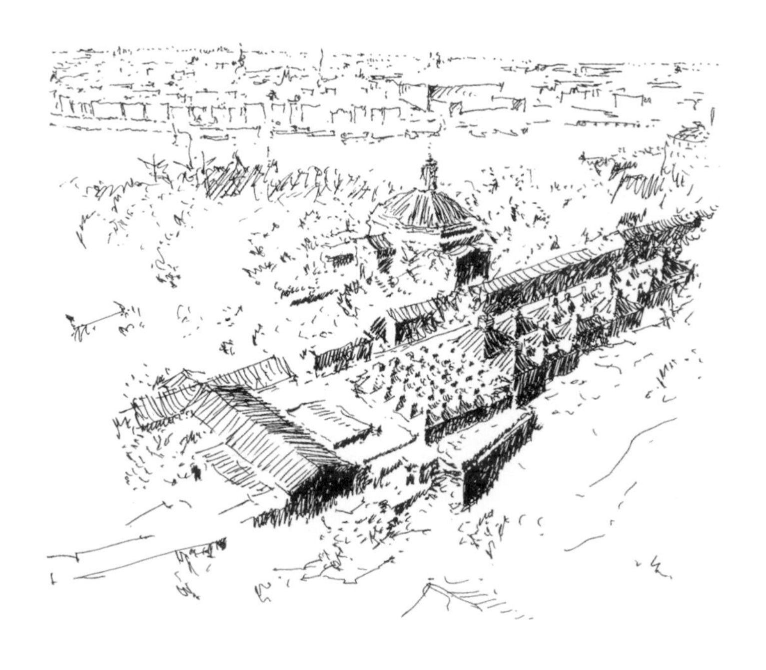

Rafael Moneo

STOCKHOLM MUSEUMS OF MODERN ART AND ARCHITECTURE

Stockholm **1998**

The island of Skeppsholmen, opposite the old town in Stockholm's archipelago, is home to two contemporary museums by Rafael Moneo: the Museum of Modern Art, or Moderna Museet, and the Architecture Museum. On rocky slopes below the dome of the Skeppsholmen Church, and adjacent to 'rather undistinguished' nineteenth century neo-Classical naval barracks,[1] Moneo succeeded in making a progammatically elaborate building of 20,000 square metres appear low key, achieving 'serenity in the complexity'.[2] The main entrance is typically modest, with only a porch announcing the break in the brick wall from the parade ground in front.

Once inside the building, a similar approach unfolds, with obvious views ahead to the sea beyond being rationed to glimpses, as 'Moneo ... seeks to entice the visitor on rather than pull out all the stops for a reverberating crescendo'.[3] The Architecture Museum lies to the right of the entrance lobby, with a line of permanent Art Museum galleries, glazed to the courtyard, extending to the left. These exhibition spaces are defined in 6-metre-square modules, and are capped with distinctive pyramidal roofs and lanterns. Indeed, 'in the absence of a "set piece" elevation serving to identify the museum, the roof determinedly takes on that role.'[4] However, the quality of light admitted through these lanterns, especially under the grey winter skies of Stockholm, is questionable.

Materiality, and more specifically colour, has been similarly debated, with Moneo's specified grey exterior finish being softened and vernacularised to terracotta. In a strangely inconsistent decision, however, the prominent lanterns have been clad in grey zinc, rather than the more vibrant and rich copper proposed by the architect.

1 James Pickard. 'Swedish Success', *Building Design*, no. 1039, 14 June 1991, p. 18.
2 Robert Bevan.'Treasure Island', *Building Design*, no. 1340, 27 Feb. 1998, p. 14.
3 Ibid., p. 17.
4 Ibid., p. 18.

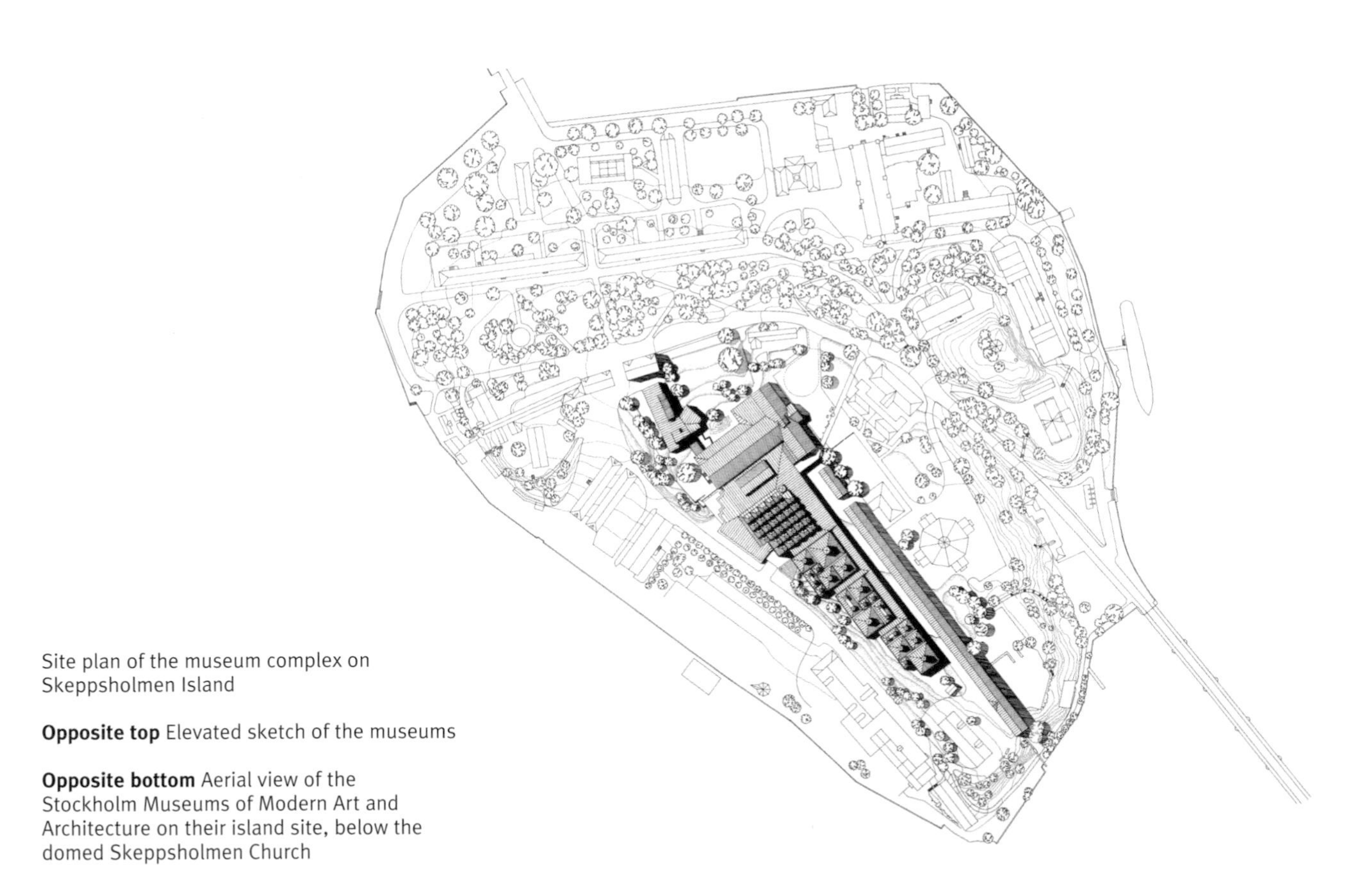

Site plan of the museum complex on Skeppsholmen Island

Opposite top Elevated sketch of the museums

Opposite bottom Aerial view of the Stockholm Museums of Modern Art and Architecture on their island site, below the domed Skeppsholmen Church

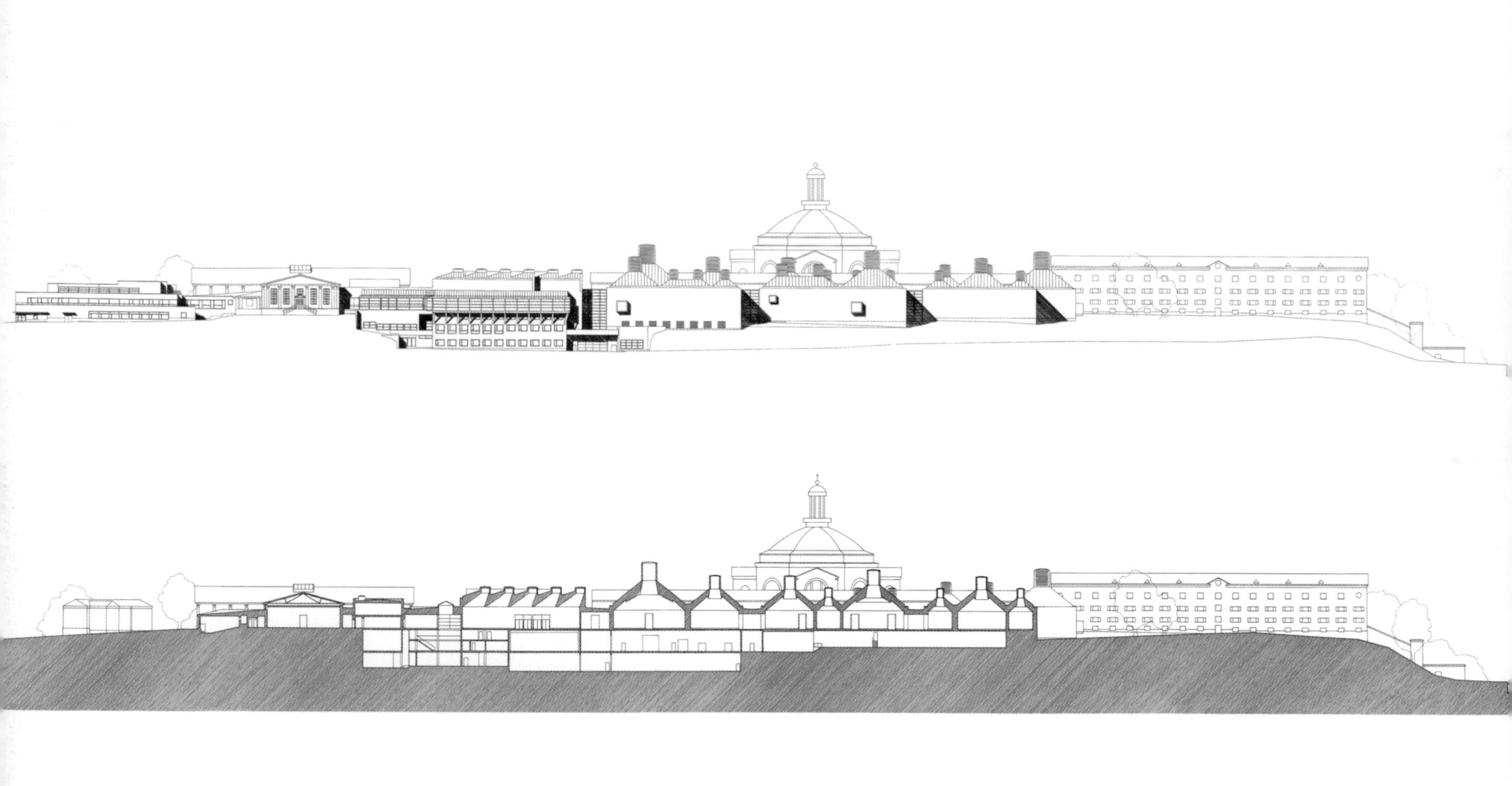

Top Longitudinal elevation, revealing Moneo's attempts to knit the new complex into the historic and densely packed surrounding urban fabric

Above The distinctive lanterned roof structure revealed in this longitudinal section was conceived by Moneo in order to draw natural light into the internal gallery spaces

Left Cross section, showing the drop in ground level across the museum complex, and its proximity to Skeppsholmen Church at the top of the hill

Opposite The distinctive lantern lights draw natural light into the gallery spaces, and create visual interest on the building's 'fifth façade'

Natural light from a lantern roof light illuminates a sculpture in one of the Art Museum's deep plan galleries

Opposite from below First, second, third and fourth floor plans, showing the relationship between the Modern Art Museum to the north, and the Architecture Museum to the south

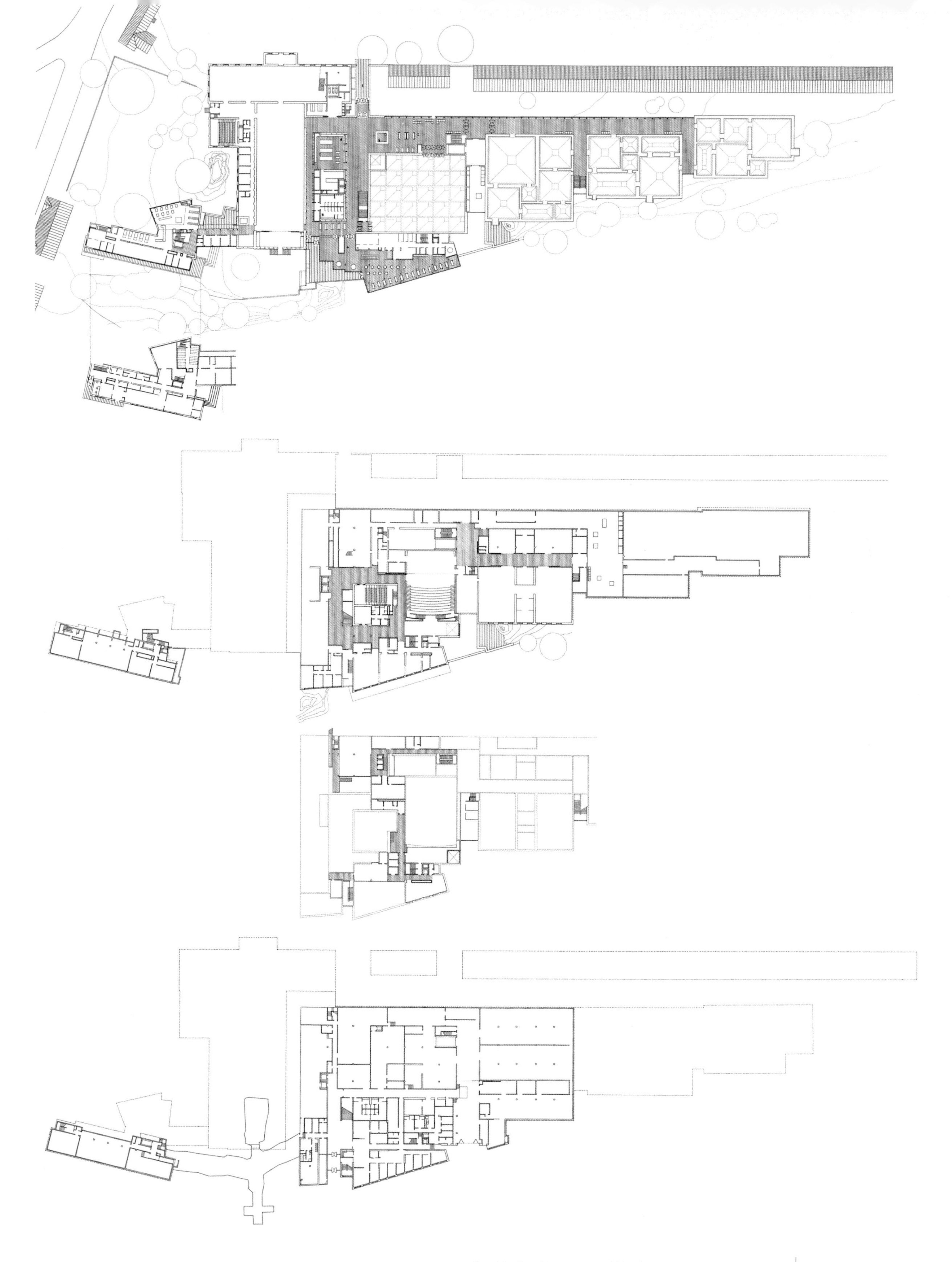

The front façade houses a recessed and ramped entry, and the shorter southern end wall appears to hover weightlessly above a horizontally sliced opening

Opposite Site plan showing the museum's proximity to the seventeenth century monastery of Santo Domingo de Bonaval

Alvaro Siza

GALICIAN CENTRE FOR CONTEMPORARY ART

Santiago de Compostela | **1997**

For his commission for the Galician Centre for Contemporary Art, Alvaro Siza travelled only a short distance northwards from his home town of Porto, to the medieval Spanish city of Santiago de Compostela. Here he derived inspiration from the hillside site, nestling between garden terraces in a rundown area of the old city, adjacent to the seventeenth century monastery of Santo Domingo de Bonaval.

In particular, the rather idiosyncratic double corner entry to the Baroque church and cloisters was mirrored by Siza in the two interlocking 'L'-shaped volumes that form the basis of his design. The smaller of these addresses the road and houses the ramped, recessed entry, whilst the larger wing to the rear creates a dialogue with the offset monastery wall. Neither is this ordering device confined to two dimensions, as 'a double-height space ... revealed as a precipice terminating the upper floor galleries ... [is] the plan's L-shape re-expressed vertically'.[1] The three-storey high triangular void between these two masses acts as an entrance atrium, and a central circulation spine of ramps and stairs appears to anchor the building to its site. The ground floor accommodates the ubiquitous bookshop and café, with the principal galleries running in a light-washed, visually stimulating enfilade along the rear wing of the floor above. The library rests atop the ground floor auditorium, and the building is crowned with a rooftop sculpture terrace, admitting views back down towards the town.

As well as suggesting the new museum's form, the monastery also influenced the palette of materials, and in particular the granite cladding. Siza's treatment of this stone was, of course, radically different, as is most evident at the southern end wall that appears to float above a full-length window incision: 'Siza's building raises the planar quality of the granite slabs to a symbolic level so that an affinity to the bonded construction of the old buildings is upheld with the simultaneous statement that the Centre's tectonic is of today.'[2]

1 David Cohn. 'Pilgrimage to Santiago: Galician Centre for Contemporary Art, Santiago de Compostela', *Architectural Record*, vol. 182, no. 10, Oct. 1994, p. 103

2 Wilfried Wang. 'Centre for Contemporary Art in Santiago de Compostela', *Domus*, no. 760, May 1994, p.15.

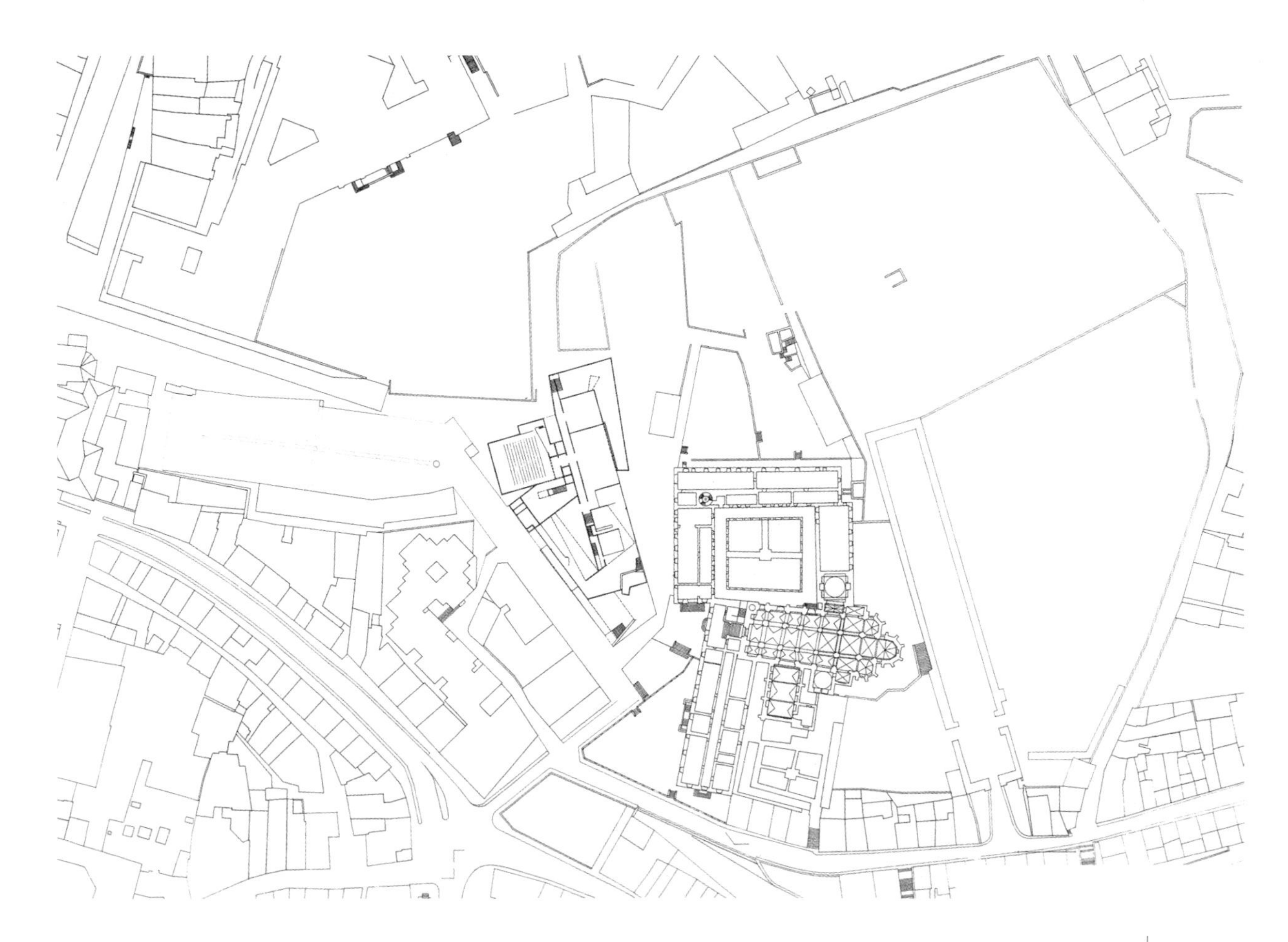

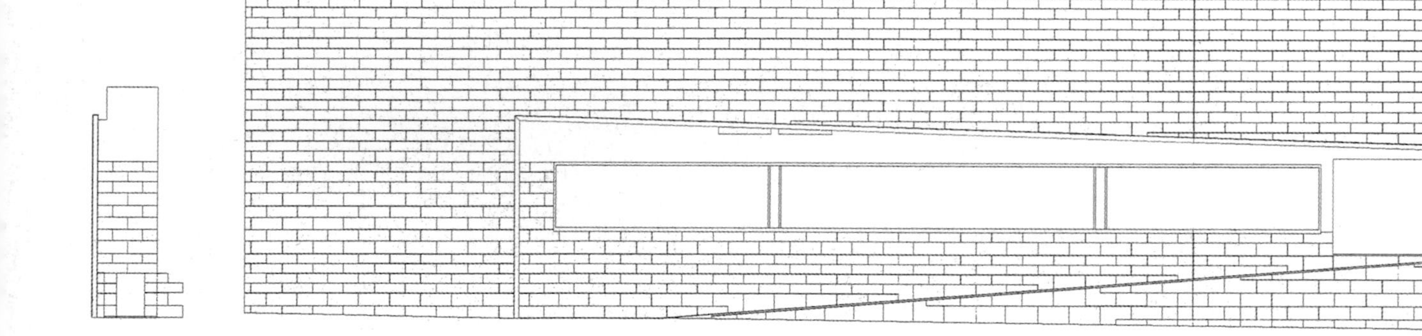

Elevational detail: the architect used granite cladding to contextualise his new intervention into the historic fabric of Santiago de Compostela

Opposite The granite cladding of the rear elevation subtly echoes the adjacent seventeenth century monastery wall

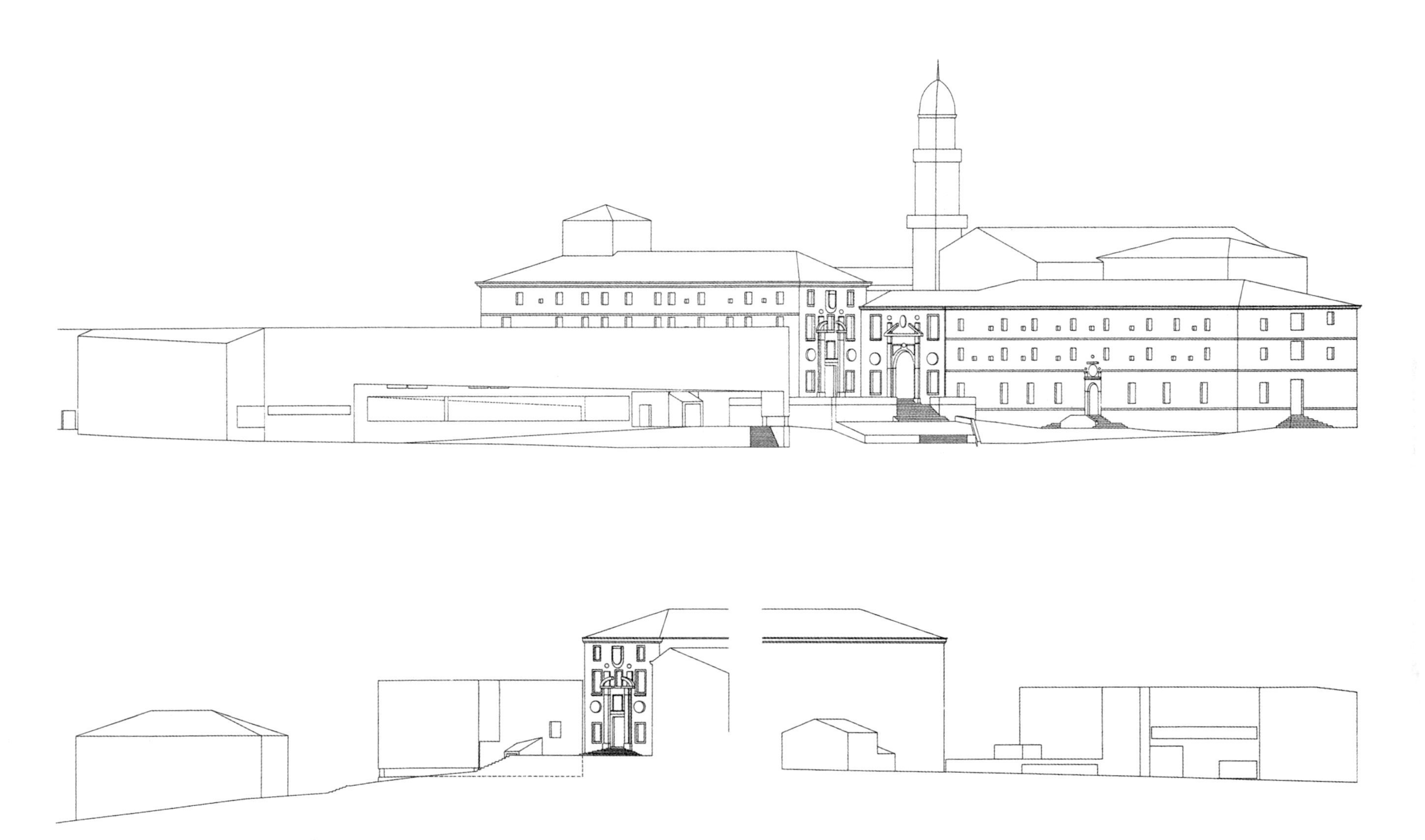

Elevations showing Siza's refined and abstracted design within its historic setting of Santiago de Compostela

Opposite The three-storey-high entrance atrium is ideal for the display of large scale installations

Left and below Sections, showing circulation routes through the museum

Bottom Siza has used a limited palette of materials and colours, allowing light and massing to create visual interest

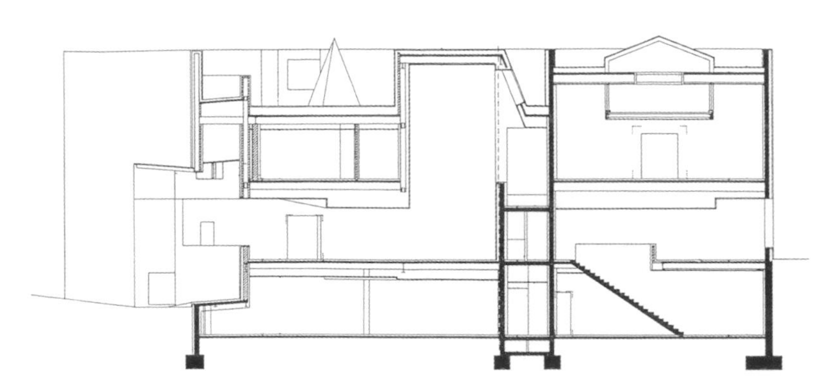

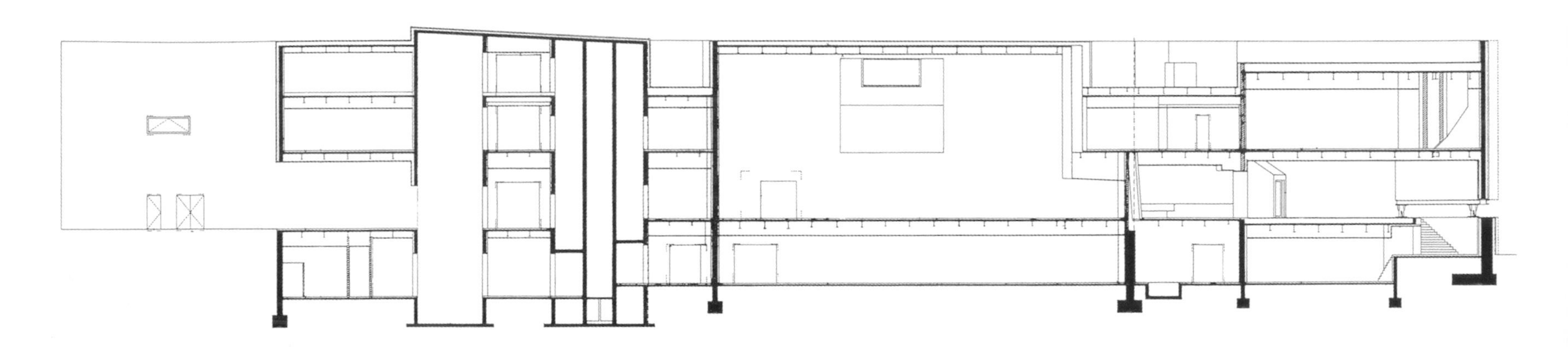

Left and below Sections, showing circulation routes through the museum

Bottom The gallery space is flooded with natural light

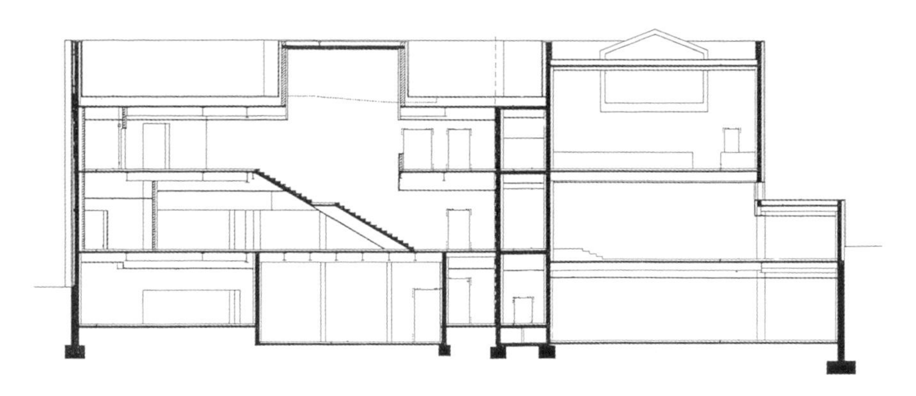

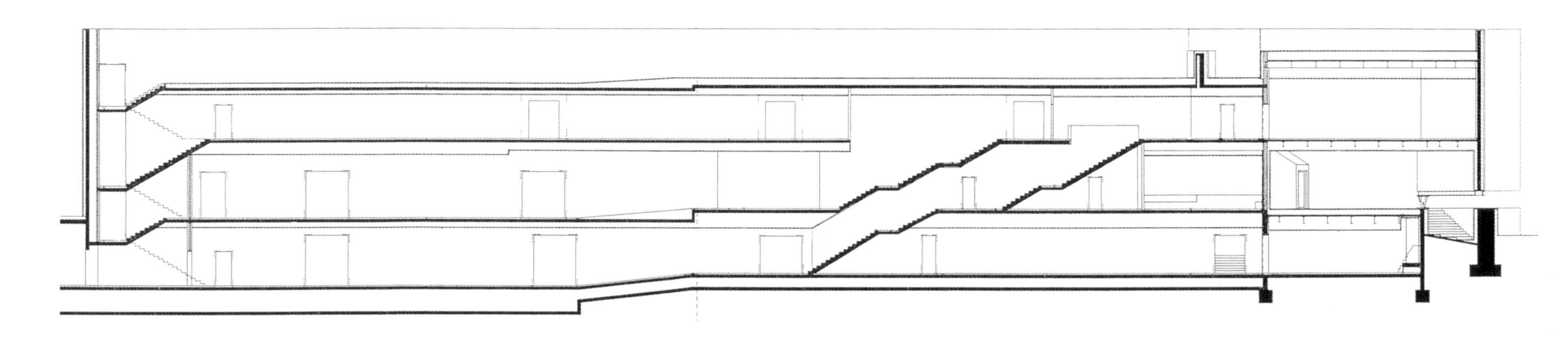

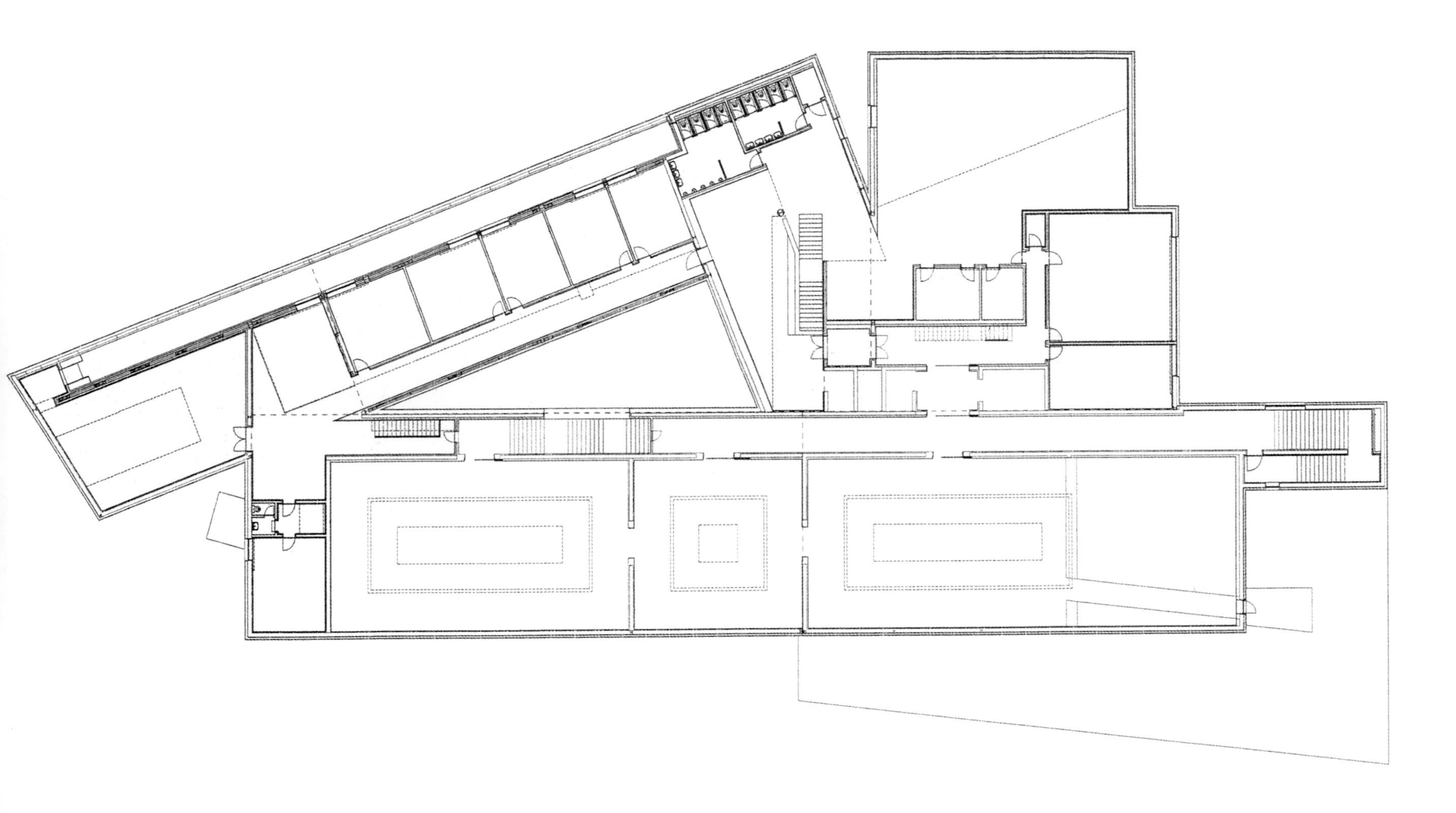

Interlocking 'L' shapes, as shown on the first floor plan, have structured the museum's form in both two and three dimensions

Opposite Siza's exhibition spaces, as in this double-height gallery, are plain and discrete in form and materiality, allowing the art work to take centre stage

The pure, white massing of Siza's museum has its roots in International Modernism

Opposite 1:500 scale site plan of the new museum within the historic Serralves Estate, with its Art Deco mansion, formal gardens and parkland

Alvaro Siza

SERRALVES MUSEUM

Oporto **1999**

Like so many other recent museum commissions, the Serralves Museum in the western suburbs of Oporto, Portugal, struggled to overcome fierce opposition from preservationists. Objections were raised – and taken as far as the European Commission in Brussels – to the proposed new building, which was to be located in the grounds of the Serralves Estate, with its Art Deco mansion, formal gardens and rural landscape. In order to gain approval, the nation's most revered architect, and son of Oporto, Alvaro Siza, designed four different schemes for two separate locations in the park. He eventually opted for the site of a former vegetable garden on the perimeter of the estate, and a design sufficiently embedded in the parkland gradient to negate views of the new complex from the villa, explaining: 'I like this indirect relation with the main house ... it is more a relation of memory, as you walk among the woods and paths.'[1]

On a national and civic scale, the Serralves was a cornerstone of Porto's reign as European Capital of Culture, 2001, whilst at an architectural level, the museum resembles 'a majestic walled garden filled with art'.[2] The building is independent from the rest of the estate, with direct access from the street, and occupies a nearly rectangular footprint contained within two strong wall elements along its longest elevations. Siza revelled in the architectural route through the building that 'like a garden walk ... is replete with branching routes, sudden turns, spatial clearings and pauses'.[3] From the second-floor entrance to the north, the visitor encounters patio, lobby, bookshop and atrium spaces, before reaching the main exhibition galleries. These are arranged in two almost parallel wings to the south, and the smaller 'L'-shaped block to the east, and occupy a total of 4,000 square metres. Ramps and stairs lead down to a 300 seat auditorium, library and storage spaces at first- and ground-floor levels. The seamless procession incorporates carefully staged vistas, and fuses internal and semi-internal spaces, such as the restaurant and verandah, with the nearby lake and parkland beyond.

1 David Cohn. 'In Oporto, Portugal, Alvaro Siza's Serralves Museum Takes Visitors into a Majestic Walled Garden Filled with Art', *Architectural Record*, vol. 187, no. 11, Nov. 1999, pp. 108.

2 Ibid., p. 103

3 Ibid.

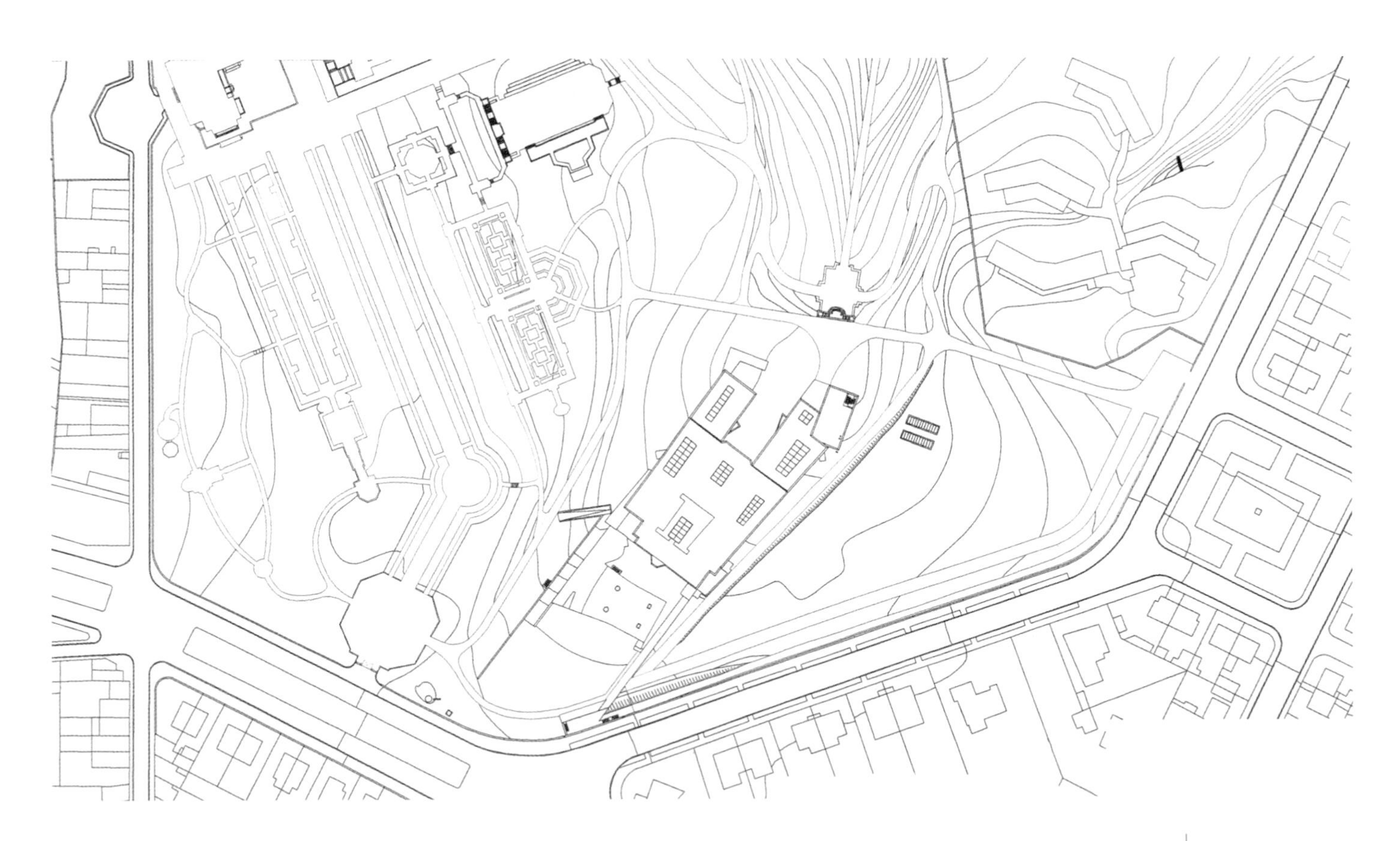

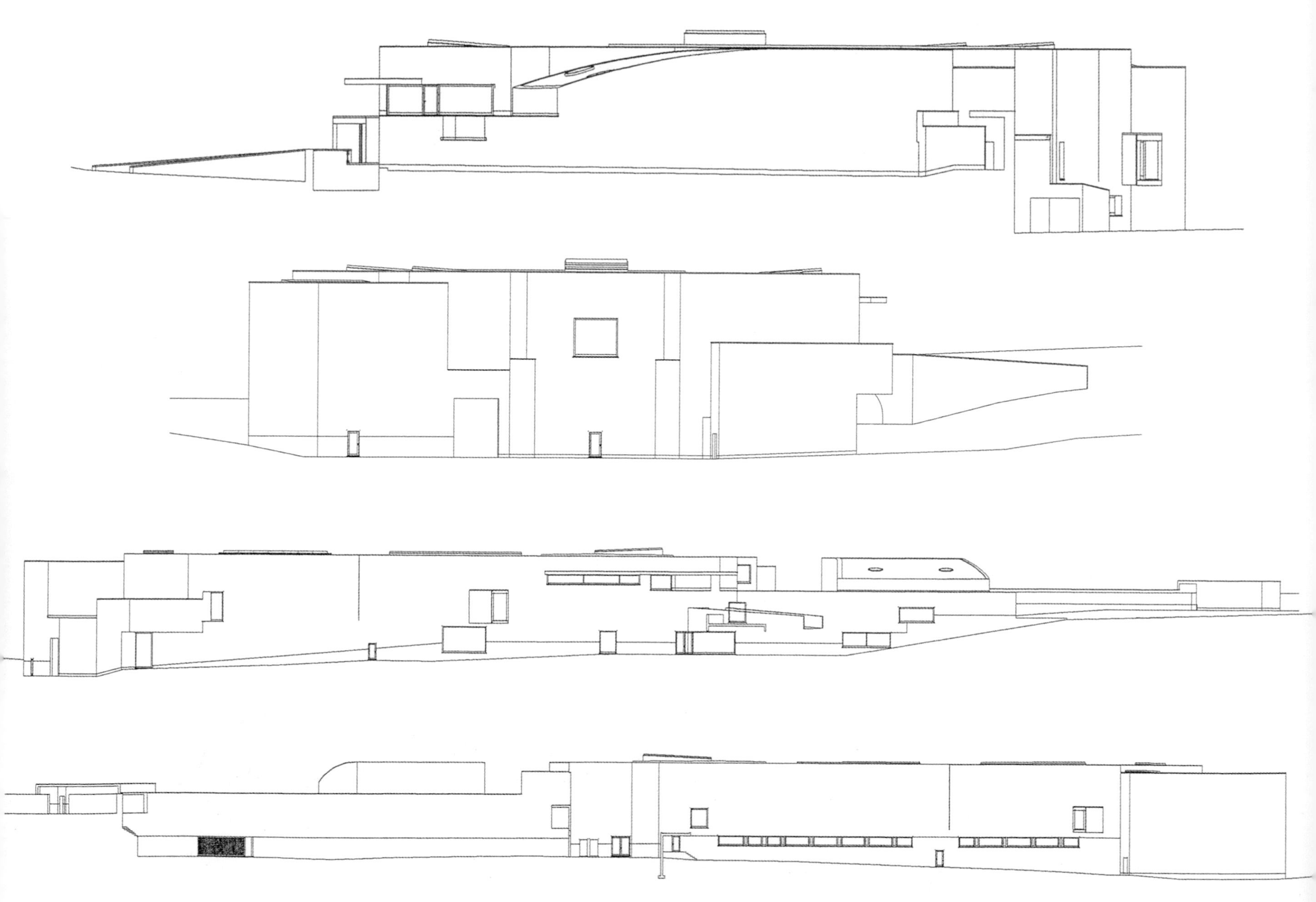

From above

The short north and south elevations reveal the simplicity of Siza's design

Long east and west elevations, showing the museum embedded in its parkland site

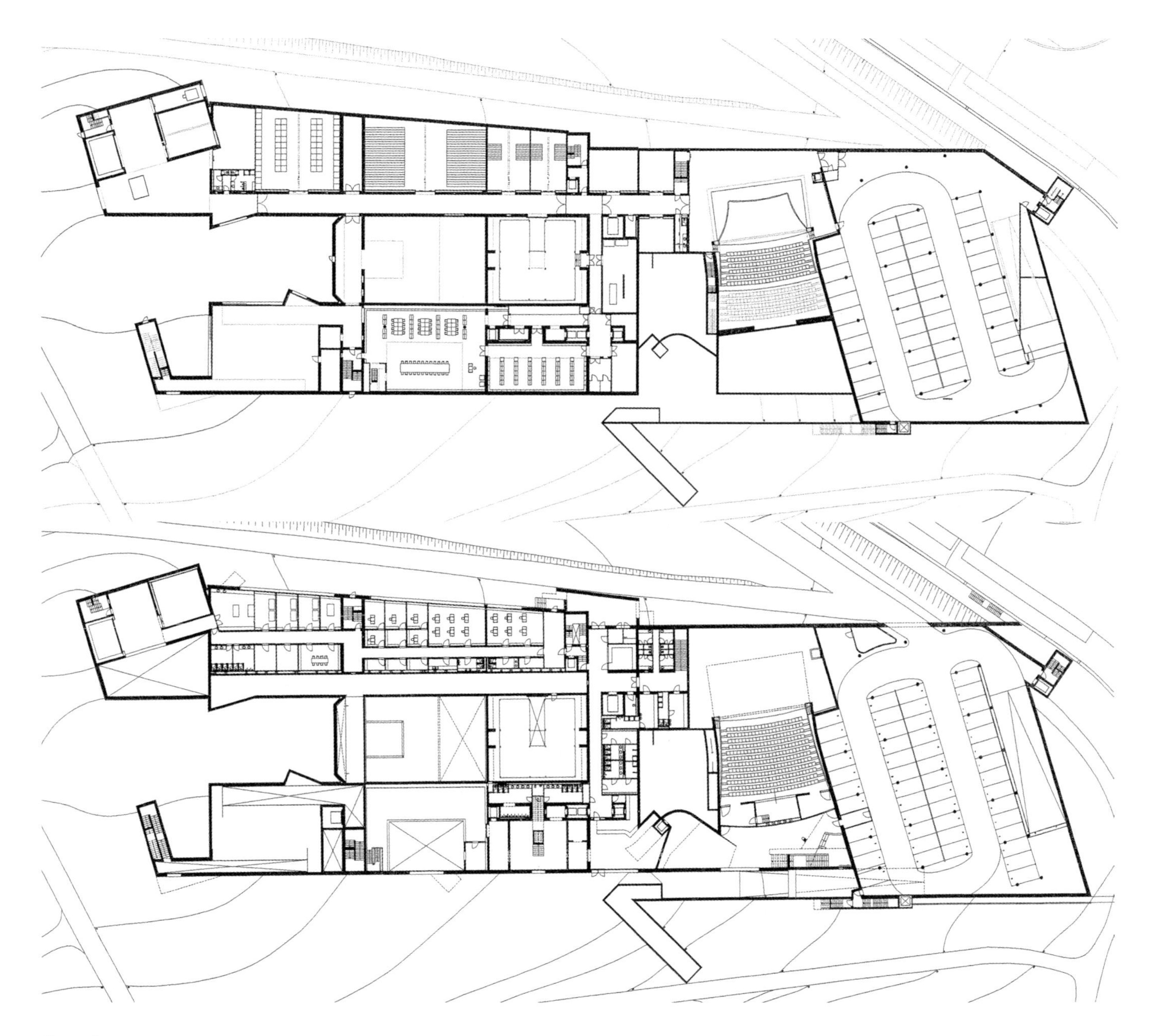

From above

First floor plan showing foyer area, auditorium and library

Ground floor plan showing exhibition galleries and related storage spaces. The plan is organised around two strong wall elements, which run from northeast to southwest

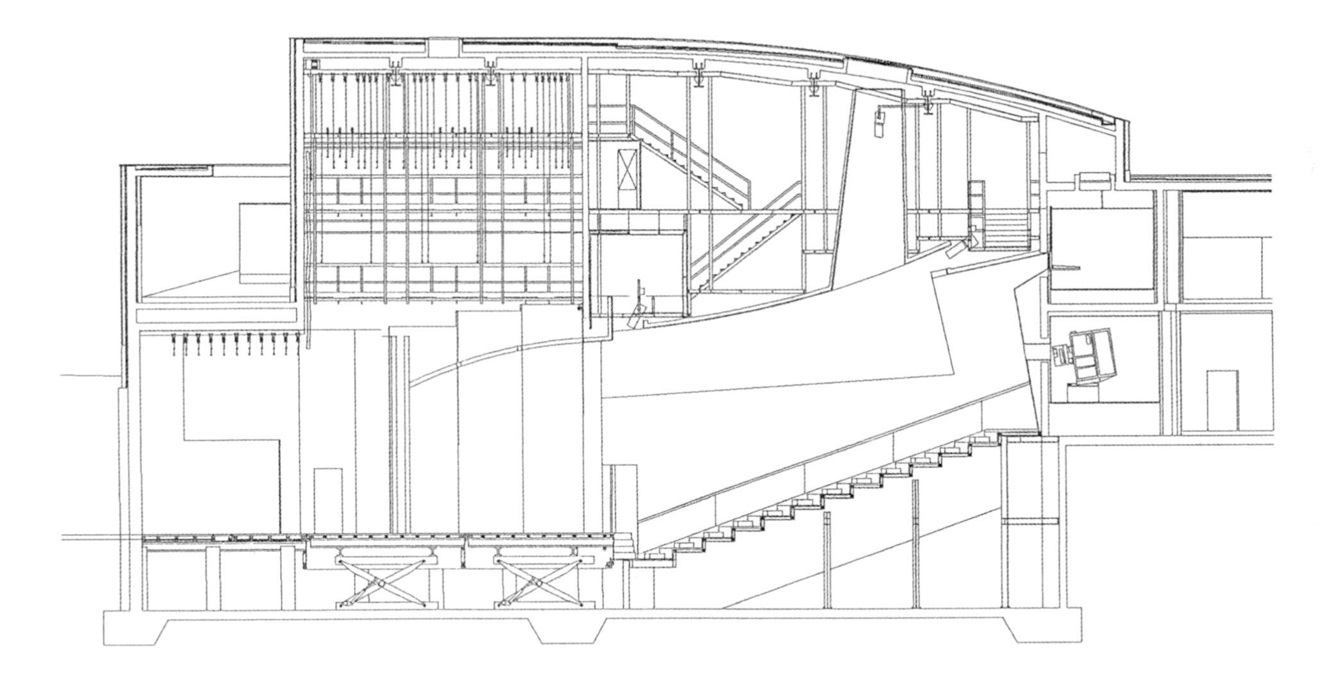

Detailed section of the auditorium, showing the raked seating and stage area

Opposite The architectural promenade around the building integrates the museum into its natural setting, and was carefully devised by Siza to instill curiosity

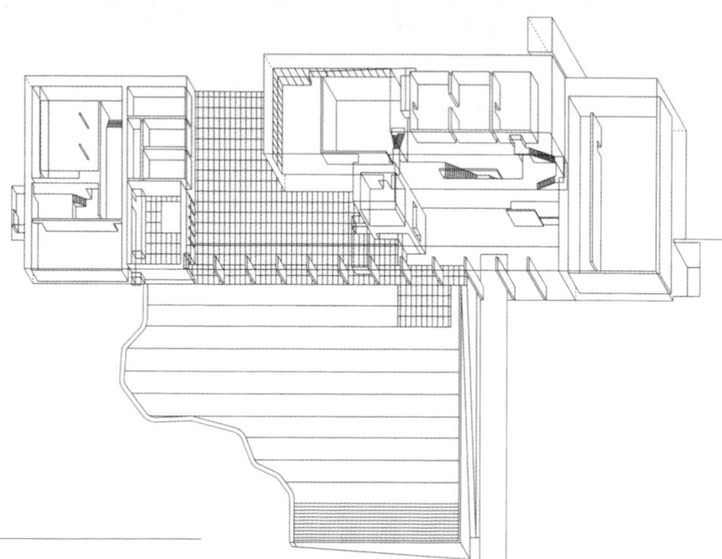

Yoshio Taniguchi

TOYOTA MUNICIPAL MUSEUM OF ART

Toyota City **1995**

Toyota City, in Japan's Aichi Prefecture, is at once both old and new, having originated as the castle town of Koroma City, before the Toyota Motor Corporation imported its manufacturing process, prompting the name change. Yoshio Taniguchi's Municipal Museum of Art is located on a sloping site adjacent to the partly reconstructed eighteenth century castle, and subtly acknowledges both aspects of the city's past, by framing views to the historic quarter to the east, and westwards to the modern urban centre.

The building itself makes full use of its graduated site, tucking administration and services below the level of the main foyer. The design hinges around three principal spaces: the green-stone clad temporary and Setsuro Takahashi galleries to the south and north façades respectively; and the permanent exhibition space, positioned between these two. This gallery is enclosed in translucent glass that provides natural lighting during the day and a beacon-like glow at night.

Landscaping is an integral part of this scheme, which Taniguchi worked on with the American landscape designer, Peter Walker. An 'L'-shaped sculpture terrace lies at the heart of the complex, and a man-made pool to the west front of the building defines the entry path and terminates at the museum's perimeter with a dignified colonnade of square arches.

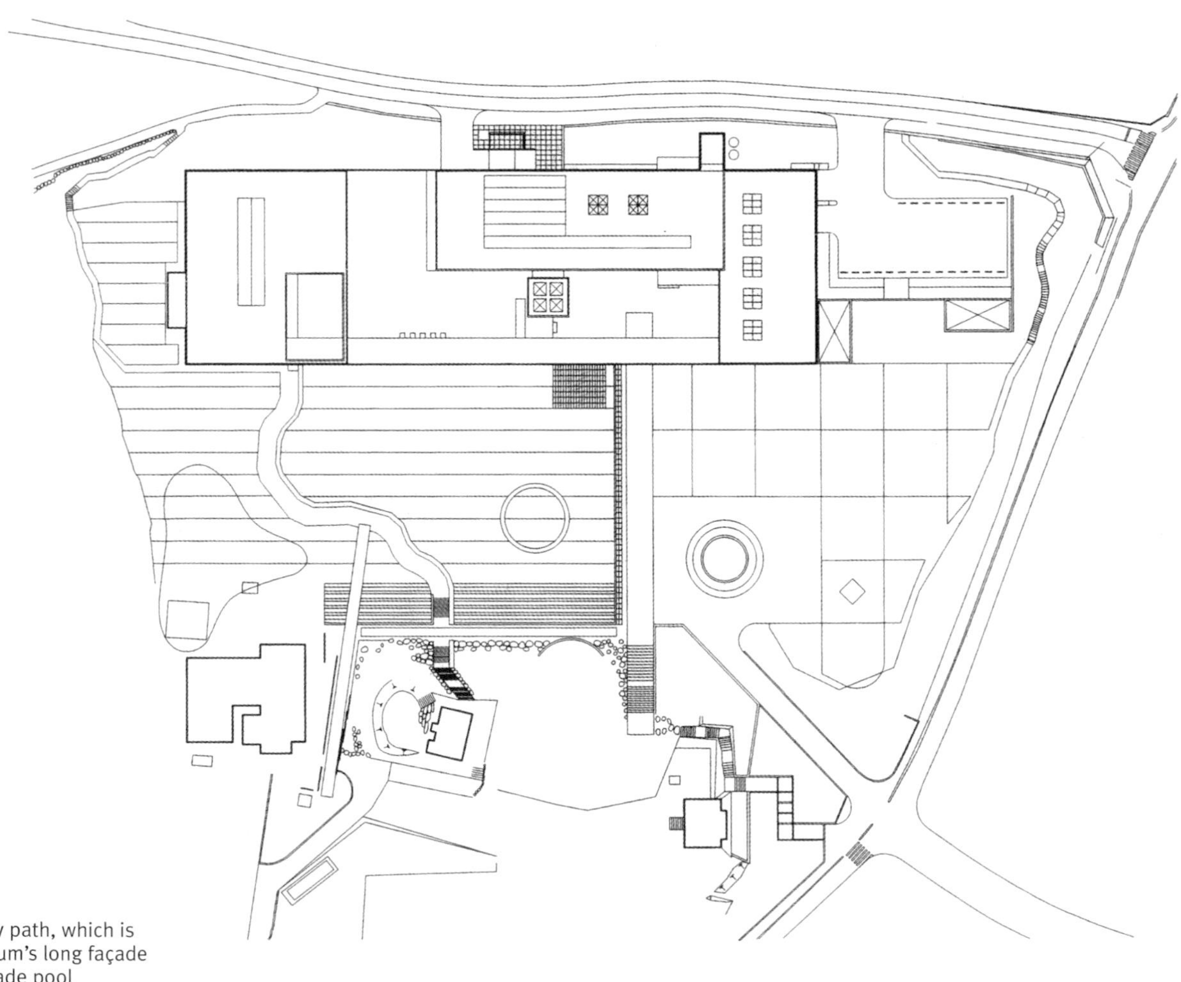

Site plan showing the entry path, which is perpendicular to the museum's long façade and defined by the man-made pool

Opposite top Principal west façade of the museum, with the entry ramp rising on the left-hand side

Opposite bottom Axonometric view showing the colonnade of square arches which spans the museum's entry façade

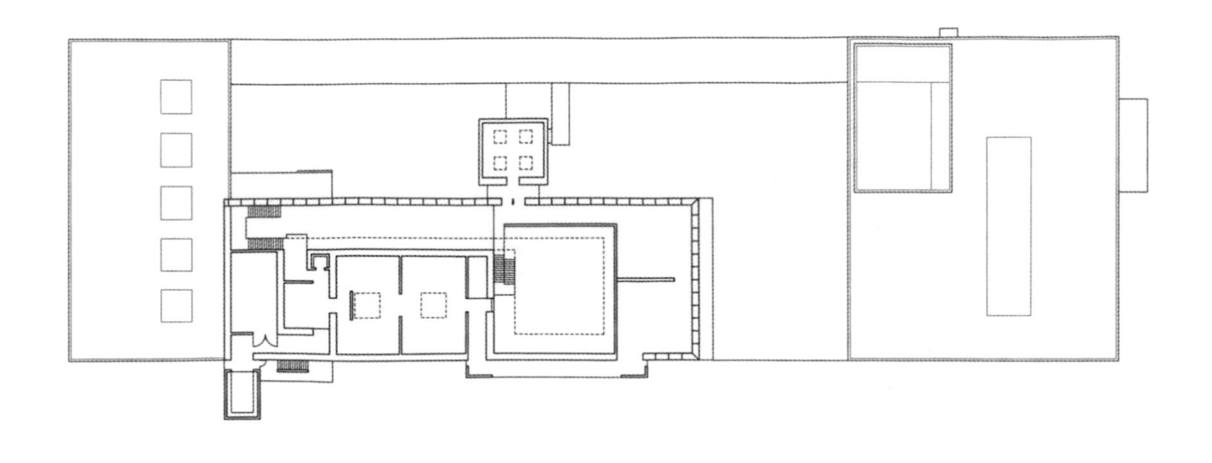

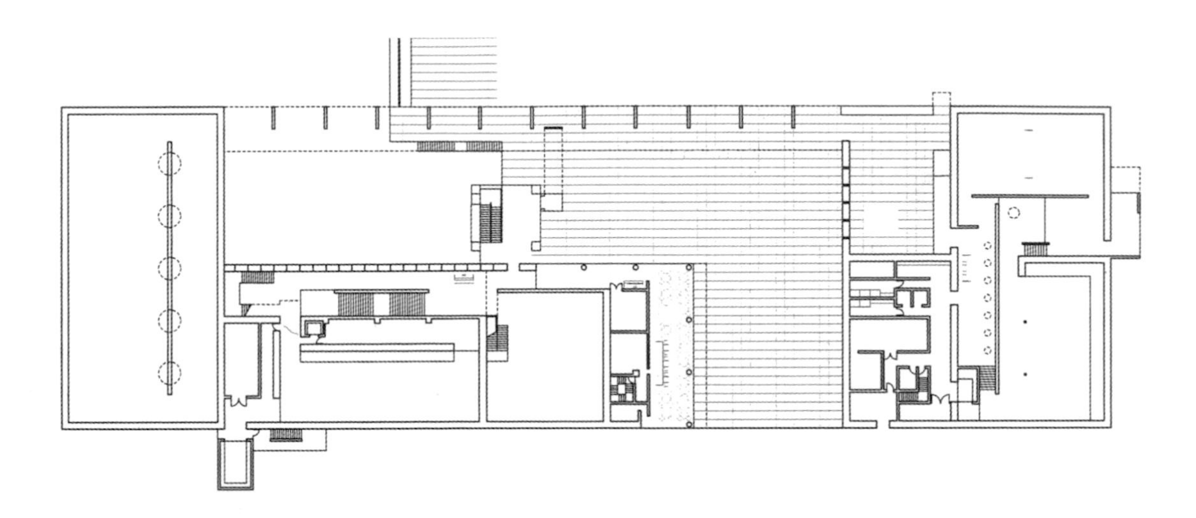

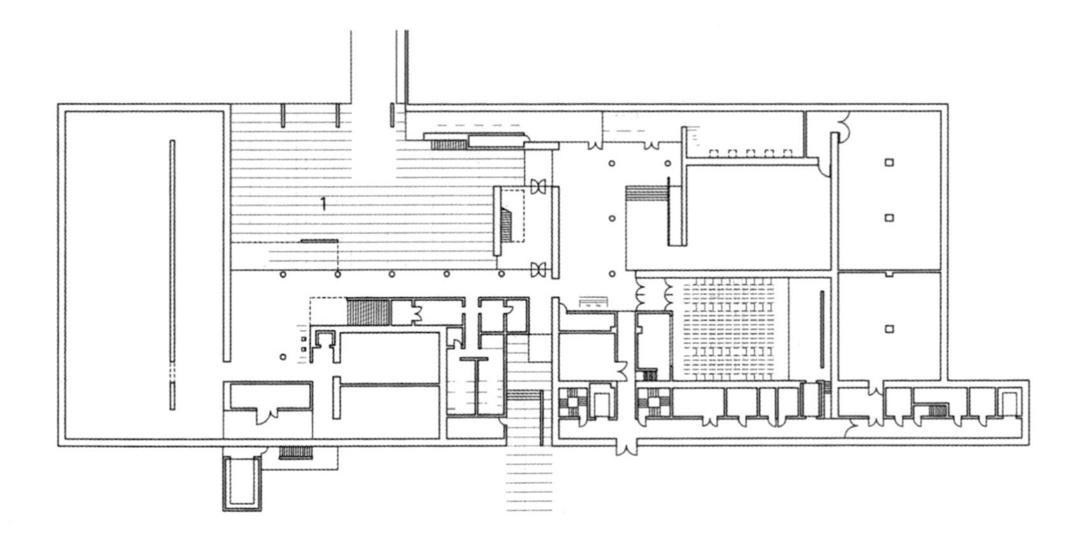
1

The American landscape designer, Peter Walker, collaborated with Taniguchi, creating calm, but formal, outdoor spaces

Opposite from below Ground, first and second floor plans, showing the sizeable areas devoted to the open-air entry court and the upper level terrace. The three principal gallery spaces: the temporary, permanent and Setsuro Takahashi galleries, are located from south to north

Artwork has impact in Taniguchi's simple and refined exhibition spaces

Opposite from above

Cross and longitudinal sections: the sloping nature of the site is maximised by housing administration and service facilities below ground

East, west and north elevations

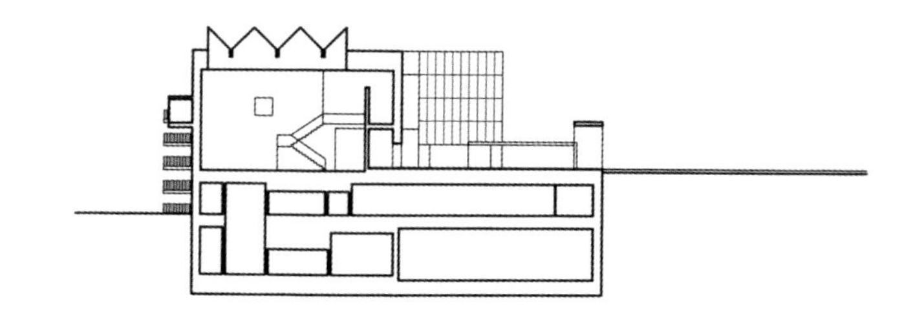

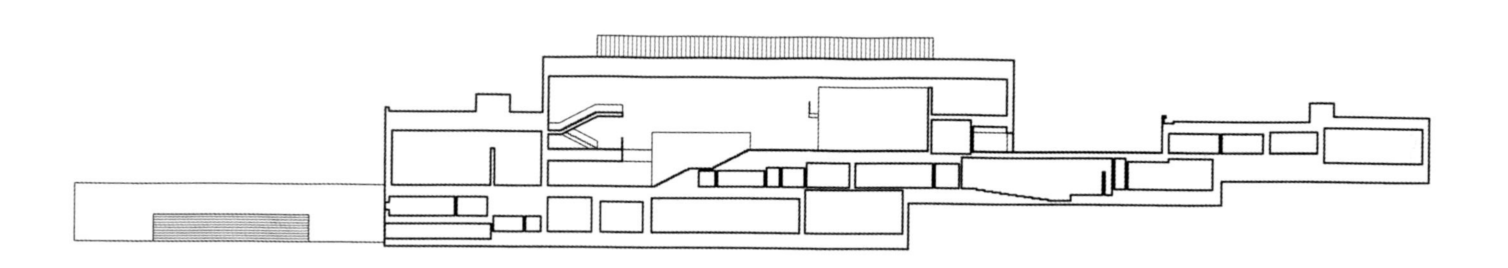

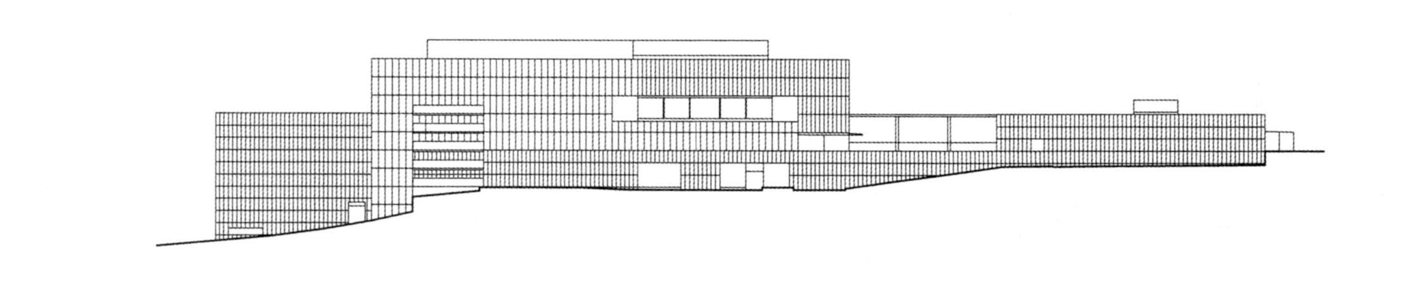

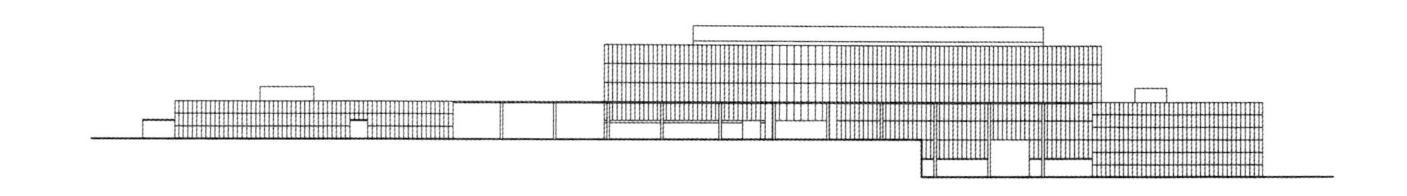

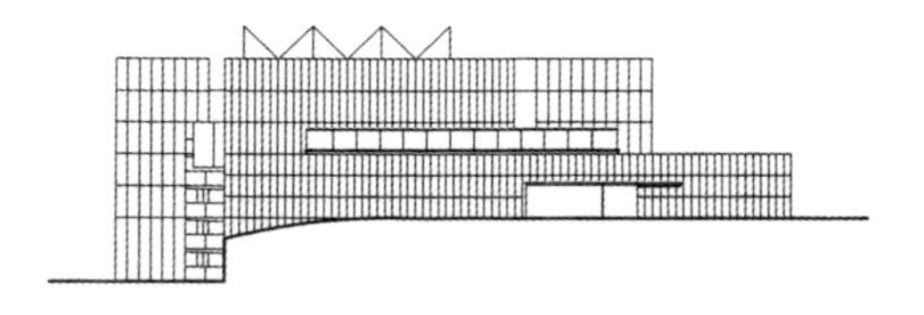

Above The museum's character is transformed at night, when the vast glazed façades glow

Below Axonometric, showing voids and projections on the roof plane

Opposite The fractal curve of the museum's façade breaks the confines of rectilinearity

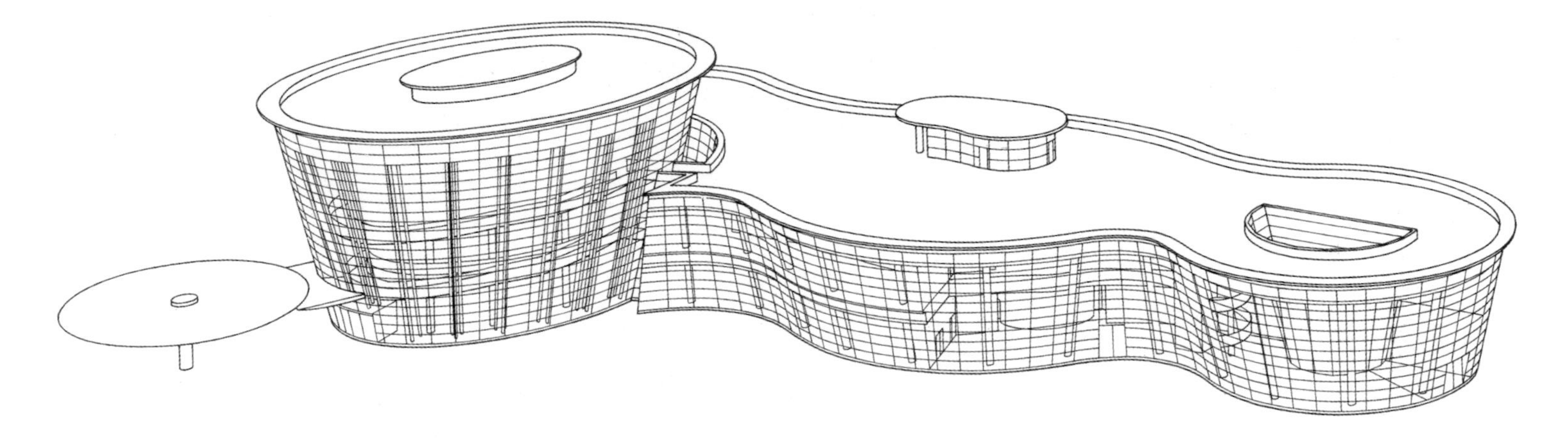

Kisho Kurokawa

FUKUI CITY MUSEUM OF ART

Fukui City **1996**

The footprint of the Fukui City Museum of Art is freely amorphous – like an oil drop on water – adhering to Kisho Kurokawa's self-proclaimed language of 'abstract symbolism'.[1] Despite its undulating form, the architect maintains careful control of the building's programme and three-dimensional spatial planning. Reposing in 4 hectares of parkland on the outskirts of the Japanese city of Fukui, the museum is relatively low-lying and completely encased with a glazed curtain wall in order to minimise its impact on the natural setting. Programmatically, the museum was designed to house three zones, although only two have been constructed to date.

The first of these areas contains a fine art exhibition, consisting of a permanent gallery devoted to the sculptures of Hiroatsu Takada, other more flexible exhibition spaces and a public studio. This two-storey volume, with storage areas at basement level, contains a tapering void of semi-circular cross-section at its far end that creates a dialogue with an irregular oval lantern projecting from the middle of the wing's roof. Abutting this pavilion is the three-storey entrance hall that, on completion of the scheme, will be the common entry point to both art zones. A ramp spirals up through this space that houses a lecture theatre as well as a café with open views of the park. The third, and still pending, element of the scheme, a performing arts wing, is to house a 1,000 capacity hall, rehearsal spaces and a library.

As the whole volume is wrapped in curtain glazing, solar gain, heat loss and deterioration of light-sensitive exhibits were all potentially problematic. To resolve these issues, Kurokawa employed 'double-framed glass, sealed heat-deflecting sashes, and semi-opaque heat- and light-deflecting rolling blinds', and angled the façade at 15 degrees to the vertical in order to minimise the direct light being admitted.[2]

1 Charles Jencks and others. *Contemporary Museums, Architectural Design*, Nov./Dec. 1997, p. 61.

2 Ibid.

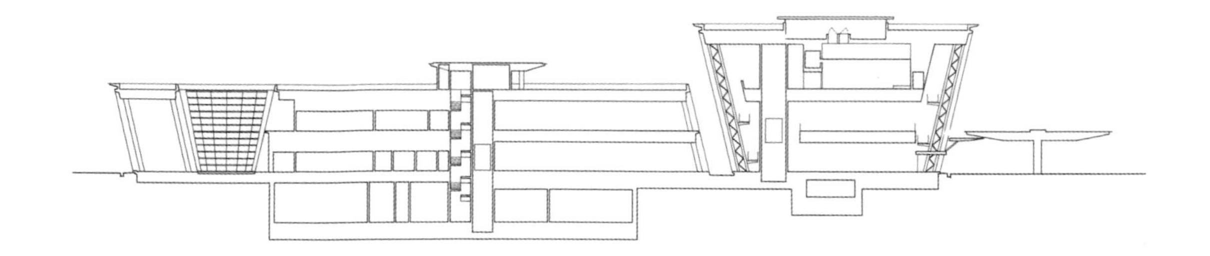

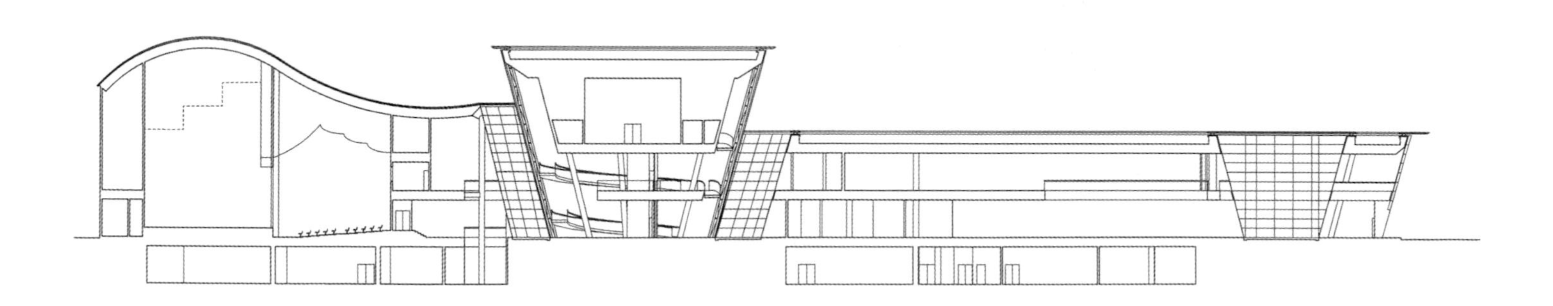

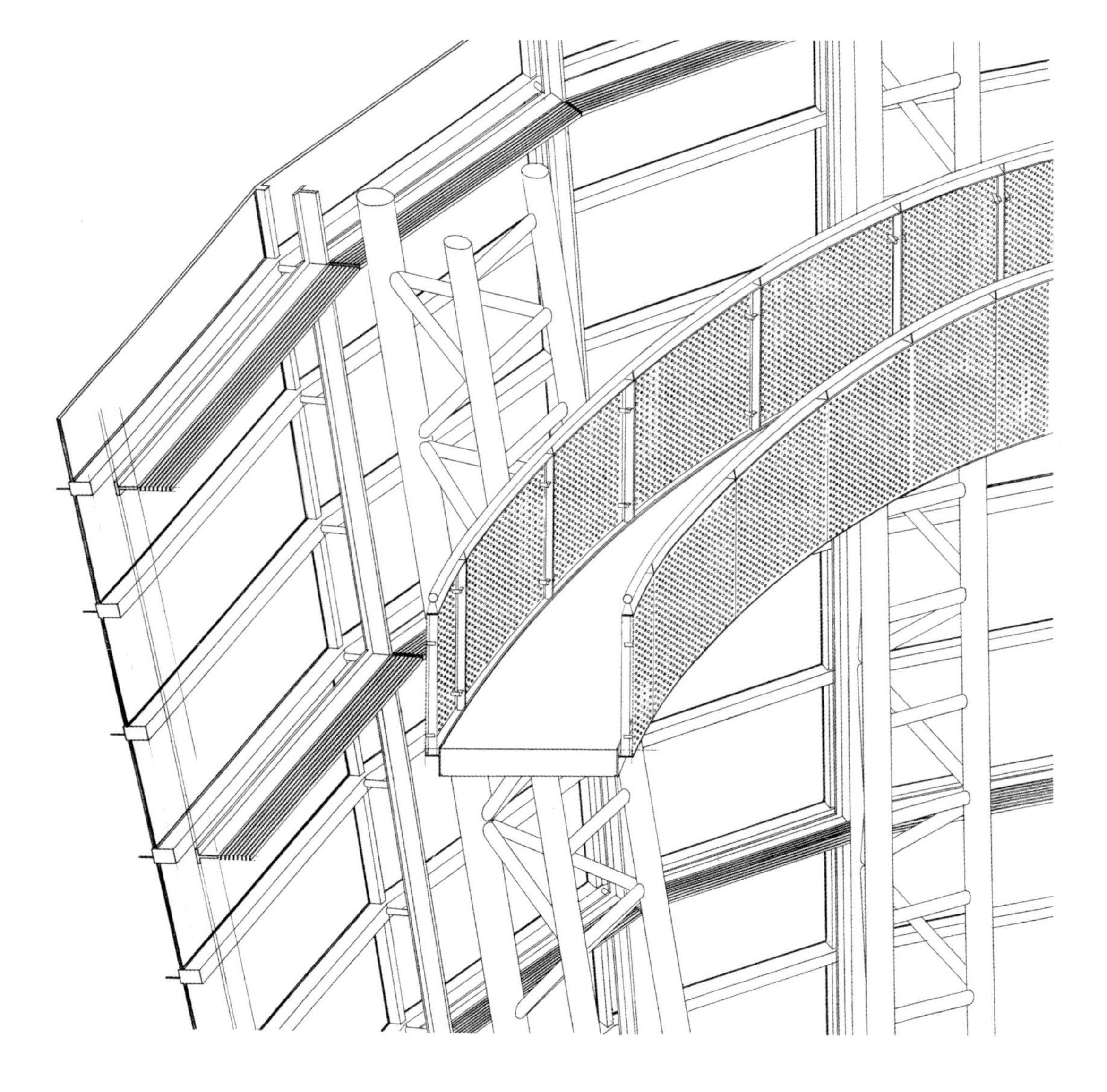

Perspective section showing the smart glazing system, trussing and bridge structure

Opposite from above

Cross section: the architect, Kisho Kurokawa, decided to hide the storage facilities at basement level

Undulating glazed curtain walling on the north side of the museum

Longitudinal section showing the still pending performing arts wing, with its wave-like roof structure hovering high above the auditorium

Museum entrance hall

Opposite top The organic, curvilinear form of the museum is startlingly obvious from this first floor plan, although Kurokawa has produced more conventional, rectilinear gallery spaces in the large exhibition wing

Opposite bottom Ground floor plan of the museum and external landscaping

Above left This view towards the exhibition room from the entrance wing gives a glimpse of vivid yellow. Kurokawa introduced such brightly coloured elements to add a vibrant and playful note to the otherwise pristine, even clinical, aesthetic

Above right The glazing bars of the curtain walling create ever-changing patterns of light and shade across the museum floor

Above left The slope of the entrance wing ensures a dynamically charged space

Above right Detail of a truss

FOR CONTEMPORARY ART

Zaha Hadid

LOIS & RICHARD ROSENTHAL CENTER FOR CONTEMPORARY ART

Cincinnati **2003**

With her design for the new Lois & Richard Rosenthal Center for Contemporary Art at a busy downtown intersection in Cincinnati, Zaha Hadid has broken new ground: it is her first project in the United States, and, remarkably, the first American art museum commission to be undertaken by a woman.

Hadid explains that 'the fundamental concept is a jigsaw puzzle of diverse exhibition spaces: long, short, broad, or tall spaces, each with different lighting conditions.'[1] These pieces of the puzzle – five massive wedges of concrete, black aluminium and glass – jostle together on the south and east façades, and 'read as a single three-dimensional face on two planes'.[2] Rather than creating an explosive effect, however, the energy of these elements is harnessed, and the whole floats on top of a recessed, transparent ground floor façade, making the mass appear strangely weightless. Internally, these volumes are expressed via the materiality of their floor and ceiling planes.

The visitor enters into the light-filled, glazed entrance lobby, from the rear of which an open ramp-stair ascends through the building, allowing vistas to people and displays beyond. Surfaces are a subdued mix of grey concrete, battleship grey and black cement and silver metal, all illuminated with white light.[3] The most unique facet of the design is surely the 'urban carpet', conceived by Hadid as one single concrete sculptural element, extending from the sidewalk into the museum to create the lobby floor, before curving up to form the rear wall of the building. This intervention creates ambiguity between inside and out, allowing the street to flow into the building and vice versa, whilst also providing a monumental backdrop to the activities of the museum.

1 Zaha Hadid. 'Zaha Hadid on the Contemporary Arts Center', *Press Kit*, Zaha Hadid Statement, p. 1.

2 'Building Study. Zaha Hadid Architects, Cincinnati', *Building Design*, 23 May 2003, p. 13.

3 Ibid.

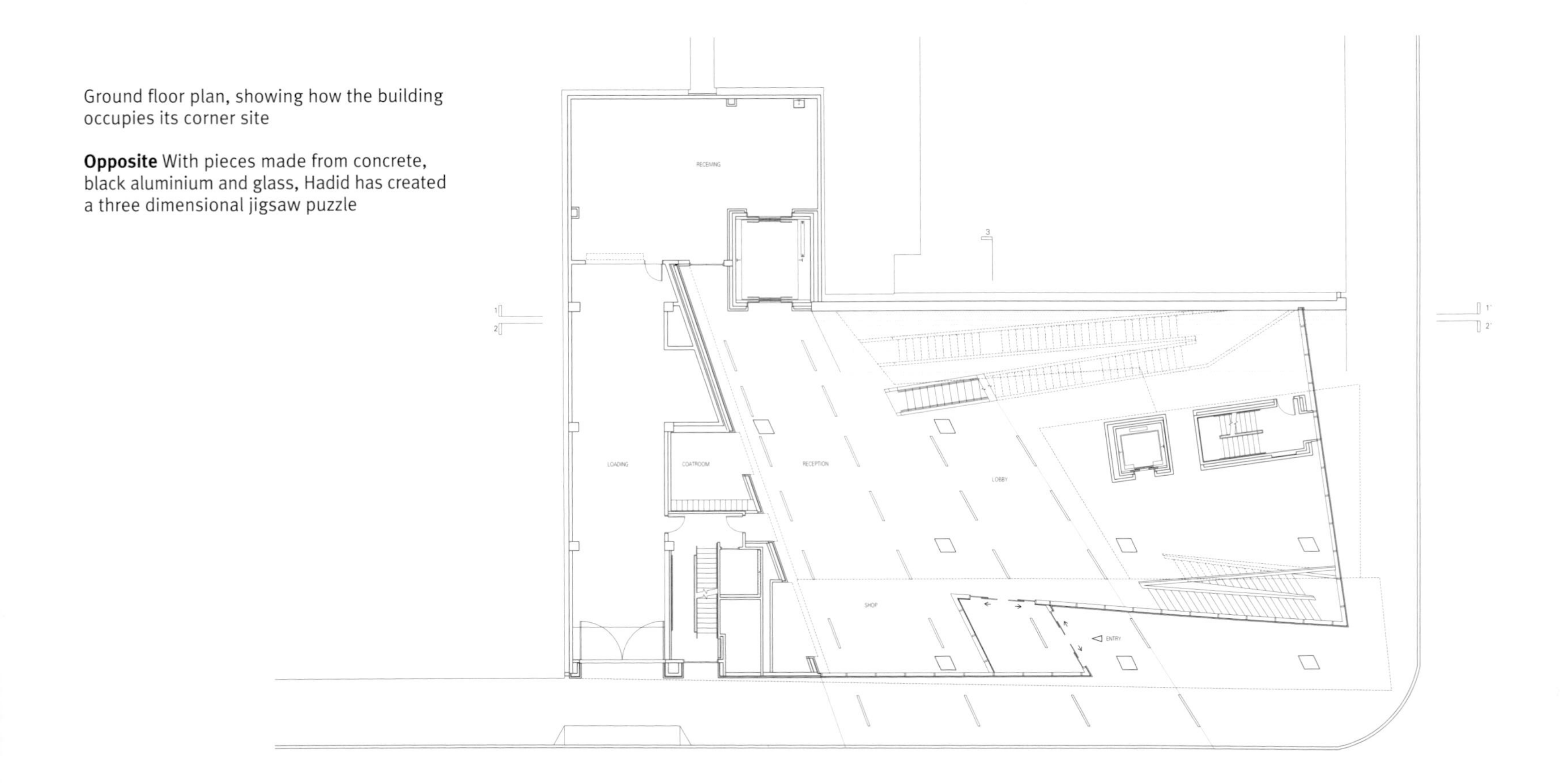

Ground floor plan, showing how the building occupies its corner site

Opposite With pieces made from concrete, black aluminium and glass, Hadid has created a three dimensional jigsaw puzzle

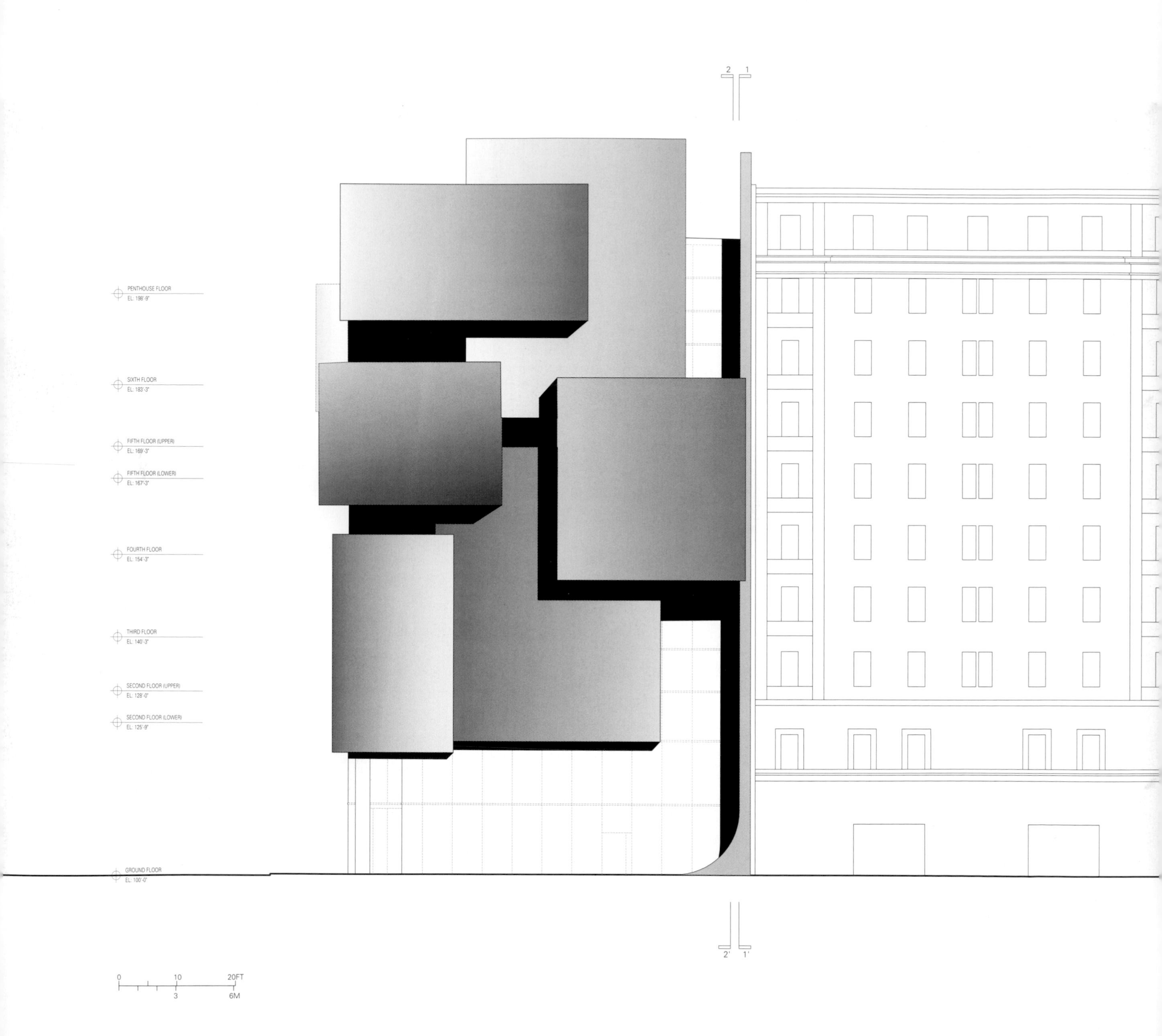
2
1
PENTHOUSE FLOOR
EL: 198'-9"
SIXTH FLOOR
EL: 183'-3"
FIFTH FLOOR (UPPER)
EL: 169'-3"
FIFTH FLOOR (LOWER)
EL: 167'-3"
FOURTH FLOOR
EL: 154'-3"
THIRD FLOOR
EL: 140'-3"
SECOND FLOOR (UPPER)
EL: 128'-0"
SECOND FLOOR (LOWER)
EL: 125'-9"
GROUND FLOOR
EL: 100'-0"
2'
1'
0
10
20FT
3
6M

Above left Zaha Hadid Architects used physical and computer rendered models to generate the center's final circulation pattern and blocked form

Above right The massed three-dimensionality of Hadid's creation is emphasized here on the Walnut Street façade

Opposite East shadow elevation

This façade strongly articulates the museum's geometry

Opposite South shadow elevation

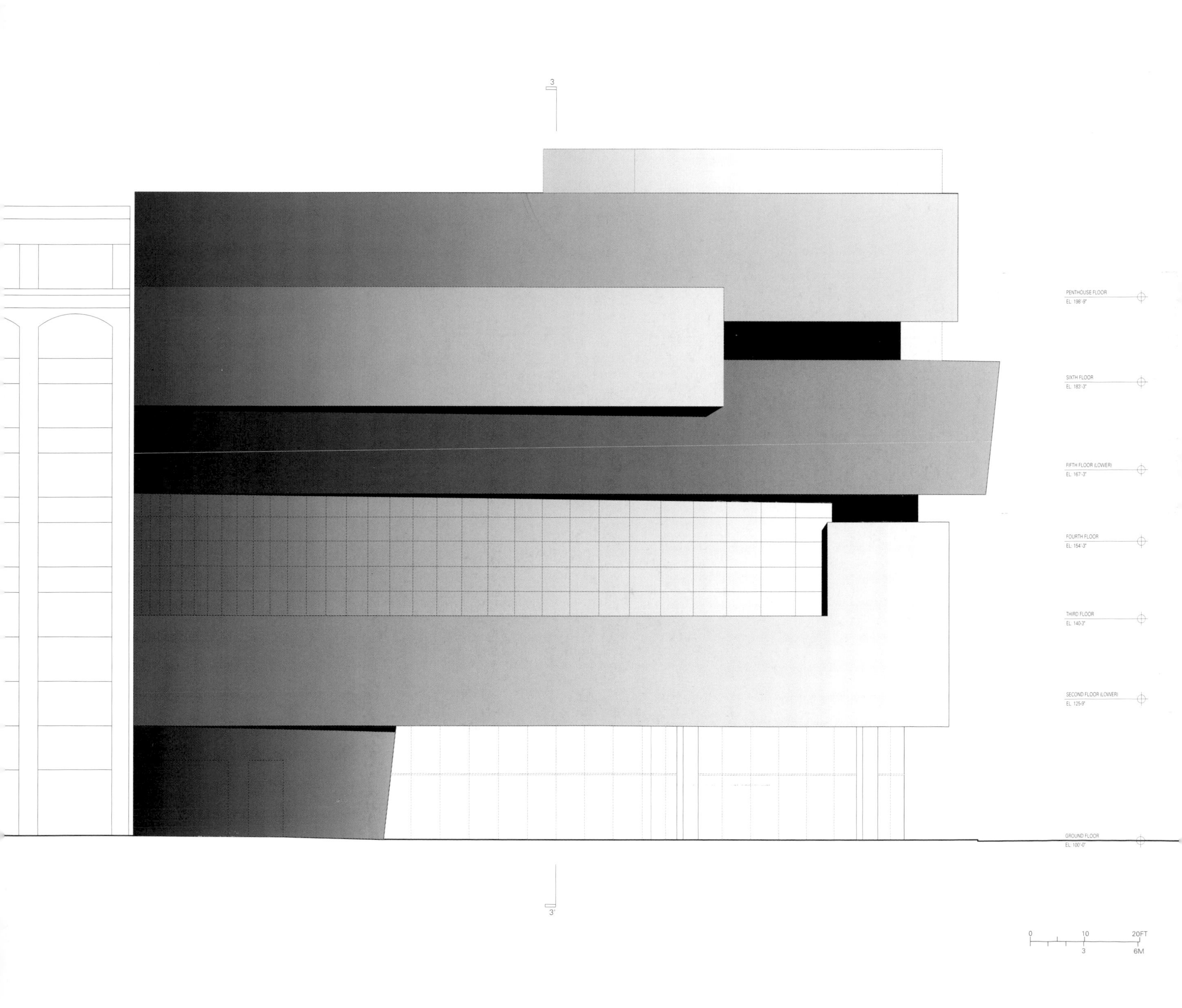
3
PENTHOUSE FLOOR
EL: 198'-9"
SIXTH FLOOR
EL: 183'-3"
FIFTH FLOOR (LOWER)
EL: 167'-3"
FOURTH FLOOR
EL: 154'-3"
THIRD FLOOR
EL: 140-3"
SECOND FLOOR (LOWER)
EL: 125-9"
GROUND FLOOR
EL: 100'-0"
3'
0
10
20FT
3
6M

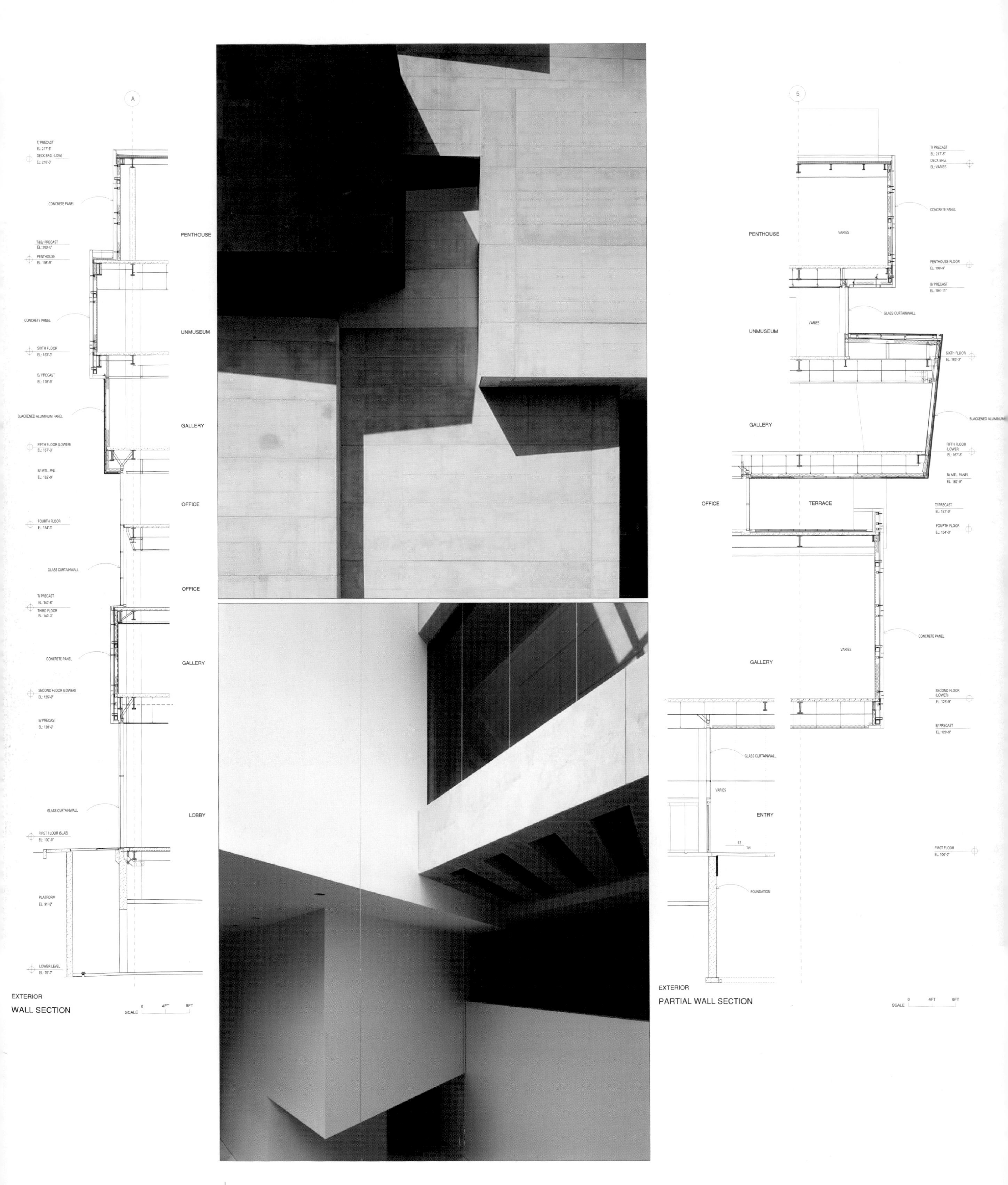
A
PENTHOUSE
UNMUSEUM
GALLERY
OFFICE
OFFICE
GALLERY
LOBBY
CONCRETE PANEL
BLACKENED ALUMINUM PANEL
GLASS CURTAINWALL
EXTERIOR
WALL SECTION
SCALE 0 4FT 8FT
5
PENTHOUSE
UNMUSEUM
GALLERY
OFFICE
TERRACE
GALLERY
ENTRY
VARIES
FOUNDATION
EXTERIOR
PARTIAL WALL SECTION
SCALE 0 4FT 8FT

This perspective painting by Zaha Hadid shows the concrete 'urban carpet', which forms the center's rear wall and floor plane, before emerging onto the Cincinnati pavement

Opposite top Close inspection of the center's façades reveals an almost Modernist abstraction

Opposite bottom The subdued palette of interior materials creates a suitably discrete background for the artwork contained within

Opposite left and right Partial exterior wall sections, showing the relation between the form of the building and the functions it houses

Above and opposite An open stair ramp, shown above between levels 2 and 3, ascends through the entire building creating visual links and a dramatic architectural promenade

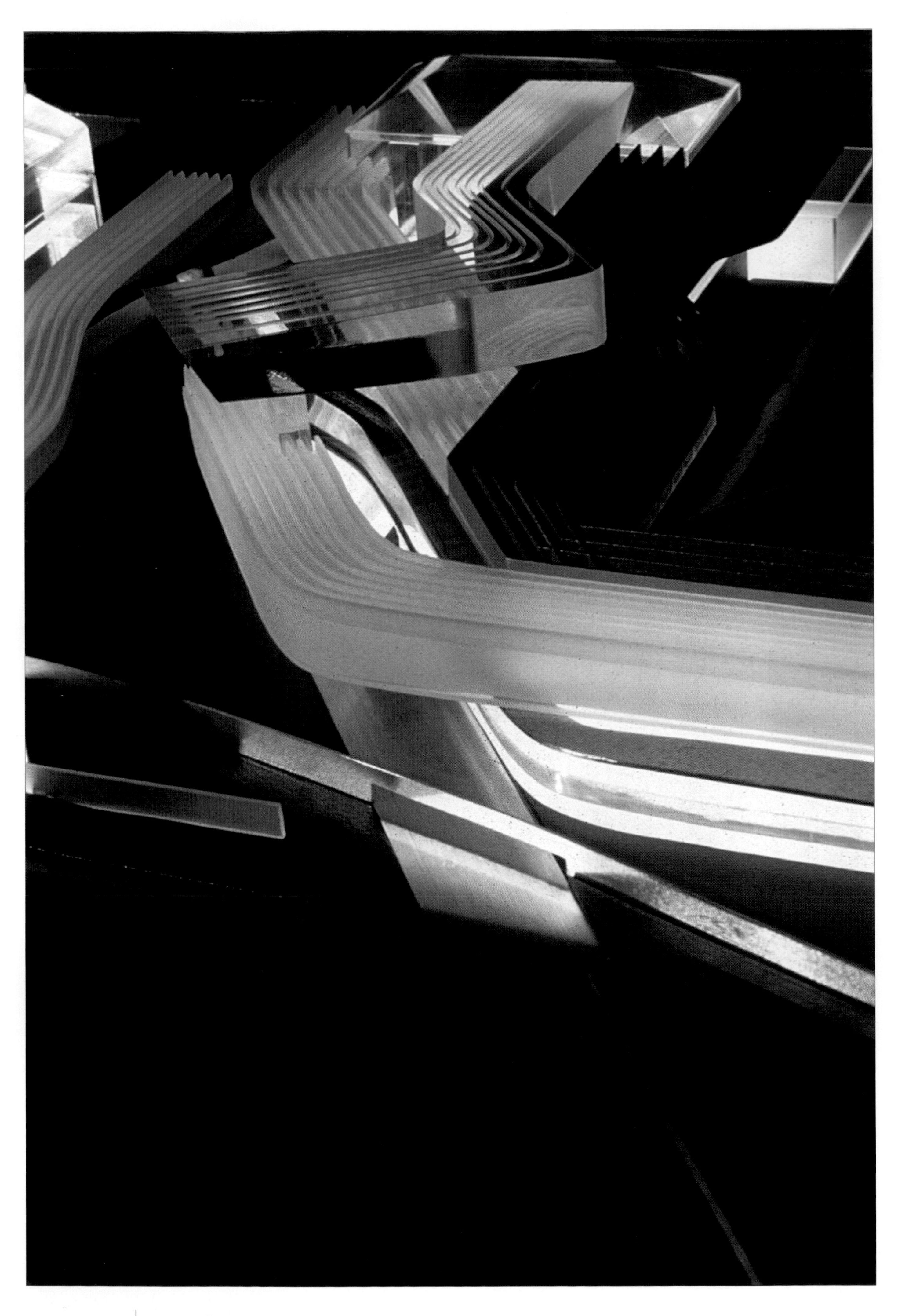

Zaha Hadid

NATIONAL CENTRE FOR CONTEMPORARY ARTS

Rome

The National Centre for Contemporary Arts in Rome is due for completion in 2005 and will form a key component of the city's new cultural district that extends from the Rome Music Performing Centre by Renzo Piano, on a site 300 metres away, to the River Tiber. Following a design competition that called for 'a solution of appropriate visual boldness and creativity, acting as a landmark of the country's commitment to design excellence and innovation', Zaha Hadid was appointed as project architect in 1999.[1]

The exhibition and building design programmes were multifaceted, requiring accommodation for the Museum of Architecture, a 21st Century Art Museum and a venue for live events, as well as all the usual museum support spaces. Hadid decided to utilise two of the former Montello barracks buildings on the site, north of Rome's historic centre, and completed the first phase of the development in February 2001.

The main concept of Hadid's scheme is a complex linearity that results in a dense, continuous space, full of branches and overlaps. 'The site is "run through" with exhibition spaces, walls that go through space. The intersection of the walls defines the interior and exterior spaces.'[2] Over the whole, a glass roof permits natural light to filter through the structural frames of the ceiling, down into the gallery spaces below.

1 http://www.gnam.arti.beniculturali.it

2 http://www.mnitalia.com

This aerial rendering of the Centre for Contemporary Arts highlights the fluidity and movement of Hadid's design, which at the same time is also 'geometrically aligned with the urban grids that join at the site'

Opposite Elevated view of the scheme's presentation model

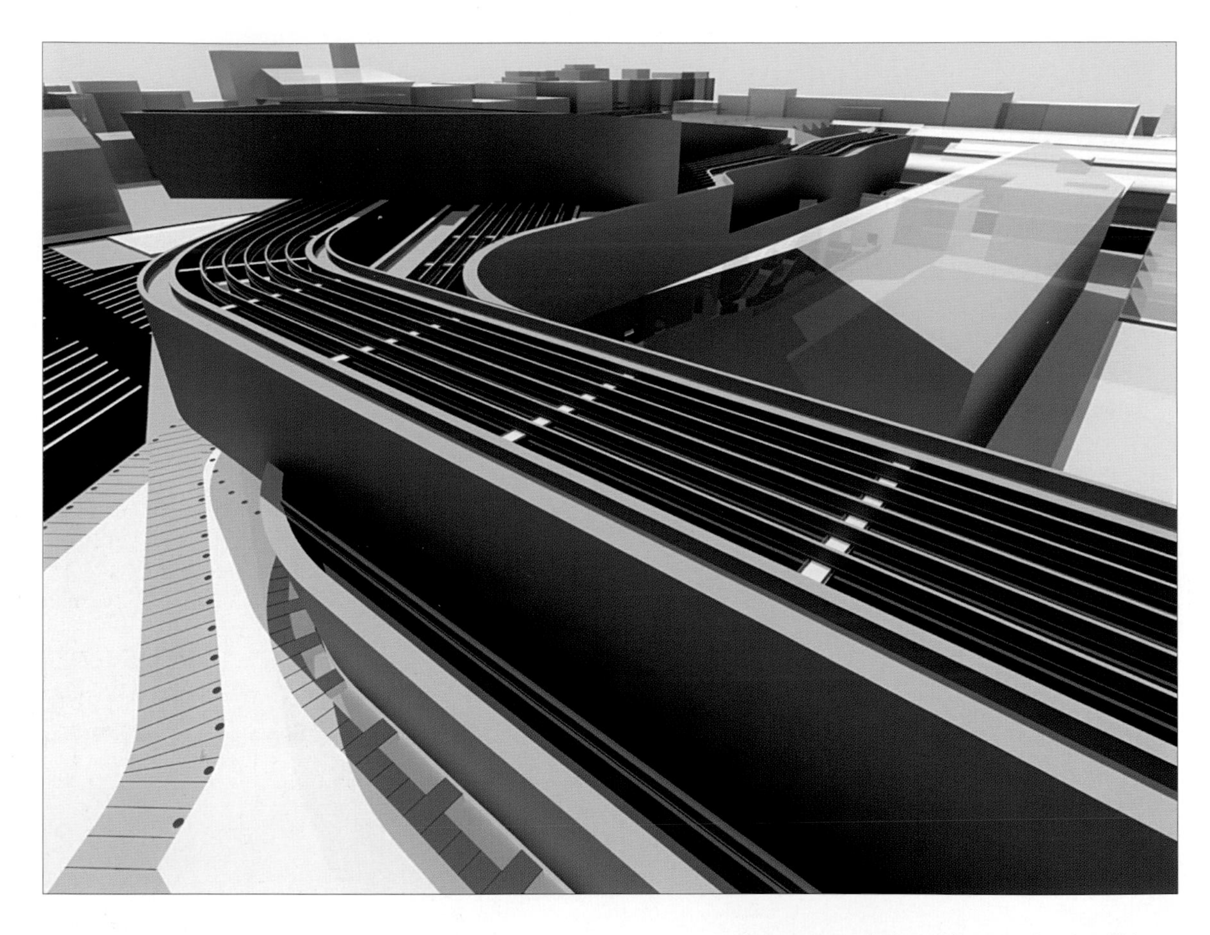

Computer rendering of the complex, in which the wall becomes a flexible and ever-changing stage for art

Opposite top Illuminated model of the centre, which 'encompasses both movement patterns extant and desired, contained within and outside'

Opposite bottom View of the centre's roof, within the densely packed urban fabric of Rome

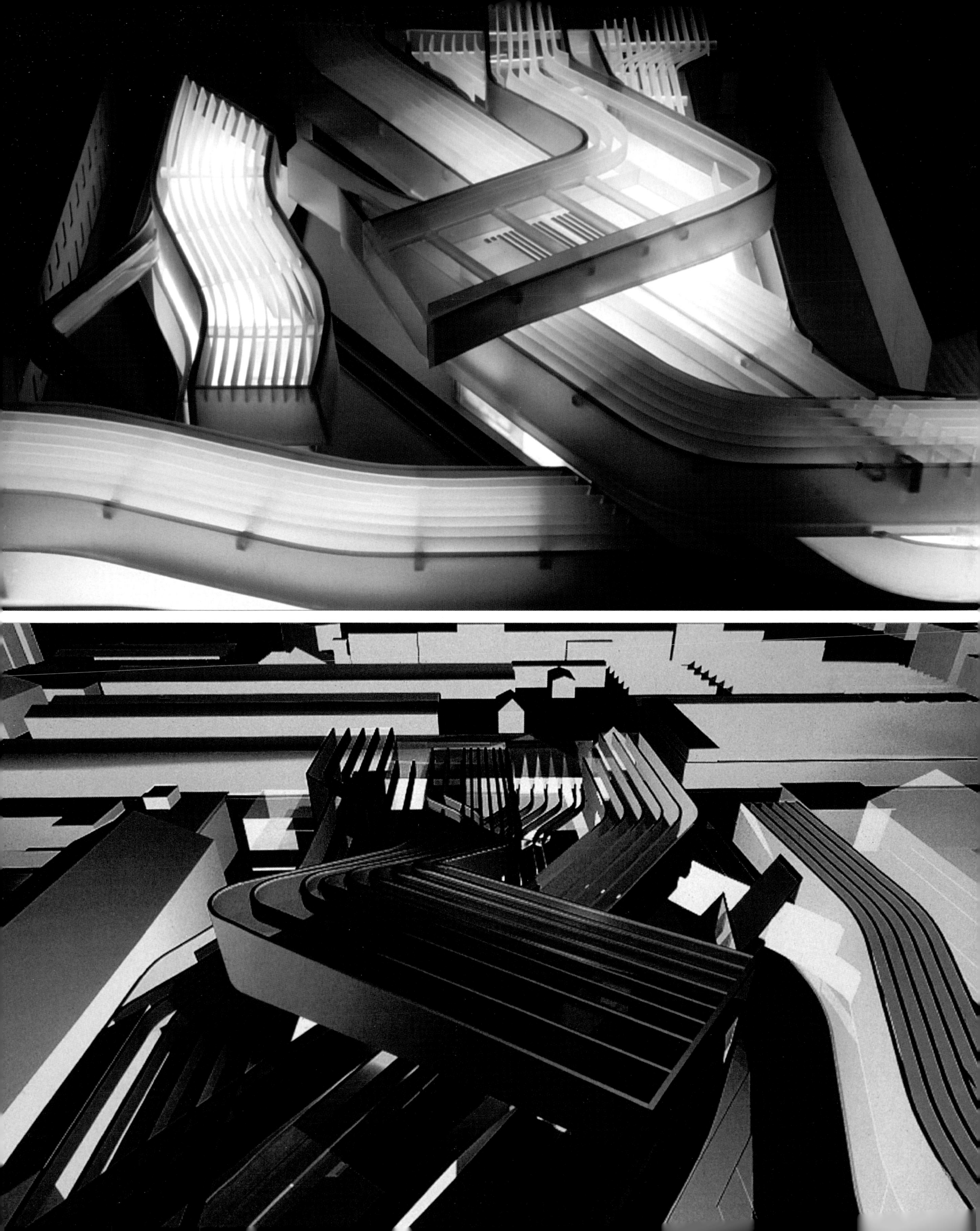

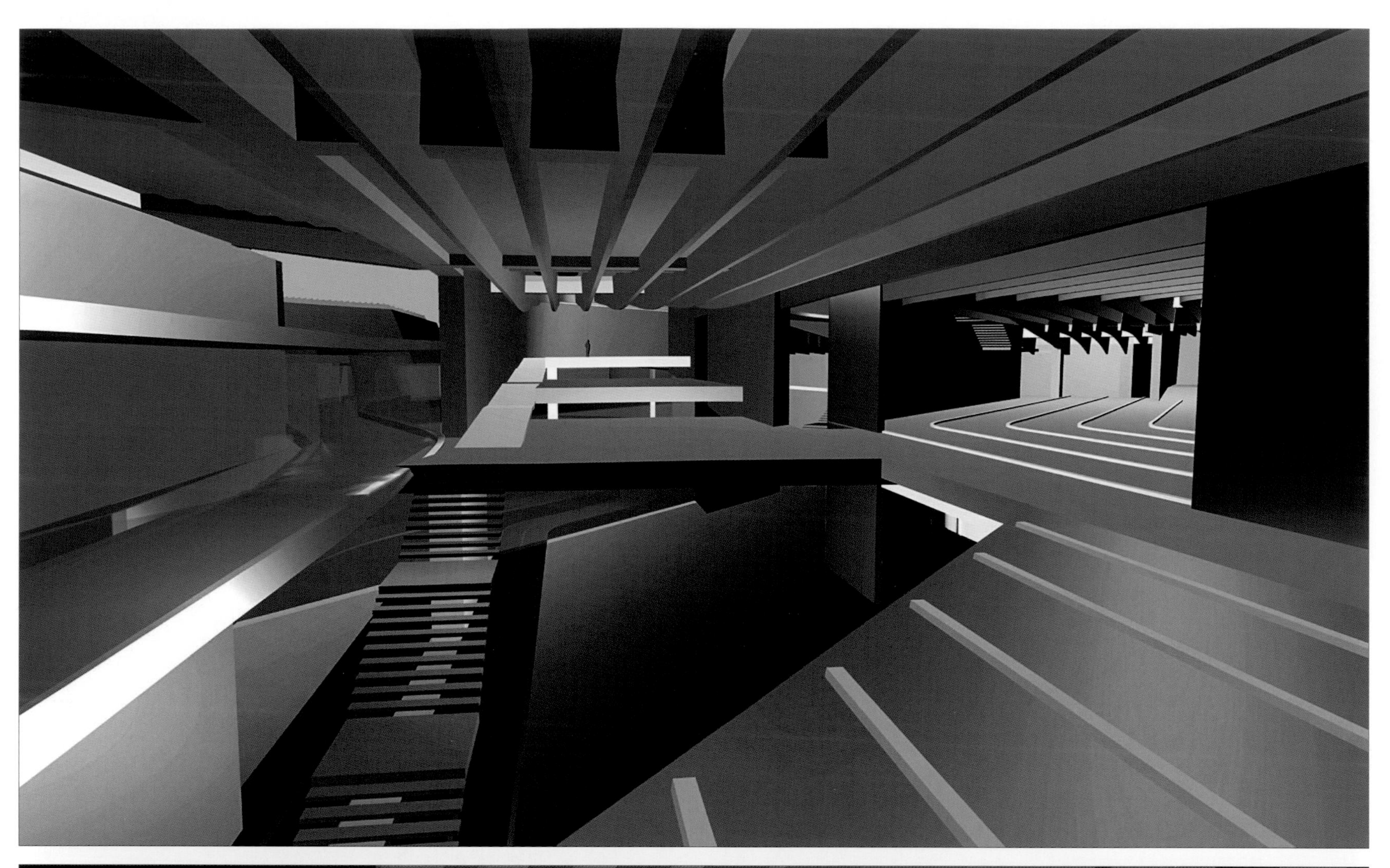

Perspective rendering of interior circulation space

Opposite top Digital rendering of internal circulation and display space

Opposite bottom Internal rendering showing the vertical openness of Hadid's scheme

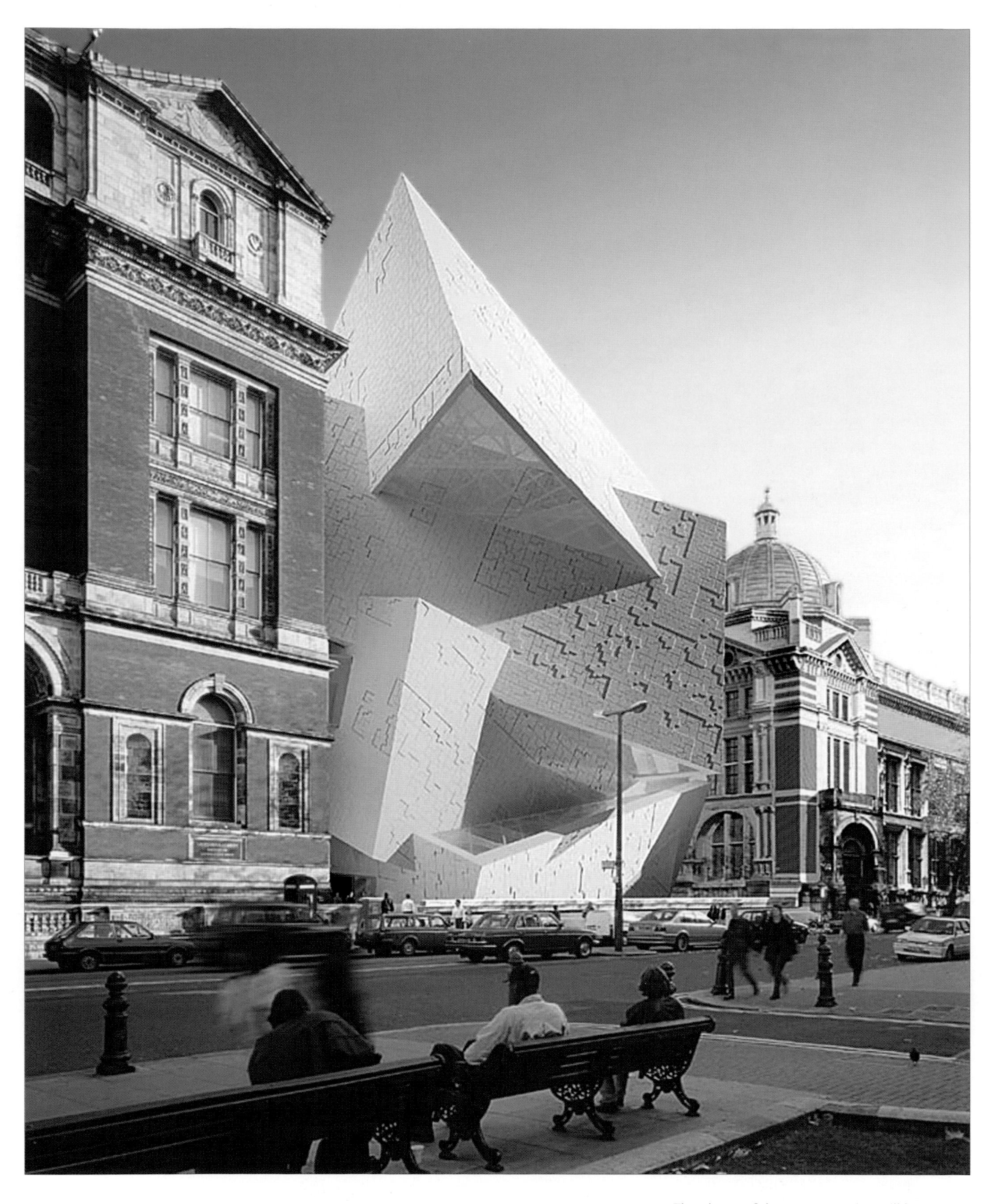

The planes of the new extension will burst out into the restrained formality of Exhibition Road

Opposite A lattice of structural elements and glazing bars in the café-restaurant space

Daniel Libeskind

SPIRAL EXTENSION TO THE VICTORIA & ALBERT MUSEUM

London

Daniel Libeskind's Spiral or Boilerhouse Extension for the Victoria & Albert Museum, has still not made the shift from drawing board – where it was conceived between 1996 and 1999 – to reality, due to a series of financial and other setbacks. The project is currently on hold, with no immediate prospect of work beginning on site

The challenge for Libeskind and his team was to design an intervention to knit into the complex and extensive existing fabric of the museum, and symbolise the V&A into the twenty first century. Three major, linked concepts informed the design: 'the spiral movement of art and history; the interlocking of inside and outside, and the labyrinth of discovery.'[1] In response to these objectives, Libeskind favoured the same basic spiral form as that employed by Wright 50 years earlier at the New York Guggenheim, arguing that it related to the building's programme: 'The trajectory of History ... is not a straight line to be projected by technocrats without spirit, or sensualists without heart, but is a subtle, imaginative and contemporary trace embodying the fullness of a poetic heritage.'[2] However, unlike Wright's traditional helix, Libeskind's contemporary vortex is much freer and less restrained, 'open[ing] a plurality of directions along many different trajectories, providing multiple routes, spaces and ambience for the visitors.'[3] This spiralling journey responds to both the museum within and the city without, bursting out into the streetscape of Exhibition Road.

The visitor will access the building via a bridge, entering directly into the two-level lobby spaces that are connected at ground level to the surrounding buildings and address a sunken garden. The upper floors house permanent galleries, administration space and an orientation centre, whilst the subterranean spaces extend under the existing building and Pirelli Gardens, to house temporary exhibitions, educational spaces and an auditorium. Externally, the interlocking planes carry on the architect's daring signature aesthetic and, where not glazed, are clad in ceramic tiles derived from fractiles.

1 Charles Jencks and others. *New Science = New Architecture?*, *Architectural Design*, Sept./Oct. 1997, p. 65.

2 http://www.daniel-libeskind.com

3 Ibid.

Libeskind has sought flexibility, designing galleries sufficiently capacious and open plan to accommodate a wide range of different displays

Top Libeskind understands the importance of views to the world beyond

Bottom Staged vistas connect the different levels of the museum extension

1046 feet

Chihuly at the V&A
Click Here Now
Entrance level
You are here
Level 9
Level 8
Level 7
Level 6
Level 5
Wednesday 10.00-22.00
Last Friday of every month 10.00-22.00
£5.00
Donatello's Ascension

Herzog and de Meuron

TATE MODERN

London **1999**

Herzog and de Meuron's Tate Modern is undoubtedly the most internationally renowned adaptive reuse museum project of recent years. By the early 1990s, the Tate wished to acquire a central and accessible London site to house its twentieth-century art collection, and Bankside Power Station in Southwark provided this opportunity. Prohibitive costs for demolition and new build led to an international design competition to transform the existing structure; a mid-twentieth-century industrial edifice, designed by Giles Gilbert Scott.

The approach of the successful architects, Herzog and de Meuron, was largely non-interventionist. Retaining the basic organisation of three elongated bays, running in parallel to the Thames, they simply removed the huge turbines from the central hall, creating a vast, ramped orientation and installation space, of 'visceral impact'.[1] The former boiler house to the north, river side of this hall was then adapted to house circulation concourses and the galleries themselves, with the south-facing switch house being earmarked for phase two of the development. Similarly, the 93 metre tower looming above the river façade was retained, and is due to become an observation platform during the second phase of building.

The architects' boldest move was the inclusion of a glazed 'light beam', which runs the entire length of the building, at roof level. 'This body of light was to pour daylight into the rooms on the top floor of the gallery and, at night, the direction of the artificial illumination would be reversed and magically shine into the London Sky.'[2]

Unlike the disastrous Millennium Dome, the Tate is fast becoming a popular icon and, on an urban scale, the museum has contributed significantly to the regeneration of the deprived borough of Southwark.

1 Rowan Moore and Raymund Ryan. *Building Tate Modern* (London: Tate Gallery Publishing, 2000), p. 12.

2 Ibid., p. 127.

Site plan of existing Bankside Power Station

Opposite The roof level 'light beam' draws natural light into the galleries during the day, and is seen to glow at night

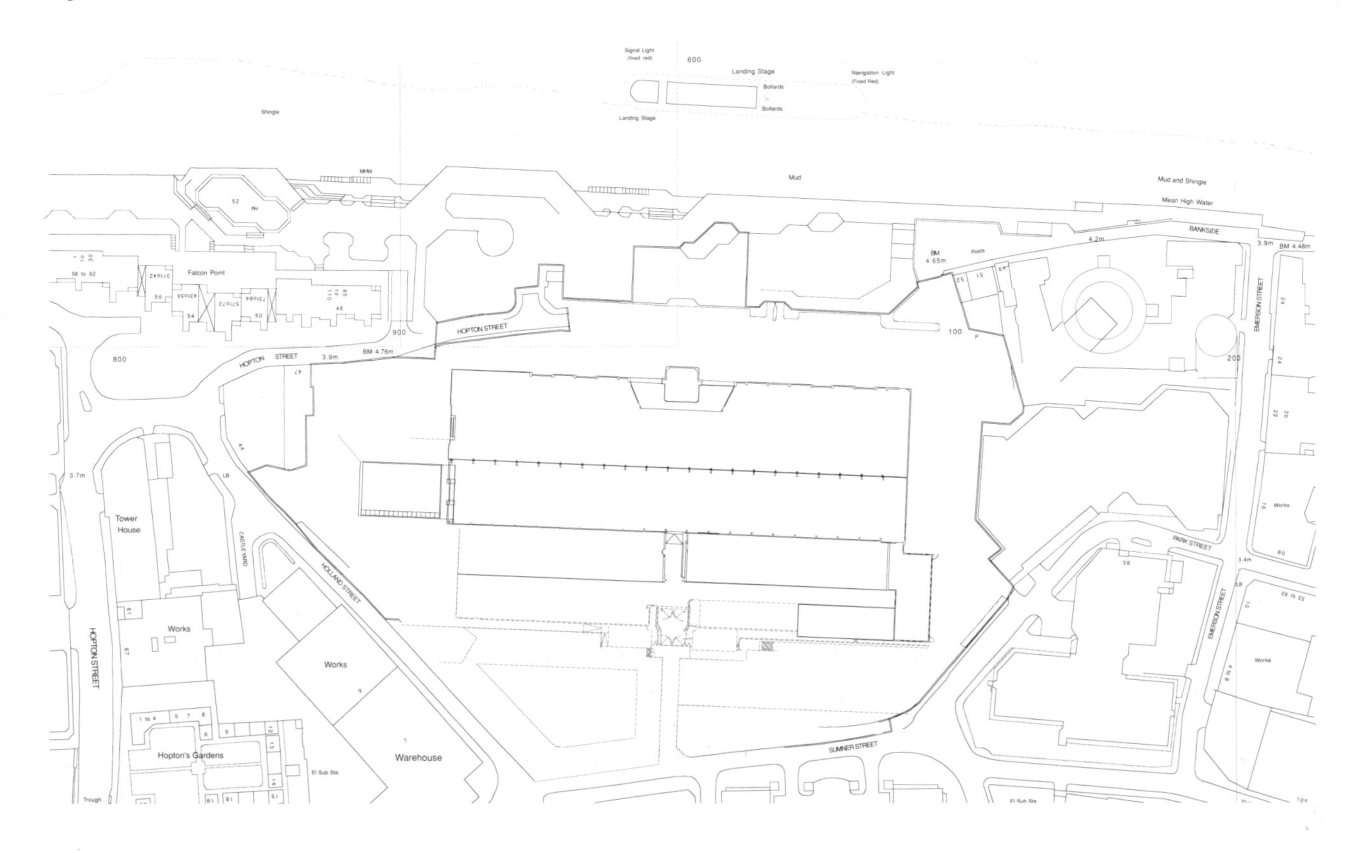

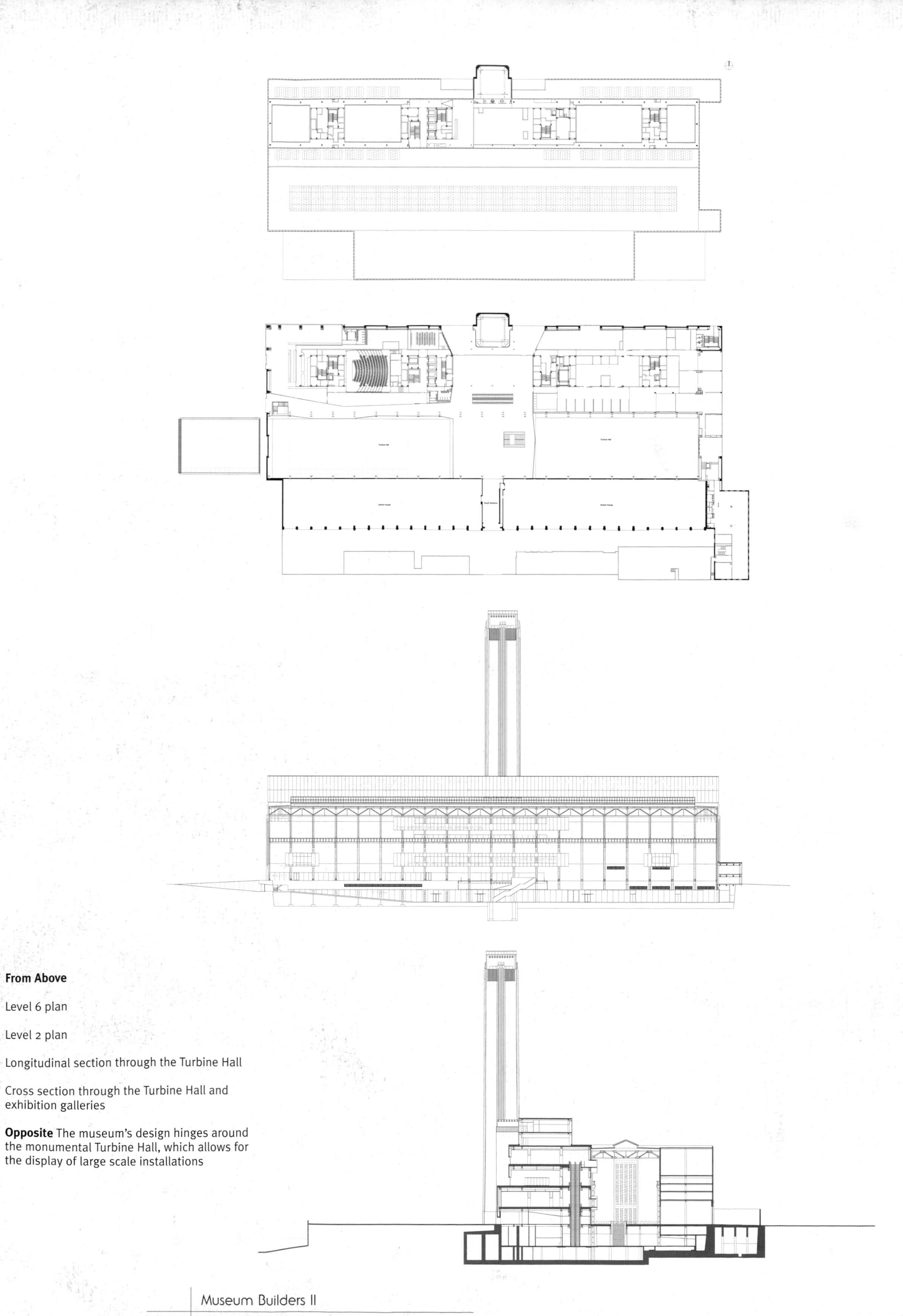

From Above

Level 6 plan

Level 2 plan

Longitudinal section through the Turbine Hall

Cross section through the Turbine Hall and exhibition galleries

Opposite The museum's design hinges around the monumental Turbine Hall, which allows for the display of large scale installations

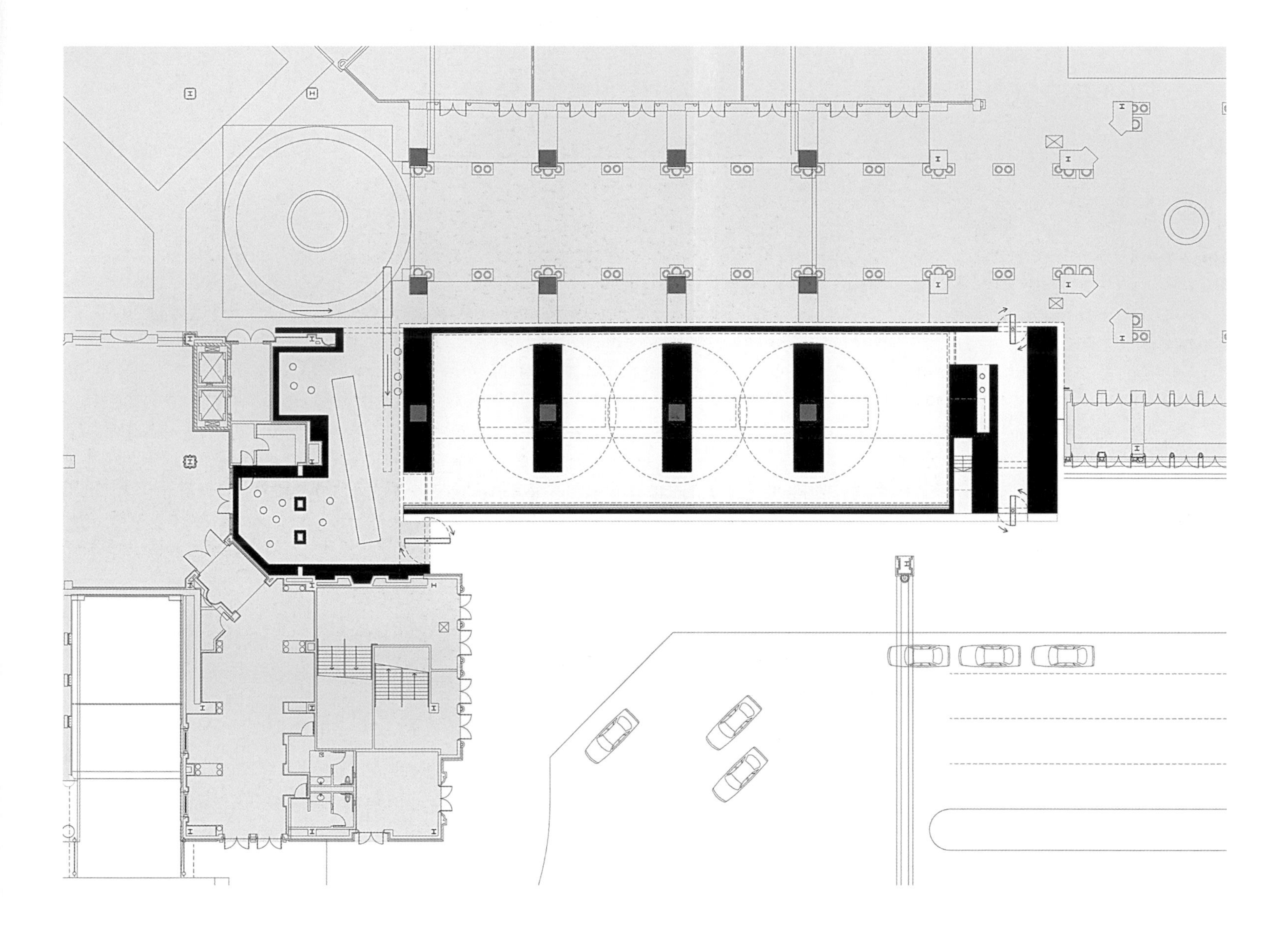

Top Ground floor plan of the Guggenheim Hermitage Museum

Bottom Main elevation of the Guggenheim Hermitage Museum

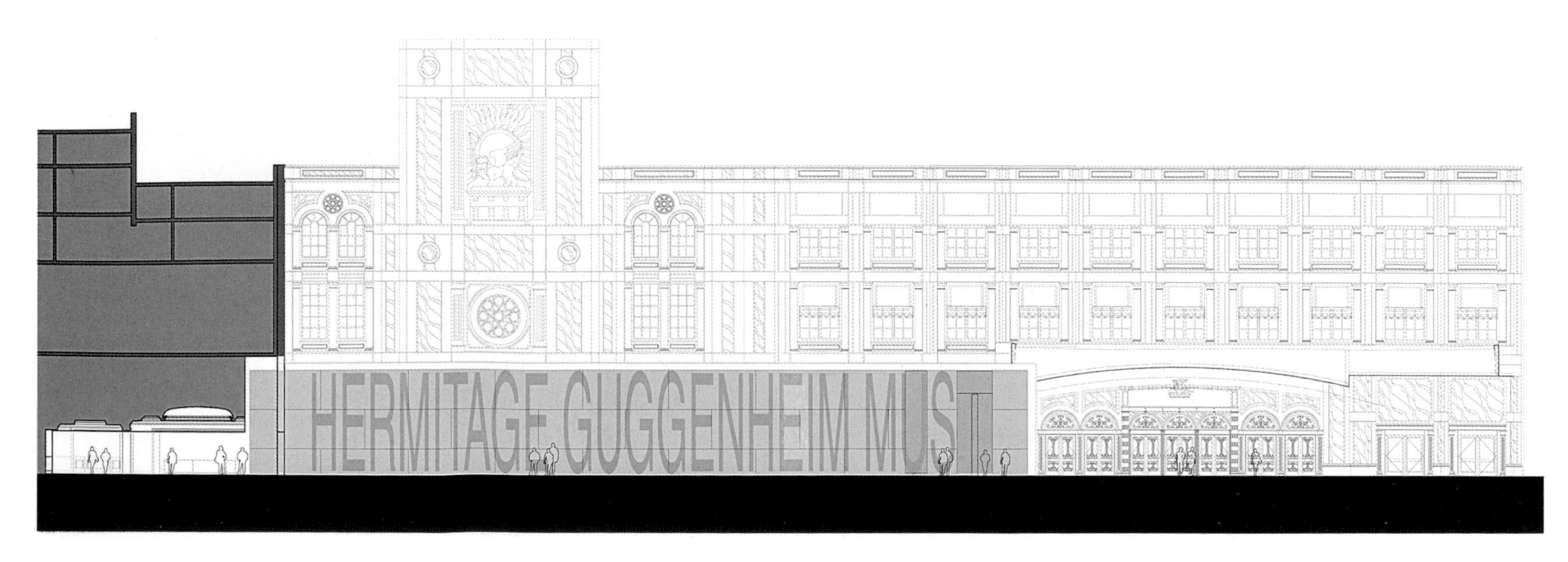

Rem Koolhaas

GUGGENHEIM LAS VEGAS AND GUGGENHEIM HERMITAGE MUSEUMS

Las Vegas **2001**

Las Vegas has become an unlikely recent outpost of the Guggenheim art empire. Rem Koolhaas, of Office for Metropolitan Architecture, was commissioned to design two museums – the Guggenheim Las Vegas and the Guggenheim Hermitage – within the Baroque pastiche of the Venetian Hotel, throwing up a startling contrast between the kitsch pop culture of Vegas, and the programme of 'high' art espoused by the Guggenheim.

The largest of the two discrete gallery spaces, the Guggenheim Las Vegas, plugs a vacant 'hole' adjacent to the hotel, with a simple, almost cubic volume. In part quasi-industrial, the space contains a large trench incised into its concrete floor, and a vast metal door, painted in black and orange chevrons, which occupies one whole façade. Flexibility is ensured, as the trench that accommodates a basement level gallery and generous stairway can be floored over with steel and glass panels to provide uninterrupted exhibition space at ground level, and the hinged door can be opened to admit large-scale installations. This cool functionalism is offset with ironic reference to high culture: a large blind depicting *God Creating Adam* from Michelangelo's Sistine Chapel ceiling provides 'a rare moment of exegesis'.[1]

A short walk from this gallery through the casino brings one to the Guggenheim Hermitage Museum that occupies a long, narrow gallery adjacent to the hotel's front façade. Although materially it is rather different from the other space, with COR-Ten steel cladding on both interior and exterior, a dialogue is created with its nearby sister gallery, as 'it represents, in both size and shape, the space excavated to form the trench in the Las Vegas Guggenheim'.[2] Most noticeable here though, is the startling collision between Koolhaas's restrained contemporary intervention and the theatrical Baroque of the existing hotel: 'It's as if a hammer has been dropped onto a large meringue pie'.[3]

1 Mark Irving. 'Another lesson from Las Vegas', *Domus*, no. 843, Dec. 2001, p. 112.
2 Ibid., p. 116.
3 Ibid.

Section through the Guggenheim Hermitage Museum, with the kitsch façade of the Venetian Hotel behind

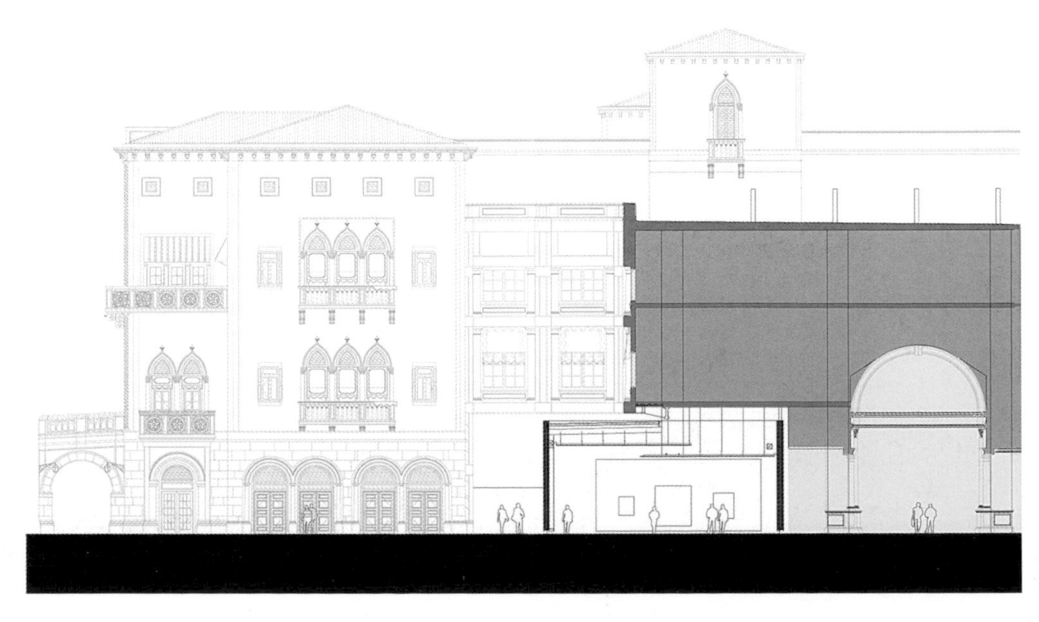

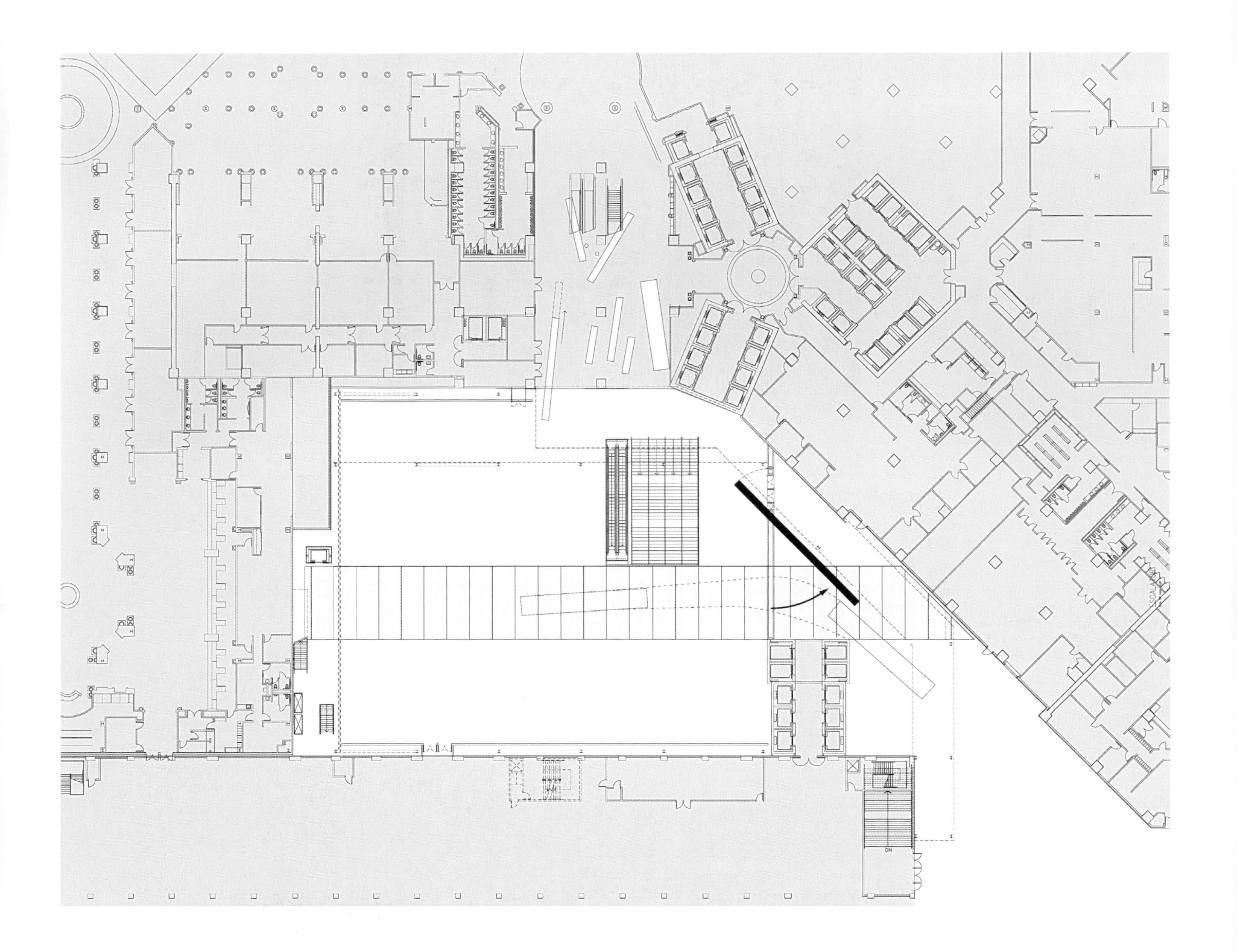

Above Plan of the Guggenheim Las Vegas, showing the large removable floor plate, which increases the display space

Below Elevated view of a model of the Guggenheim Hermitage Museum, which runs along the front façade of the Venetian Hotel

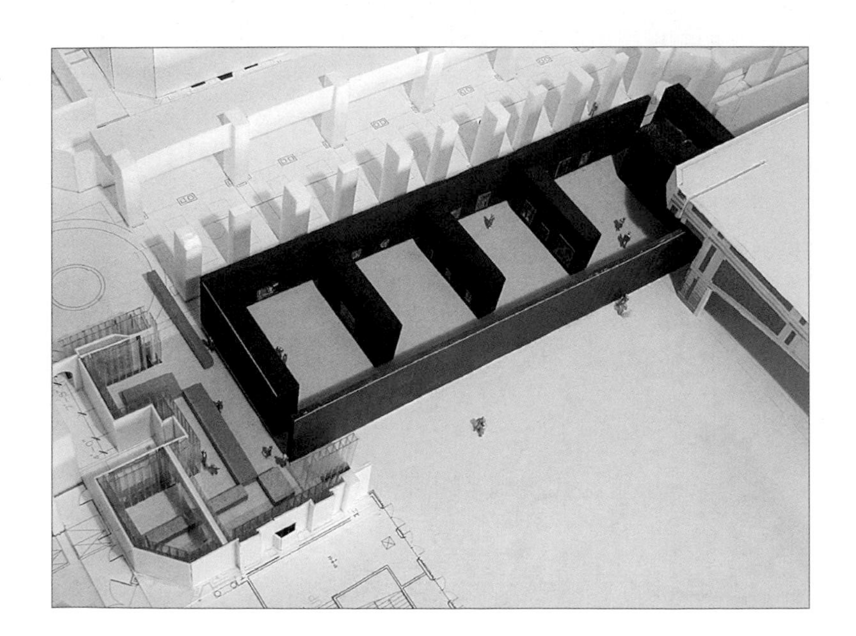

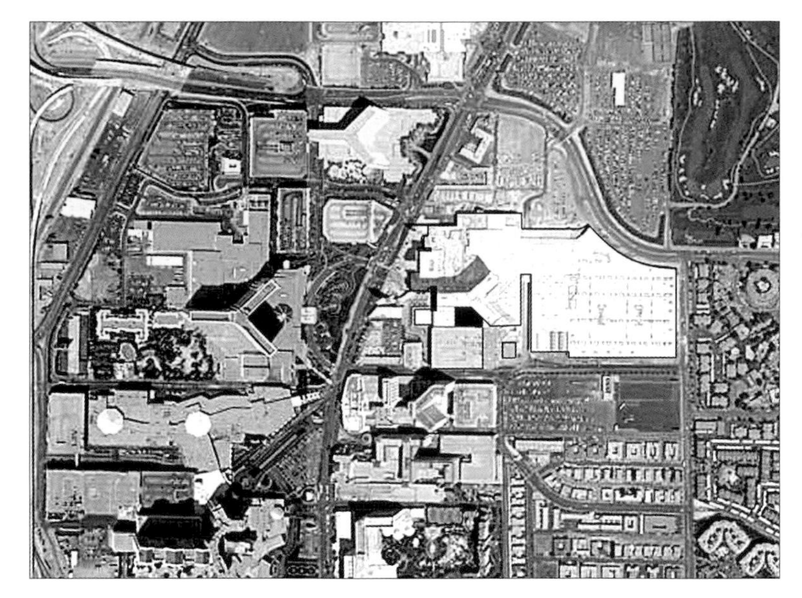

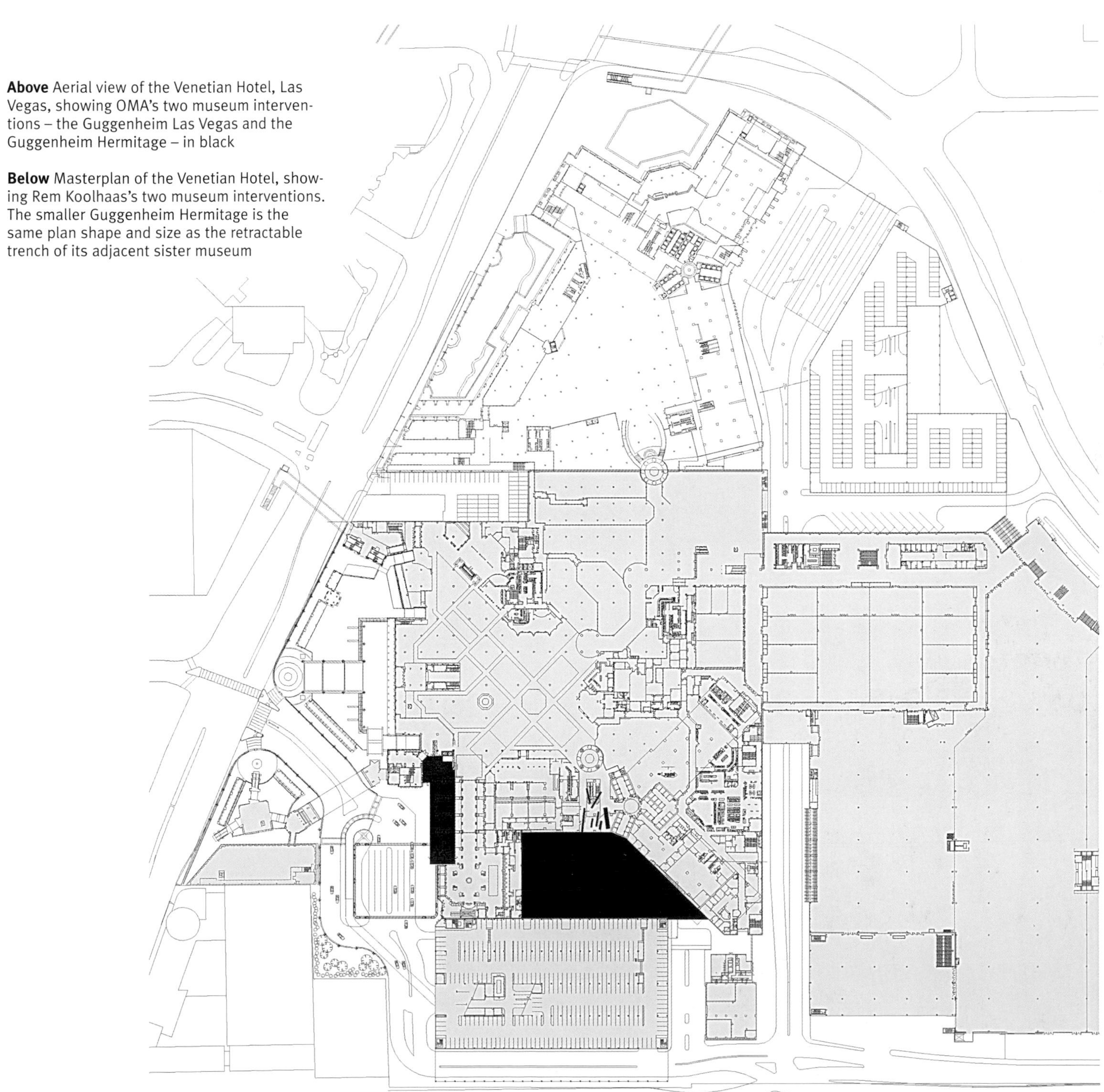

Above Aerial view of the Venetian Hotel, Las Vegas, showing OMA's two museum interventions – the Guggenheim Las Vegas and the Guggenheim Hermitage – in black

Below Masterplan of the Venetian Hotel, showing Rem Koolhaas's two museum interventions. The smaller Guggenheim Hermitage is the same plan shape and size as the retractable trench of its adjacent sister museum

Glazed curtain walling and a rooftop viewing box are anchored between the corner service towers of the retained brick planes

Dominic Williams with Ellis Williams Architects

BALTIC THE CENTRE FOR CONTEMPORARY ART

Gateshead **2002**

BALTIC the Centre for Contemporary Art, located on the south bank of the River Tyne, embodies two of the most prevalent themes in contemporary museum architecture: urban regeneration and the transformation of industrial building stock for cultural use.

Urban regeneration lies at the heart of this project, which is the flagship of a 15-year scheme to redevelop Gateshead quayside and the surrounding area, and to create 1,840 new homes and 1,500 new jobs. The Baltic Flour Mill, completed in 1950, was chosen to house the new centre, and, in 1994, Dominic Williams with Ellis Williams Architects were appointed as project architects. They pronounced their intention to 'retain as much of the existing character and fabric of the building as possible, whilst clearly and unambiguously announcing the structure's new purpose'.[1]

The original mill building was strongly vertical, being essentially composed of two parallel, sheer brick façades, running from east to west, sandwiched between which was a tightly packed grillage of concrete silos. The architects chose to retain the imposing brick layers, whilst removing practically all the silos within, which were incompatible with the new art space function. Four new horizontal steel floors were then inserted inside the skin, and the east and west façades were fully glazed, to flood light into the galleries and enable dramatic views of the river, both up- and down-stream. Corner service towers, a projecting rooftop viewing box, a discrete low-rise visitor facility and careful external landscaping completed the major elements of the scheme.

Externally, then, the building has retained much of its former character, enlivened by the newly transparent east and west façades, which symbolically open the centre to the public. Internally, however, the transformation required to produce flexible display and support spaces was much more radical, although as the architect explains, the original process of production is echoed in the building's new life: 'The original function of the building was to collect, contain and distribute flour through the unseen workings of the silos. In many ways these activities will be unchanged, with the building now refocused to a new use. Works will come, be created, and travel on from the place, the function less secret though still housed between its sheer walls'.[2]

1 Ellis Williams Architects. 'The Baltic Flour Mills – International Gallery of the Contemporary Arts', *Design Report, Stage D*, 3 July 1996.

2 'Baltic Flour Mills, Overview Document', *Gateshead MBC*, 1996.

Night view towards the BALTIC, through the Gateshead Millennium Bridge

Perspective sketch, highlighting the strong verticality of the scheme

Opposite top Interior perspective of the Level 4 art space

Opposite bottom Reflections of visitors and the River Tyne beyond in the centre's glazing

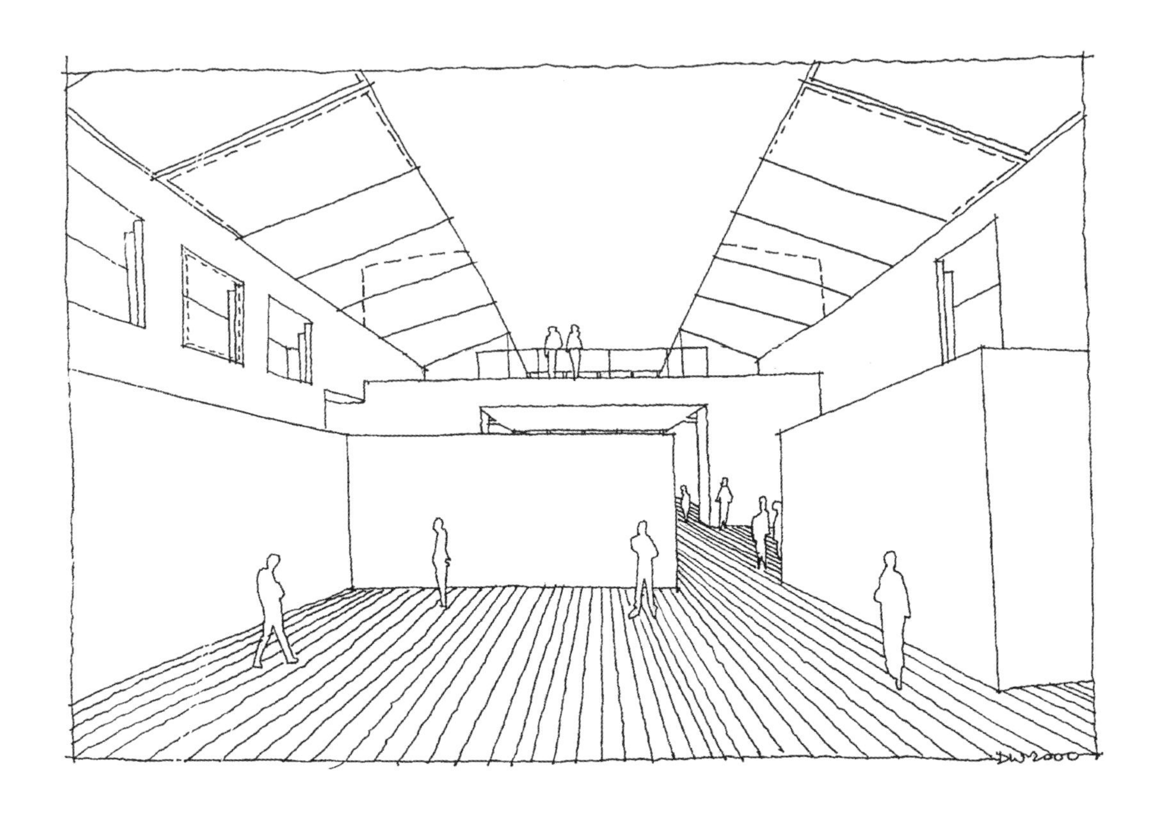
DW2000

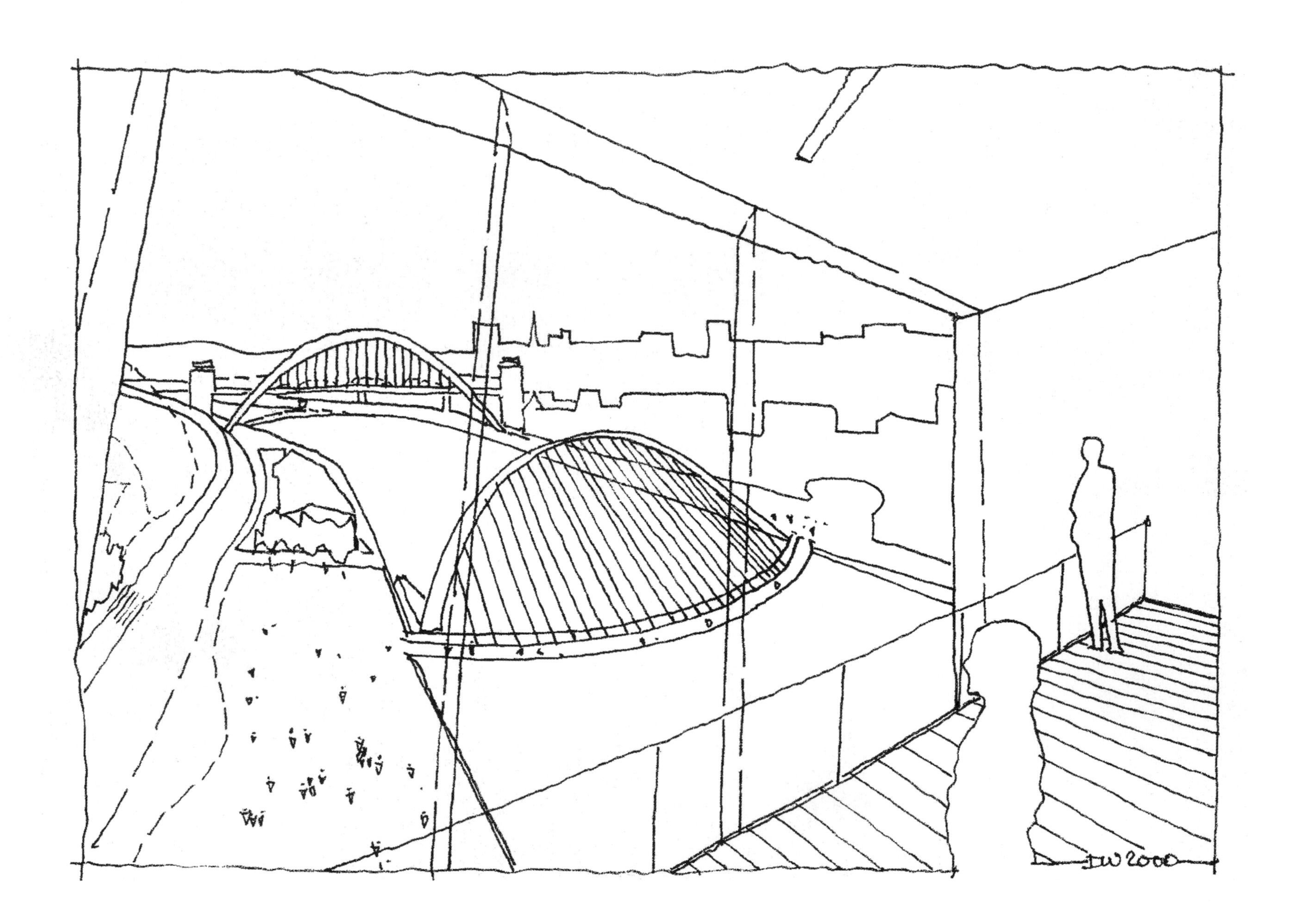
DW2000

Opposite top The glazed east and west façades allow river views up- and down-stream, and open the building to its new public

Opposite bottom Architect's impression of the vista from the level 5 viewing box down river towards the Gateshead Millennium and Tyne bridges

Below View up the transparent lift shaft

PROJECT INFORMATION

The following information has been collated from material provided by the architects. All costs should be taken as a guide only.

MUSEUM OF SCOTLAND
Location: Edinburgh, Scotland
Architect: Benson + Forsyth
Project Manager: Turner & Townsend Project Management
Structural Engineer: Anthony Hunt Associates
Service Engineer: Waterman Gore
Quantity Surveyor: Davis Langdon & Everest
Contractor: Bovis
Lighting Consultant: Kevan Shaw Lighting Design
Acoustic Consultant: Arup Acoustics
Date of Design: 1991
Period of Construction: 1996–1998
Total Floor Area: 12,489 m²
Building Cost: £64 million

CANADIAN MUSEUM OF CIVILIZATION
Location: Hull, Quebec, Canada
Client: Government of Canada; Canada Museums Construction Corporation
Architect: Douglas J. Cardinal Architect Ltd., and Tetreault, Parent, Languedoc and Associates
Construction Manager: Concordia Construction Management Company
Structural Engineer: Asselin, Benoit, Boucher, Ducharme, Lapointe, Inc.
Mechanical Engineer: Bouthillette, Parizeau and Associates
Electrical Engineer: Dessau Consultants
Landscape Architect: EDA Collaborative Inc./ Parent, Latreille and Associates
Date of Completion: June 1989

TE PAPA TONGAREWA THE NATIONAL MUSEUM OF NEW ZEALAND
Location: Wellington, New Zealand
Client: Museum of New Zealand Project Development Board
Architect: Jasmax Architects Ltd.
Competition Authors: Ivan Mercep, Pete Bossley, Pip Cheshire
Project Manager: Carson Group Project Management Ltd.
Civil and Structural Engineer: Holmes Arup Joint Venture
Geotechnical Engineer: Tonkin and Taylor Ltd.
Mechanical/Hydraulics
Engineer: Connell Wagner Rankine & Hill Ltd.
Landscape Architect: Boffa Miskell Partners Ltd.
Acoustic Consultant: Marshall Day Associates Ltd.
Date of Completion: 1998

IMPERIAL WAR MUSEUM NORTH
Location: Manchester, England
Client: The Trustees of the Imperial War Museum, London
Architect: Studio Daniel Libeskind
Associate Architect: Leach Rhodes Walker
Project Manager: Gardiner and Theobald Management Services
Structural Engineer: Arup
Services Engineer: Mott MacDonald
Quantity Surveyor: Turner and Townsend
Exhibition Designer: Event and Real Studios
Contractor: Sir Robert McAlpine, Ltd.
Date of Competition: 1997
Date of Completion: 2001
Date of Opening: 2002
Structure: Steel structure on concrete, aluminium cladding, rendered façade
Site Area: 9,000 m²
Total Floor Area: 6,500 m²
Building Cost: £15.6 million

JEWISH MUSEUM
Location: Berlin, Germany
Client: Land Berlin
Architect: Studio Daniel Libeskind
Structural Engineer: GSE Tragwerkplaner, IGW Ingenieurgruppe Wiese
Civil Engineer: Cziesielski + Partner
Structure: Reinforced concrete with zinc façade
Landscape Architect: Müller, Knippschild, Wehberg
Cost and Site Control: Arge Beusterirn and Lubic
Lighting Consultant: Lichtplanung Dinnebier KG, Wuppertal
Date of Competition: 1989
Date of Completion: 1999
Date of Opening: 2001
Site Area: 15,000 m²
Total Floor Area: 12,000 m²
Building Cost: US$ 40.05 million

UNITED STATES HOLOCAUST MEMORIAL MUSEUM
Location: Washington D.C., USA
Client: The United States Holocaust Memorial Council
Architect: Pei Cobb Freed & Partners James Ingo Freed
Associate Architect: Notter Finegold & Alexander
Structural Engineer: Weiskopf & Pickworth
Mechanical/Electrical
Engineer: Cosentini Associates LLP
Lighting Consultant: Jules Fisher & Paul Marantz
Exhibition Consultant: Ralph Appelbaum Associates, Inc.
Theatre Consultant: Jules Fishers Associates
Site Area: 1.7 acres
Total Floor Area: 258,000 ft²
Period of Design: Oct. 1986–Oct. 1989
Period of Construction: Oct. 1989–April 1993

CHIKATSU-ASUKA HISTORICAL MUSEUM
Location: Minamikawachi-gun, Osaka, Japan
Architect: Tadao Ando
Structural Engineer: Ascoral Engineering Associates
Structure: 2 storeys and 1 basement, rigid frame reinforced, concrete
Period of Design: April 1990–Nov. 1991
Period of Construction: Dec. 1991–Mar. 1994
Site Area: 14,318 m²
Building Area: 3,408 m²
Total Floor Area: 5,925 m²

VULCANIA: THE EUROPEAN CENTRE OF VOLCANISM
Location: St Ours-les-Roches, Auvergne, France
Client: Auvergne Regional Council President V. Giscard d'Estaing
Architect: Hans Hollein
Environmental Consultant/ Landscape Architect: Gilles Clement
Project Manager: S.E.M. Volcans
Scenography: Rainer Verbizh
Site Area: 57 hectares
Date of Conception: 1992
Period of Design: 1994–1996
Period of Construction: July 1997–Feb. 2002

FUKUI PREFECTURAL DINOSAUR MUSEUM
Location: Katsuyama City, Fukui Prefecture, Japan
Client: Fukui Prefectural Government
Architect: Kisho Kurokawa Architect & Associates
Structural Engineer: Takumi Orimoto Structural Engineers and Associates
Mechanical Engineer: Inuzuka Engineering Consultants
Contractor: Kumagaigumi, Maeda Construction
Period of Design: 1996–1998
Period of Construction: 1998–2000
Structure: Steel structure, steel reinforced concrete, and reinforced concrete, 1 basement + 3 storeys
Total Floor Area: 15,000 m^2

DOMUS, HOME OF MAN
Location: La Coruña, Spain
Client: La Coruña Council
Programme: Interactive science centre
Architects: Arata Isozaki and Cesar Portela Associate
Associate Architects: T. Tange; M. Hori; N. Ogawa; I. Peraza; A. Casares; F.Garrido; J.L. Gahona; P. Sánchez; F. José; A. Suárez
Structure: Reinforced concrete structure, granite cladding
Total Floor Area: 3300 m^2
Date of Completion: April 1995
Building Cost: 1500 million Pesetas

NATIONAL MARITIME MUSEUM CORNWALL
Location: Falmouth, Cornwall, England
Client: Southwest of England Regional Development Authority
Architect: Long & Kentish Architects
Engineer: Ove Arup & Partners
Quantity Surveyor: Davis Langdon Everest
Contractor: Alfred McAlpine Construction
Superstructure: Interserve
Exhibition Designer: Land Design Studio
Exhibition: Scena
Period of Design: 1996–1999
Period of Construction: 1999–2002

KUNSTHAL ROTTERDAM
Location: Rotterdam, Netherlands
Client: City of Rotterdam
Architect: Office for Metropolitan Architecture, Rem Koolhaas
Associate Architects: Fuminori Hoshino; Tony Adams; Isaac Batenburg; Leo van Immerzeel; Herman Jacobs; Edu Arroyo; Jim Njoo; Marc Peeters; Ron Steiner; Jeroen Thomas; Patricia Blaisse
Engineer: Ove Arup; Cecil Balmond
Period of Design: 1988–1989
Date of Completion: Oct. 1992
Total Floor Area: 3400 m^2
Building Cost: 14.5 million Euros

CARTIER FOUNDATION FOR CONTEMPORARY ART
Location: Paris, France
Client: Cartier S.A.
Architect: Jean Nouvel
Project Architect: Didier Braoult
Associate Architects: P.A. Bohnet; L. Ininguez; P.Mathieu; V. Morteau; G. Potel; S. Ray; S. Robert
Structural Engineer: Ove Arup & Partners
Façade Consultant: Arnaud de Bussière et Associés
Air Conditioning: Reidweg et Gendre
Landscaping: Ingénieur et Paysage
Period of Construction: 1991–1994

SAN FRANCISCO MUSEUM OF MODERN ART
Location: San Francisco, California, USA.
Client: Museum of Modern Art Foundation, San Francisco
Architect: Mario Botta
Associate Architect: Hellmuth, Obata and Kassabaum Inc.
Project Manager: Bechtel International Company
Period of Design: 1989–1992
Period of Construction: 1992–1995
Total Floor Area: 18,500 m^2
Volume: 100,000 m^2
Dimensions: Length 60m x 83m, height 44m

MODERN AND CONTEMPORARY ART MUSEUM OF TRENTO AND ROVERETO
Location: Rovereto, Province of Trento, Italy
Client: City of Rovereto, Autonomous Province of Trento
Architect: Mario Botta
Associate Architect: Giulio Andreolli
Project Manager: Contec Ing. Maurizio Cossato
Technical Engineer: Manens Intertecnica
Contractor: Lamaro Appalti Spa
Programme: Exhibition galleries, auditorum, administration, offices, library and historic archives with exhibition rooms and reading hall
Period of Design: 1992–1993
Period of Construction: 1996–2002
Total Floor Area: 20,800 m^2
Volume: 140,000 m^2
Building Cost: US$ 55 million

CHICAGO MUSEUM OF CONTEMPORARY ART
Location: Chicago, Illinois, USA
Architect: Kleihues + Kleihues
Project Manager: Schal Bovis, Inc.
Engineer: Ove Arup
Landscape Architect: Daniel Weinbach & Partners
Lighting Consultant: Claude R. Engle
Period of Design: 1991–1995

Period of Construction: 1994–1996
Programme: Museum of contemporary art, services, parking and exterior landscaping
Total Floor Area: 10,000 m²
Building Cost: US$ 45 million

GUGGENHEIM MUSEUM BILBAO
Location: Bilbao, Spain
Architect: Frank O. Gehry
Associate Architects: Randy Jefferson; Vano Haritunians; Douglas Hanson; Edwin Chan
Scheme: Museum of contemporary art
Programme: Exhibition halls, conservation rooms, auditorium,restaurant, shops, stores and outdoor plaza for public use
Date of Design: 1990
Date of Completion: 1997

STOCKHOLM MUSEUMS OF MODERN ART AND ARCHITECTURE
Location: Stockholm, Sweden
Client: Swedish National Board of Public Works
Architect: Rafael Moneo
Associate Architect: White Architecture
Collaborators: Michael Bischoff; Robert Robinowitz; Lucho Marcial
Structural Engineer: Tyrens Byggkonsult
Lighting Engineer: KTH Arkitektur/belysningslara
Lighting Consultant: Fisher Marantz Renfro Stone
Acoustic Consultant: Ingemanssons Akustik
Date of Design: 1991
Period of Construction: 1994–1997
Museum of Modern Art: 20,000 m²
Museum of Architecture: 6,000 m²
Cost: US$ 52.5 million

GALICIAN CENTRE FOR CONTEMPORARY ART
Location: Santiago de Compostella, Spain
Client: Santiago City Hall
Architect: Alvaro Siza; Joan Falgueras; Mona Trautman; Jordi Fossas; Rafael Soto; Angel Fibla; Joan Genis; Joan Claudi- Minguel; Jordi Maristany; Yves Stump; João Sabugúerio; Jane Considine; Tiago Faria; Anton Graf; Cecilia Lau; Elsiario Miranda; Luis Cardoso; Miguel Nery; Carles Muro
Engineer: EuroConsult
Landscape Architect: Isabel Aguirre
Contractor: Construtora S. José
Programme: Exhibition halls, auditorium, library, documentation and administration centres, book-shop, cafeteria, service areas, administrative offices, management office and viewing terrace
Date of Completion: 1997

SERRALVES MUSEUM
Location: Serralves Park, Oporto, Portugal
Architect: Alvaro Siza; Clemente Menéres Semide; Tiago Faria; Christian Gaenshirt; Sofia Thenaisie Coelho; Edison Okumura; Abilio Mourão; Avelino Silva; João Sabugueiro; Cristina Ferreirinha; Taichi Tomuro; Daniela Antonucci; Francesca Montalto; Francisco Raina Guedes de Carvalho
Structural Engineer: GOP-João Maria Sobraira
Mechanical Engineer: GET-Alfredo Costa Pereira
Landscape Architect: João Gomes da Silva
Contractor: Edifer, S.A.
Programme: Exhibition galleries, administrative offices, book shop, gift shop, auditorium, restaurant, terrace and exterior landscaping
Date of Completion: June 1999

TOYOTA MUNICIPAL MUSEUM OF ART
Location: Toyota City, Aichi Prefecture, Japan
Client: Toyota City
Architect: Taniguchi and Associates
Structural Engineer: Masao Saito + Kozo Keikaku Plus One
Mechanical Engineer: Chiku Engineering Consultants
Lighting Consultant: TL Yamagiwa Laboratory Inc.
Landscape Architect: Peter Walker, William Johnson and Partners
Contractors: Joint venture of Taisei Corporation, Taikei Construction Co., Ltd., and Ito Construction Co., Ltd.
Structure: Reinforced concrete, partly steel frame and reinforced concrete; 2 basements + 3 storeys
Period of Design: Nov. 1991–Mar. 1993
Period of Construction: Aug. 1993–June 1995
Site Area: 30,041 m²
Total Floor Area: 11,238 m²

FUKUI CITY MUSEUM OF ART
Location: Fukui City, Fukui Prefecture, Japan
Client: Fukui Municipal Government
Architect: Kisho Kurokawa
Structural Engineer: Zoken Consultant Inc.
Mechanical Engineer: Tatsuya Urashima; Inuzuka Engineering Consultants
Fire Prevention: Ataka Fire Safety Design Office
Contractor: Muranaka, Maekawa, and Marusho Corporation
Period of Design: Nov. 1993–Dec. 1994
Period of Construction: Mar. 1995–Sept. 1996
Structure: Steel structure, partly reinforced concrete 3 storeys + 1 basement
Total Floor Area: 5,262.84 m²
Cost: 2,874,800,000 Yen

LOIS & RICHARD ROSENTHAL CENTER FOR CONTEMPORARY ART
Location: Cincinnati, USA
Architect: Zaha Hadid Architects
Associate Architect: KZF Design, Inc.
Structural Engineer: THP Limited, Inc.
Construction Manager: Turner Construction Company
Acoustic Consultant: Ove Arup & Partners
Lighting Consultant: Office for Visual Interaction, Inc.
Services Consultant: Heapy Engineering
Security Consultant: Steven R. Keller & Associates
Theatre Consultant: Charles Cosler Theater

Security Consultant: Steven R. Keller & Associates
Theatre Consultant: Charles Cosler Theater Design, Inc.
Period of Construction: May 2001–May 2003
Total Floor Area: 87,000 ft²
Total Cost: US$ 35.7 million

NATIONAL CENTRE FOR CONTEMPORARY ARTS
Location: Rome, Italy
Client: Italian Ministry of Culture
Architect: Zaha Hadid Architects
Associate Architect: ABT, Rome
Structural Engineers: Anthony Hunt Associates; The OK Design Group
Services Engineer: Max Fordham and Partners
Lighting Consultant: Equation Lighting
Acoustic Consultant: Paul Gillieron Acoustic
Costing: MDA International
Curator: Bruce McAllister
Period of Project: 1998–2005
Total Surface Area: 30,000 m²

SPIRAL EXTENSION TO THE VICTORIA & ALBERT MUSEUM
Location: South Kensington, London, England
Client: City of London
Architect: Studio Daniel Libeskind
Structural Engineer: Arup; Cecil Balmond
Structure: Steel, ceramic tile cladding
Date of Competition: 1996
Date of Completion: 2006
Net Area: 8,200 m²
Gross Area: 10,000 m²
Building Cost: US$ 54.5 million
Total Cost: US$ 90.75 million (fully fitted and art installed)

TATE MODERN
Location: London, England
Client: Tate Gallery
Architect: Herzog & de Meuron
Associate Architect: Sheppard Robson + Partners
Construction Manager: Schal International Management Ltd.
Structural Engineer: Ove Arup Partner
Services Engineer: Arup Services
Acoustic/
Lighting Consultant: OAP – Ove Arup Partner
Landscape Architect: Herzog & de Meuron in collaboration with Kienast Vogt + Partner
Façade Consultant: Emmer Phenniger
Interior Designers: Herzog & de Meuron in collaboration with Office for Design, Lumsden Design Partnership
Cost Consultant: Davis Langdon & Everest
Period of Competition: 1994–1995
Period of Design: 1995–1997
Period of Construction: 1997–2000
Total Floor Area: 34,000 m²
Total Exhibition Space: 6,000 m²
Building Cost: £134 million

GUGGENHEIM LAS VEGAS & GUGGENHEIM HERMITAGE MUSEUMS
Location: The Venetian Casino Resort, Las Vegas, USA
Client: The Venetian Casino Resort and the Solomon R. Guggenheim Foundation
Architect: Office for Metropolitan Architecture, Rem Koolhaas
Associate Architect: Stubbins Assoc.; Easley Hammer; Curtis Smith; Chris Leary
Consultants: Martin & Martin; Ove Arup & Partners; MSA Engineering; Syska & Hennessy; Rolf Jensen Associates
Contractor: Taylor International; Jim Mason; Bill Mason
Material: Guggenheim Las Vegas: steel, concrete, aluminium, glass Guggenheim Hermitage: Cor ten steel and wood
Programme: Guggenheim Las Vegas : flexible exhibition space and museum store of total 63,700 ft² Guggenheim Hermitage: flexible exhibition space and museum store of total 7,660 ft²
Exhibition Designer: The Art of the Motorcycle, design by The Gehry Partnership; Michelle Kaufmann; George Metzger
Period of Construction: Oct. 2000–Oct. 2001

BALTIC THE CENTRE FOR CONTEMPORARY ART
Location: Gateshead, England
Client: Gateshead Metropolitan Borough Council
Architect: Ellis Williams Architects Dominic Williams
Structural Engineer: Atelier One
Landscape Architect: Gateshead Metropolitan Borough Council Landscape Architects
Interior Designer: Julina Opie; Prof. Axelsson
Graphic Designer: Ulf Greger Nilsson and Henrik Nygren
Date of Competition: 1994
Date of Completion: July 2002
Area per floor: 750 m²

BIBLIOGRAPHY

Issues of Identity

Bennett, Tony. *The Birth of the Museum* (London and New York: Routledge, 1995).

Benson, Gordon and Alan Forsyth. *Museum of Scotland* (London: August Media in association with Benson + Forsyth, 1999).

Benson, Gordon. 'Benson + Forsyth', *Mac Mag*. Nov. 1991.

Bevan, Robert. 'Treasure Island', *Building Design*, no. 1340, 27 Feb. 1998.

Bossley, Pete. 'Concepts in Culture', *Architecture New Zealand*, 'The Designing of Te Papa', Special Edition, 1998.

Bossley, Pete. 'Redirect, Redevelop', *Architecture New Zealand*, 'The Designing of Te Papa', Special Edition, 1998.

Bossley, Pete. *Te Papa. An Architectural Adventure*, (Wellington: Te Papa Press, 1998).

Bossley, Pete. 'The Treaty', *Architecture New Zealand*, 'The Designing of Te Papa', Special Edition, 1998.

Calder, Jenni. *Museum of Scotland* (Edinburgh: NMS Publishing, 1998).

Cardinal, Douglas. *A Vision for the National Museum of Man* (Hull: Canadian Museum of Civilization, 1983).

Crowe, Norman. *Nature and the Idea of a Man-Made World*, (Cambridge, MA and London: MIT Press, 1995).

Curtis, William J.R. *Modern Architecture since 1900* (London: Phaidon Press, 1997).

French, Anne. 'Setting Standards', *Architecture New Zealand*, 'The Designing of Te Papa', Special Edition, 1998.

Giddens, Anthony. *The Consequences of Modernity* (Cambridge: Polity Press, 1990).

Hannah, Edith B. *Story of Scotland in Stone* (Edinburgh and London: Oliver Boyd, 1934).

Hay, George. *Architecture of Scotland* (London: Oriel Press, 1977).

Heumann Gurian, Elaine. 'A Ray of Hope', *Architecture New Zealand*, 'The Designing of Te Papa', Special Edition, 1998.

Hooper-Greenhill, Eilean. *Museums and the Shaping of Knowledge* (London and New York: Routledge, 1992).

Hunt, John. 'Process of Selection', *Architecture New Zealand*, 'The Designing of Te Papa', Special Edition, 1998.

Jackson, Martin. *Reflections* (Falmouth: National Maritime Museum Cornwall, 2002).

Jencks, Charles and others. 'New Science = New Architecture?', *Architectural Design*, vol. 67, no. 9/10, Sept./Oct. 1997.

Karp, Ivan and Steven D. Lavine. *Exhibiting Cultures. The Poetics and Politics of Museum Display* (Washington and London: Smithsonian Institution Press, 1991).

Keay, John and Julia. *Collins Encyclopedia of Scotland*, (London: HarperCollins Publishers, 1994).

Laforet, Andrea. *The Book of the Grand Hall* (Hull: Canadian Museum of Civilization,1992).

Libeskind, Daniel. *The Space of Encounter, Between the Lines* (New York: Universe Publishing, 2000).

Macdonald, George F. and Stephen Alsford. *A Museum for the Global Village* (Hull: Canadian Museum of Civilization, 1989).

Macdonald, Sharon and Gordon Fyfe. *Theorizing Museums. Representing Identity and Diversity in a Changing World* (Oxford and Cambridge: Blackwell Publishers, 1996).

McCrone, David. *Understanding Scotland: The Sociology of a Stateless Nation* (London and New York: Routledge, 1992).

McKay, Graham. 'Old Paradigm Jencks', *Architectural Review*, vol. 213, no. 1274, Apr. 2003.

McKean, Charles. *The Making of the Museum of Scotland* (Edinburgh: National Museums of Scotland Publishing, 2000).

Sarup, Madan. *Identity, Culture and the Postmodern World* (Edinburgh: Edinburgh University Press, 1996).

Steele, James. *Museum Builders* (London: Academy Editions, 1994).

Primary Sources

Architecture and Planning Group, National Museums of Canada. *Architectural Programme Synopsis*, 1983.

Te Papa Tongarewa the National Museum of New Zealand, *Architectural Brief*, Wellington, 1989.

Canadian Museum of Civilization. Grand Hall, *Exhibition Text.*

Imperial War Museum North. *Wall Text.*

Museum of Scotland

Baillieu, Amanda. 'Record Entry for Scottish Museum Competition', *Building Design*, no. 1031, 19 Apr. 1991, p. 3.

Baillieu, Amanda. 'Stars Eclipsed in Edinburgh', *Building Design*, no. 1035, 17 May 1991, p. 1.

Baillieu, Amanda and John Welsh. 'A Profession United ... A Press Divided; Act of Union', *Building Design*, no. 1046, 16/23 Aug. 1991, pp. 3, 12–13.

Benson + Forsyth. *Museum of Scotland* (London: August Media, 1999).

Benson, Gordon. 'Benson + Forsyth', *Mac Mag*, Nov. 1991.

Cannon, Dick. 'Scotland's Brave Heart', *RIBA Journal*, vol. 105, no. 12, Dec. 1998, pp. 18–19.

'Benson & Forsyth Scots Showcase', *Architects' Journal*, vol. 194, no. 7, 14 Aug. 1991, p. 9.

'Berth of a Nation III', *Building Design*, no. 1043, 12 July 1991, pp. 16–18, 20.

'Creating a Scottish Modern Tradition', *Architects' Journal*, vol. 194, no. 8/9, 21/28 Aug. 1991, p. 10.

'National Museum of Scotland', *RIBA Journal*, vol. 98, no. 9, Sept. 1991, p. 15.

'Prince Quits in Row Over Museum Contest', *Building*, vol. 256, no. 7709 (32/33), 16 Aug. 1991, p. 8.

'Wales Welshes on Scotland', *Architectural Review*, vol. 189, no. 1135, Sept. 1991, p. 9.

Jencks, Charles and others. 'Contemporary Museums', *Architectural Design*, vol. 67, no. 11/12, Nov./Dec. 1997, pp. 72–75.

Keown, Richard. 'Edinburgh Seeks Competition Entries for 25 Million Pound Museum', *Building Design*, no. 1014, 30 Nov. 1990, p. 4.

McKean, Charles. *The Making of the Museum of Scotland* (Edinburgh: NMS Publishing, 2000).

Macmillan, Duncan. 'A National Tragedy', *Museums Journal*, vol. 91, no. 11, Nov. 1991, pp. 20–21.

Macneil, James 'Hard Craft', *Building*, vol. 262, no. 7991 (20), 23 May 1997, pp. 42–47.

Melhuish, Clare. 'Scotch Missed', *Building Design*, no. 1047, 6 Sept 1991, pp. 18–19.

Murphy, Richard and others. 'Edinburgh Tour de Force', *Architects' Journal*, vol. 209, no. 8, 25 Feb. 1999, pp. 26–35.

Powell, Kenneth. 'Made for Scotland', *Architects' Journal*, vol. 207, no. 18, 7 May 1998, pp. 28–29.

Psarra, Sophia and Tadeusz Grajewski. 'Architecture, Narrative and Promenade in Benson & Forsyth's Museum of Scotland', *ARQ: Architectural Research Quarterly*, vol. 4, no. 2, 2000, pp. 122–136.

Singmaster, Deborah. 'Scotland Today', *Architects' Journal*, vol. 207, no. 18, 7 May 1998, pp. 33–47.

Solomon, Shoshanna. 'Museum Shortlist: The Famous Five', *Architects' Journal*, vol. 194, no. 10, 4 Sept. 1991, pp. 12–13.

Spalding, Julian. 'Scotland's Real Story Hidden in the Detail', *Museums Journal*, vol. 99, no. 6, June 1999, pp. 20–21.

Spens, Michael and others. 'Special Issue. Cultural Contexts', *Architectural Review*, vol. 205, no. 1226, Apr. 1999, pp. 38–39.
Spring, Martin. 'The Rock: The National Museum of Scotland, Edinburgh', *Building*, vol. 263, no. 8057 (39), 25 Sept. 1998, pp. 42–49.
Thompson, Jessica Cargill. 'Competition Unveiled for 25 Million Pound Scottish Museum', *Building Design*, no. 970 (26), Jan. 1990, p. 10.
Welsh, John. 'Berth of a Nation', *Building Design*, no. 1039, 14 June 1991, pp. 18, 20, 22–25, 30–37.

Canadian Museum of Civilization

Architecture and Planning Group, National Museums of Canada. *Architectural Programme Synopsis* (Ottawa: National Museums of Canada, 1983).
Banerji, Anupam. 'Canadian Museum of Civilization', *A&U*, no. 7 (238), July 1990, pp. 7–39.
Boddy, Trevor. *The Architecture of Douglas Cardinal* (Edmonton: NeWest Press, 1989).
Bohigas, Oriol. 'A Museum in the Style of American Grand Speculation', *Section a*, vol.2, no. 2, Apr./May 1984, pp. 29–32.
Bonomo, Fabrizio. 'Canadian Museum of Civilization in Ottawa', *Arca*, no. 49, May 1991, pp. 97–98.
Bressani, Martin. 'Canadian Museum of Civilization, Hull, Quebec', *Canadian Architect*, vol. 34, no. 11, Nov. 1989, pp. 18–31.
'Douglas Cardinal's Design for the Canadian National Museum of Man', *International Journal of Museum Management and Curatorship*, vol. 4, no. 1, Mar. 1985, pp. 97–100.
Freedman, Adele. ' "Right-Sided" Museum for Ottawa', *Progressive Architecture*, vol. 70, no. 9, Sept. 1989, pp. 21, 24.
Hume, Christopher. 'Carved by Wind and Water', *Landscape Architecture*, vol. 79, no. 8, Oct. 1989, pp. 51–53.
MacDonald, George. 'Streets Are In At This Museum', *Canadian Heritage*, vol. 10, no. 5, Dec./Jan. 1984/1985, pp. 30–33, 49.
MacDonald, George and Douglas Cardinal. 'Building Canada's National Museum of Man: An Interprofessional Dialogue', *Museum*, vol. 38, no. 1 (149), 1986, pp. 9–15.
MacDonald, George F. and Stephen Alsford. *A Museum for the Global Village* (Hull: Canadian Museum of Civilization, 1989).
Sachner, Paul. 'Collective Memory', *Architectural Record*, vol. 178, no. 2, Feb. 1990, pp. 88–93.
Sharp, Dennis. 'Cardinal Virtues', *Building Design*, no. 1000, 24 Aug. 1990, pp. 12–13.

Te Papa Tongarewa the National Museum of New Zealand

Bohling, Steve. 'Do Cultures Clash or Click at New Zealand's National Museum?' *Architectural Record*, vol. 186, no. 4, Apr. 1998, p. 37.
Bossley, Pete. *Te Papa. An Architectural Adventure* (New Zealand: Te Papa Press, 1998).
Connolly, Pippa 'Museum of New Zealand Te Papa Tongarewa', *Arup Journal*, vol. 32, no. 3, 1997, pp. 3–9.
Cook, Nigel and John Hunt. 'Nationalistic Expression', *Architecture New Zealand*, Nov./Dec. 1990, pp. 18–23.
'Museum of New Zealand Te Papa Tongarewa', *Architecture New Zealand*, July/Aug. 1990, pp. 31–41.
'Museum of New Zealand Te Papa Tongarewa', *Constructional Review*, vol. 66, no. 2, May 1993, pp. 8–9.
'Te Papa Museum, Wellington', *Architecture Australia*, vol. 87, no. 3, May/June 1998, p. 20.
Eisenstadt Belasco, Claire. 'Combining Cultures in a New Zealand Museum', *Progressive Architecture*, vol. 71, no. 9, Sept. 1990, p. 27.
Harper, Jenny and Mark Taylor. 'Moller-fied?', *Architecture New Zealand*, no. 2, Mar./Apr. 2002, pp. 26–33.
Hunt, John and others. 'Special Issue. Te Papa: Concepts, Context, Structure', *Architecture New Zealand*, Feb. 1998, pp. 14–104.
Jasmax Competition Entry, 1990.
Niven, Stuart. 'Bicultural Condition at Museum's Heart', *Architecture New Zealand*, Sept./Oct. 1992, pp. 35–42.
Sutherland, John. 'National Symbol Evolves', *Architecture New Zealand*, Nov./Dec. 1995, pp. 76–79.
Te Papa Tongarewa Design Brief, 1989.

Imperial War Museum North

Andersen, Hans-Christian. 'War & Order: The Imperial War Museum North', *Museums Journal*, vol. 102, no. 8, Aug. 2002, p. 34.
Cork, Richard. 'Apocalypse North', *The Times*, 3 July 2002, p. 5.
Croft, Catherine. 'Rise & Shine', *Building Design. Supplement*, June 2001, pp. 10–13.
Dunster, David and others. 'Devastation into Destination: Libeskind in Salford', *Architecture Today*, no. 130, July 2002, pp. 42–57.
'A Globe Ripped to Pieces', *Daily Telegraph*, 29 June 2002.
'Seeing Action', *Blueprint*, no. 196, June 2002, p. 22.
'What's the Spec?', *Building*, vol. 267, no. 8225(10), 15 Mar. 2002, p. 70.
Gibson, Grant. 'Theatre of Battle', *Blueprint*, no. 199, Sept. 2002, p. 119.
Glancey, Jonathan. 'War and Peace and Quiet', *Guardian*, 22 April 2002, pp. 10–13.
Greaves, Katy. 'Mother of All Museums', *Blueprint*, no. 177, Nov. 2000, p. 30.
Griffin, Phil. 'The War Zone', *Building Design*, no. 1537, 14 June 2002, pp. 12–15.
Libeskind, Daniel. *Countersign* (London: Academy Editions, 1991).
Libeskind, Daniel. *Daniel Libeskind: The Space of Encounter* (London: Thames & Hudson, 2001).
Libeskind, Daniel. *Traces of the Unborn* (Ann Arbor, MI: The University of Michigan, College of Architecture & Urban Planning, c. 1995).
McLaren, Leah. 'Triumph Over Adversity', *The Globe and Mail*, 6 July 2002, p. R5.
Merry, Alison. *Daniel Libeskind: An Interpretation*, 1993.
Morrison, Richard. 'A Mind Like a Furnace', *The Times*, 3 July 2002, pp. 4–5.
Mulhearn, Deborah. 'A Life in Architecture: Jim Forrester', *Architects' Journal*, vol. 216, no. 1, 4 July 2002, p. 24.
Spring, Martin. 'War Poetry', *Building*, vol. 266, no. 8209(45), 9 Nov. 2001, pp. 40–47.
Street-Porter, Janet. 'Philosopher Who Creates Buildings that Perform to the Public', *The Independent*, 6 July 2002.
Sudjic, Deyan. 'War and Pieces', *The Observer*, 30 June 2002, Review.
Williams, Austin. 'Conflict Resolution', *Architects' Journal*, vol. 212, no. 14, 19 Oct. 2000, pp. 28–33.

Jewish Museum

Bunschoten, Raoul. *A Passage Through Silence and Light: Daniel Libeskind's Jewish Museum Extension to the Berlin Museum* (London: Black Dog Publishing, c. 1997).
De Michelis, Marco. 'The Jewish Museum, Berlin', *Domus*, no. 820, Nov. 1999, pp. 32–41.
'Berlin Museum with the Jewish Museum, Berlin', *GA Document*, no. 43, 1995, pp. 56–61.
Haslam, Michael. 'Jewish Museum, Berlin', *Architecture*

Today, no. 84, Jan. 1998, pp. 6–9.
Libeskind, Daniel. *Daniel Libeskind: Countersign* (London: Academy Editions, 1991).
Libeskind, Daniel. *The Space of Encounter: Between the Lines* (New York: Universe Publishing, 2000).
Libeskind, Daniel. 'The Jewish Museum, Berlin', *A&U*, no. 12(381), Dec. 1998, pp. 102–121.
Libeskind, Daniel and Helene Binet. *Jewish Museum Berlin* (Amsterdam: G+B Arts International, 1999).
Patterson, Richard and others. 'Special Issue: The Tragic in Architecture', *Architectural Design*, vol. 70, no. 5, Oct. 2000, pp. 68–75.
Schneider, Bernhard. *Jewish Museum Berlin: Between the Lines* (Munich and London: Prestel, 1999).

United States Holocaust Memorial Museum

Alden Branch, Mark. 'Museums', *Progressive Architecture*, vol. 71, no. 5, May 1990, pp. 124–128.
Dannatt, Adrian. 'Bearing Witness', *Building Design*, no. 1131, 2 July 1993, pp. 10–13.
'Auschwitz Inspiration for Memorial', *Architects' Journal*, vol. 187, no. 17, 27 Apr. 1988, p. 12.
'The United States Holocaust Memorial Museum', *Assemblage*, no. 9, June 1989, pp. 58–79.
'US Holocaust Memorial Museum Challenges Literal Architectural Interpretations of History', *Architectural Record*, vol. 181, no. 5, May 1993, p. 27.
Freiman, Zira. 'Memory too Politic', *Progressive Architecture*, vol. 76, no. 10, Oct. 1995, pp. 62–69.
Henderson, Justin. *Museum Architecture* (Gloucester, MA: Rockport Publishers, 1998).
Johnson, Mairi. 'Once Upon a Sign: Relationships of Architecture and Narrative in the United States Holocaust Memorial Museum', *Journal of Architecture*, vol. 1, no. 3, Autumn 1996, pp. 207–225.
Knesl, John. 'Accidental Classicists: Freed in Washington, Libeskind in Berlin', *Assemblage*, no. 16, Dec. 1991, pp. 98–101.
Murphy, Jim and others. 'Memorial to Atrocity', *Progressive Architecture*, vol. 74, no. 2, Feb. 1993, pp. 60–79.
Oppenheimer Dean, Andrea. 'Holocaust Museum Opens to Acclaim' *Progressive Architecture*, vol. 74, no. 6, June 1993, pp. 19–20.
Pearson, Clifford. 'Breaking Out of the Display Case, Exhibits Reach Out and Touch', *Architectural Record*, vol. 182, no. 9, Sept. 1994, pp. 28–33.
Russell, James S. 'Permanent Witness: United States Holocaust Memorial Museum, Washington DC.', *Architectural Record*, vol. 181, no. 7, July 1993, pp. 58–67.
Slessor, Catherine. 'Special Issue. Museums & Libraries', *Architectual Review*, vol. 194, no. 1164, Feb. 1994, pp. 57–63.
Weinberg, Jeshajahu and Rina Elieli. *The Holocaust Museum in Washington* (New York: Rizzoli, 1995).
Young, James E. *The Art of Memory: Holocaust Memorials in History* (London: Thames & Hudson, 1994).

Chikatsu-Asuka Historical Museum

Ando, Tadao and others. 'Special Issue. Tadao Ando 1989/1992', *Croquis*, vol. 12, no. 1(58), 1993, pp. 166–169.
Ando, Tadao and others. 'Special Issue. Tadao Ando', *Japan Architect*, no. 1, Jan. 1991, pp. 76–79.
Baglione, Chiara. 'Chikatsu-Asuka Historic Museum', *Casabella*, vol. 59, no. 622, Apr. 1995, pp. 52–57, 71.
Bognar, Botond and others. 'Japanese Architecture II', *Architectural Design*, vol. 62, no. 9/10, Sept./Oct. 1992, pp. 52–57.
Chow, Phoebe. 'House of Shadows – Chikatsu-Asuka Historical Museum, Osaka', *Architectural Review*, vol. 198, no. 1182, 1995, pp. 40–44.
Doi, Yoshitake and others. 'Special Issue. Japan '94', *GA Document*, no. 39, 1994, pp. 16–21.
Frampton, Kenneth. *Tadao Ando* (New York: Museum of Modern Art/Abrams, 1991, 1993).
Furuyama, Masao. 'Special Issue. 1994 Annual (Part 1)', *Japan Architect*, no. 17(1), Spring 1995, pp. 12–15.
Hein, Carola. 'Modern References to Japanese Tradition: The New Museum in Chikatsu Asuka', *Archis*, no. 2, Feb. 1996, pp. 40–45.
Henderson, Justin. *Museum Architecture*, (Gloucester, MA: Rockport Publishers, 1998).
Montaner, Josep Maria. *Museum for the New Century* (Barcelona: Gili, 1995).
Pollock, Naomi R. 'Realms of the Living and Dead', *Architectural Record*, vol. 183, no.11, Nov. 1995, pp. 72–77.
Rodermond, Janny and others. 'Special Issue. Museums', *Architect (The Hague)*, vol. 27, dossier 1, July 1996, pp. 62–65.
Slessor, Catherine. *Concrete Regionalism* (London: Thames & Hudson, 2000).

Vulcania: The European Centre of Volcanism

Baudrillard, Jean and others. 'Special Issue. Truth, Radicality and Beyond in Contemporary Architecture', *New Architecture*, no. 5, July 2000, pp. 76–79.
Downy, Claire. 'Hollein's Volcano Museum Fires Up', *Architectural Record*, vol. 182, no. 12, Dec. 1994, p. 13.
'Volcano Museum in St Ours-les-Roches', *Detail*, vol. 42, no. 4, Apr. 2002, p. 395.
Escher, Gudrun. 'Vulcania: Cryptic Architecture for an Outstanding Natural Phenomenon', *Deutsche Bauzeitschrift*, vol. 50, no. 6, June 2002, p. 24.
Jodidio, Philip. 'Architects on a Volcano', *Connaissance des Arts*, no. 510, Oct. 1994, p. 30.
Ponte, Alessandra and others. 'Special Issue. Topographic Extremes', *Diadalos*, no. 63, Mar. 1997, pp. 86–89.
Smith, Harry and others. 'Special Issue. Landscapes', *ViA Arquitectura*, no. 3 (6), 1999, pp. 28–32.
Spens, Michael. 'Museums and Galleries', *Architectural Review*, vol. 198, no. 1182, 1995, pp. 72–75.
Vidler, Antony and others. 'Special Issue. Being and Nothingness', *ANY:Architecture New York*, no. 27, 2000, p. 8B.

Fukui Prefectural Dinosaur Museum

Castellano, Aldo. 'Special Issue. Museums', *Arca*, no. 142, Nov. 1999, pp. 14–17.
Kurokawa, Kisho Architect and Associates, 'Fukui Dinosaur Museum: Design Concept', *KKAA In-house Publication*, 2002.
Kurokawa, Kisho. Architect and Associates, 'Fukui Dinosaur Museum: Concrete Work', *KKAA In-house Publication*, 2002.
Kurokawa, Kisho. *Kisho Kurokawa: Museums* (Milan: L'Arca, 2002).
Sharp, Dennis. *Kisho Kurokawa: Metabolism + Recent Work* (London: Book Art, 2001).
Stucchi, Silvano. 'Dinosaur Museum, Katsuyama', *Industria delle Costruzioni*, vol. 35, no. 355, May 2001, pp. 48–57.

Domus, Home of Man

Carolyn Jarvitts. 'Cavern of Life – La Casa del Hombre, La Coruña, Spain', *Architectural Review*, vol. 198, no. 1183, Sept. 1995, pp. 58–62.
Dal Co, Francesco. 'Deconstructive Deformations', *Casabella*, vol. 60, no. 633, Apr. 1996, pp. 35–37.
Justo Isasi, 'Domus – La Casa del Hombre, La Coruña, Spain', *Arquitectura Vivi*, no. 43, July/Aug. 1995, pp. 38–41.
Doi, Yoshitake and others. 'Special Issue. Japan '94', *GA Document*, no. 39, 1994, pp. 50–53.
Doi, Yoshitake and others. 'Special Issue. 1995 Annual (Part1)', *Japan Architect*, no. 20(4), Winter 1995, pp. 38–41.
'Arata Isozaki – Current Works in Europe', *Japan Architect*, no. 19(3), Autumn 1995, pp. 6–27.
'Domus: Interactive Museum about Humans', *GA Document*, no. 44, 1995, pp. 74–83.
'The House of Man Interactive Museum', *Deutsche Bauzeitschrift*, vol. 44, no. 1, Jan. 1996, pp. 28–29.
Fernandez-Galiano, Luis and others. 'Special Issue. Spanish Yearbook 1996', *A&V Monografias*, no. 57/58, Jan./Apr. 1996, pp. 38–41.
Gleiniger, Andrea and others. 'Hommage to Tinguely', *Bauwelt*, vol. 87, no. 40, 25 Oct. 1996, pp. 2306–2309.
Montaner, Josep Maria and others. 'Special Issue. Spanish Architecture 1995: Modernism, Avant Garde

and Neo-Avant Garde', *Croquis*, vol. 14, no. 5(76), 1995, pp. 78–91.
Rodermond, Janny and others. 'Special Issue. Museums', *Architect (The Hague)*, vol. 27, dossier 1, July 1996, pp. 34–39.
Wislocki, Peter. 'Fun and Serious Games', *World Architecture*, no. 39, 1995, pp. 124–127.
Wislocki, Peter. 'Museum of Mankind, La Coruña, *Architektura Murator*, no. 6(21), June 1996, pp. 38–39.

National Maritime Museum Cornwall
Baldock, Hannah. 'Cornish Museum Stalled by Dispute', *Building*, vol. 263, no. 8052 (33), 14 Aug. 1998, p. 10.
Bevan, Robert. 'Messing about with Boatsheds', *Building Design*, no. 1308, 16 May 1997, pp. 12–13.
Croft, Catherine. 'Shore Winner', *Building Design*, 22 Nov. 2002, pp. 12–17.
Jackson, Martin. *Reflections* (Falmouth: National Maritime Museum Cornwall, 2002).
Jackson, Martin. *Setting Sail* (Falmouth: National Maritime Mueum Cornwall, n.d.).
Long, M.J. 'Anatomy of Architecture', *Building Design*, no. 1345, 3 Apr. 1998, p. 21.
Long, M.J. *Architect's Story* (London: Long & Kentish Architects, 2003).
Thompson, Jessica Cargill. 'Tyro Power: Rising Stars', *Building*, vol. 262, no. 7980 (9), 7 Mar. 1997, pp. 44–47.
Williams, Austin. 'Ship Shape in Cornwall', *Architects' Journal*, vol. 215, no. 4, 31 Jan. 2002, pp. 36–38.

Kunsthal, Rotterdam
Kunsthal Rotterdam (Rotterdam: Kunsthal Rotterdam/a+t ediciones, 2002).
'Le Kunsthal de Rotterdam', *Architecture d'Aujourd Hui*, no. 285, Feb. 1993, pp. 6–14.
'Popular Culture', *Blueprint*, no. 93, Dec./Jan., 1992/1993, pp. 16–19.
Field, Marcus. 'The Cult of Koolhaas', *Blueprint*, no. 141, July/Aug. 1997, p. 50.
Giovannini, Joseph and others, 'Special Issue. European Architecture', *Architecture (AIA)*, vol. 82, no. 9, Sept. 1993, pp. 67–119.
Lucan, Jacques, *OMA – Rem Koolhaas: Architecture 1970–1990* (Princeton, NJ: Princeton Architectural Press, 1991).
MacNair, Andrew. 'Kunsthal, Rotterdam, Netherlands', *A&U*, no. 8 (287), Aug. 1994, pp. 108–143.
Marvin, Charles Jeremy. *Rem Koolhaas: The Architect of Modern Life* (1995).
Metz, Tracy. 'Show Piece: KunstHAL Rotterdam', *Architectural Record*, vol. 181, no. 3, Mar. 1993, pp. 66–73.
Provoost, Michelle. *Dutchtown: City Centre Design by OMA/Rem Koolhaas* (Rotterdam: NAi Publishers, 1999).
Sigler, Jennifer, *Rem Koolhaas, S, M, L, XL: Small, Medium, Large, Extra-large* (New York: Monacelli Press, 1995).
Speaks, Michael. 'Rem Koolhaas and OMA Lead the Dutch onto New Turf', *Architectural Record*, vol. 188, no. 7, July 2000, pp. 92–99.
Welsh, John. 'Double Dutch', *Building Design*, no. 964, 1 Dec. 1989, pp. 18–21.

Cartier Foundation for Contemporary Art
Boyer, Charles-Arthur. 'Two Recent Buildings by Jean Nouvel', *Archis*, no. 6, June 1994, pp. 13–16.
Cerver, Francisco Asensio. *Arata Isozaki, Legorreta Arquitectos, Jean Nouvel, Steven Holl* (Barcelona: Cerver, 1997).
'Art in a Void', *Blueprint*, no. 107, May 1994, pp. 38–40.
'Jean Nouvel', *GA Document*, no. 41, Nov. 1994, pp. 86–95.
'New Headquarters for Cartier by Jean Nouvel', *Progressive Architecture*, vol. 75, no. 6, June 1994, p. 65.
'The New Building of the Fondation Cartier in Paris', *Domus*, no. 766, Dec. 1994, pp. 23–33.
Evans, David. 'Machines d'Architecture', *AA Files*, no. 24, Autumn 1992, pp. 86–93.
Futagawa, Yoshio. 'Special Issue. Jean Nouvel', *GA Document Extra*, no. 7, 1996, pp. 64–77.
Manser, Jose. 'Cartier Foundation', *Interiors*, vol. 153, no. 12, Dec. 1994, pp. 44–47.
Melhuish, Clare. 'Peering into the Void', *Building Design*, no. 1166, 1 April 1994, pp. 8–9.
Morgan, Conway Lloyd and others. 'Jean Nouvel', *World Architecture*, no. 31, 1994, pp. 26–49.
Riley, Terence. *Light Construction* (New York: Museum of Modern Art/Abrams, 1995).
Shortt, Barbara. 'Parisian Jewel', *Architecture (AIA)*, vol. 83, no. 9, Sept. 1994, pp. 64–69.
Slessor, Catherine. *Eco-Tech: Sustainable Architecture and High Technology* (London: Thames & Hudson, 1997).
Spring, Martin. 'Screen Play: Cartier Foundation Gallery', *Building*, vol. 259, no. 7852(28), 15 July 1994, pp. 38–41.
Zaira, Alejandro and Jean Nouvel. 'Special Issue. Jean Nouvel 1987–1994', *Croquis*, vol. 13, no. 2(65/66), 1994, pp. 234–253.

San Francisco Museum of Modern Art
Brogan, James and others. 'Light in Architecture', *Architectural Design*, vol. 67, no. 3/4, Mar./Apr. 1997, pp. 64–67.
'A European in San Francisco', *Building Design*, no. 1012, 16 Nov. 1990, pp. 30–32.
'Botta's New San Francisco MOMA Opens', *Progressive Architecture*, vol. 76, no. 2, Feb. 1995, p. 37.
'Short List for San Fran Museum', *Progressive Architecture*, vol. 69, no. 8, Aug. 1988, p. 26.
Ellis, John. 'San Francisco Visions', *Architecture (AIA)*, vol. 79, no. 8, Aug. 1990, p. 37.
Frampton, Kenneth. 'The New San Francisco Museum of Modern Art', *Domus*, no. 767, Jan. 1995, pp. 8–22.
Henderson, Justin. *Museum Architecture* (London: Mitchell Beazley, 1998).
Henderson, Justin. *San Francisco Museum of Modern Art*, (San Francisco,CA: San Francisco Museum of Modern Art, 2000).
Powell, Ken and others. 'New Museums', *Architectural Design*, vol. 61, no. 11/12, 1991, pp. 78–79.
Stein, Karen D. and Aaron Betsky. 'Monument to Art: San Francisco Museum of Modern Art', *Architectural Record*, vol. 182, no. 11, Nov. 1994, pp. 74–83.
Woodbridge, Sally. 'SF MoMA Unveils Botta Design', *Progressive Architecture*, vol. 71, no. 11, Nov. 1990, p. 24.

Modern and Contemporary Art Museum of Trento and Rovereto
Botta, Mario. 'Museum of Modern and Contemporary Art, Rovereto, 2002', *Casabella*, vol. 67, no. 710, April 2003, pp. 34–47.
Botta, Mario. *The Museum of Modern and Contemporary Art of Trento and Rovereto* (Milan: Skira, 1995).
'Museum for Modern and Contemporary Art, Rovereto', *Bauwelt*, vol. 94, no. 1/2, 10 Jan. 2003, p. 6.
Hartmann, Rahel. 'Museum of Modern and Contemporary Art, Rovereto', *Bauwelt*, vol. 86, no. 29/30, 11 Aug. 1995, p. 1603.
Ingersoll, Richard. 'New (M)art: Museum of Modern and Contemporary Art of Trento and Rovereto, Italy', *Architecture (New York)*, vol. 92, no. 2, Feb. 2003, pp. 22.

Chicago Museum of Contemporary Art
'A Walk Through the Museum of Contemporary Art's New Building', *Museum Information Pack*, MCA, Chicago.
'Go West: Museum of Contemporary Art in Chicago', *AIT*, no. 9, Sept. 1996, p. 28.
Hower, Barbara K. 'Unveiling the MCA', *Inland Architect*, vol. 36, no. 3, May/June 1992, pp. 24, 59.
Kamin, Blair. 'Chicago Museum Design Unveiled', *Architecture (AIA)*, vol. 81, no. 5, May 1992, p. 23.
Kent, Cheryl. ' "Poetic Rationalism" for Chicago Museum', *Progressive Architecture*, vol. 73, no. 5, May 1992, p. 27.
Kent, Cheryl. 'Chicago Museum Rises', *Progressive Architecture*, vol. 76, no. 12, Dec. 1995, p. 30.
Kent, Cheryl. 'Kleihues Defies Skepticism to Create

Chicago Landmark', *Architectural Record*, vol. 184, no. 8, Aug. 1996, pp. 80–87.
Kleihues, Josef Paul. 'Museum of Contemporary Art, Chicago', *Domus*, no. 739, June 1992, pp. 48–53.
Krohe Jr., James. 'New Contemporary Museum Scheme Bows to Mies', *Architectural Record*, vol. 180, no. 5, May 1992, p. 23.
Martin, Nicola and Andrew Sedwick. 'Chicago Museum of Contemporary Art', *Arup Journal*, vol. 31, no. 3, 1996, pp. 3–5.
Melvin, Jeremy and Nicola Martin. 'Restraining Influence', *Building Design*, no. 1274, 9 Aug. 1996, pp. 12–13.
Mesecke, Andrea and Thorsten Scheer. *Josef Paul Kleihues: Themes and Projects* (Basel: Birkhäuser, 1996).
Mesecke, Andrea and Thorsten Scheer. *Museum of Contemporary Art Chicago: Josef Paul Kleihues* (Berlin: Mann, 1996).
Schulze, Franz. 'Museum by Kleihues Opens in Chicago', *Architecture (AIA)*, vol. 85, no. 6, June 1996, pp. 38–39.

Guggenheim Museum Bilbao

De Jong, Judith K. 'Walking Around the Guggenheim', *Landscape Architecture*, vol. 91, no. 12, Dec. 2001, pp. 114–116.
'Bursting on the Scene; Frank Gehry's Bilbao Guggenheim', *Architecture Today*, no. 82, Oct. 1997, pp. 16–23.
Fairs, Marcus. 'Bilbao', *Building*, vol. 265, no. 8160(44), 3 Nov. 2000, pp. 46–49.
Foster, Kurt W. *Frank O. Gehry: Guggenheim Bilbao Museum* (Stuttgart and London: Menges, 1998).
Henderson, Justin. *Museum Architecture* (Gloucester, MA: Rockport Publishers, 1998).
Jencks, Charles and others. 'Contemporary Museums', *Architectural Design*, vol. 67, no. 11/12, Nov./Dec. 1997.
Rattenbury, Kester. 'Adventures in Toon Town', *Building Design*, no. 1324, 10 Oct. 1997, pp. 12–16.
Rattenbury, Kester. 'Viva la Difference', *Building Design*, no. 1449, 14 July 2000, pp. 30, 31.
Slessor, Catherine. 'Special Issue. Museums', *Architectural Review*, vol. 202, no. 1210, Dec. 1997, pp. 30–42, 43–45.
Stein, Karen D. 'Project Diary: Frank Gehry's Dream Project, the Guggenheim Museum Bilbao, Draws the World to Spain's Basque Country', *Architectural Record*, vol. 185, no. 10, Oct. 1997, pp. 74–87.
Taylor, David. 'Gehry Slams "Rust" Stories but Takes Basques to Task ... and Says Computers Will Revive the "Master Builder" ', *Architects' Journal*, vol. 212, no. 15, 26 Oct. 2000, p. 24.
Thompson, Jessica Cargill. 'Wow in Bilbao', *Building*, vol. 262, no. 7996(25), 27 June 1997, pp. 38–45.
Van Bruggen, Coosje. *Frank O. Gehry: Guggenheim Museum Bilbao* (New York: Guggenheim Museum Publications, 1998).
Von der Becke, Alex. 'A Futurist Triumph for Spain', *Museums Journal*, vol. 98, no. 1, Jan. 1998, p. 25.

Stockholm Museums of Modern Art and Architecture

Andersson, Ola. 'Stockholm Serenity: Moneo's Museum of Modern Art', *Architecture Today*, no. 91, Sept., pp. 32–41.
Anstey, Tim. 'Moneo Gives Stockholm an Architectural Delight', *Architects' Journal*, vol. 207, no. 7, 19 Feb. 1998, p. 24.
Barrett, Clear. ' "Mouldy" Rafael Moneo Museum Closes', *World Architecture*, no. 103, Feb. 2002, p. 8.
Bevan, Robert. 'Treasure Island', *Building Design*, no. 1340, 27 Feb. 1998, pp. 14–19.
Capezzuto, Rita. 'Modern Art and Architecture Museums Complex, Stockholm', *Domus*, no. 806, July/Aug. 1998, pp. 18–27.
'The Better Part of Modern Valor', *Progressive Architecture*, vol. 76, no. 9, Sept. 1995, p. 31.
'Mouldy Moneo Museums Close', *Building Design*, no. 1520, 15 Feb. 2002, p. 5.
Ericsson, Edith. 'Special Issue. Colour', *Architectural Review*, vol. 204, no. 1221, Nov. 1998, pp. 36–41.
Hultin, Olof. 'Museum of Modern Art, Stockholm', *Arkitektur (Stockholm)*, vol. 96, no. 1, Jan./Feb. 1996, pp. 38–41.
Lindvall, Jordan. 'The Museum of Modern Art and the Museum of Architecture in Stockholm', *Living Architecture*, 1998, pp. 50–67.
Melvin, Jeremy. 'Picture Perfect', *RIBA Journal*, vol. 105, no. 2, Feb. 1998, pp. 16–19.
Moneo, Rafael. *Modern Museum and Swedish Museum of Architecture in Stockholm* (Stockholm: Arkitektur Forlag, 1998)
Pickard, James and John Welsh. 'Swedish Success', *Building Design*, no. 1039, 14 June 1991, pp. 18, 20.
Slessor, Catherine. 'Northern Lights: Modern Museum, Stockholm', *Architecture (New York)*, vol. 87, no. 6, June 1998, pp. 114–121.
Wortmann, Arthur. 'Moneo in Stockholm', *Archis*, no. 12, Dec. 1997, pp. 30–33.

Galician Centre for Contemporary Art

Beaudouin, Laurent and others. 'Special Issue. Alvaro Siza', *Architecture D'Aujourd'Hui*, no. 278, Dec. 1991, pp. 120–123.
Bussel, Abby. 'Searching for Siza', *Progressive Architecture*, vol. 76, no. 4, Apr. 1995, pp. 62–63.
Cerver, Francisco Asensio. *Plans of Architecture: Building Details* (Barcelona: Arco, 1997).
Cohn, David. 'Pilgrimage to Santiago: Galician Center of Contemporary Art, Santiago de Compostela', *Architectural Record*, vol. 182, no. 10, Oct. 1994, pp. 102–107.
Cuito, Aurora. *Alvaro Siza* (London: teNeues, 2002).
'Galician Center for Contemporary Art, Santiago de Compestela, Spain', *GA Document*, no. 36, 1993, pp. 76–77.
'Galician Center for Contemporary Art', *GA Document*, no. 38, 1994, p. 98–115.
Futagawa, Yoshio. 'Special Issue. Alvaro Siza', *GA Document Extra*, no. 11, 1998, pp. 50–69.
Montaner, Josep M. *New Museums* (London: Architecture Design & Technology Press, 1990).
Siza, Alvaro. 'Galician Center of Contemporary Art, Santiago de Compostela', *A&U*, no.6(297), June 1995, pp. 4–27.
Siza, Alvaro and others. 'Special Issue. Alvaro Siza – Recent Works', *A&U*, no. 4(355), Apr. 2000, pp. 56–73.
Testa, Peter and Peter Brinkert. 'The Plan for Macao and Other Recent Projects by Alvaro Siza Vieira', *Casabella*, vol. 53, no. 559, July/Aug. 1989, pp. 4–26, 59–60.
Wang, Wilfried. 'Centre for Contemporary Art in Santiago de Compostela', *Domus*, no. 760, May 1994, pp. 7–17.

Serralves Museum

Barry, Samuel W. 'Still Life with Siza', *Architecture (New York)*, vol. 88, no. 9, Sept. 1999, p. 39.
Cohn, David. 'In Oporto, Portugal, Alvaro Siza's Serralves Museum Takes Visitors into a Majestic Walled Garden Filled with Art', *Architectural Record*, vol. 187, no. 11, Nov. 1999, pp. 102–109.
Cohn, David and others. 'The Iberian Peninsula: Country Focus', *World Architecture*, no.73, Feb. 1999, p. 94.
Cuito, Aurora. *Alvaro Siza* (London: teNeues, 2002).
Curtis, William J.R. and others. 'Alvaro Siza 1995–1999. Notes on Intervention' *Croquis*, 1999, pp. 154–185.
Editor. 'Siza the Day', *Blueprint*, July/Aug. 1999, p. 13.
Editor. 'The Unadorned Walls of Alvaro Siza', *Techniques & Architecture*, no. 445, Oct./Nov. 1999, pp. 94–99.
Ganshirt, Christian and others. 'Three Museums and a Gallery', *Bauwelt*, vol. 90, no. 32, 20 Aug. 1999, pp. 1740–1747.
Hammer, Gerd. 'Contemporary Art in Oporto: The Serralves Museum', *Baumeister*, July 1999, p. 6.
Moore, Guy and others. 'Inside', *Architectural Review*, Aug. 1999, pp. 28–33.
Siza, Alvaro. 'Contemporary Art Museum of Oporto', *GA Document*, no. 59, July 1999, pp. 10–37.
Trulove, James Grayson. *Designing the New Museum: Building a Destination*, (Gloucester, MA: Rockport Publishers, 2000).
Wild, David. 'Alvaro Siza's Museu Serralves', *Architecture Today*, Sept. 1999, pp. 20–22, 25–28, 31.

Toyota Municipal Museum of Art

Bognar, Botond and others. 'Special Issue. Japan at the Cutting Edge', *New Architecture*, no. 3, 1999, pp. 80–85.

Castle, Helen. *Modernism and Modernization in Architecture* (London: Academy Editions, 1999).

Gillette, Jane Brown. 'The Rough and the Smooth', *Landscape Architecture*, vol. 88, no. 5, May 1998, pp. 66–73, 102, 105–107.

Jewell, Linda and others. 'Special Issue. Peter Walker William Johnson and Partners: Art and Nature', *Process: Architecture*, no. 118, 1994, pp. 110–113.

Maki, Fumihiko and Andrea Maffei. 'Stillness and Plentitude: The Architecture of Yoshio Taniguchi', *Casabella*, vol. 62, no. 661, Nov. 1998, pp. 78–83.

Maki, Fumihiko and others. 'Special Issue, Yoshio Tamiguchi', *Japan Architect*, no. 21(1), Spring 1996, pp. 28–49.

Miyazaki, Hioshi and others. 'Special Issue. The Landscape of Detail: Its Art and Techniques', *SD*, no. 9(408), Sept. 1998, pp. 36–43.

Nanba, Kazuhika and others. 'Special Issue. 1996 Yearbook: Japanese Architectural Scene in 1996 (Part 1)', *Japan Architect*, no. 24(4), Winter 1996, pp. 14–17.

Reid, T.R. and others. 'New Buildings in Japan', *Architecture (AIA)*, vol. 85, no. 10, Oct. 1996, pp. 100–103.

Russell, James S. 'Yoshio Who? MOMA's New Architect', *Archi-tectural Record*, vol. 186, no. 1, Jan. 1998, p. 29.

Shannon, Kelly and others. 'Special Issue. Japanese Immaterials', *Arquitectura Viva*, no. 52, Jan./Feb. 1997, pp. 46–49.

Taniguchi, Yoshio. *The Architecture of Yoshio Taniguchi* (New York and London: Abrams, 1999).

Walker, Peter and Leah Levy. 'Special Issue: The Works of Peter Walker: Minimalism and the Landscape Architecture', *SD*, no. 358(7), July 1994, pp. 83–85.

Fukui City Museum of Art

Chirat, Sylvie. 'Kisho Kurakawa: To Think of Symbiosis', *Architecture Interieure Cree*, no. 281, 1998, pp. 46–47.

Dall'Olio, Lorenzo. 'Art Museum in Fukui, Japan', *Industria Delle Costruzioni*, vol. 33, no. 335, Sept. 1999, pp. 22–35.

Jencks, Charles and others. 'Contemporary Museums', *Architectural Design*, vol. 67, no. 11/12, Nov./Dec. 1997, pp. 60–61.

Kurokawa, Kisho and Aldo Castellano. *Kisho Kurakawa: Abstract Symbolism* (Milano: Arca Edizioni, 1996).

Kurokawa, Kisho and others. 'Special Issue. Kisho Kurokawa 1988–1995', *Japan Architect*, no. 18 (2), Summer 1995, pp. 76–79.

Peressut, Luca Basso. *Musei: Architetture 1990–2000* (Milan: Motta, 1999).

Suzuki, Hiroyuki and others. 'Special Issue. Japan '96', *GA Document*, no. 47, 1996, pp. 74–77.

Vogliazzo, Maurizio. 'Special Issue. Emotion', *Arca*, no. 125, Apr. 1998, pp. 18–27.

Lois & Richard Rosenthal Center for Contemporary Art

Ando, Tadao and others. 'Special Issue. International "99" ', *GA Document*, no. 58, Apr. 1999, pp. 26–27.

Baldock, Hannah. 'Hadid's U.S. Arts Centre Design Revealed', *Building*, vol. 263, no. 8057 (39), 25 Sept. 1998, pp. 16–17.

Betsky, Aaron. *Zaha Hadid: The Complete Buildings and Projects* (London: Thames & Hudson, 1998).

Clark, Phil and others, 'Building Does America', *Building*, vol. 265, no. 8162 (46), 17 Nov. 2000, p. 53

Cook, Peter and others. 'Zaha Hadid', *A&U*, no. 11 (374), Nov. 2001, pp. 90–93.

'Building Study. Zaha Hadid Architects, Cincinnati', *Building Design*, 23 May 2003, pp. 12–14.

'Hadid's Contemporary Arts Centre Design Goes on Show', *Architects' Journal*, vol. 208, no. 21, 3/10 Dec. 1998, p. 17.

Hadid, Zaha. 'Zaha Hadid on the Contemporary Arts Center', *Press Kit*, Zaha Hadid Statement.

Litt, Steven. 'Hadid Takes Cincinnati', *Architecture (New York)*, vol. 87, no. 4, Apr. 1998, p. 26.

Mornement, Adam. 'Hadid – First Amongst Americans', *World Architecture*, no. 66, May 1998, p. 21.

Morton, David Simon. 'In Cincinnati, Hadid Gets Her First American Commission', *Architectural Record*, vol. 186, no. 4, Apr. 1998, p. 35.

Mostafavi, Mohsen and others. 'Special Issue, Zaha Hadid 1996–2001', *Croquis*, no. 5 (103), 2000 (2001), pp. 166–173.

Taylor, David. 'Zaha Hadid Becomes the Newest Cincinnati Kid', *Architects' Journal*, vol. 207, no. 10/12, Mar. 1998, p. 18.

National Centre for Contemporary Arts

Ando, Tadao and others. 'International 2000', *GA Document*, no. 61, Apr. 2000, pp. 20–24.

'Competition for Contemporary Arts Centre Near the Foro Italico, Rome; Winning Design: Zaha Hadid', *Architects' Journal*, vol. 209, no. 8, 25 Feb. 1999, pp. 4–5.

'Zaha Hadid Wins Rome Arts Complex', *Building*, vol. 264, no. 8076 (8), 26 Feb. 1999, p. 11.

'Zaha Steals the Day', *Blueprint*, no. 159, Mar. 1999, p. 13.

Giovannini, Jospeh. 'Exhibitions. Zaha Hadid Imagines a New Stratum Added to Rome's Architectural Riches', *Architectural Record*, vol. 190, no. 8, Aug. 2002, pp. 71–72.

Gubitosi, Alessandro. 'Transparency', *Arca*, May 1999, pp. 76–79.

O'Connor, Michael J. 'Hadid Says, "Ciao, Italia" ', *Architecture (New York)*, vol. 88, no. 5, May 1999, pp. 50–51.

Redecke, Sebastian and others. 'The Eternal City', *Bauwelt*, vol. 90, no. 14, 9 Apr. 1999, pp. 760–761.

Sharif, Mohamed. 'Figuring Ground: Notes on Recent Work by the Office of Zaha Hadid', *ARQ: Architectural Research Quarterly*, vol. 5, no. 3, Sept. 2001, pp. 286–288.

Spiral Extension to the Victoria & Albert Museum

Baillieu, Amanda. '40 Million Pound Competition for 'Bold' New V&A Addition', *Architects Journal*, vol. 202, no. 19, 16 Nov. 1995, p.7.

Baillieu, Amanda and Marcus Field. 'V&A Promises to Fight All the Way for Libeskind Building; Libeskind at the V&A', *Architects' Journal*, vol. 203, no. 20, 23 May 1996, pp. 7–9.

Baldock, Hannah. 'Straight Up, With a Twist: V&A Extension', *Building*, vol. 263, no. 8067(49), 4 Dec.1998, pp.18–19.

Bates, Donald L. and others. 'Special Issue. Daniel Libeskind 1987–1996', *Croquis*, vol. 15, no. 4(80), 1996, pp.168–181.

Blackler, Zoe. 'Libeskind's Spiral on Track as V&A Begins 150 Million Pounds Overhaul', *Architects' Journal*, vol. 215, no. 16, 25 Apr. 2002, p. 18.

Booth, Robert. 'New Man at V&A Falls for Daniel Libeskind's Spiral', *Architects' Journal*, vol. 213, no. 6, 15 Feb. 2001, p. 13.

Butler, Toby. 'Libeskind's V&A Spiral May be Revised', *Museum Journal*, vol. 101, no. 6, June 2001, p. 9.

Buxton, Pamela. 'V&A's Libeskind Extension Could Be Funded by PFI', *Building Design*, no. 1275, 23 Aug. 1996, p. 4.

'Boilerhouse Extension, Victoria & Albert Museum, London', *AIT*, no. 10, Oct. 1996, p. 20.

'Newspapers Fuel Controversy Over Libeskind's V&A Design', *Architects' Journal*, vol. 203, no. 21, 30 May 1996, p. 11.

'Revised Scheme for 50 Million Pounds V&A Museum Unveiled', *Building*, vol.261, no. 7961(41), 11 Oct. 1996, p. 12.

'Millennium Setback of Libeskind V&A Building', *Building Design*, no. 1281, 11 Oct. 1996, p. 3.

'EH Praises Libeskind's Boilerhouse Extension', *Building Design*, no. 1297, 28 Feb.1997, p. 3.

'Libeskind's V&A Scheme on Upward Popularity Spiral', *Architects' Journal*, vol. 208, no. 9, 10 Sept. 1998, p. 12.

'Cut Price Spiral for V&A', *Architects' Journal*, vol. 213, no. 18, 10 May 2001, p. 14.

'V&A Needs Nineteen Million Pounds to Start Work on Spiral', *Building Design*, no. 1530, 26 Apr. 2002, p. 5.

Eisenman, Peter and others. 'Formless. From Eisenman to Gehry, Beneath the Sign of Bataille', *Arquitectura Viva*, no. 50, Sept./Oct. 1996, pp. 42–45.

Fisher, James. 'V&A Spiral Condemned as "The Voice of Road Rage" ', *Building Design*, no. 1360, 24 July 1998, p. 1.
Jencks, Charles and others. 'New Science = New Architecture?', *Architectural Design*, vol. 67, no. 9/10, Sept./Oct. 1997, pp. 64–67.
Knutt, Elaine. 'V&A Spiral Inspires Strong Reaction', *Building*, vol. 261, no. 7942(21), 24 May 1996, p. 14.
Libeskind, Daniel. *Daniel Libeskind & Cecil Balmond: Unfolding* (Rotterdam: Nai, 1997).
Lubbock, Jules. 'Libeskind – Morris Would Approve', *Architects' Journal*, vol. 203, no. 25, 27 June 1996, pp. 22–23.
Mallet, Lee. 'Shaken and Stirred', *Building Design*, no. 1271, 28 June 1996, p. 12.
Melhuish, Claire. 'Clare Melhuish Reviews ... the V&A's Gwyn Miles on Libeskind's Spiral Project', *Architects' Journal*, vol. 212, no. 13, 12 Oct. 2000, p. 12.
Melvin, Jeremy. 'V&A Judge Slams Contest: Keeping in with the Neighbours', *Building Design*, no. 1266, 24 May 1996, pp. 1, 8, 24.
Slavid, Ruth. 'Revised Boilerhouse Goes On Show at the V&A', *Architects' Journal*, vol. 204, no. 13, 10 Oct. 1996, pp. 10, 16.
Slavid, Ruth. 'RFAC Backs "Daring and Innovative" V&A Plan', *Architects' Journal*, vol. 205, no. 4, 30 Jan. 1997, p. 9.
Slavid, Ruth. '140 Million Pounds to Heritage Projects, But Not the V&A', *Architects' Journal*, vol. 205, no. 8, 28 Feb. 1997, p. 16.
Taylor, David. 'Libeskind to Alter V&A Plans After Public Consultation', *Architects' Journal*, vol. 204, no. 6, 15 Aug. 1996, p. 12.
Taylor, David. 'V&A Garners 20 Million Pounds Donation for Spiral', *Architects' Journal*, vol. 209, no. 17, 29 Apr. 1999, p. 10.

Tate Modern

Buxton, Pamela. 'Power Struggles', *Building Design*, no. 1434, 31 Mar. 2000, pp. 20–21.
Curtis, William J.R. 'Herzog & de Meuron's Architecture of Luminosity and Transparency Transforms an Old Power Station on the Thames into the New Tate Gallery of Modern Art', *Architectural Record*, vol. 188, no. 6, June 2000, pp. 102–115, 244.
Darwent, Charles. 'All Mod Cons', *Blueprint*, no. 173, June 2000, p. 73.
Fretton, Tony. 'Into the Void: Herzog and de Meuron's Tate Modern', *Architecture Today*, no. 109, June 2000, pp. 34–57.
Melvin, Jeremy. 'Modern Times', *Blueprint*, no. 171, Apr. 2000, pp. 22–26.
Moore, Rowan and Raymund Ryan. *Building Tate Modern* (London: Tate Gallery Publishing, 2000).
Palmer, Henry. 'The Regeneration Game', *Museums Journal*, vol. 101, no. 10, Oct. 2001, pp. 20–23.
Powell, Kenneth and others. 'Powerhouse', *Architects' Journal*, vol. 211, no. 16, 27 Apr. 2000, pp. 24–33.
Rattenbury, Kester. 'Behold the Pyramid', *Building Design*, no. 1443, 2 June 2000, p. 2.
Rattenbury, Kester. 'Ideas Above and Within Their Station', *Building Design*, no. 1442, 26 May 2000, p. 23.
Rattenbury, Kester. 'Let There Be Light', *Building Design*, no. 1440, 12 May 2000, pp. 16–29.
Sabbagh, Karl. *Power into Art* (London: Allen Lane, 2000).
Spring, Martin. 'The Troubled Marriage of Art and Industry', *Building*, vol. 265, no. 8132(15), 14 Apr. 2000, pp. 14–17.
Taylor, David. 'Modern Masterpiece at the Tate', *Architects' Journal*, vol. 211, no. 13, 6 Apr. 2000, p. 16.
Taylor, David. 'Tate Modern Seeks Funds for 3.5 Million Pounds Chimney-Top Gallery', *Architects' Journal*, vol. 211, no. 14, 13 Apr. 2000, p. 15.
Taylor, David. 'Tate of the Nation', *Architects' Journal*, vol. 214, no. 16, 1 Nov. 2001, pp. 24–25.

Guggenheim Las Vegas and Guggenheim Hermitage Museums

Halliday, Tom. 'Koolhaas Leads World Guggenheim Plan', *Building Design*, no. 1451, 28 July 2000, p. 5.
Irving, Mark. 'Another Lesson from Las Vegas', *Domus*, no. 843, Dec. 2001, pp. 106–119.
Jones, Will. 'Guggenheim Hits Las Vegas', *World Architecture*, no. 101, Nov./Dec. 2001, p. 8.
Pearson, Clifford A. 'Rem Koolhaas Plugs the Guggenheim and Hermitage Museums into the High-Voltage Setting of the Las Vegas Strip', *Architectural Record*, vol. 190, no. 1, Jan. 2002, pp. 101–107.
Ryan, Zoe. 'Bucking the Odds in Vegas', *Blueprint*, no. 190, Dec. 2001, pp. 30–33.
Viray, Erwin J.S. and others. 'Museum', *A&U*, no. 1, (376), Jan. 2002, pp. 15–114.
Young, Eleanor. 'Viva Las Vegas', *RIBA Journal*, vol. 108, no. 11, Nov. 2001, pp. 8–9.

BALTIC the Centre for Contemporary Art

Cadji, Miriam. 'A Very Industrious Year', *RIBA Journal*, vol. 108, no. 1, Jan. 2001, pp. 8–9.
Carill, Nancy and Martin Spring. 'Tyneside', *Building*, 2 July 1999, pp.36–47.
Delargy, Melanie. 'HBG Favourite for 46 Million Pound Gateshead Gallery', *Building*, 23 July 1999, p.12.
'Art and Industry', *Building*, vol. 266, no. 8186 (21), 25 May 2001, pp. 42–47.
'Delayed Opening for Baltic Centre', *Building Design*, no. 1516, 18 Jan. 2002, p. 3.
'Flour Power in Gateshead as Ellis Williams' Gallery Opens', *RIBA Journal*, vol. 109, no. 7, July 2002, p.13.
Ellis Williams Architects. 'The Baltic Flour Mills – International Gallery of the Contemporary Arts', *Design Report, Stage D*, 3 July 1996.
Evamy, Michael. 'Art for Art's Sake', *Blueprint*, no. 193, Mar. 2002, pp. 42–48.
Fairs, Marcus. 'Where there's a Mill ...', *Building*, vol. 267, no. 8241 (26), 5 July 2002, pp. 20–27.
Gregory, Rob. 'Rise and Shine', *Building Design*, no. 1542, 11 July 2002, pp. 10-13.
Kloocke, Agnes and others. 'Art and Culture Factories', *Bauwelt*, vol. 93, no. 32, 23 Aug. 2002, pp. 10–31.
Martin, Sarah and Emma Thomas. *Baltic: The Art Factory* (Gateshead: Baltic, 2002).
Morris, Jane. 'Wanna B: Baltic, the Centre for Contemporary Art', *Museums Journal*, vol. 102, no. 8, Aug. 2002, pp. 35–36.
Williams, Austin and others. 'Flour Power', *Architects' Journal*, vol. 216, no. 5, 1/8 Aug. 2002, pp. 20–31.
Wulf, Andrea. 'Man about the Art House', *Architects' Journal*, vol. 216, no.5, 1/8 Aug. 2002, pp.16–17.